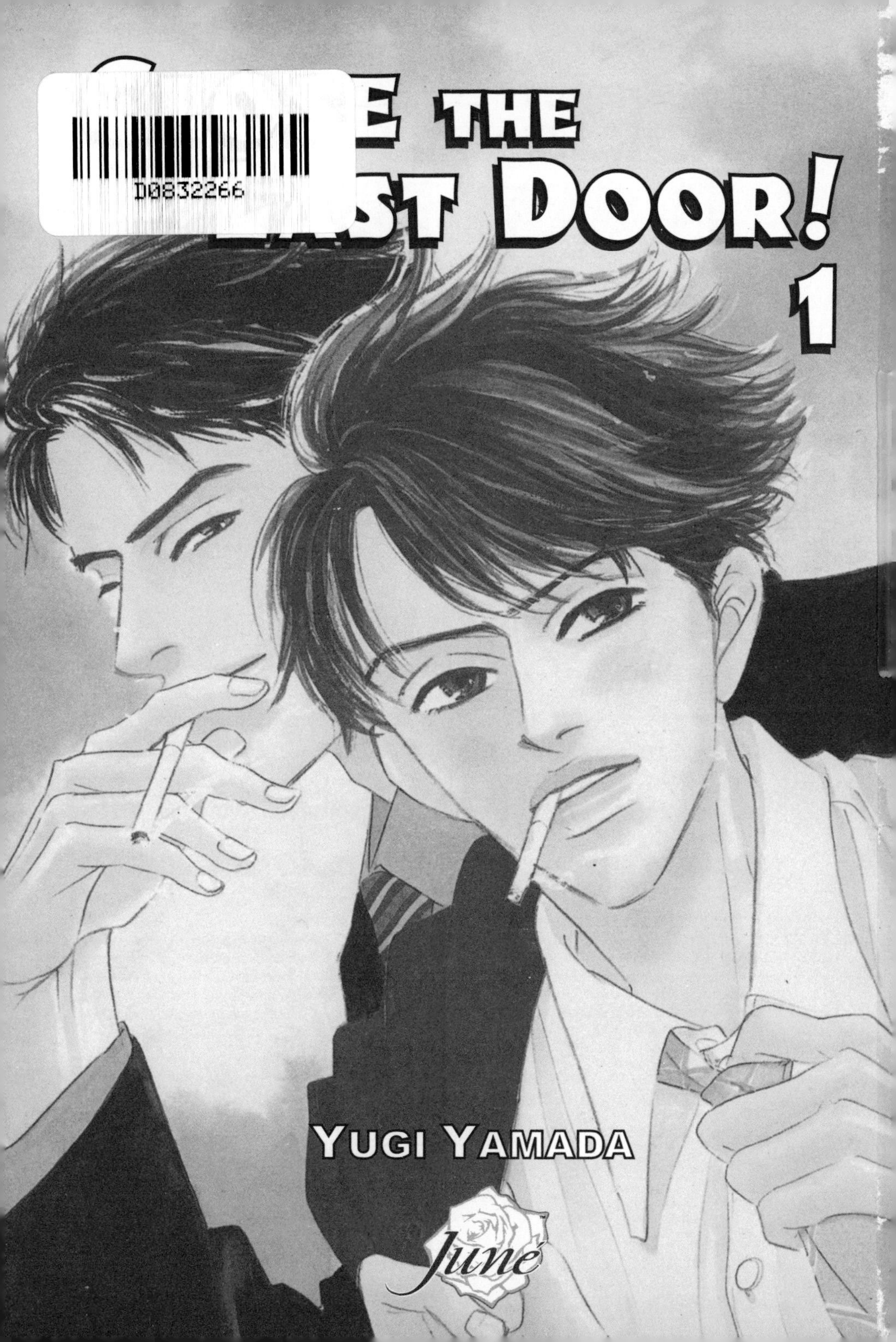
E THE
AST DOOR!
1
YUGI YAMADA
June

CLOSE THE LAST DOOR! 1

CONTENTS

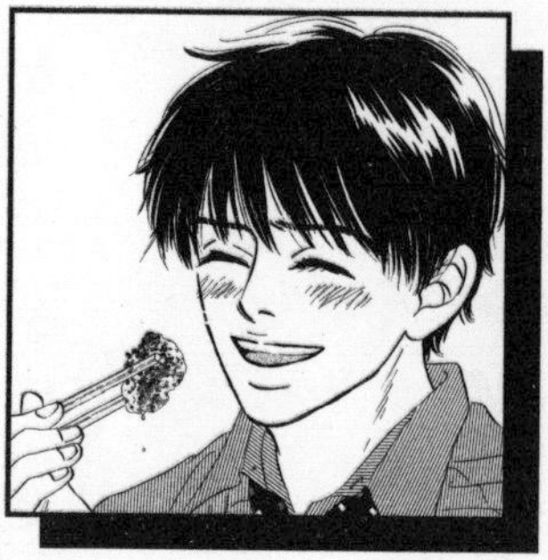

Translation	Melanie Schoen
Lettering	John Ott
Graphic Design	Wendy Lee
Editing	Stephanie Donnelly
Editor in Chief	Fred Lui
Publisher	Hikaru Sasahara

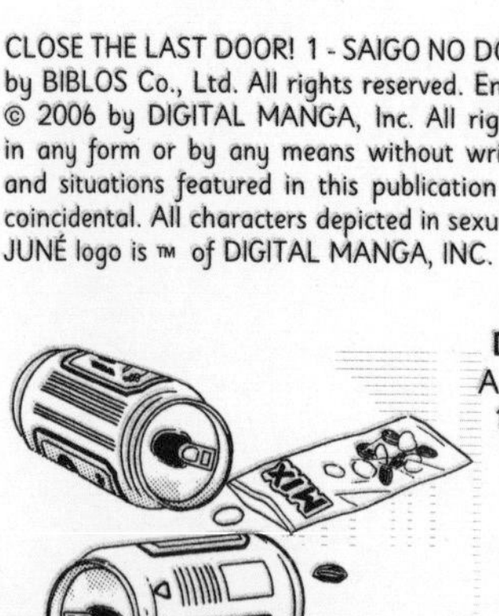
MIX

English Edition Published by
DIGITAL MANGA PUBLISHING
A division of DIGITAL MANGA, Inc.
1487 W. 178th Street, Suite 300
Gardena, CA 90248

www.dmpbooks.com

First Edition: September 2006
ISBN: 1-56970-883-5

1 3 5 6 9 10 8 6 4 2

Printed in China

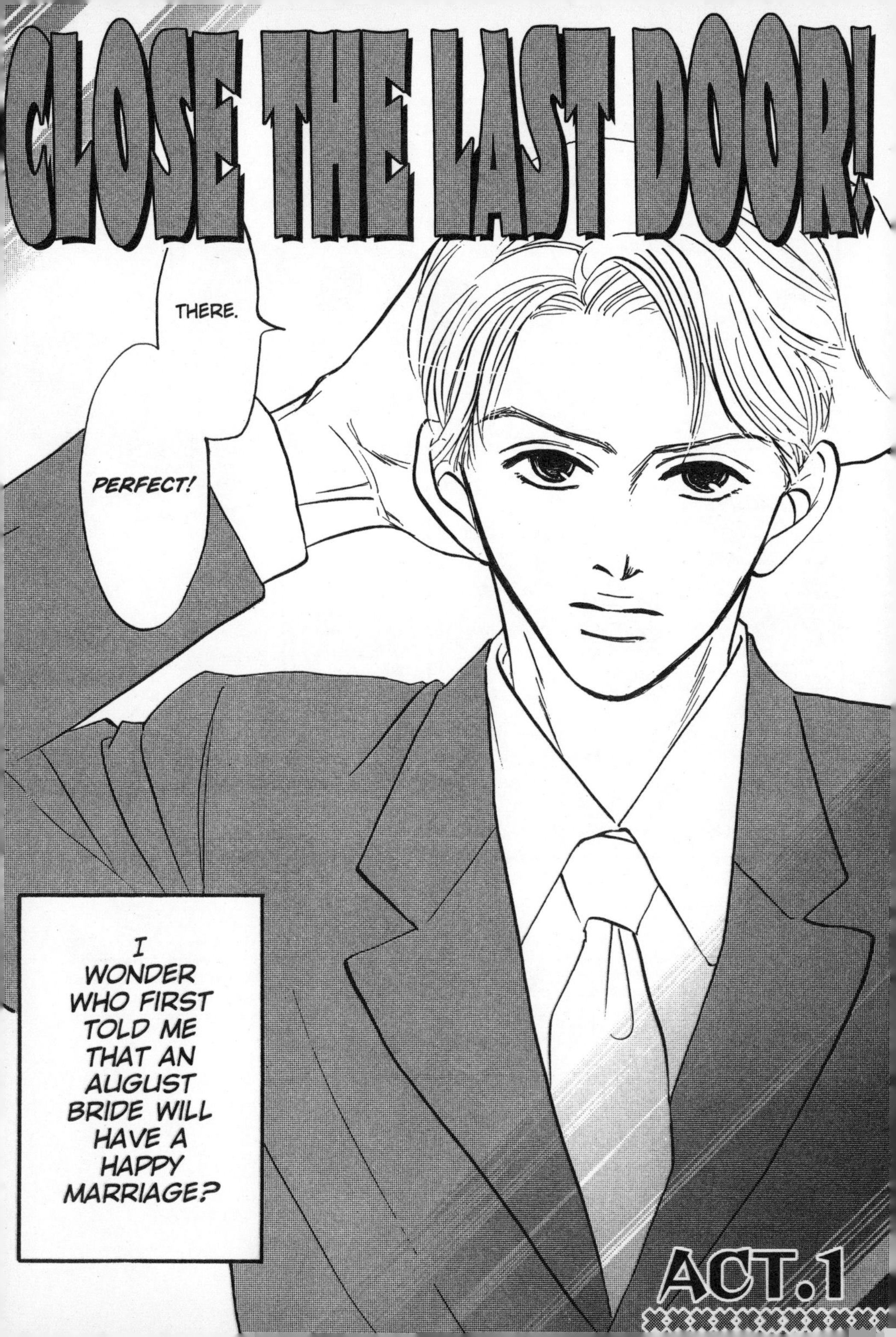
CLOSE THE LAST DOOR!
THERE.
PERFECT!
I WONDER WHO FIRST TOLD ME THAT AN AUGUST BRIDE WILL HAVE A HAPPY MARRIAGE?
ACT.1

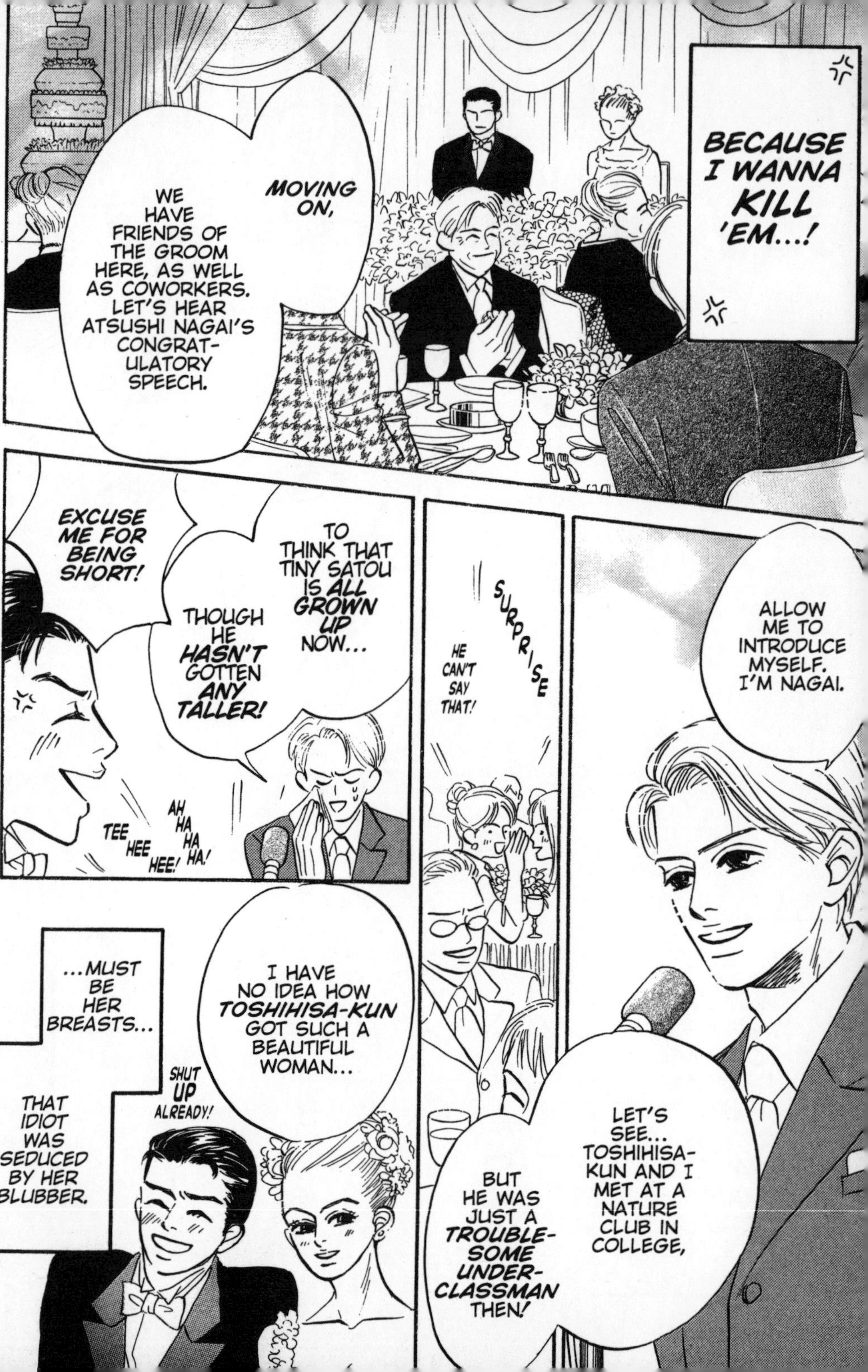

BECAUSE I WANNA KILL 'EM...!
MOVING ON,
WE HAVE FRIENDS OF THE GROOM HERE, AS WELL AS COWORKERS. LET'S HEAR ATSUSHI NAGAI'S CONGRAT-ULATORY SPEECH.
ALLOW ME TO INTRODUCE MYSELF. I'M NAGAI.
LET'S SEE... TOSHIHISA-KUN AND I MET AT A NATURE CLUB IN COLLEGE,
BUT HE WAS JUST A TROUBLE-SOME UNDER-CLASSMAN THEN!
SURPRISE
HE CAN'T SAY THAT!
TO THINK THAT TINY SATOU IS ALL GROWN UP NOW...
THOUGH HE HASN'T GOTTEN ANY TALLER!
EXCUSE ME FOR BEING SHORT!
AH HA HA HA!
TEE HEE HEE!
I HAVE NO IDEA HOW TOSHIHISA-KUN GOT SUCH A BEAUTIFUL WOMAN...
...MUST BE HER BREASTS...
SHUT UP ALREADY!
THAT IDIOT WAS SEDUCED BY HER BLUBBER.

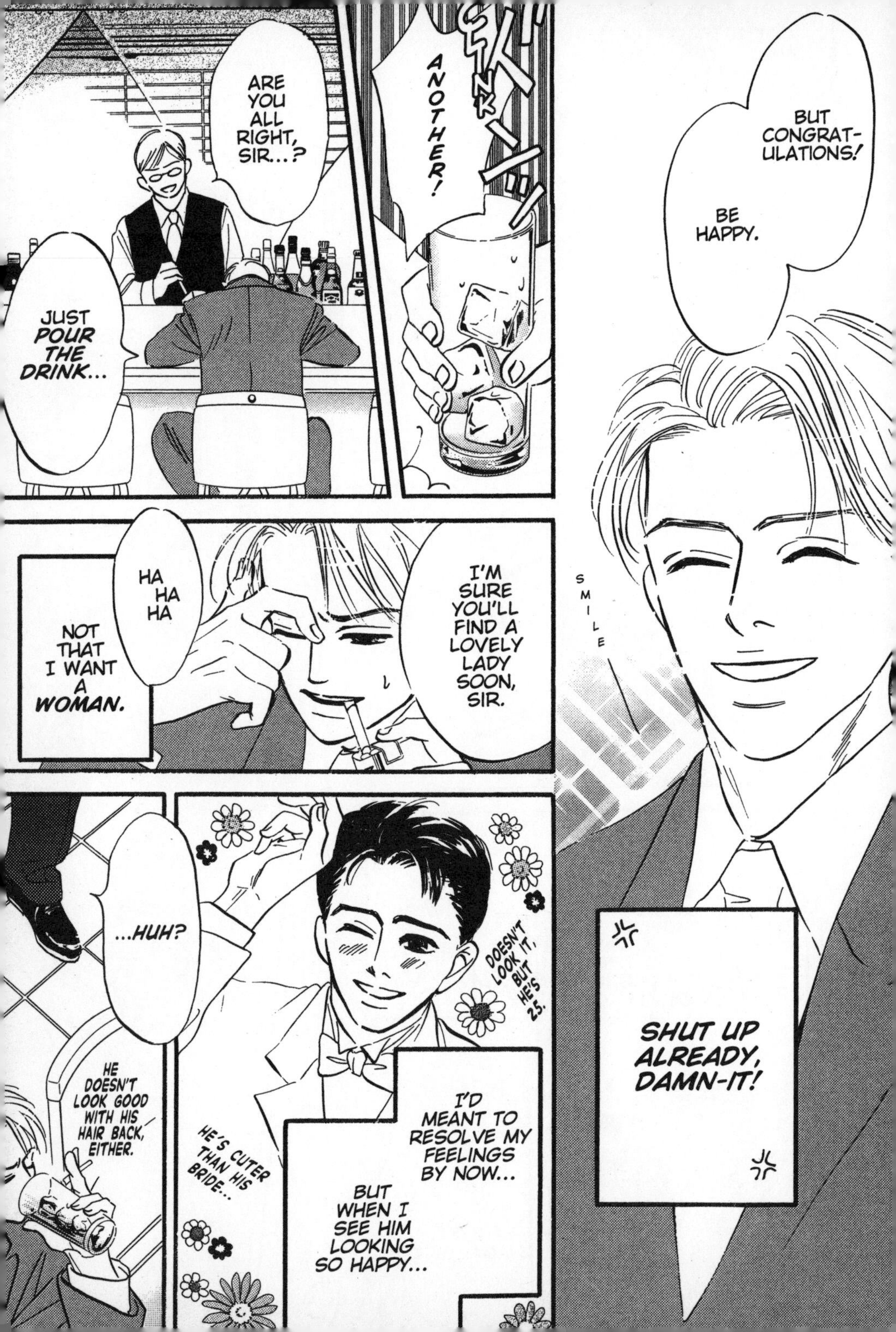
BUT CONGRATULATIONS!
BE HAPPY.
SMILE
SHUT UP ALREADY, DAMN-IT!
KLINK
ANOTHER!
ARE YOU ALL RIGHT, SIR...?
JUST POUR THE DRINK...
I'M SURE YOU'LL FIND A LOVELY LADY SOON, SIR.
HA HA HA
NOT THAT I WANT A WOMAN.
DOESN'T LOOK IT, BUT HE'S 25.
I'D MEANT TO RESOLVE MY FEELINGS BY NOW...
BUT WHEN I SEE HIM LOOKING SO HAPPY...
HE'S CUTER THAN HIS BRIDE...
...HUH?
HE DOESN'T LOOK GOOD WITH HIS HAIR BACK, EITHER.

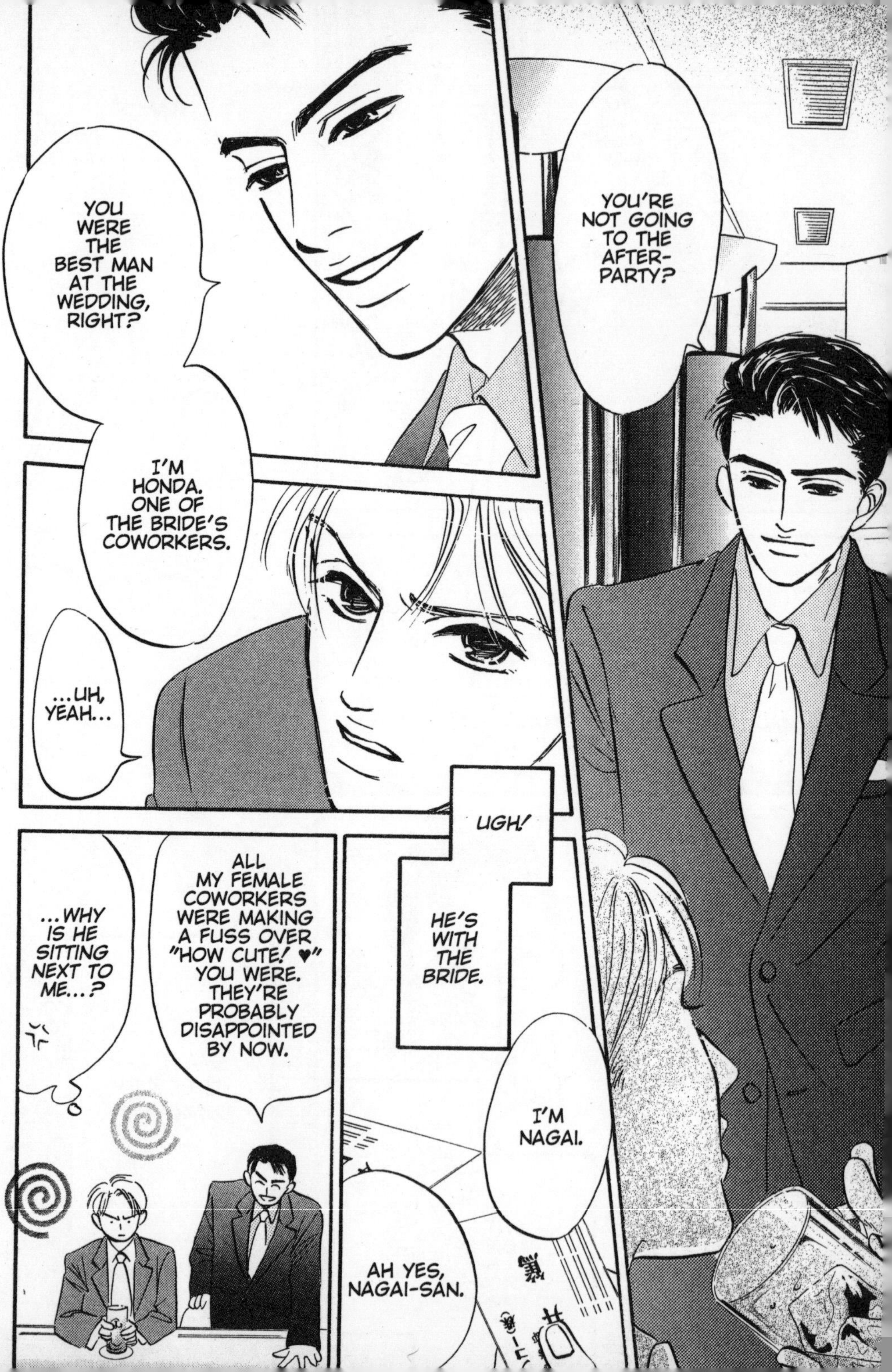
YOU'RE NOT GOING TO THE AFTER-PARTY?
I'M NAGAI.
YOU WERE THE BEST MAN AT THE WEDDING, RIGHT?
I'M HONDA. ONE OF THE BRIDE'S COWORKERS.
...UH, YEAH...
UGH!
HE'S WITH THE BRIDE.
AH YES, NAGAI-SAN.
ALL MY FEMALE COWORKERS WERE MAKING A FUSS OVER "HOW CUTE! ♥" YOU WERE. THEY'RE PROBABLY DISAPPOINTED BY NOW.
...WHY IS HE SITTING NEXT TO ME...?

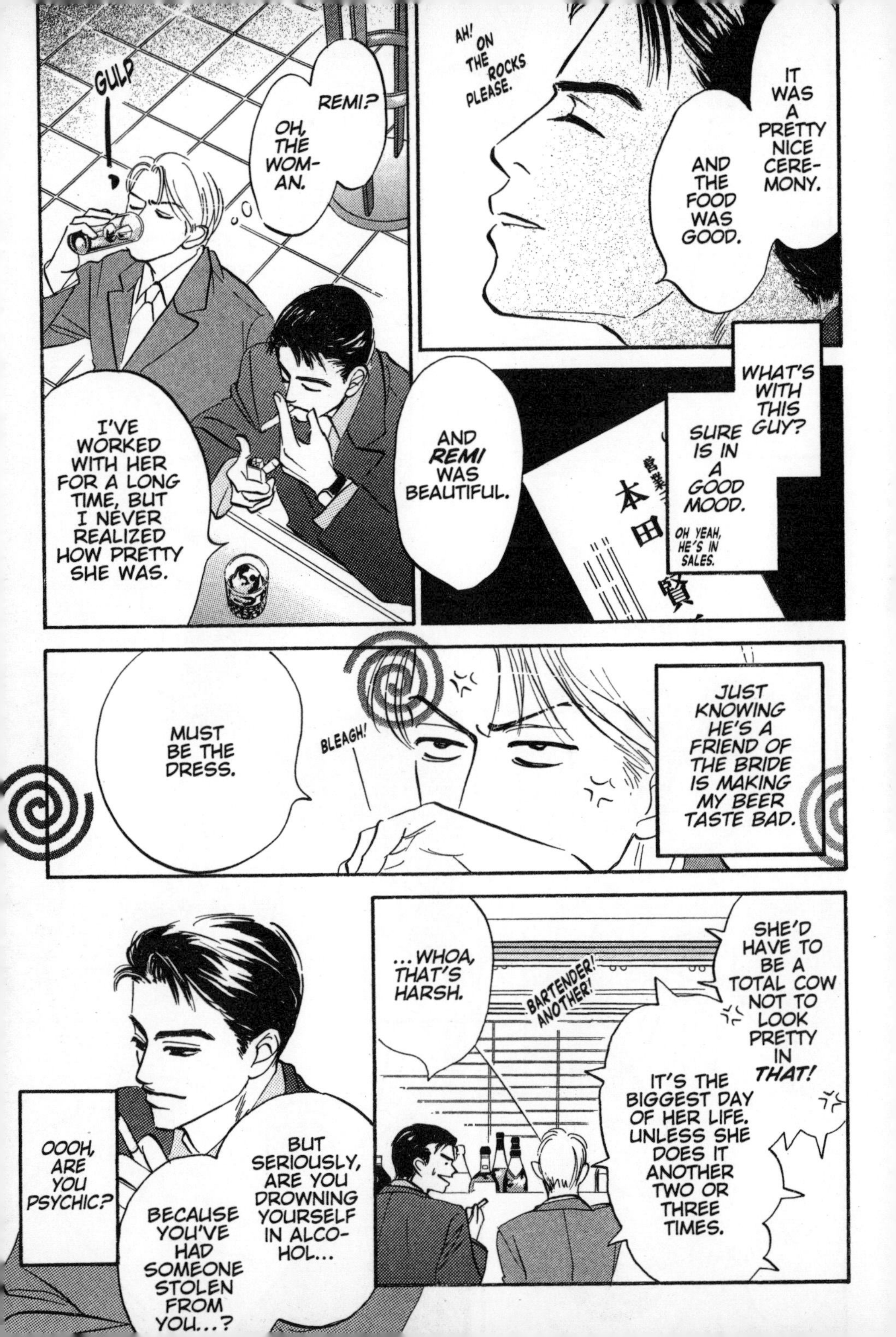
AH! ON THE ROCKS PLEASE.
IT WAS A PRETTY NICE CEREMONY.
AND THE FOOD WAS GOOD.
WHAT'S WITH THIS GUY?
SURE IS IN A GOOD MOOD.
営業
本田 賢
OH YEAH, HE'S IN SALES.
AND ***REMI*** WAS BEAUTIFUL.
GULP
REMI?
OH, THE WOMAN.
I'VE WORKED WITH HER FOR A LONG TIME, BUT I NEVER REALIZED HOW PRETTY SHE WAS.
JUST KNOWING HE'S A FRIEND OF THE BRIDE IS MAKING MY BEER TASTE BAD.
BLEAGH!
MUST BE THE DRESS.
SHE'D HAVE TO BE A TOTAL COW NOT TO LOOK PRETTY IN ***THAT!***
IT'S THE BIGGEST DAY OF HER LIFE. UNLESS SHE DOES IT ANOTHER TWO OR THREE TIMES.
BARTENDER! ANOTHER!
...WHOA, THAT'S HARSH.
BUT SERIOUSLY, ARE YOU DROWNING YOURSELF IN ALCOHOL...
BECAUSE YOU'VE HAD SOMEONE STOLEN FROM YOU...?
OOOH, ARE YOU PSYCHIC?

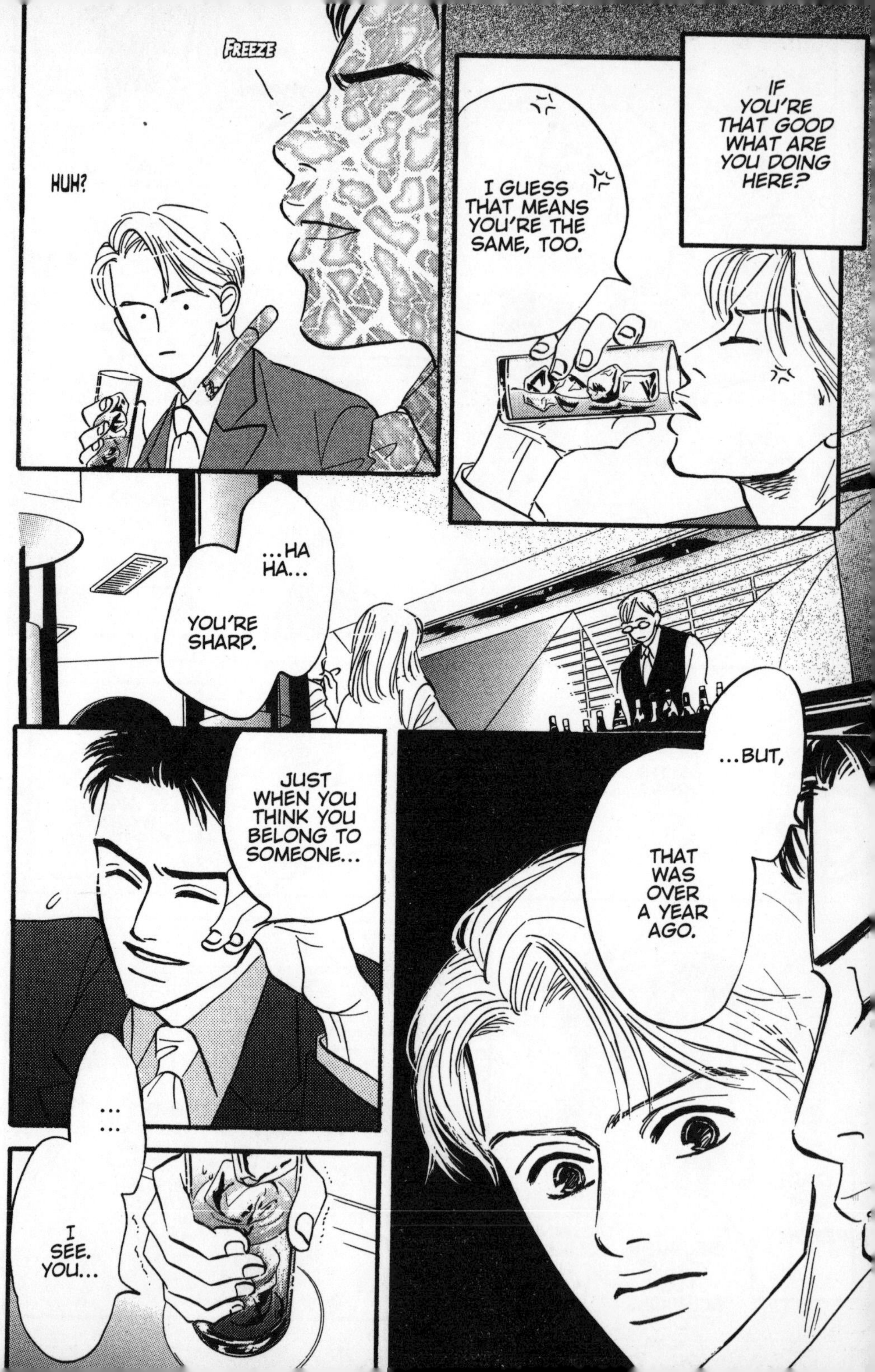
IF YOU'RE THAT GOOD WHAT ARE YOU DOING HERE?
I GUESS THAT MEANS YOU'RE THE SAME, TOO.
FREEZE
HUH?
...HA HA...
YOU'RE SHARP.
...BUT,
THAT WAS OVER A YEAR AGO.
JUST WHEN YOU THINK YOU BELONG TO SOMEONE...
......
I SEE. YOU...

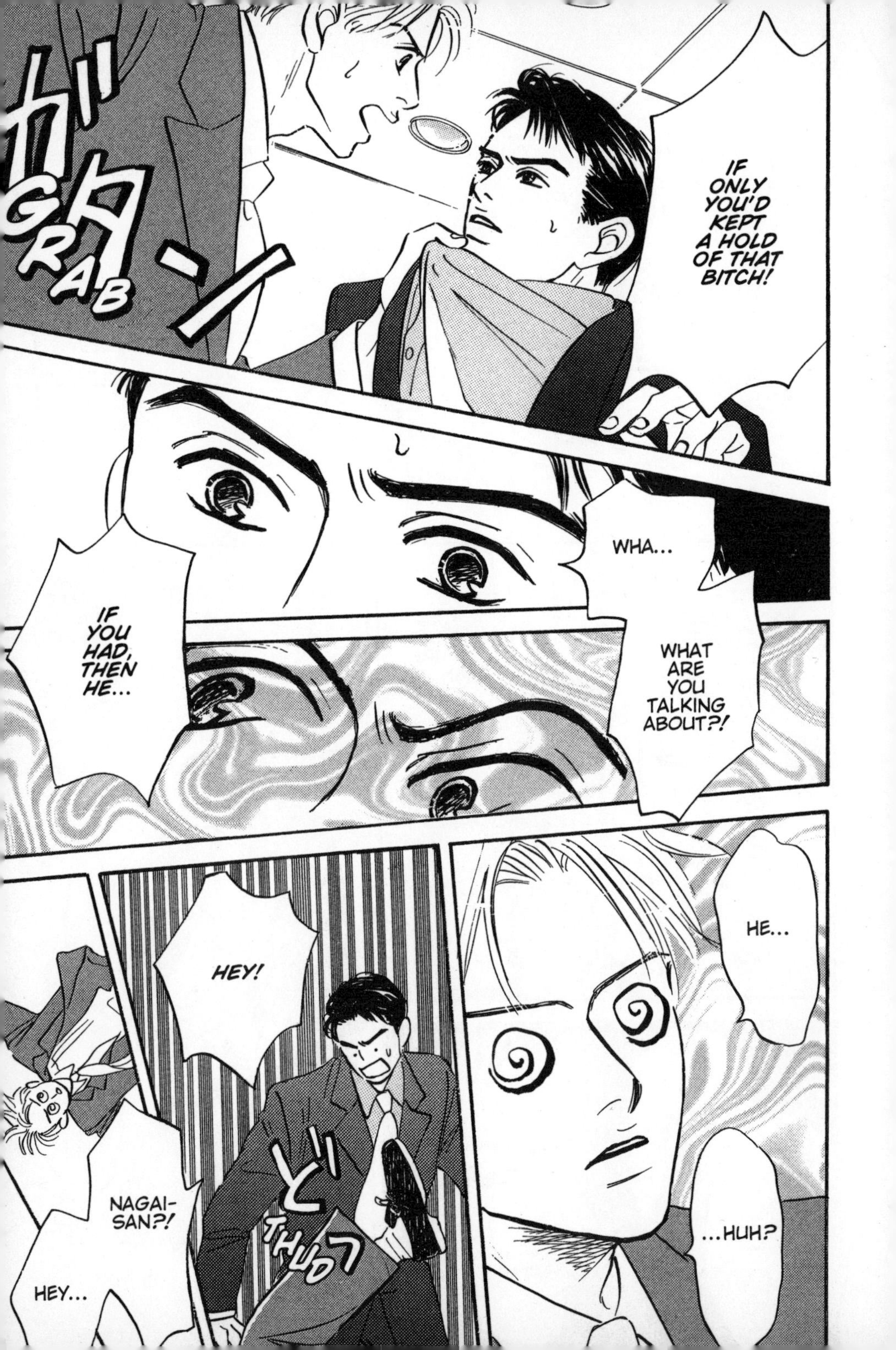
GRAB
IF ONLY YOU'D KEPT A HOLD OF THAT BITCH!
WHA...
WHAT ARE YOU TALKING ABOUT?!
IF YOU HAD, THEN HE...
HE...
...HUH?
HEY!
THUD
NAGAI-SAN?!
HEY...

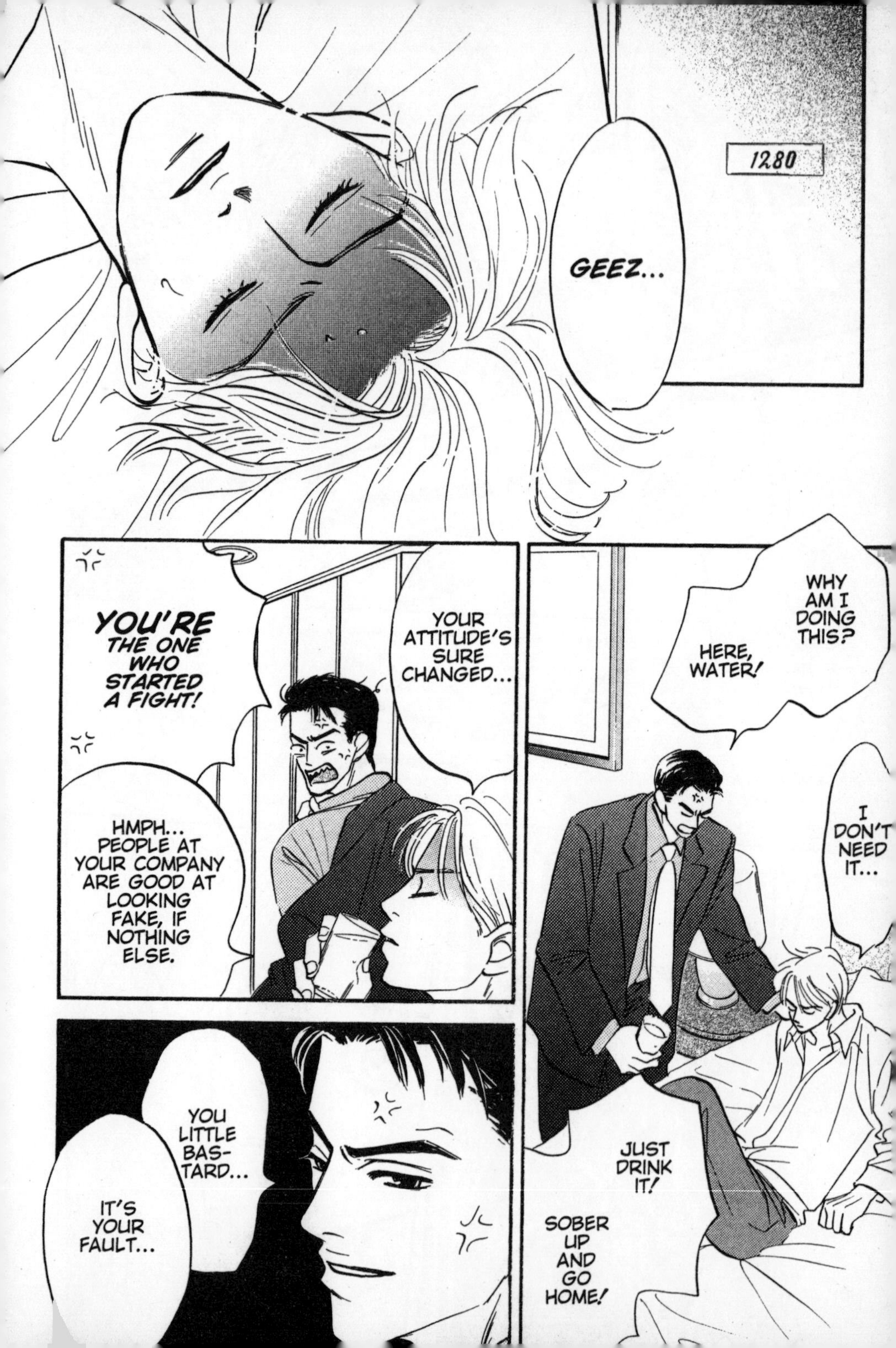
1280
GEEZ...
WHY AM I DOING THIS?
HERE, WATER!
I DON'T NEED IT...
JUST DRINK IT!
SOBER UP AND GO HOME!
YOUR ATTITUDE'S SURE CHANGED...
YOU'RE THE ONE WHO STARTED A FIGHT!
HMPH... PEOPLE AT YOUR COMPANY ARE GOOD AT LOOKING FAKE, IF NOTHING ELSE.
YOU LITTLE BAS-TARD...
IT'S YOUR FAULT...

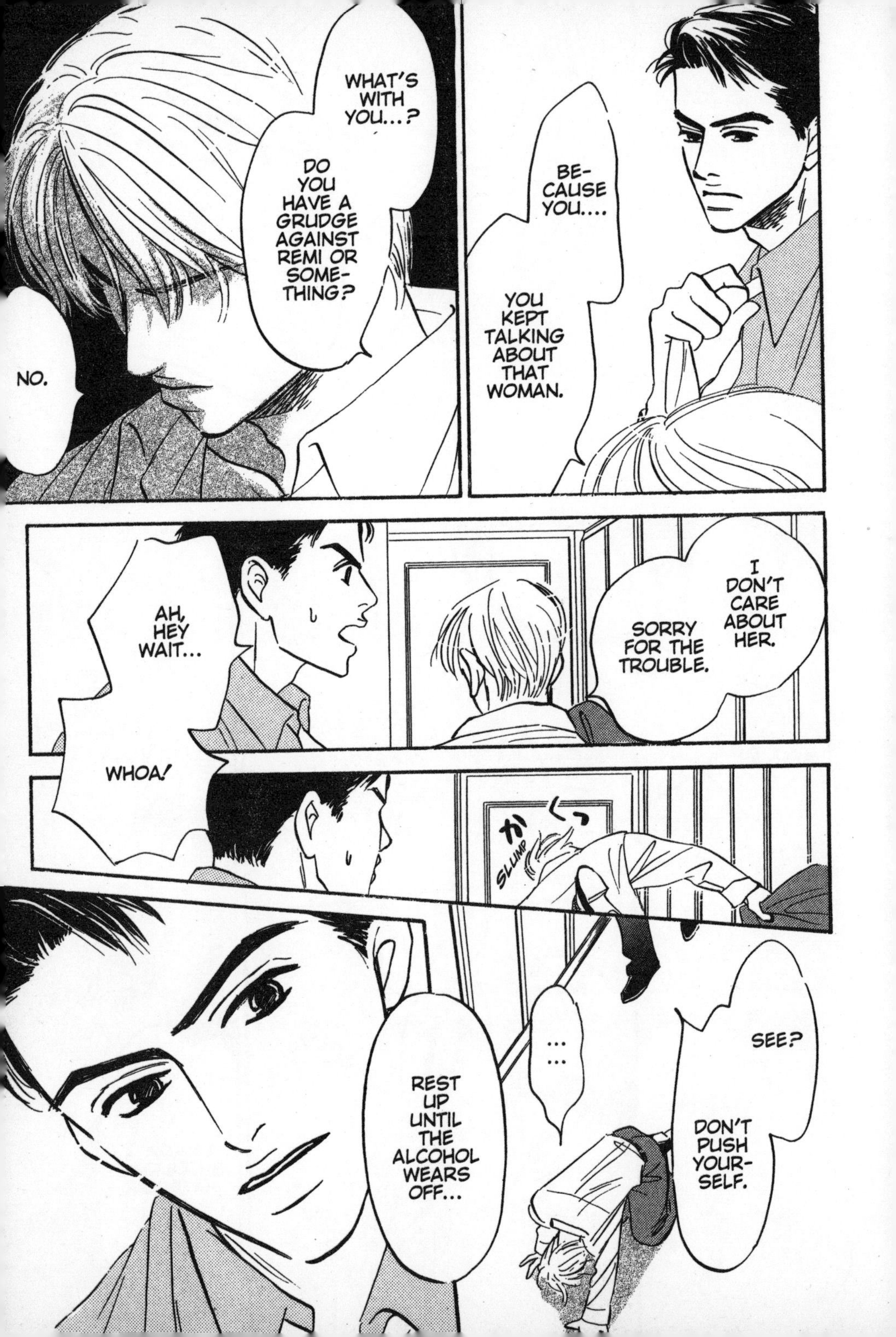
BE-CAUSE YOU....
YOU KEPT TALKING ABOUT THAT WOMAN.
WHAT'S WITH YOU...?
DO YOU HAVE A GRUDGE AGAINST REMI OR SOME-THING?
NO.
I DON'T CARE ABOUT HER.
SORRY FOR THE TROUBLE.
AH, HEY WAIT...
くっ
か
SLUMP
WHOA!
SEE?
DON'T PUSH YOUR-SELF.
......
REST UP UNTIL THE ALCOHOL WEARS OFF...

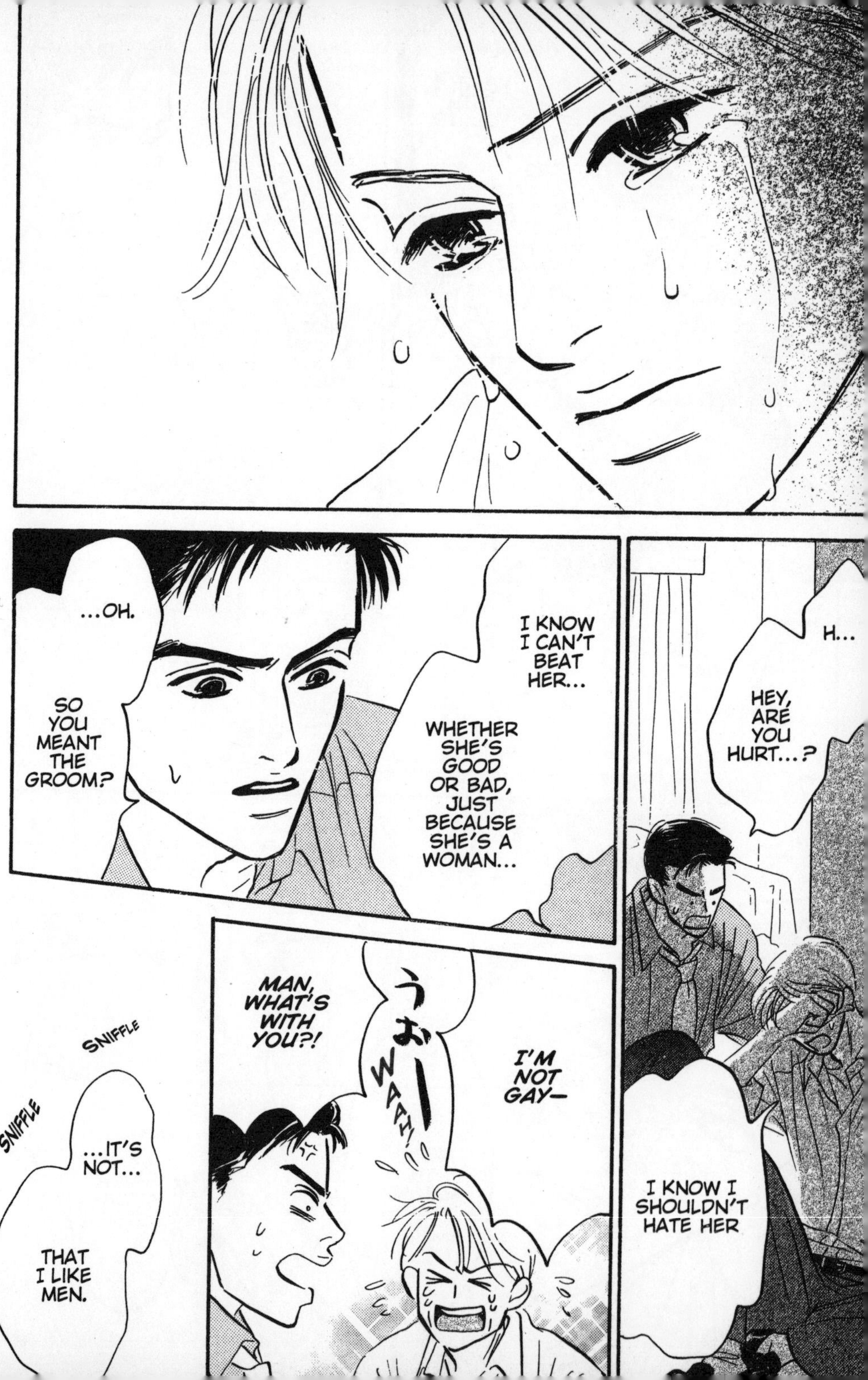
H...
HEY, ARE YOU HURT...?
I KNOW I SHOULDN'T HATE HER
I KNOW I CAN'T BEAT HER...
WHETHER SHE'S GOOD OR BAD, JUST BECAUSE SHE'S A WOMAN...
...OH.
SO YOU MEANT THE GROOM?
I'M NOT GAY—
うぉー
WAAH!
MAN, WHAT'S WITH YOU?!
SNIFFLE
SNIFFLE
...IT'S NOT...
THAT I LIKE MEN.

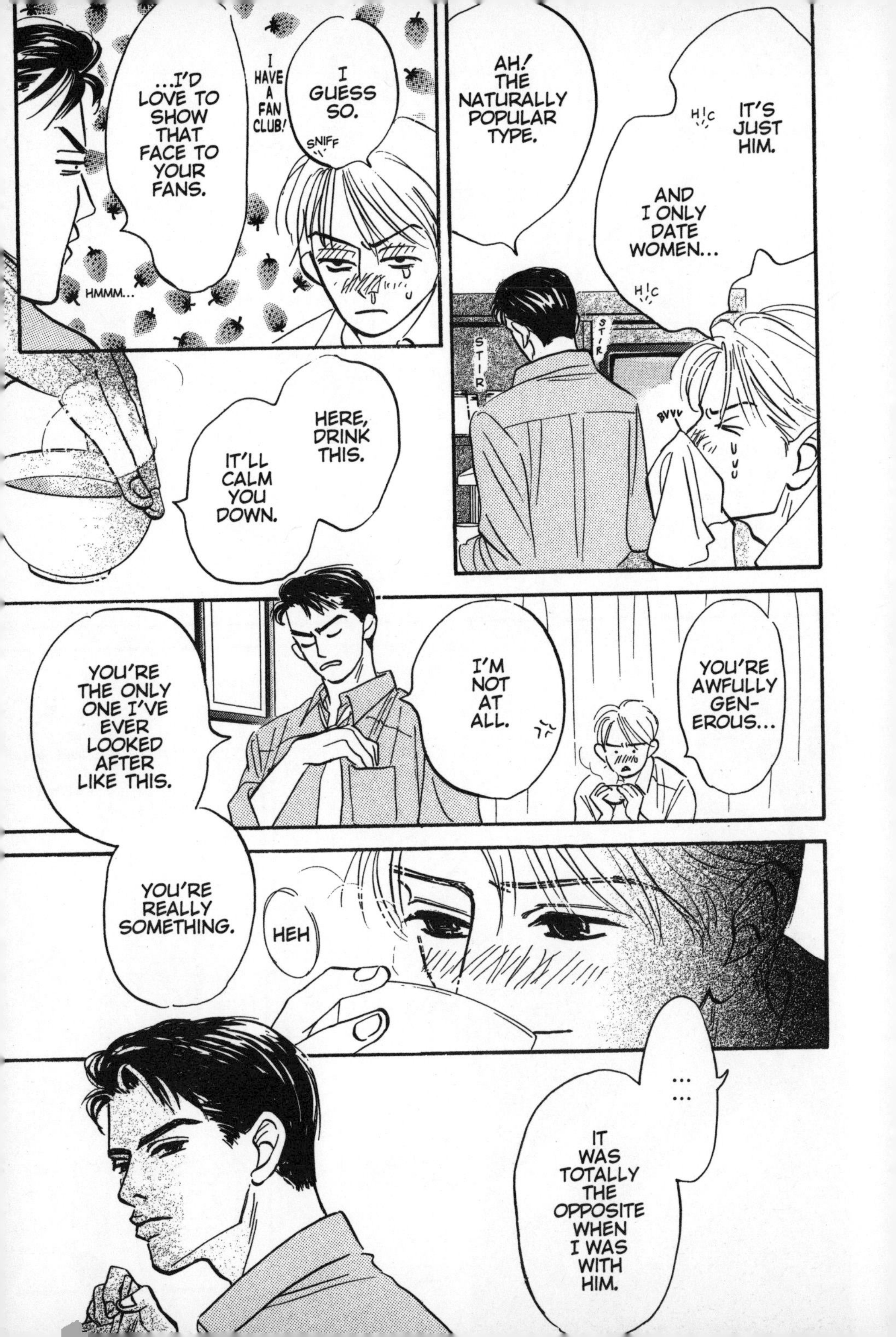
AH! THE NATURALLY POPULAR TYPE.
H!C
IT'S JUST HIM.
AND I ONLY DATE WOMEN...
H!C
STIR
STIR
BVVV
UUU
I GUESS SO.
I HAVE A FAN CLUB!
SNIFF
...I'D LOVE TO SHOW THAT FACE TO YOUR FANS.
HMMM...
HERE, DRINK THIS.
IT'LL CALM YOU DOWN.
YOU'RE AWFULLY GEN-EROUS...
I'M NOT AT ALL.
YOU'RE THE ONLY ONE I'VE EVER LOOKED AFTER LIKE THIS.
HEH
YOU'RE REALLY SOMETHING.
......
IT WAS TOTALLY THE OPPOSITE WHEN I WAS WITH HIM.

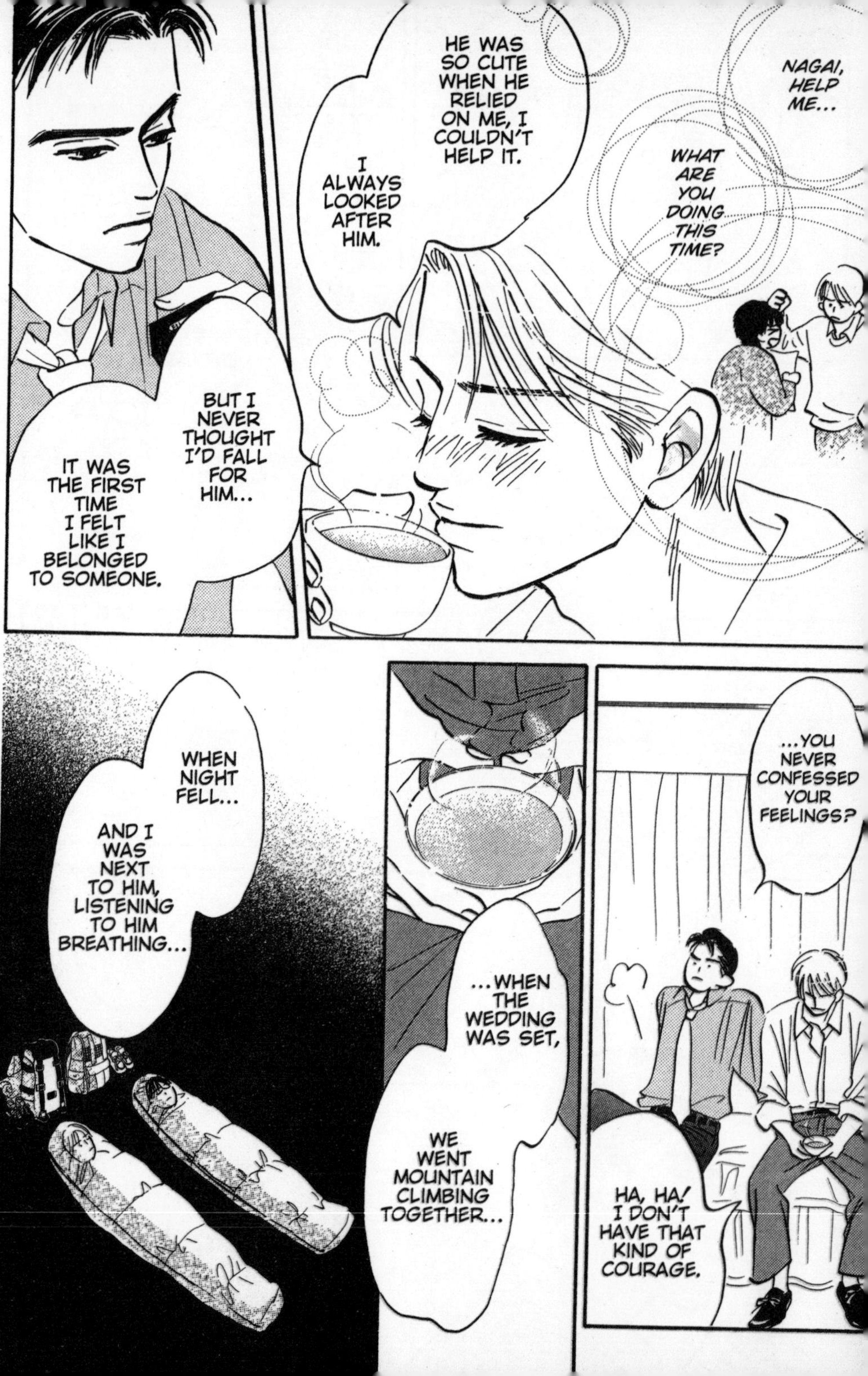
NAGAI, HELP ME...
WHAT ARE YOU DOING THIS TIME?
HE WAS SO CUTE WHEN HE RELIED ON ME, I COULDN'T HELP IT.
I ALWAYS LOOKED AFTER HIM.
BUT I NEVER THOUGHT I'D FALL FOR HIM...
IT WAS THE FIRST TIME I FELT LIKE I BELONGED TO SOMEONE.
...YOU NEVER CONFESSED YOUR FEELINGS?
HA, HA! I DON'T HAVE THAT KIND OF COURAGE.
...WHEN THE WEDDING WAS SET,
WE WENT MOUNTAIN CLIMBING TOGETHER...
WHEN NIGHT FELL...
AND I WAS NEXT TO HIM, LISTENING TO HIM BREATHING...

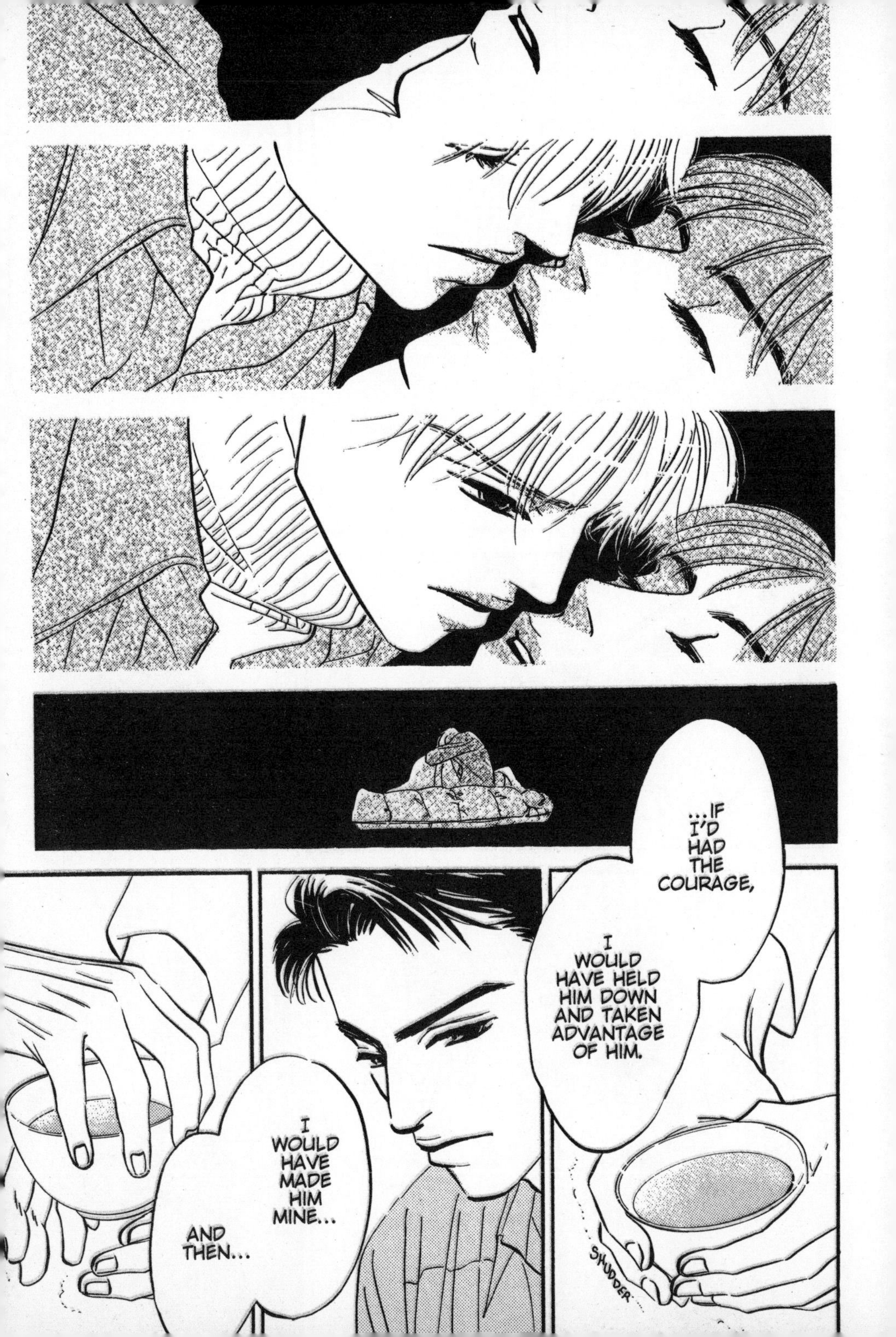
...IF I'D HAD THE COURAGE,
I WOULD HAVE HELD HIM DOWN AND TAKEN ADVANTAGE OF HIM.
SHUDDER
I WOULD HAVE MADE HIM MINE...
AND THEN...

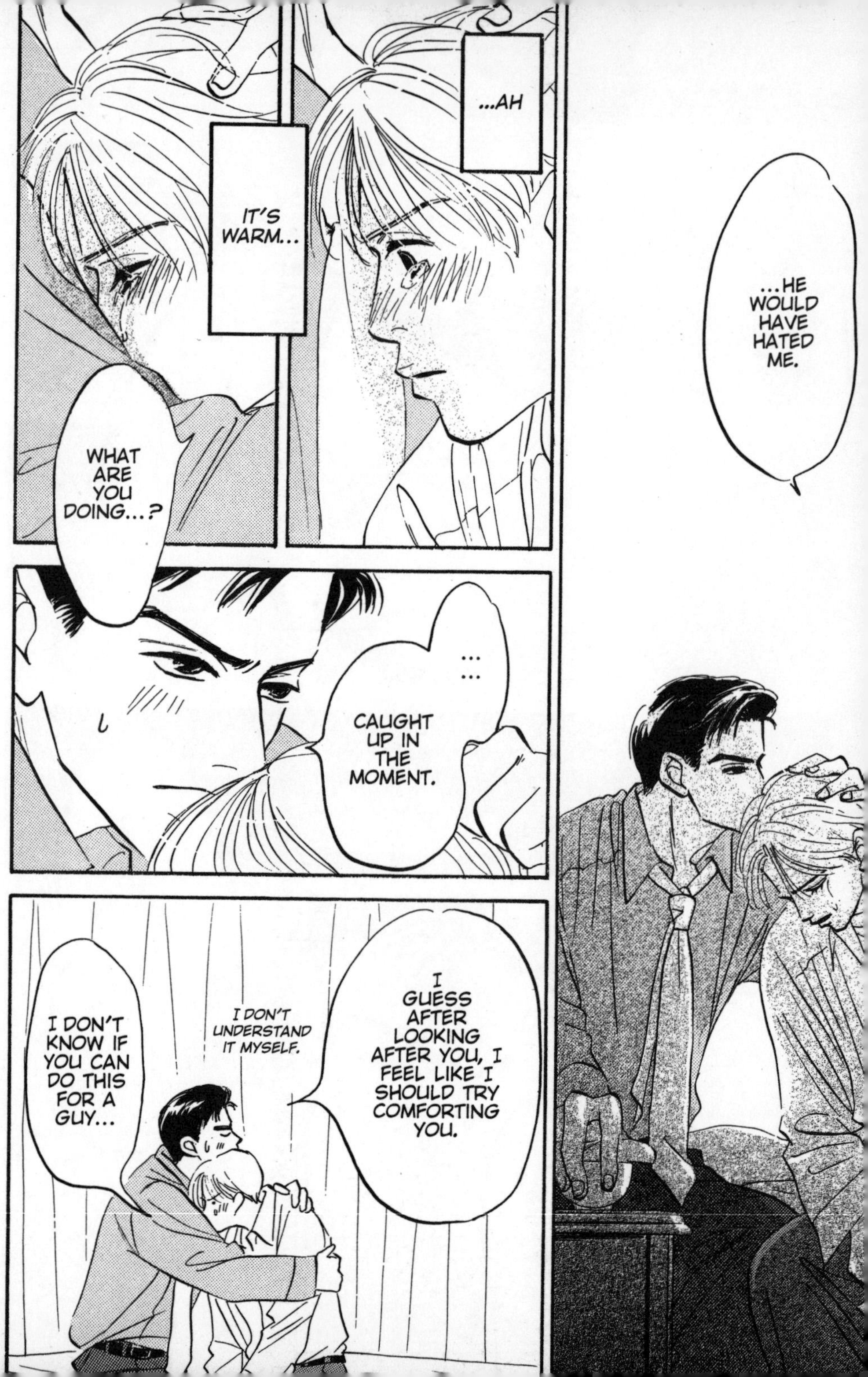
...HE WOULD HAVE HATED ME.
...AH
IT'S WARM...
WHAT ARE YOU DOING...?
......
CAUGHT UP IN THE MOMENT.
I GUESS AFTER LOOKING AFTER YOU, I FEEL LIKE I SHOULD TRY COMFORTING YOU.
I DON'T UNDERSTAND IT MYSELF.
I DON'T KNOW IF YOU CAN DO THIS FOR A GUY...

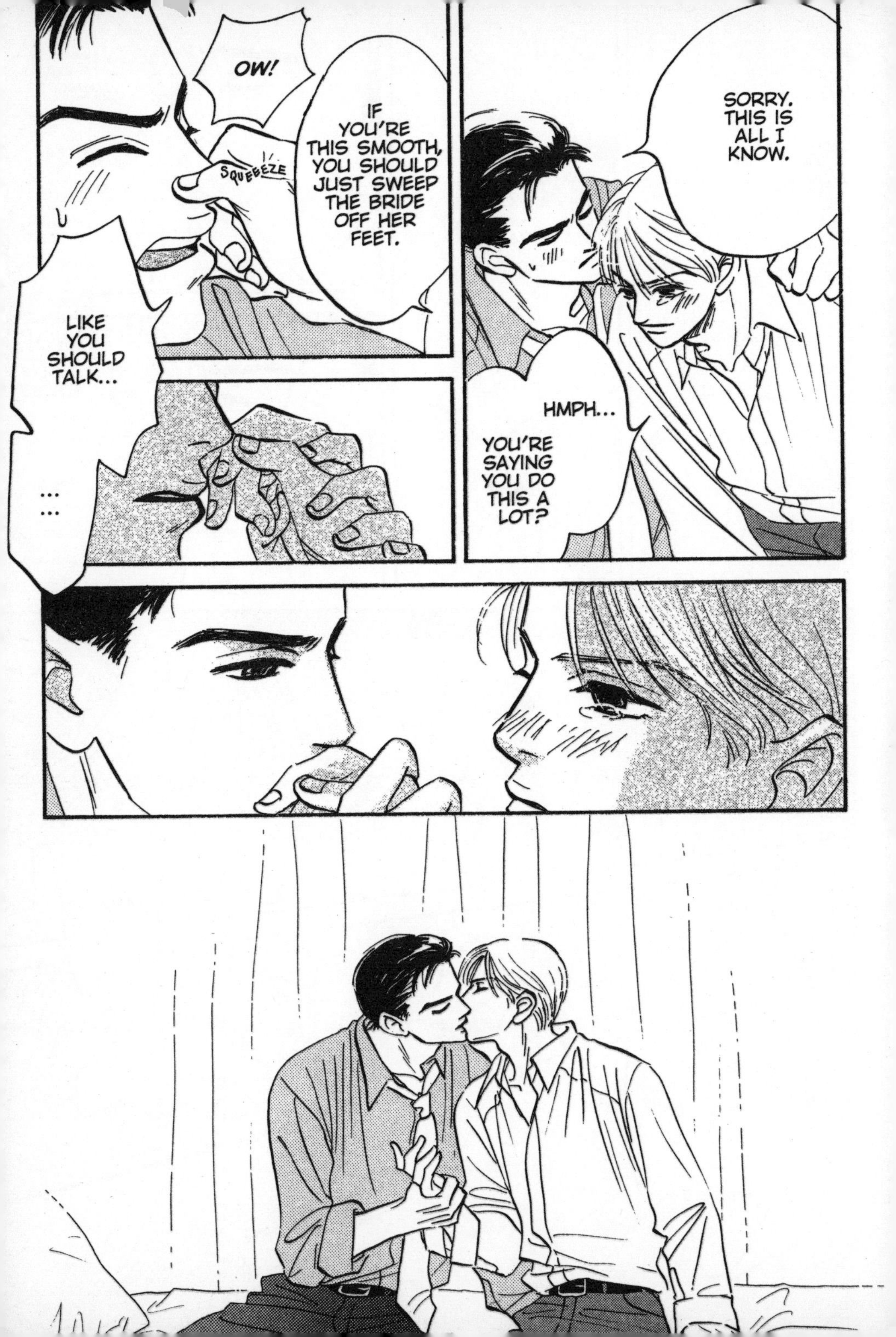
SORRY. THIS IS ALL I KNOW.
HMPH...
YOU'RE SAYING YOU DO THIS A LOT?
OW!
SQUEEEZE
IF YOU'RE THIS SMOOTH, YOU SHOULD JUST SWEEP THE BRIDE OFF HER FEET.
LIKE YOU SHOULD TALK...
...
...

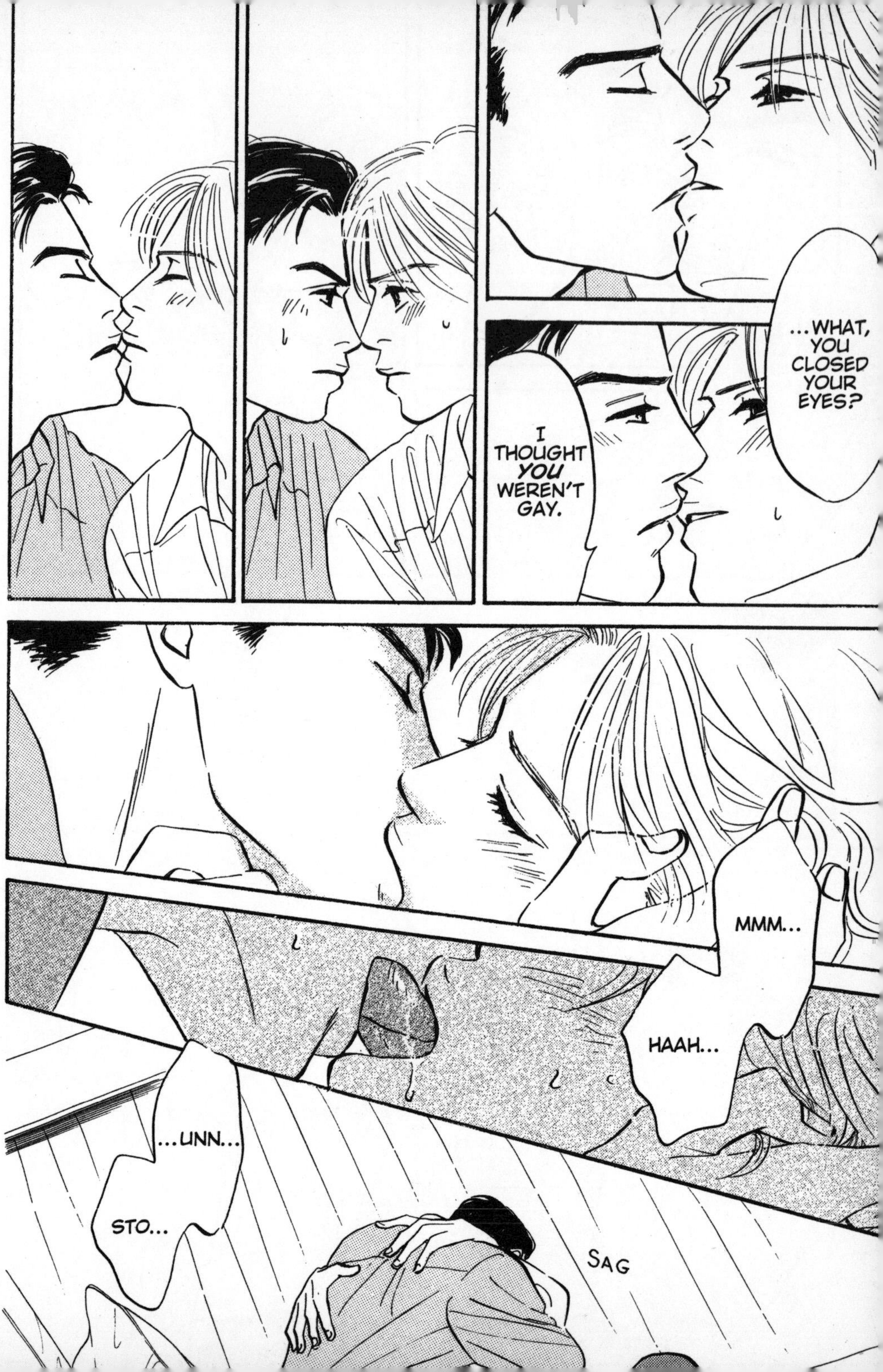
...WHAT, YOU CLOSED YOUR EYES?
I THOUGHT *YOU* WEREN'T GAY.
MMM...
HAAH...
...UNN...
STO...
SAG

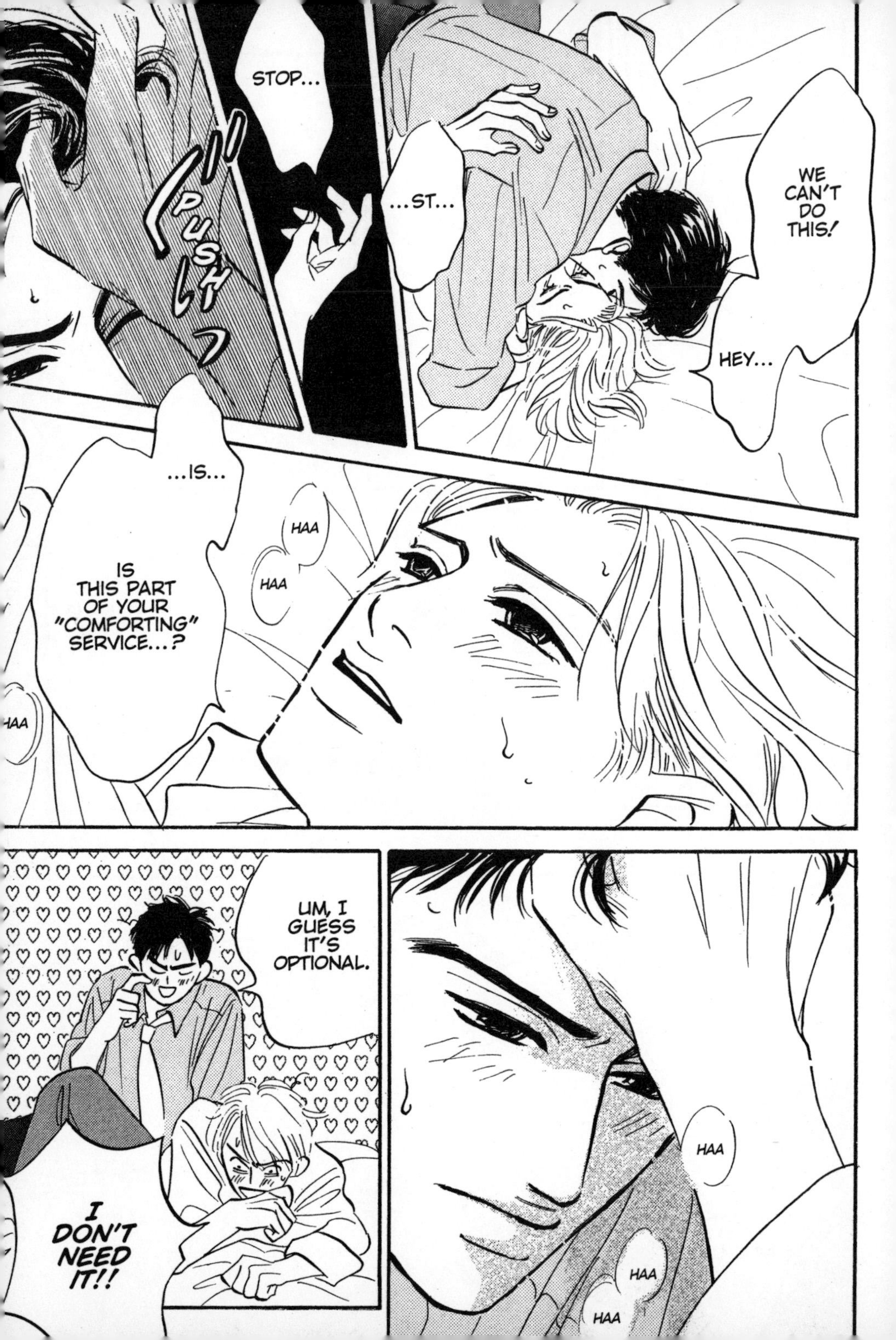
WE CAN'T DO THIS!
HEY...
...ST...
STOP...
PUSH
HAA
HAA
...IS...
IS THIS PART OF YOUR "COMFORTING" SERVICE...?
HAA
HAA
HAA
HAA
UM, I GUESS IT'S OPTIONAL.
I DON'T NEED IT!!

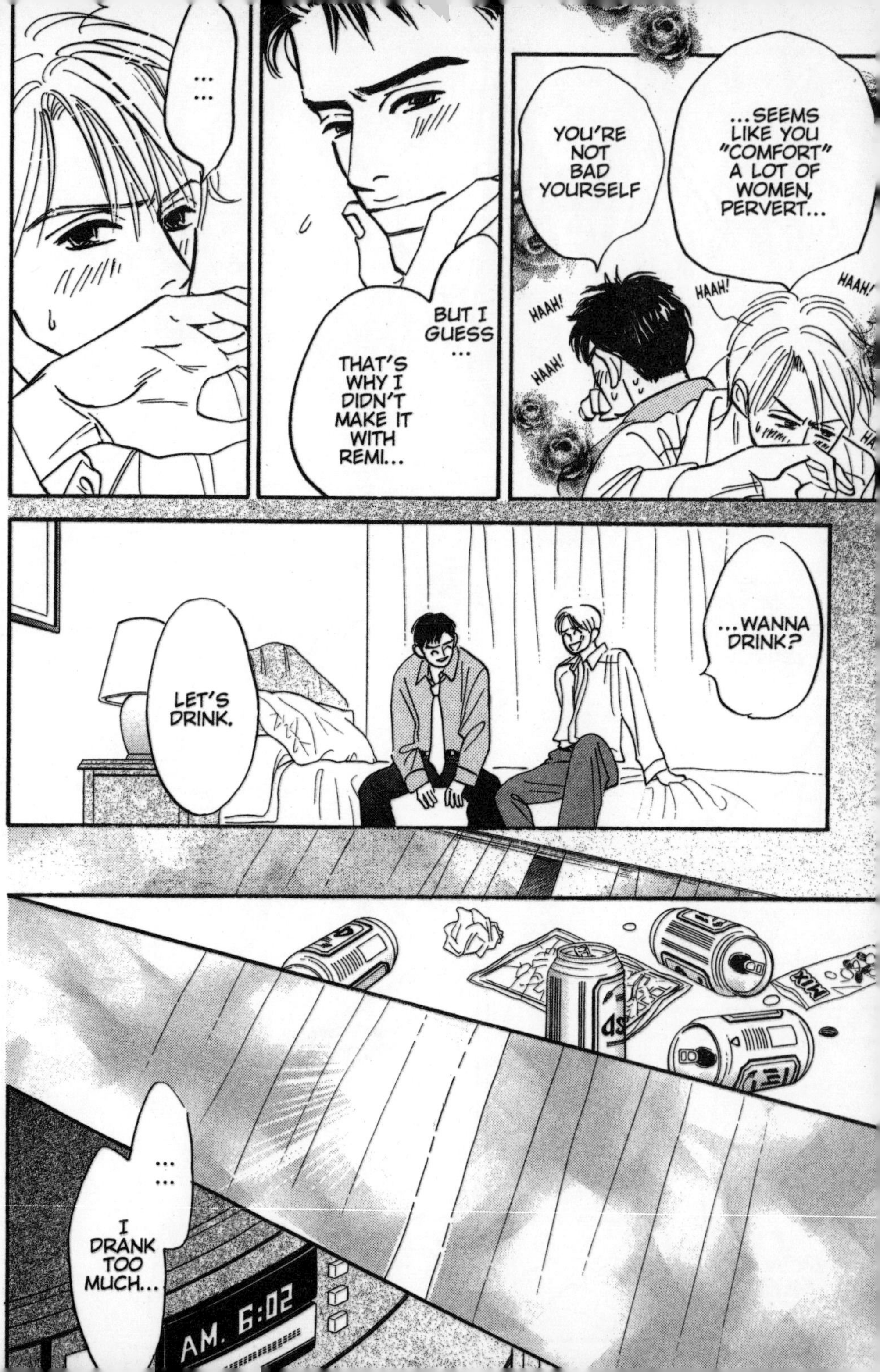
...SEEMS LIKE YOU "COMFORT" A LOT OF WOMEN, PERVERT...
YOU'RE NOT BAD YOURSELF
HAAH!
HAAH!
HAAH!
HAAH!
BUT I GUESS...
THAT'S WHY I DIDN'T MAKE IT WITH REMI...
......
...WANNA DRINK?
LET'S DRINK.
MIX
......
I DRANK TOO MUCH...
AM. 6:02

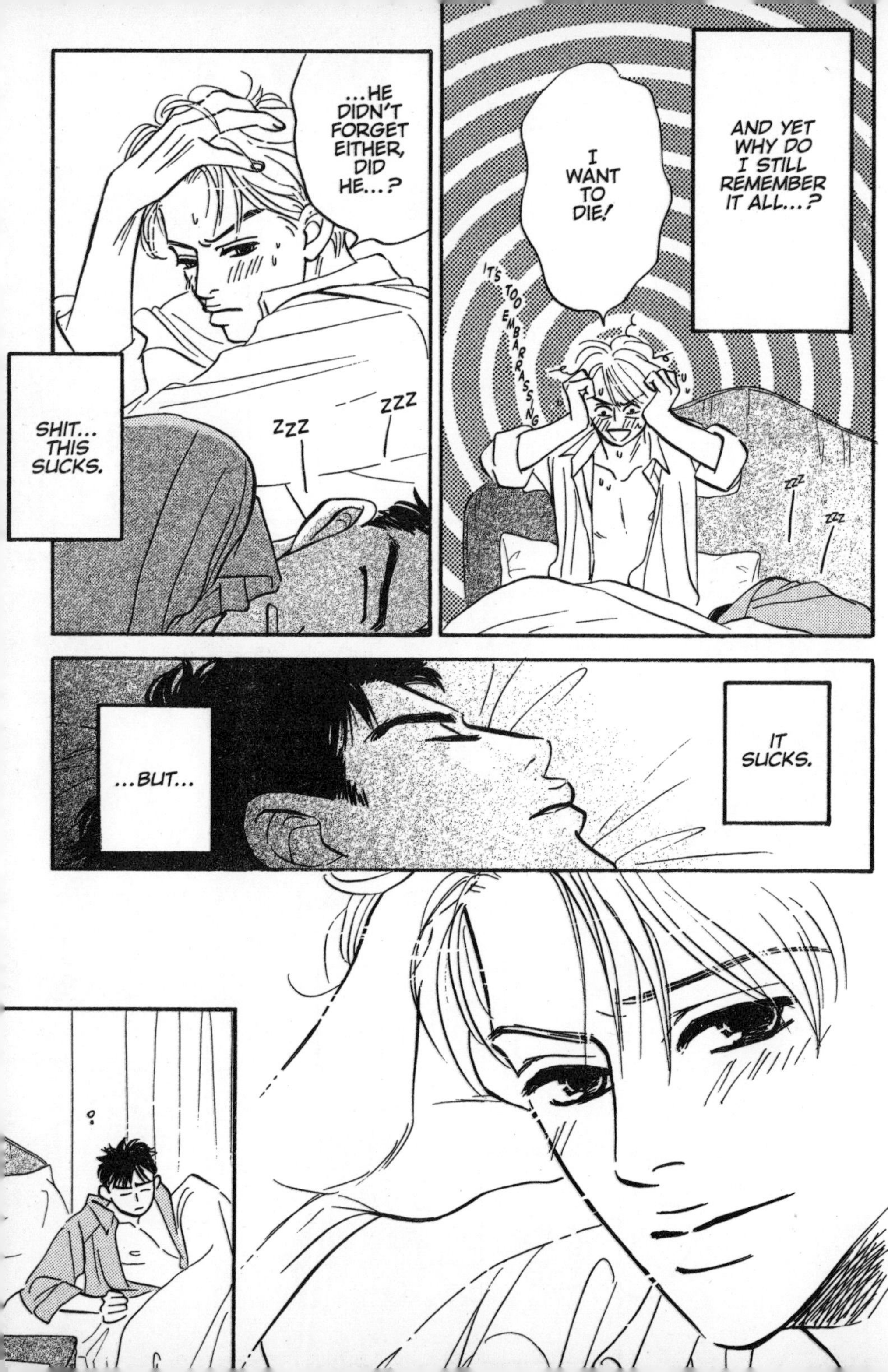
AND YET WHY DO I STILL REMEMBER IT ALL...?
I WANT TO DIE!
IT'S TOO EMBARRASSING
ZZZ
ZZZ
...HE DIDN'T FORGET EITHER, DID HE...?
ZZZ
ZZZ
SHIT... THIS SUCKS.
IT SUCKS.
...BUT...

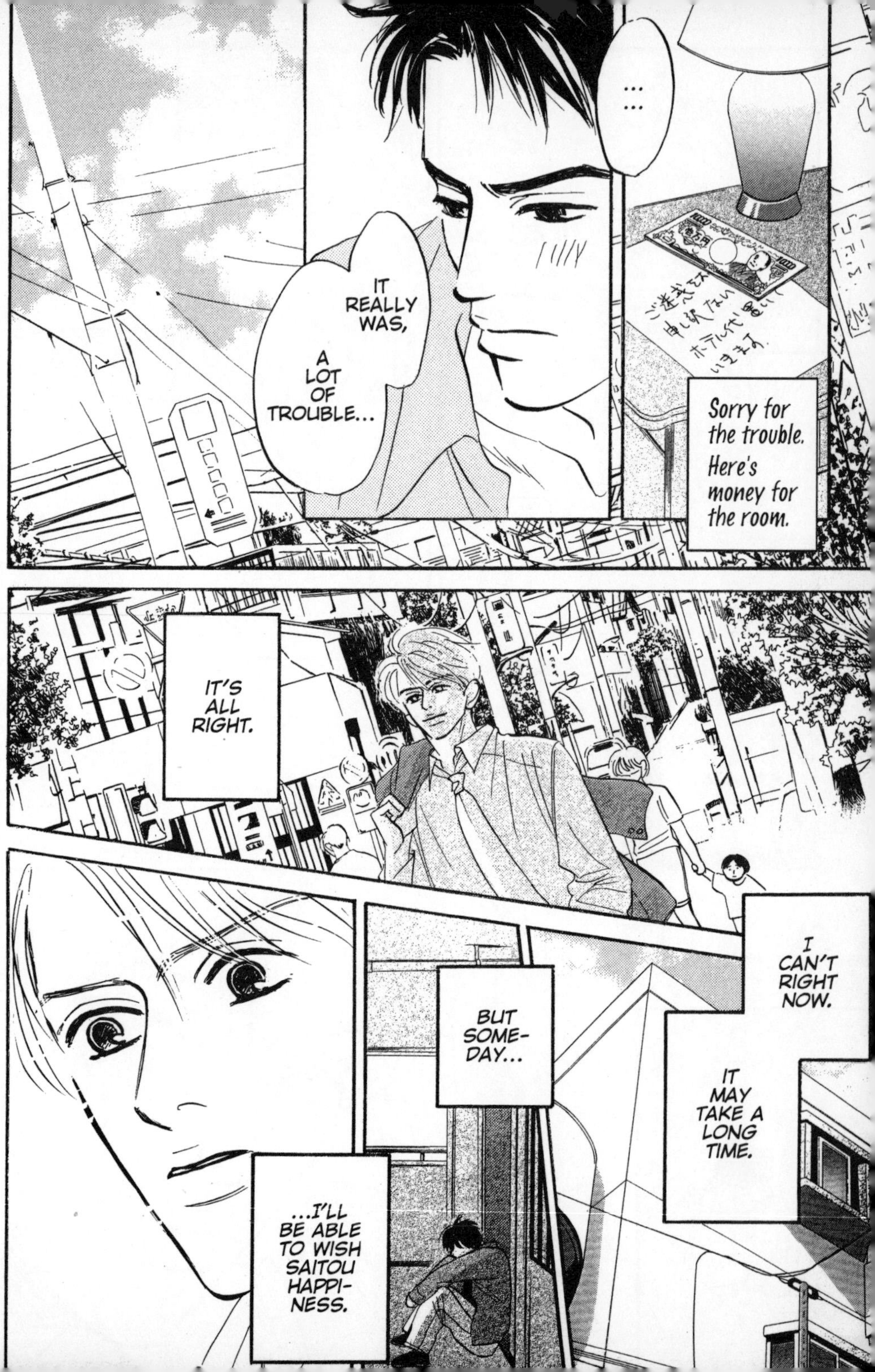

ご迷惑をかけ申し訳ない ホテル代置いていきます
Sorry for the trouble. Here's money for the room.
... ...
IT REALLY WAS, A LOT OF TROUBLE...
IT'S ALL RIGHT.
I CAN'T RIGHT NOW.
IT MAY TAKE A LONG TIME.
BUT SOME-DAY...
...I'LL BE ABLE TO WISH SAITOU HAPPI-NESS.

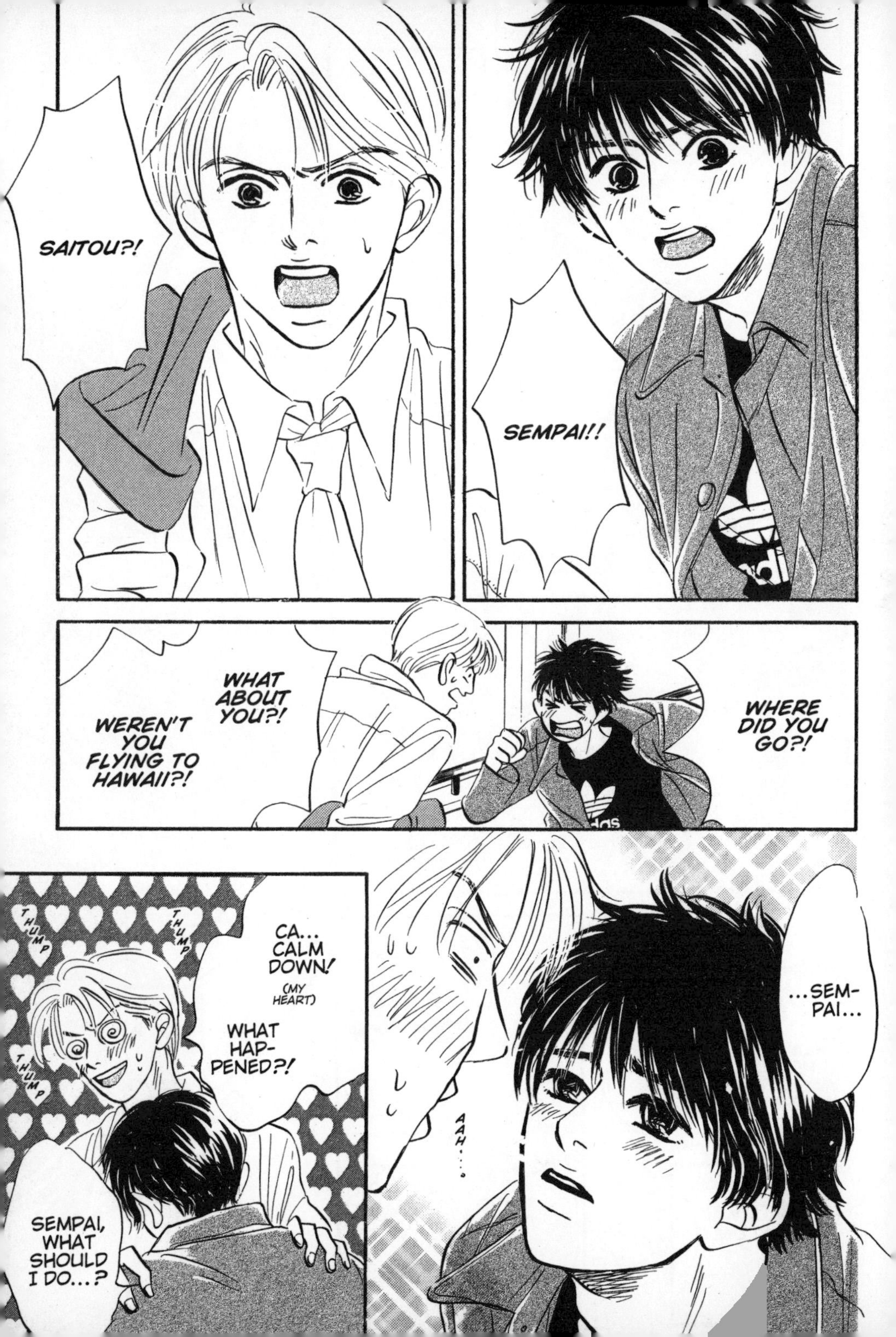
SEMPAI!!
SAITOU?!
WHERE DID YOU GO?!
WHAT ABOUT YOU?!
WEREN'T YOU FLYING TO HAWAII?!
...SEMPAI...
AAH...
THUMP
THUMP
CA... CALM DOWN!
(MY HEART)
WHAT HAPPENED?!
THUMP
SEMPAI, WHAT SHOULD I DO...?

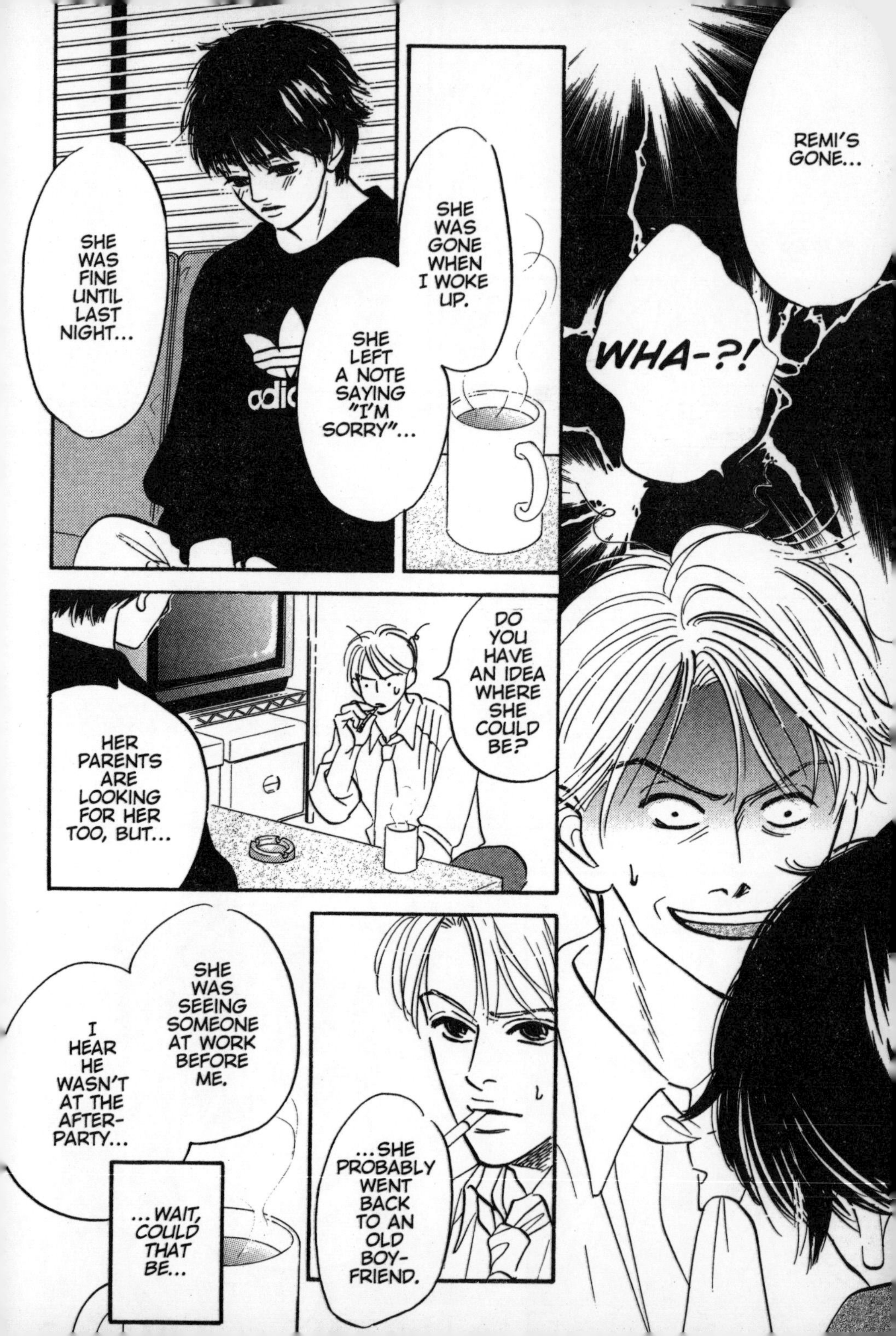
REMI'S GONE...
WHA-?!
SHE WAS GONE WHEN I WOKE UP.
SHE LEFT A NOTE SAYING "I'M SORRY"...
SHE WAS FINE UNTIL LAST NIGHT...
DO YOU HAVE AN IDEA WHERE SHE COULD BE?
HER PARENTS ARE LOOKING FOR HER TOO, BUT...
...SHE PROBABLY WENT BACK TO AN OLD BOY-FRIEND.
SHE WAS SEEING SOMEONE AT WORK BEFORE ME.
I HEAR HE WASN'T AT THE AFTER-PARTY...
...WAIT, COULD THAT BE...

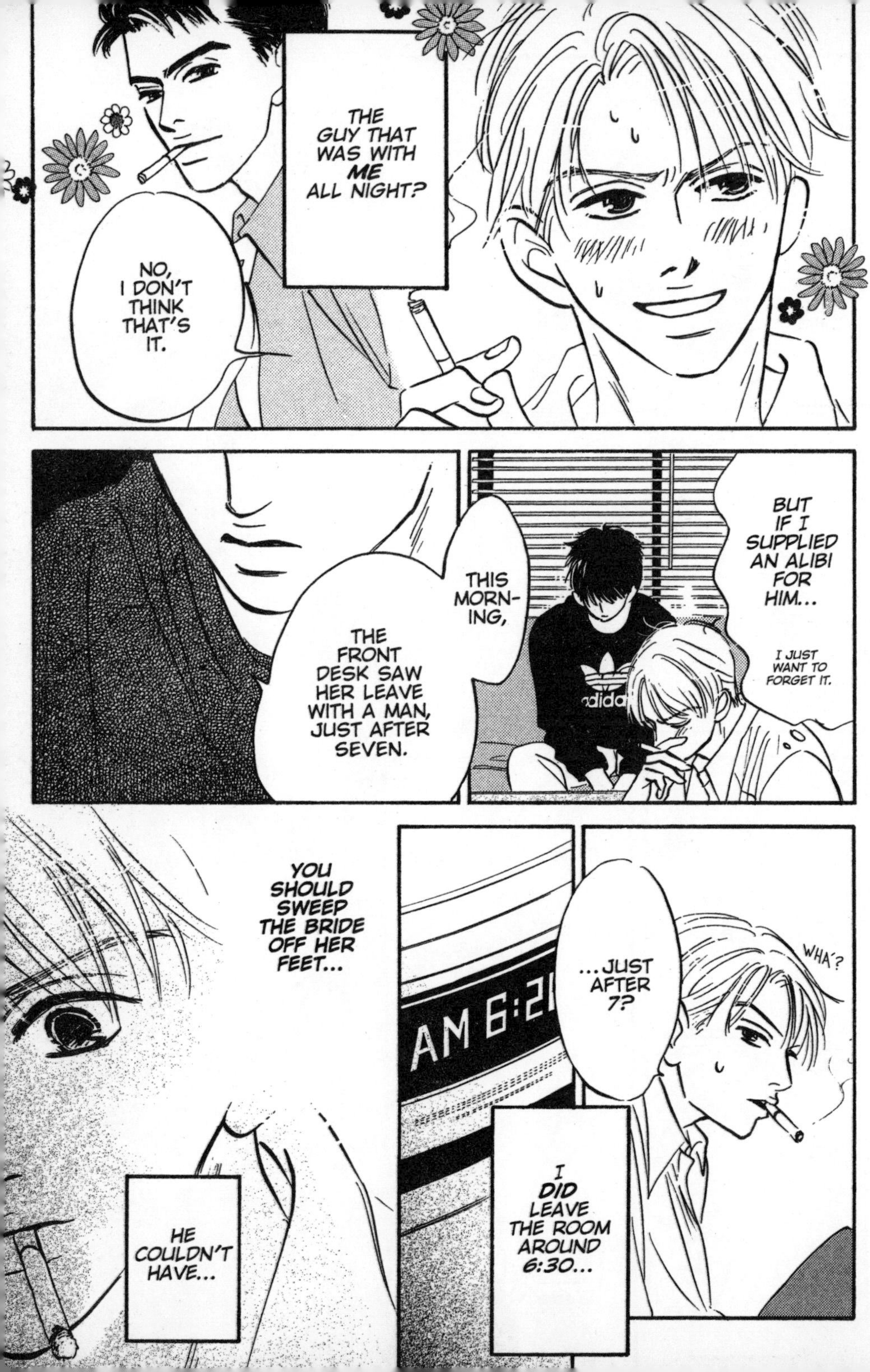
THE GUY THAT WAS WITH ME ALL NIGHT?
NO, I DON'T THINK THAT'S IT.
BUT IF I SUPPLIED AN ALIBI FOR HIM...
I JUST WANT TO FORGET IT.
THIS MORNING,
THE FRONT DESK SAW HER LEAVE WITH A MAN, JUST AFTER SEVEN.
WHA'?
...JUST AFTER 7?
I DID LEAVE THE ROOM AROUND 6:30...
AM 6:21
YOU SHOULD SWEEP THE BRIDE OFF HER FEET...
HE COULDN'T HAVE...

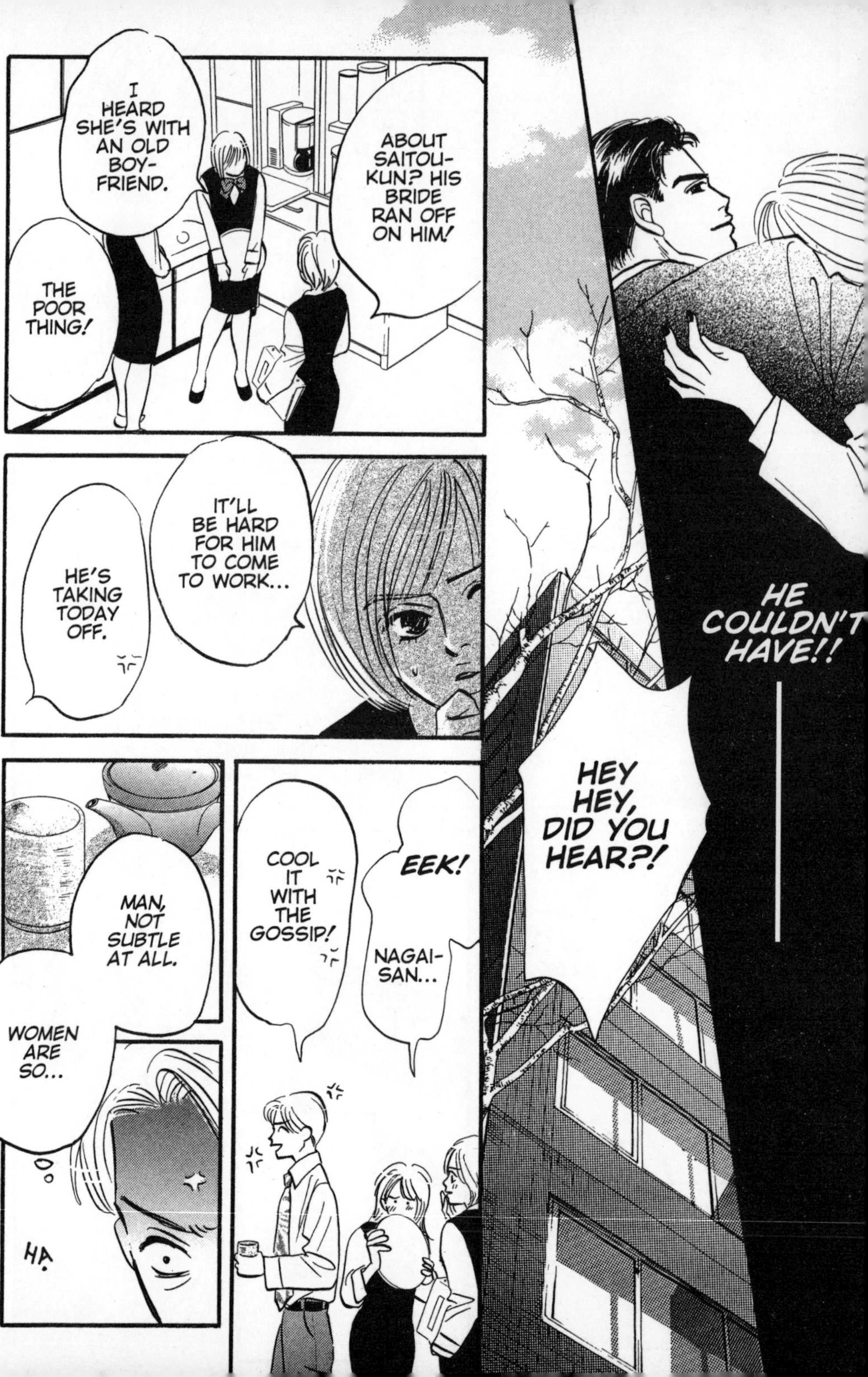
HE COULDN'T HAVE!!
HEY HEY, DID YOU HEAR?!
ABOUT SAITOU-KUN? HIS BRIDE RAN OFF ON HIM!
I HEARD SHE'S WITH AN OLD BOY-FRIEND.
THE POOR THING!
IT'LL BE HARD FOR HIM TO COME TO WORK...
HE'S TAKING TODAY OFF.
EEK!
NAGAI-SAN...
COOL IT WITH THE GOSSIP!
MAN, NOT SUBTLE AT ALL.
WOMEN ARE SO...
HA

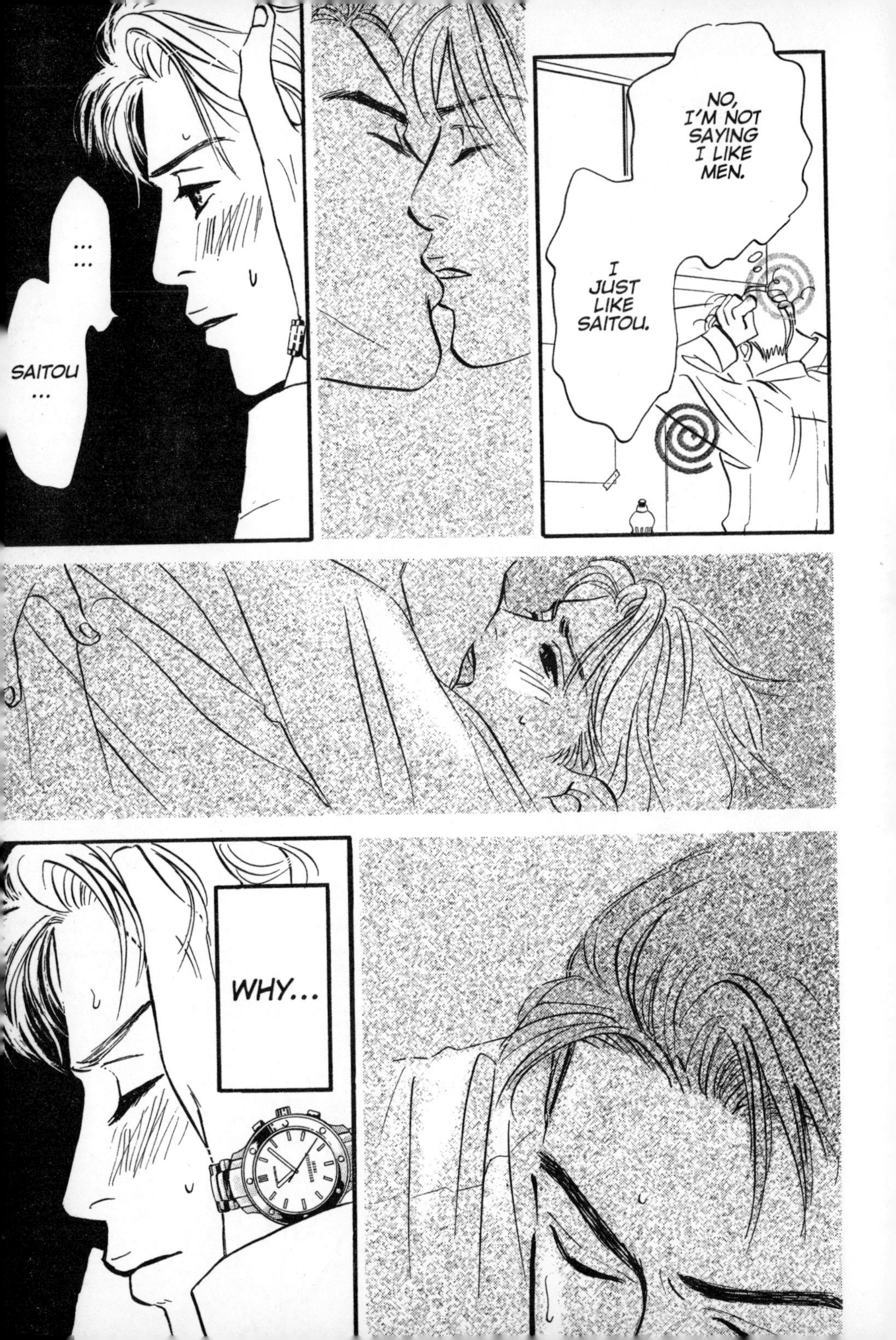
NO, I'M NOT SAYING I LIKE MEN.
I JUST LIKE SAITOU.
... ...
SAITOU ...
WHY...

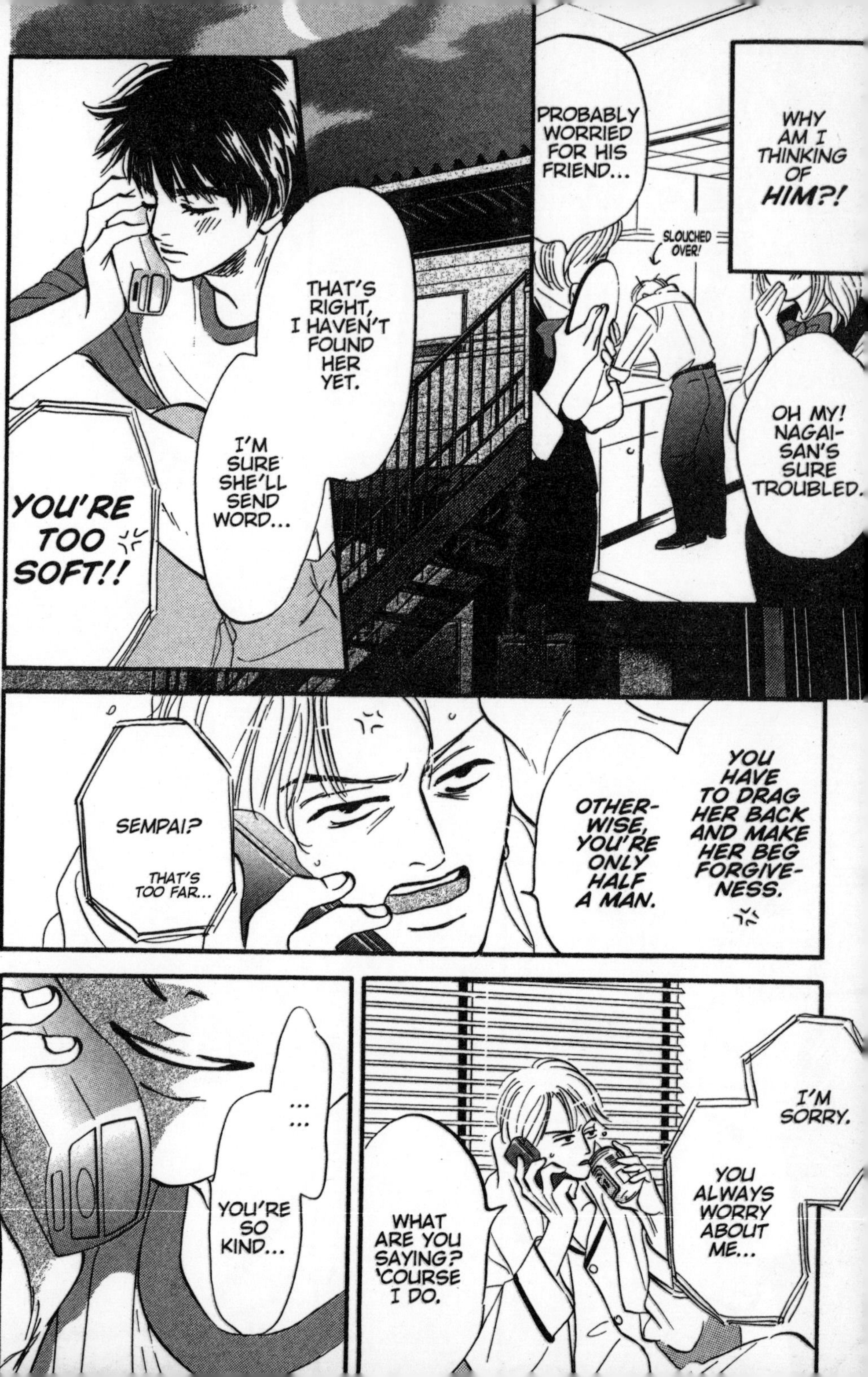
WHY AM I THINKING OF *HIM?!*
PROBABLY WORRIED FOR HIS FRIEND...
SLOUCHED OVER!
OH MY! NAGAI-SAN'S SURE TROUBLED.
THAT'S RIGHT, I HAVEN'T FOUND HER YET.
I'M SURE SHE'LL SEND WORD...
YOU'RE TOO SOFT!!
YOU HAVE TO DRAG HER BACK AND MAKE HER BEG FORGIVENESS.
OTHERWISE, YOU'RE ONLY HALF A MAN.
SEMPAI?
THAT'S TOO FAR...
I'M SORRY.
YOU ALWAYS WORRY ABOUT ME...
WHAT ARE YOU SAYING? 'COURSE I DO.
......
YOU'RE SO KIND...

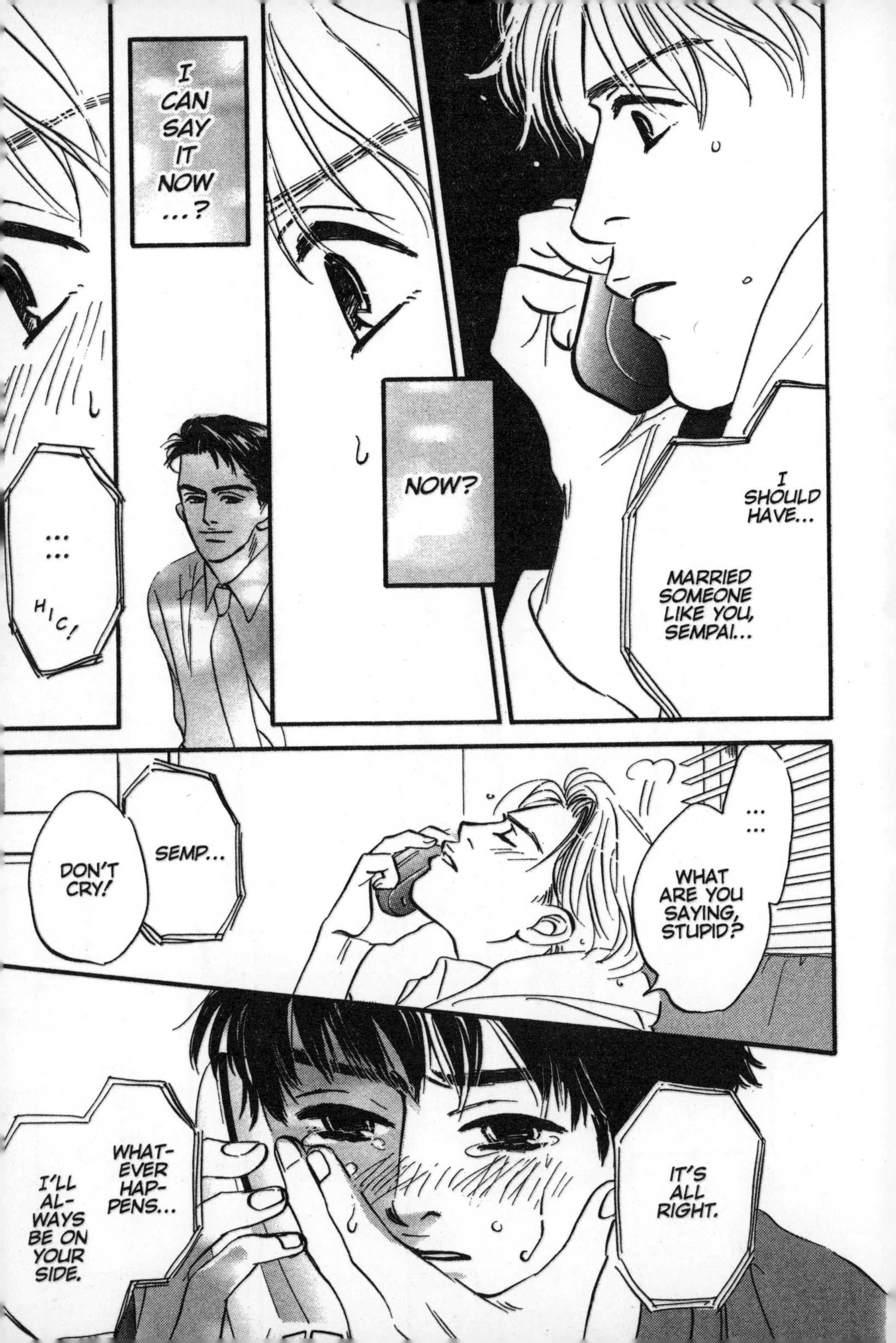
I SHOULD HAVE...
MARRIED SOMEONE LIKE YOU, SEMPAI...
NOW?
I CAN SAY IT NOW...?
...
...
HIC!
...
...
WHAT ARE YOU SAYING, STUPID?
SEMP...
DON'T CRY!
IT'S ALL RIGHT.
WHAT-EVER HAP-PENS...
I'LL AL-WAYS BE ON YOUR SIDE.

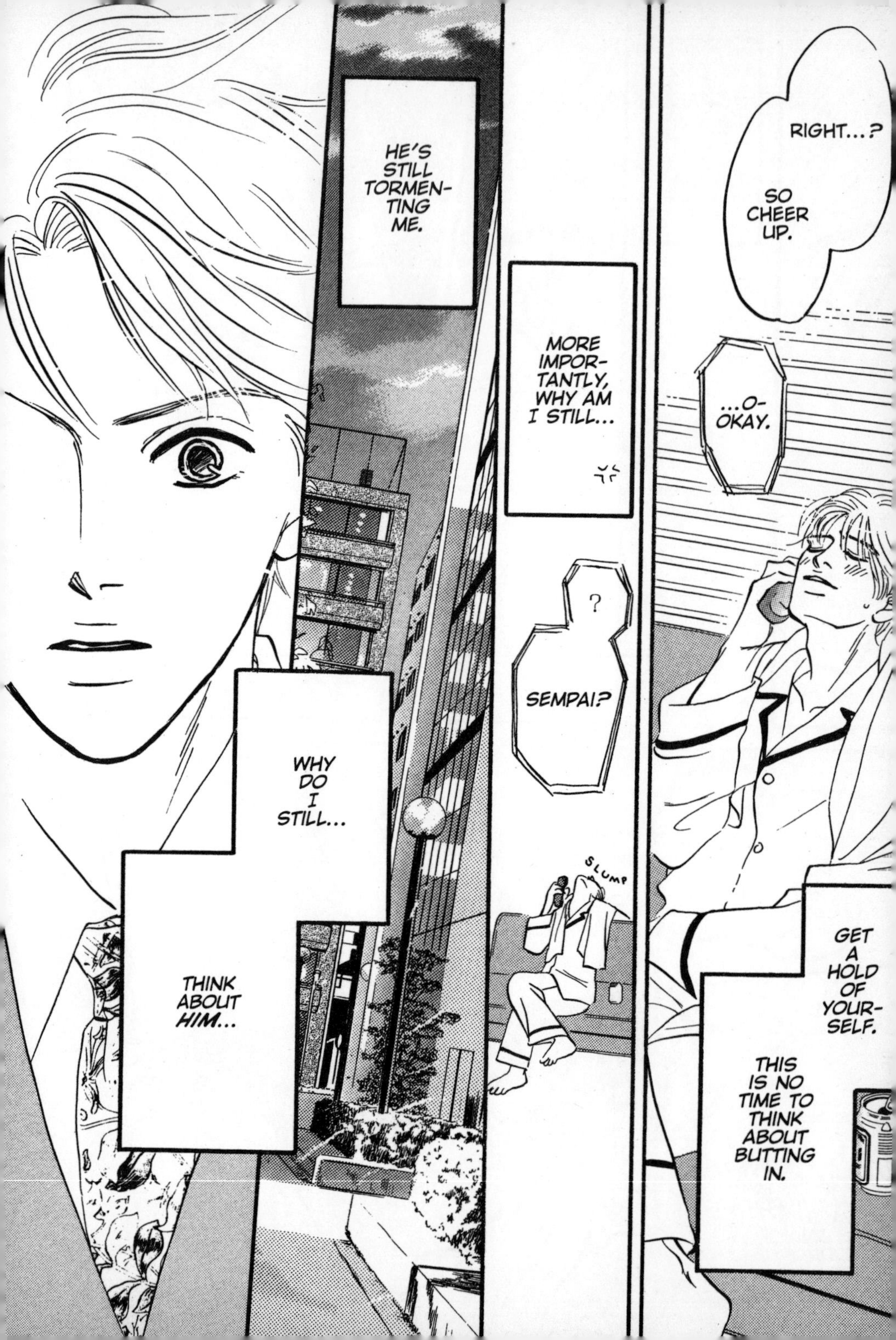
RIGHT...?
SO CHEER UP.
...O-OKAY.
GET A HOLD OF YOURSELF.
THIS IS NO TIME TO THINK ABOUT BUTTING IN.
MORE IMPORTANTLY, WHY AM I STILL...
?
SEMPAI?
SLUMP
HE'S STILL TORMENTING ME.
WHY DO I STILL...
THINK ABOUT HIM...

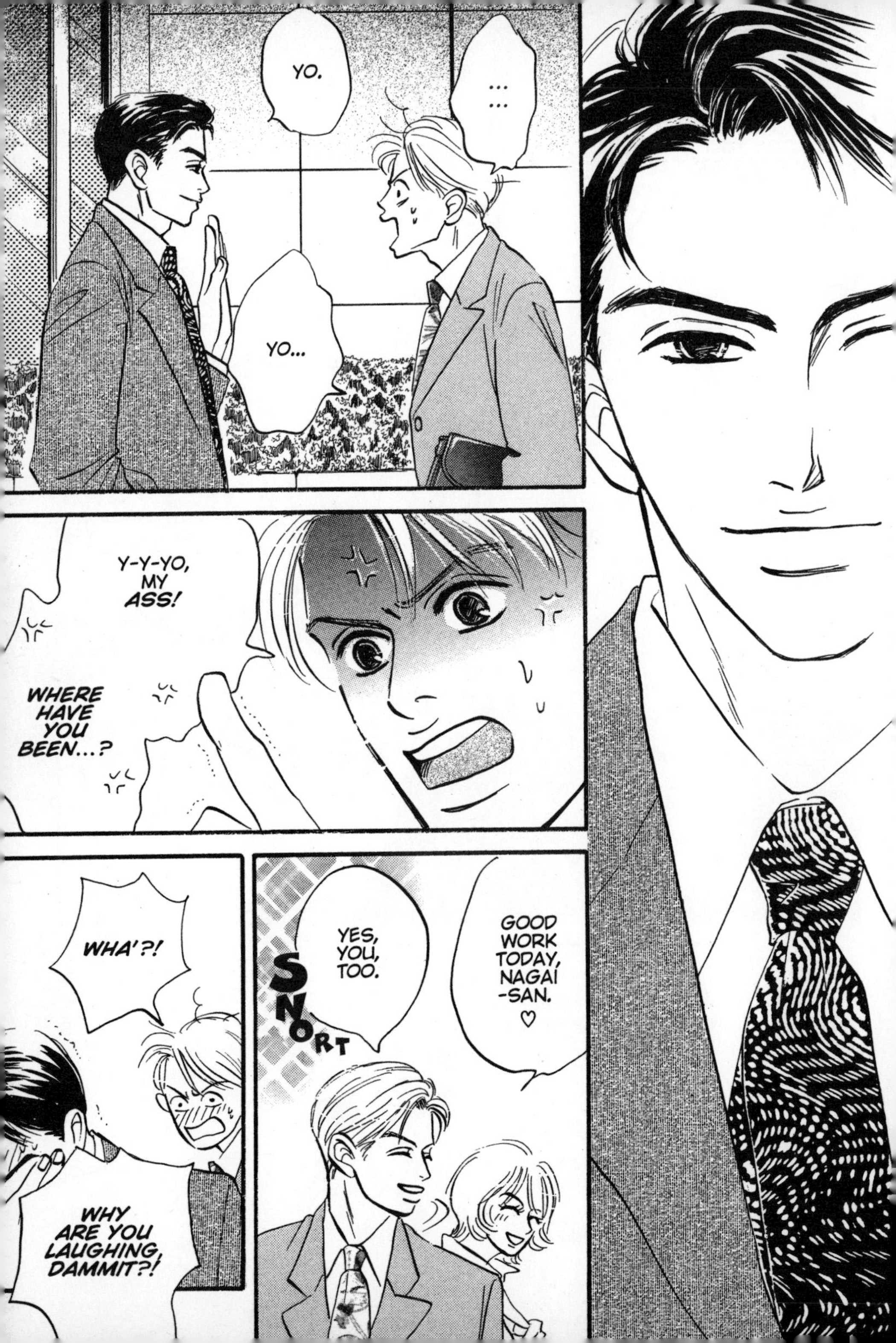
YO.
......
YO...
Y-Y-YO, MY ASS!
WHERE HAVE YOU BEEN...?
GOOD WORK TODAY, NAGAI -SAN. ♡
YES, YOU, TOO.
SNORT
WHA'?!
WHY ARE YOU LAUGHING, DAMMIT?!

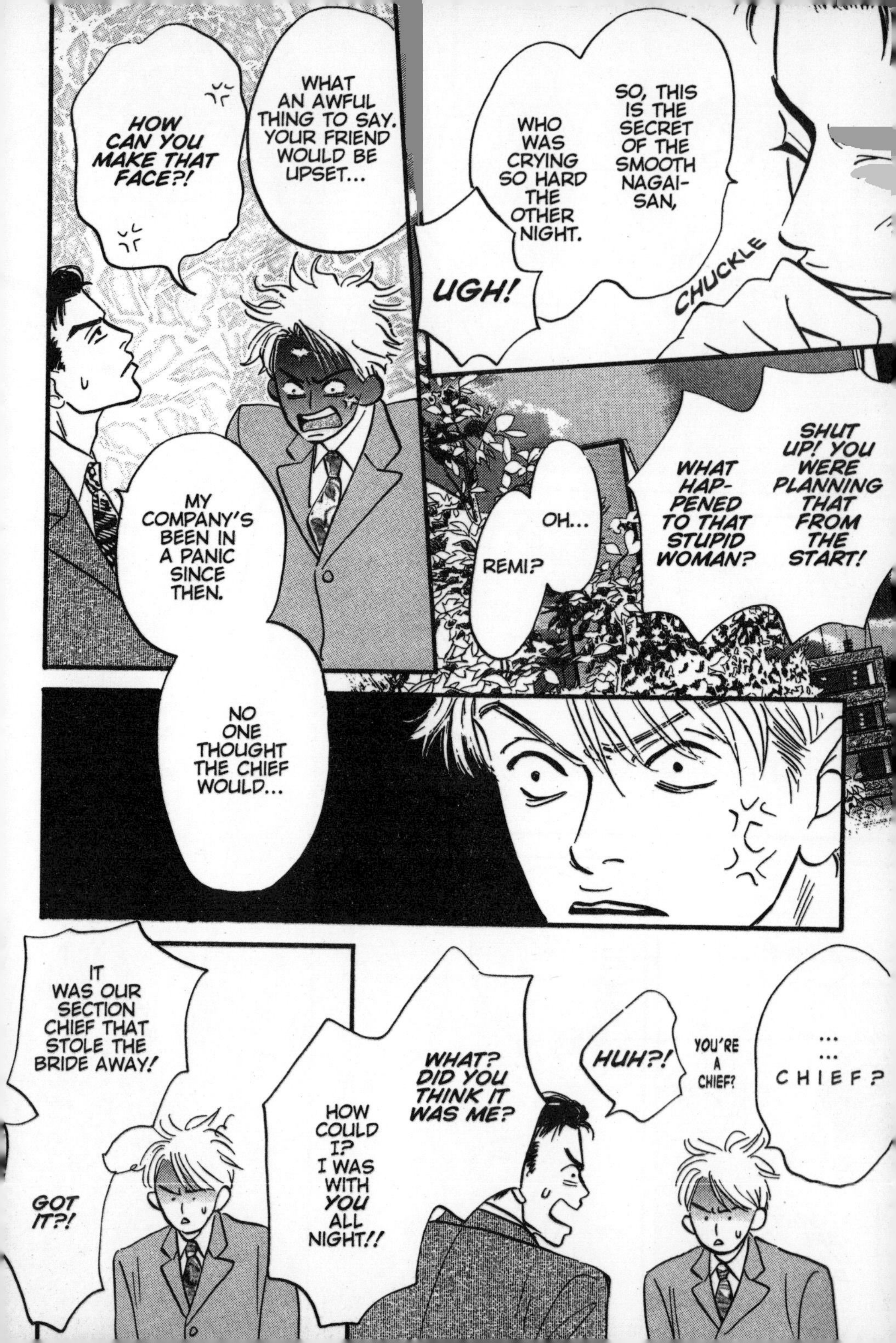
SO, THIS IS THE SECRET OF THE SMOOTH NAGAI-SAN,
WHO WAS CRYING SO HARD THE OTHER NIGHT.
CHUCKLE
UGH!
SHUT UP! YOU WERE PLANNING THAT FROM THE START!
WHAT HAP-PENED TO THAT STUPID WOMAN?
OH... REMI?
WHAT AN AWFUL THING TO SAY. YOUR FRIEND WOULD BE UPSET...
HOW CAN YOU MAKE THAT FACE?!
MY COMPANY'S BEEN IN A PANIC SINCE THEN.
NO ONE THOUGHT THE CHIEF WOULD...
... ... CHIEF?
YOU'RE A CHIEF?
HUH?!
WHAT? DID YOU THINK IT WAS ME?
HOW COULD I? I WAS WITH YOU ALL NIGHT!!
IT WAS OUR SECTION CHIEF THAT STOLE THE BRIDE AWAY!
GOT IT?!

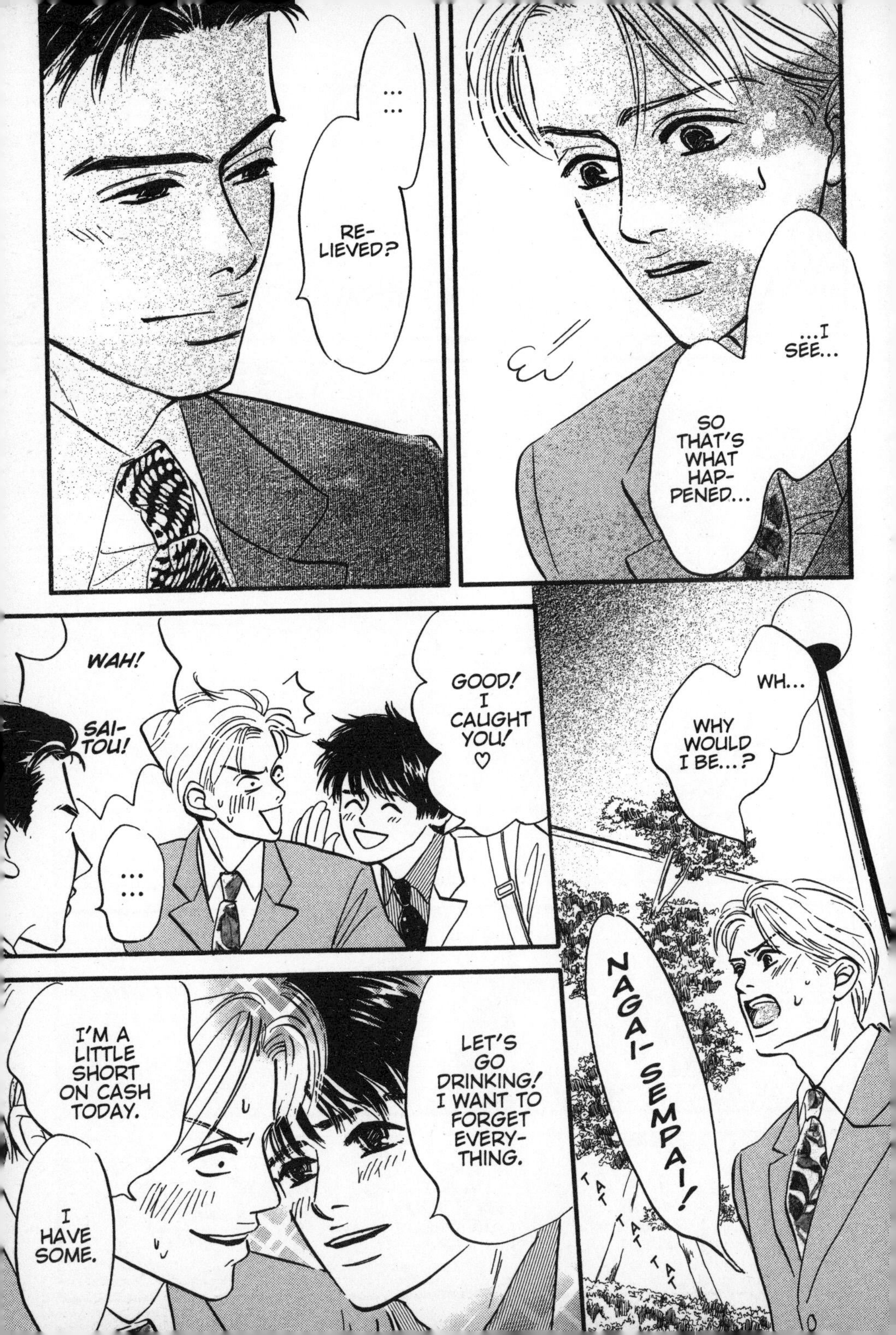
...I SEE...
SO THAT'S WHAT HAPPENED...
......
RE-LIEVED?
WH...
WHY WOULD I BE...?
NAGAI-SEMPAI!
TAT TAT TAT TAT
GOOD! I CAUGHT YOU! ♡
WAH!
SAI-TOU!
......
LET'S GO DRINKING! I WANT TO FORGET EVERYTHING.
I'M A LITTLE SHORT ON CASH TODAY.
I HAVE SOME.

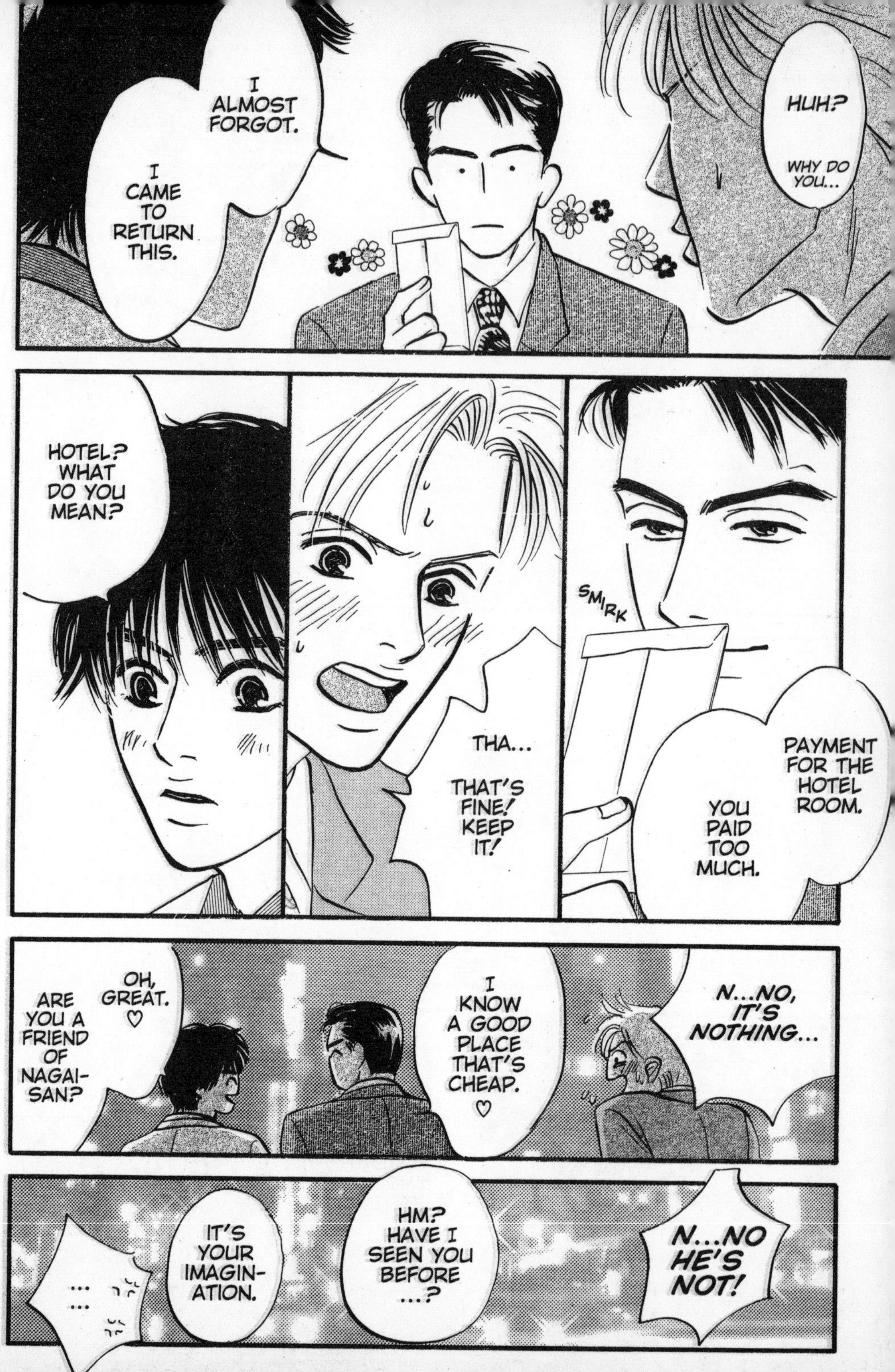
HUH?
WHY DO YOU...
I ALMOST FORGOT.
I CAME TO RETURN THIS.
PAYMENT FOR THE HOTEL ROOM.
YOU PAID TOO MUCH.
SMIRK
THA...
THAT'S FINE! KEEP IT!
HOTEL? WHAT DO YOU MEAN?
N...NO, IT'S NOTHING...
I KNOW A GOOD PLACE THAT'S CHEAP. ♡
OH, GREAT. ♡
ARE YOU A FRIEND OF NAGAI-SAN?
N...NO HE'S NOT!
HM? HAVE I SEEN YOU BEFORE ...?
IT'S YOUR IMAGINATION.
... ...

ACT.2

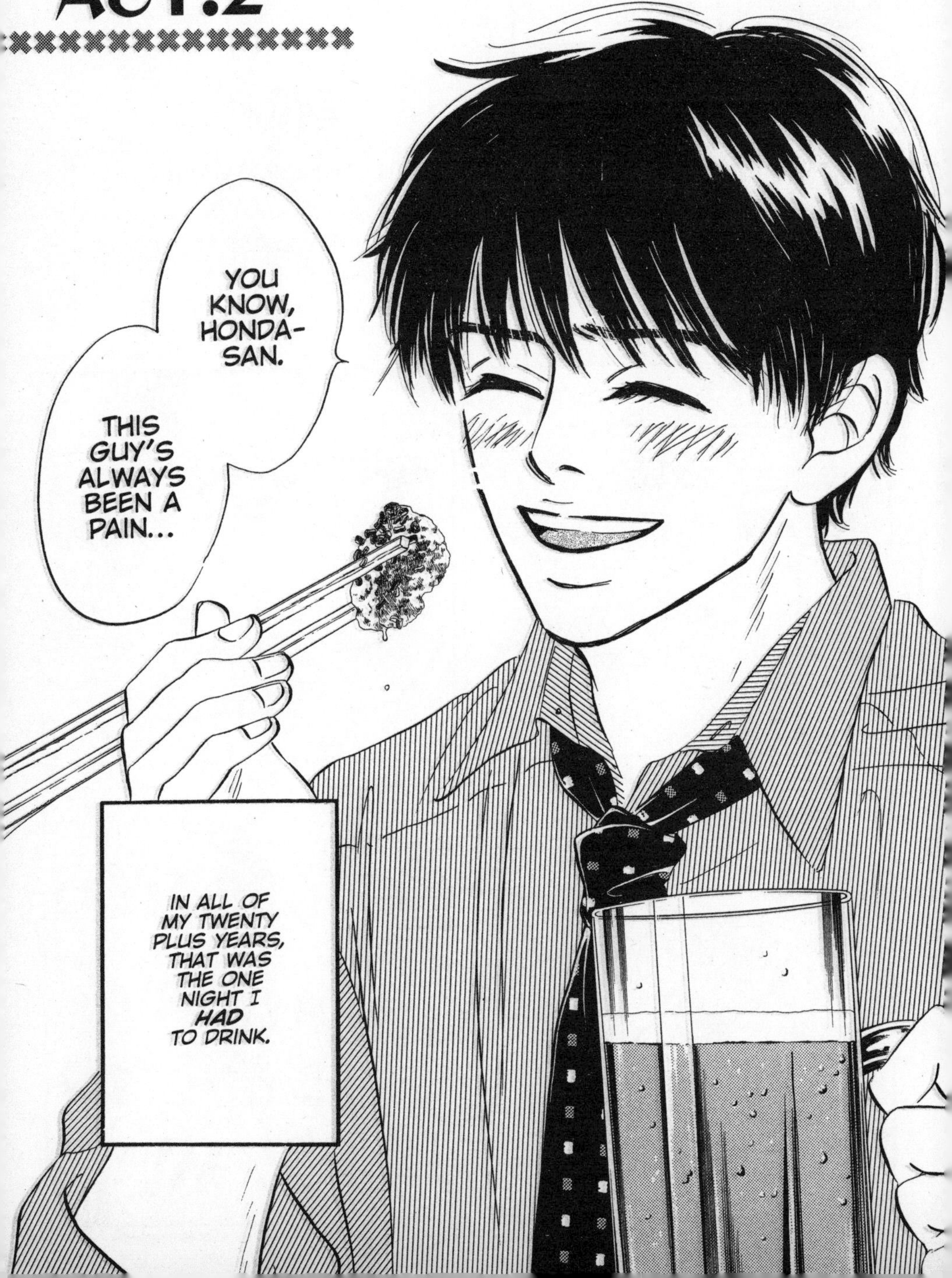
YOU KNOW, HONDA-SAN.
THIS GUY'S ALWAYS BEEN A PAIN...
IN ALL OF MY TWENTY PLUS YEARS, THAT WAS THE ONE NIGHT I *HAD* TO DRINK.

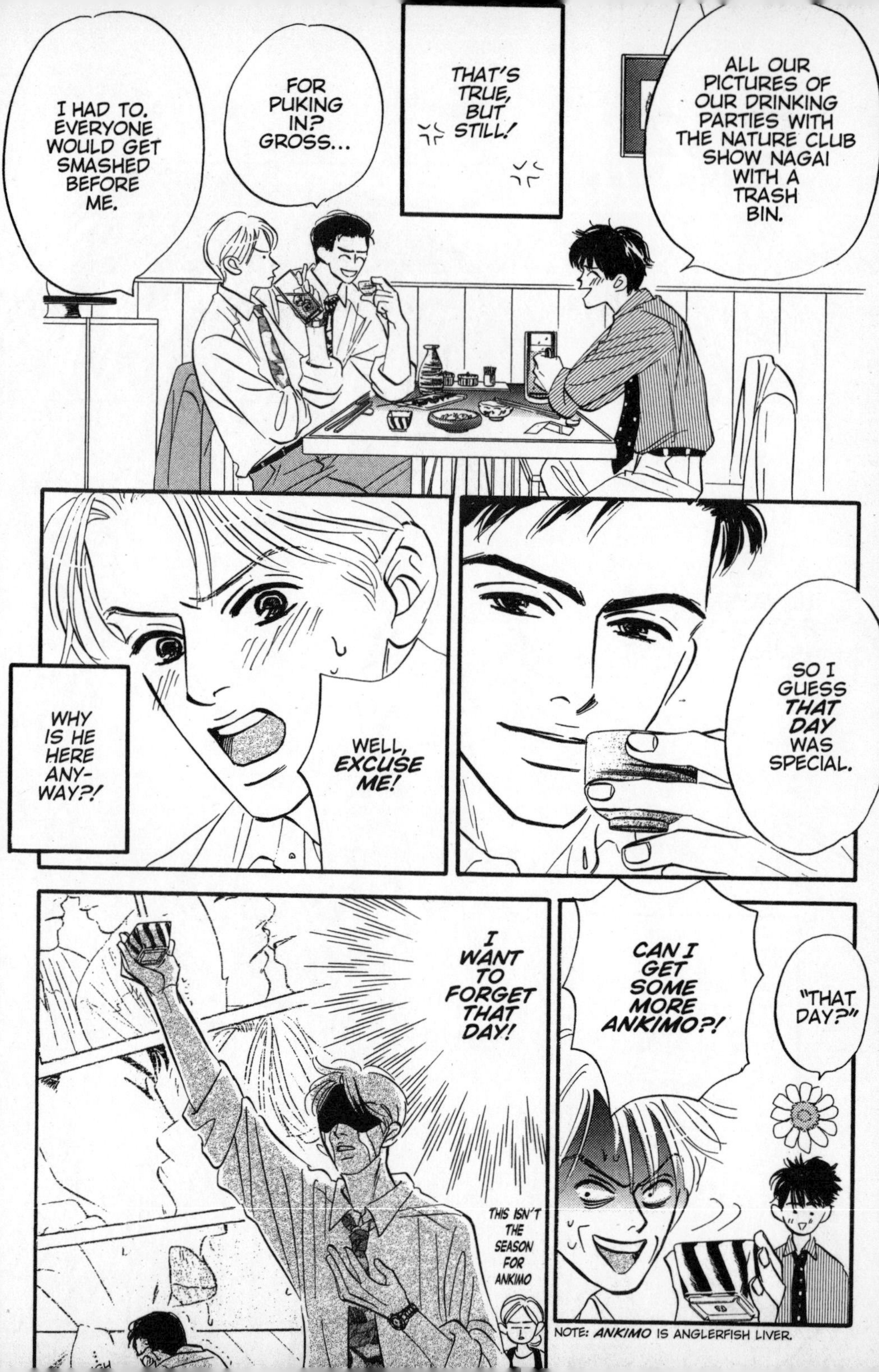
ALL OUR PICTURES OF OUR DRINKING PARTIES WITH THE NATURE CLUB SHOW NAGAI WITH A TRASH BIN.
THAT'S TRUE, BUT STILL!
FOR PUKING IN? GROSS...
I HAD TO. EVERYONE WOULD GET SMASHED BEFORE ME.
SO I GUESS THAT DAY WAS SPECIAL.
WELL, EXCUSE ME!
WHY IS HE HERE ANY-WAY?!
"THAT DAY?"
CAN I GET SOME MORE ANKIMO?!
NOTE: ANKIMO IS ANGLERFISH LIVER.
I WANT TO FORGET THAT DAY!
THIS ISN'T THE SEASON FOR ANKIMO

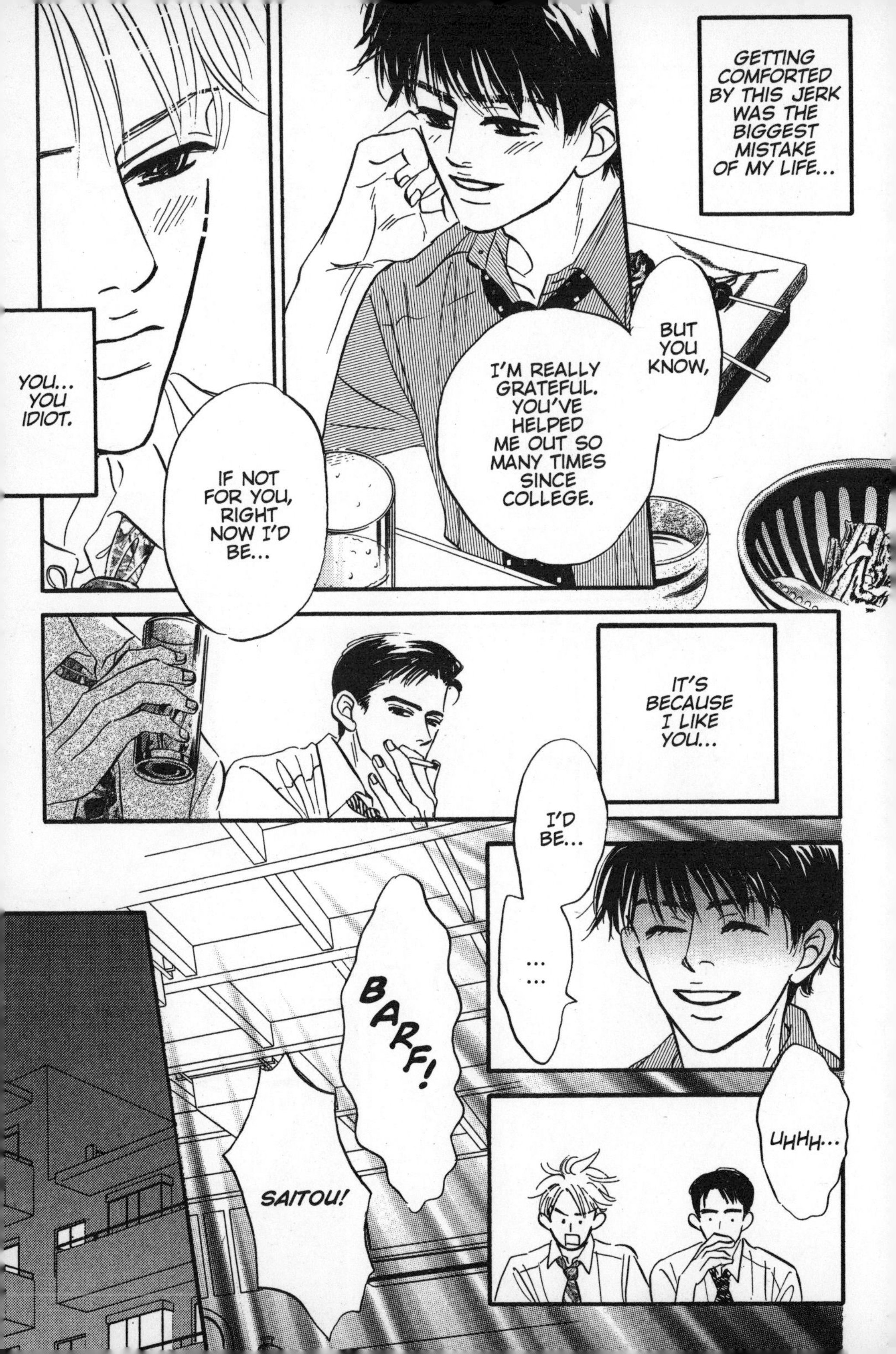
GETTING COMFORTED BY THIS JERK WAS THE BIGGEST MISTAKE OF MY LIFE...
BUT YOU KNOW,
I'M REALLY GRATEFUL. YOU'VE HELPED ME OUT SO MANY TIMES SINCE COLLEGE.
IF NOT FOR YOU, RIGHT NOW I'D BE...
YOU... YOU IDIOT.
IT'S BECAUSE I LIKE YOU...
I'D BE...
...
...
UHHH...
BARF!
SAITOU!

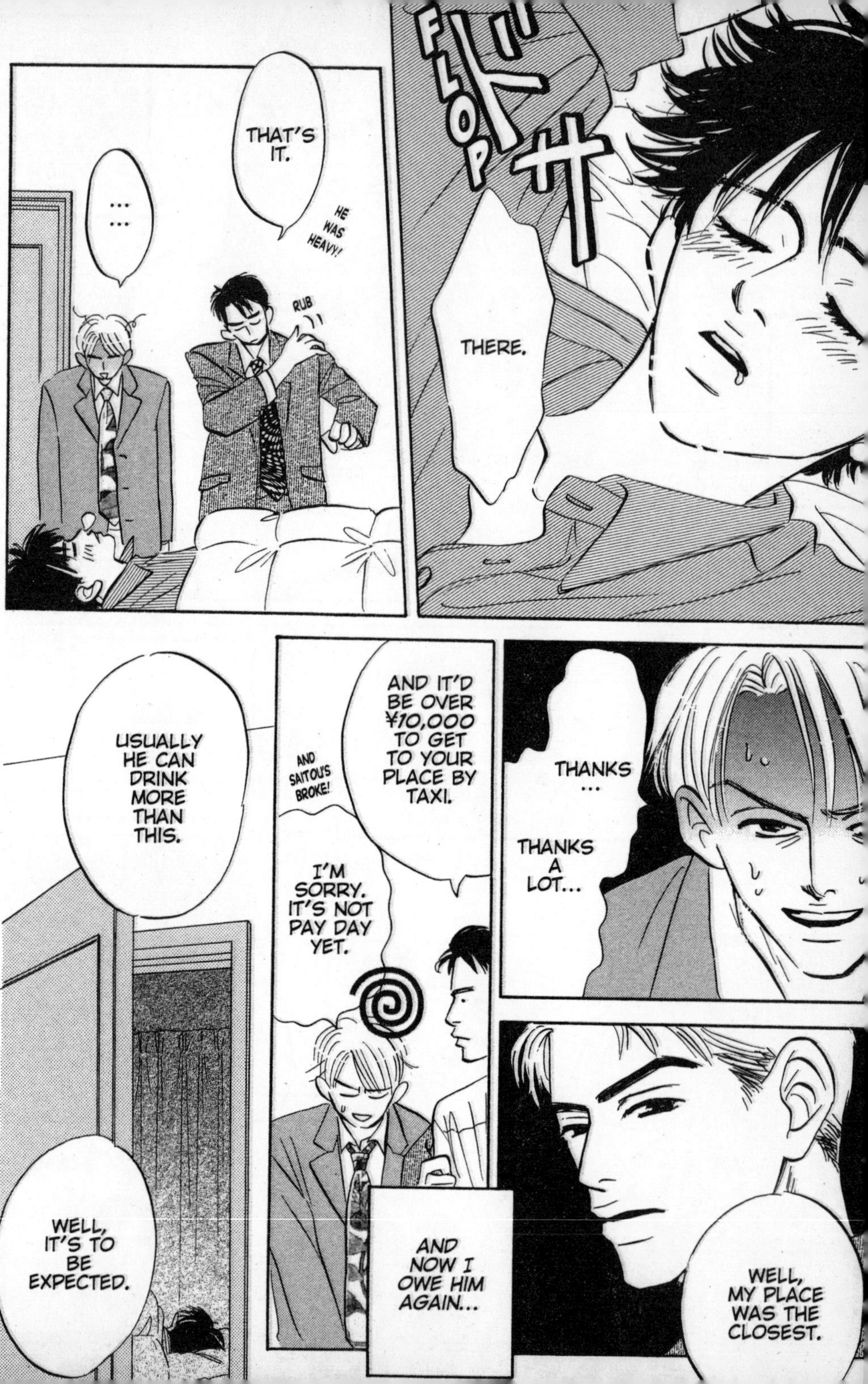
FLOP
THERE.
THAT'S IT.
......
HE WAS HEAVY!
RUB
THANKS... THANKS A LOT...
WELL, MY PLACE WAS THE CLOSEST.
AND IT'D BE OVER ¥10,000 TO GET TO YOUR PLACE BY TAXI.
AND SAITOU'S BROKE!
I'M SORRY. IT'S NOT PAY DAY YET.
AND NOW I OWE HIM AGAIN...
USUALLY HE CAN DRINK MORE THAN THIS.
WELL, IT'S TO BE EXPECTED.

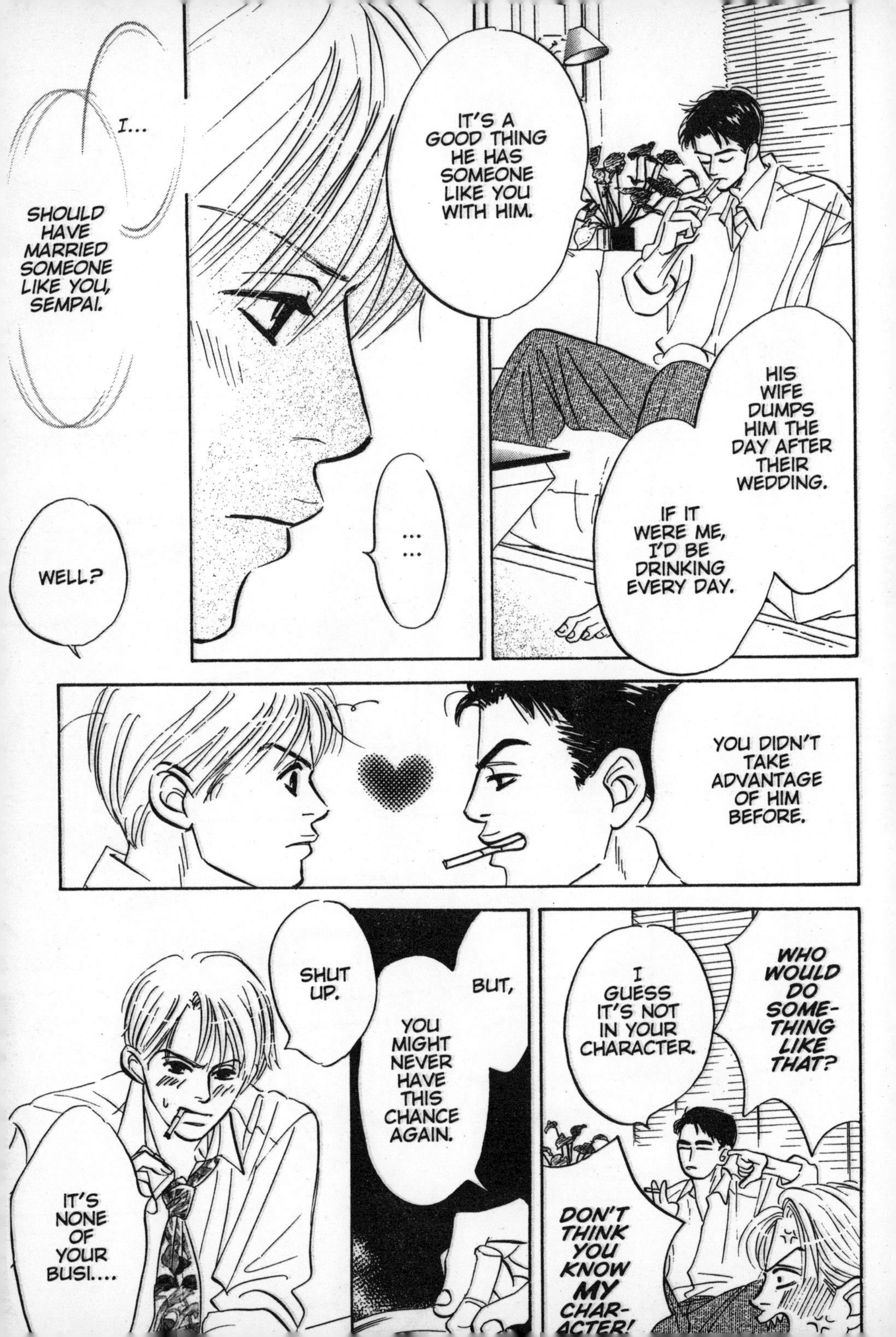
IT'S A GOOD THING HE HAS SOMEONE LIKE YOU WITH HIM.
HIS WIFE DUMPS HIM THE DAY AFTER THEIR WEDDING.
IF IT WERE ME, I'D BE DRINKING EVERY DAY.
......
I...
SHOULD HAVE MARRIED SOMEONE LIKE YOU, SEMPAI.
WELL?
YOU DIDN'T TAKE ADVANTAGE OF HIM BEFORE.
I GUESS IT'S NOT IN YOUR CHARACTER.
WHO WOULD DO SOMETHING LIKE THAT?
DON'T THINK YOU KNOW MY CHARACTER!
BUT,
YOU MIGHT NEVER HAVE THIS CHANCE AGAIN.
SHUT UP.
IT'S NONE OF YOUR BUSI....

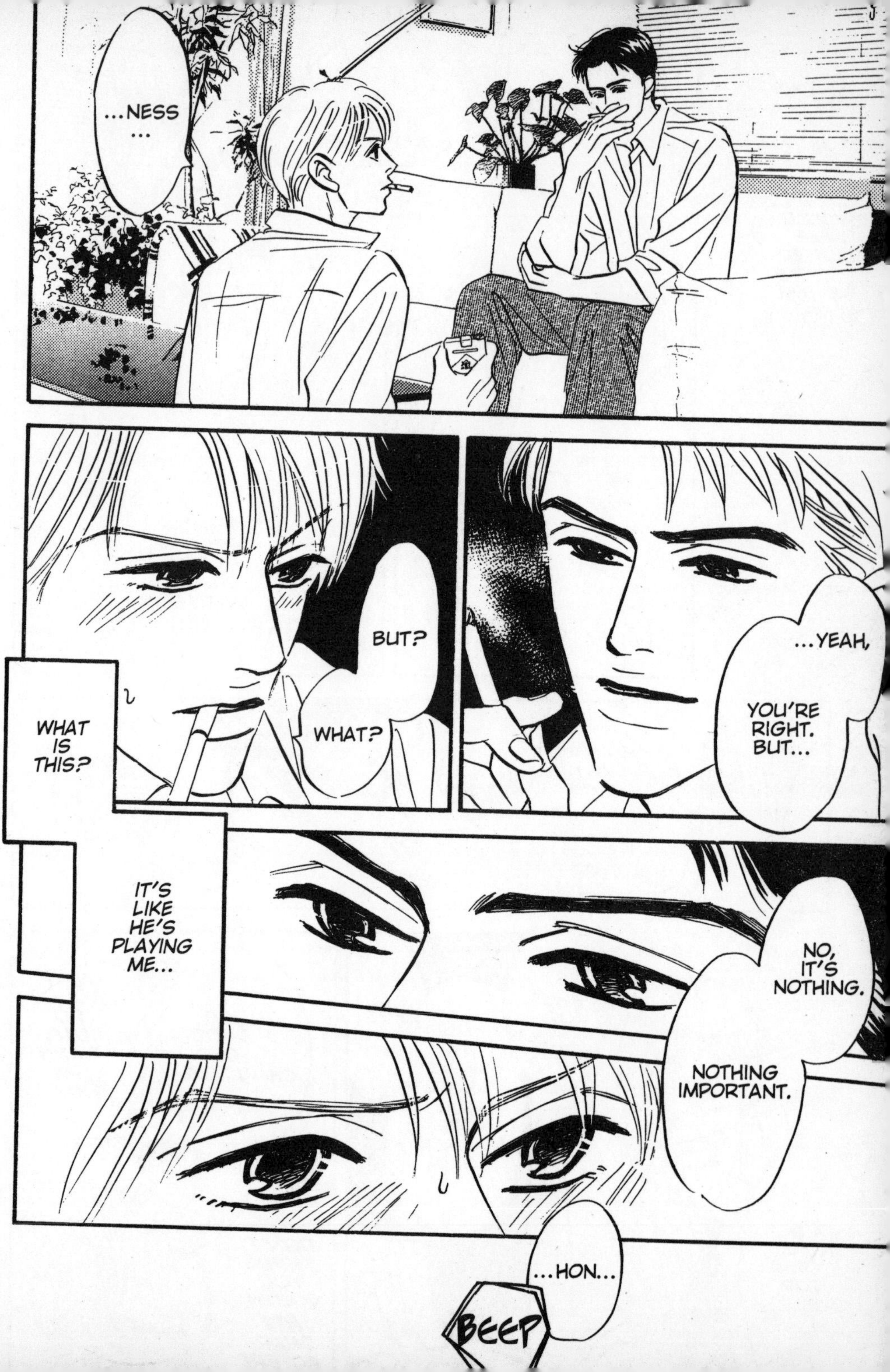
...NESS ...
...YEAH,
YOU'RE RIGHT. BUT...
BUT?
WHAT?
WHAT IS THIS?
NO, IT'S NOTHING.
NOTHING IMPORTANT.
IT'S LIKE HE'S PLAYING ME...
...HON...
BEEP

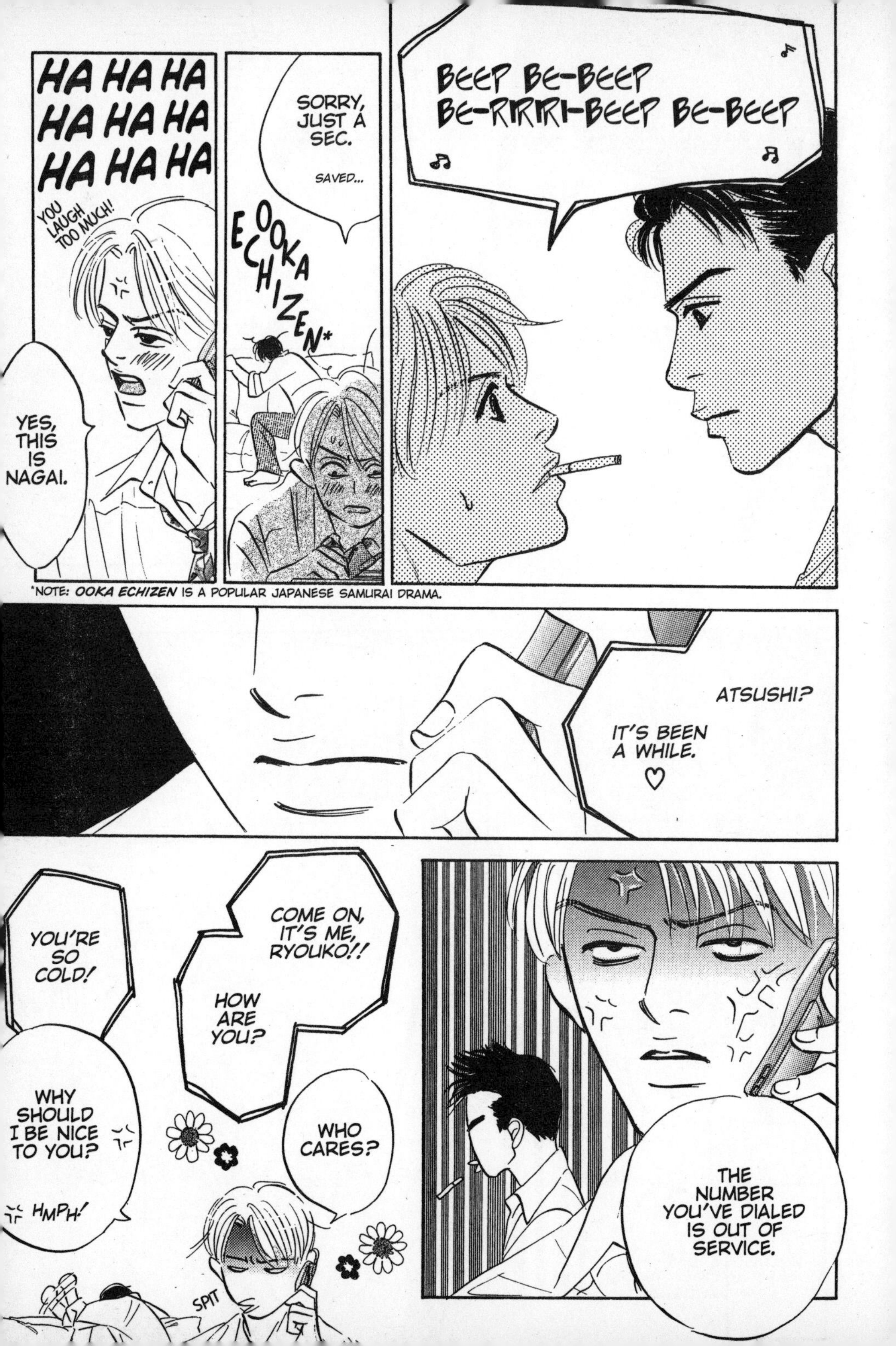
BEEP BE-BEEP BE-RIRIRI-BEEP BE-BEEP
SORRY, JUST A SEC.
SAVED...
OOKA ECHIZEN*
HA HA HA HA HA HA HA HA HA
YOU LAUGH TOO MUCH!
YES, THIS IS NAGAI.
ATSUSHI?
IT'S BEEN A WHILE. ♡
THE NUMBER YOU'VE DIALED IS OUT OF SERVICE.
COME ON, IT'S ME, RYOUKO!!
HOW ARE YOU?
YOU'RE SO COLD!
WHO CARES?
WHY SHOULD I BE NICE TO YOU?
HMPH!
SPIT

*NOTE: *OOKA ECHIZEN* IS A POPULAR JAPANESE SAMURAI DRAMA.

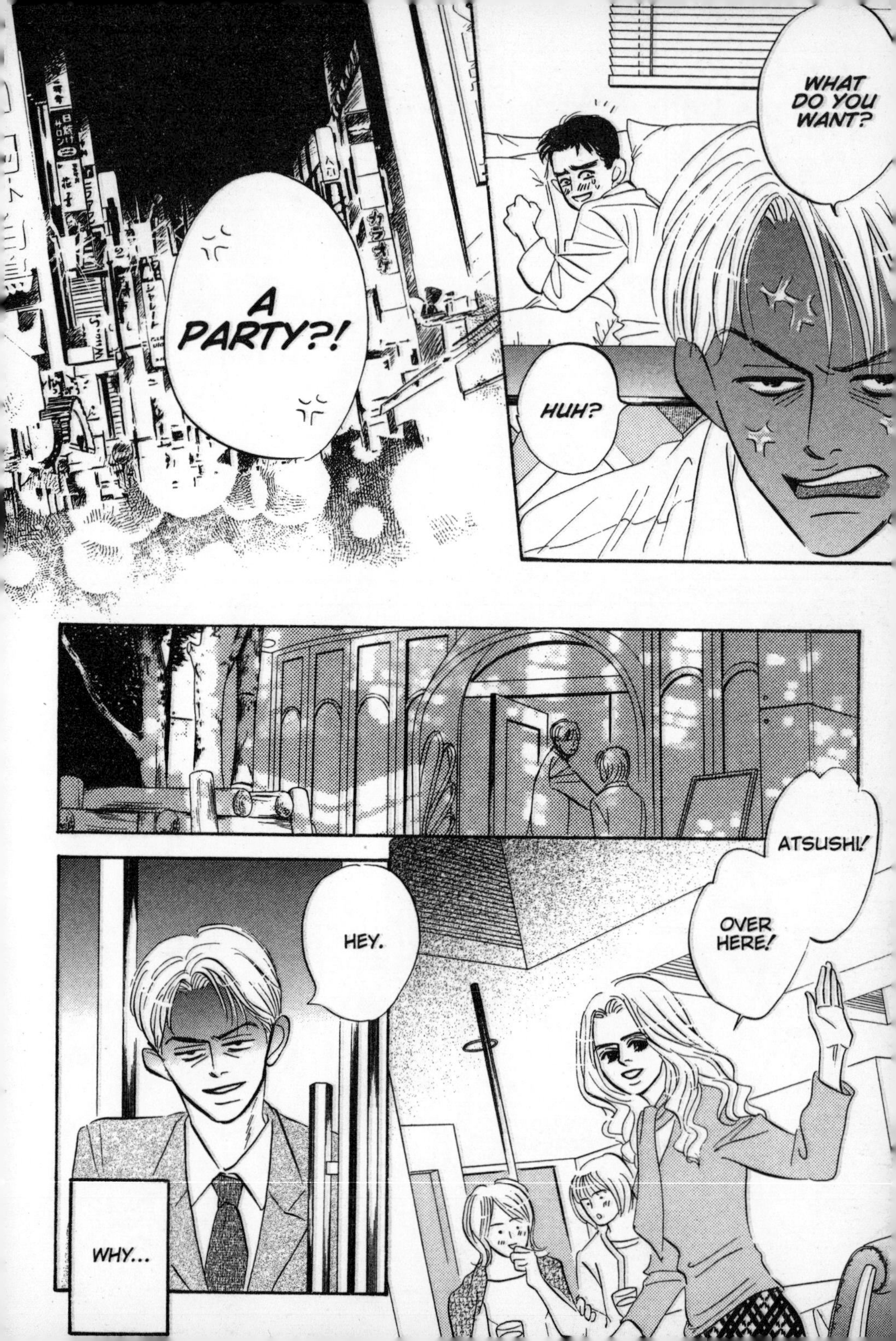
WHAT DO YOU WANT?
HUH?
A PARTY?!
ATSUSHI!
OVER HERE!
HEY.
WHY...

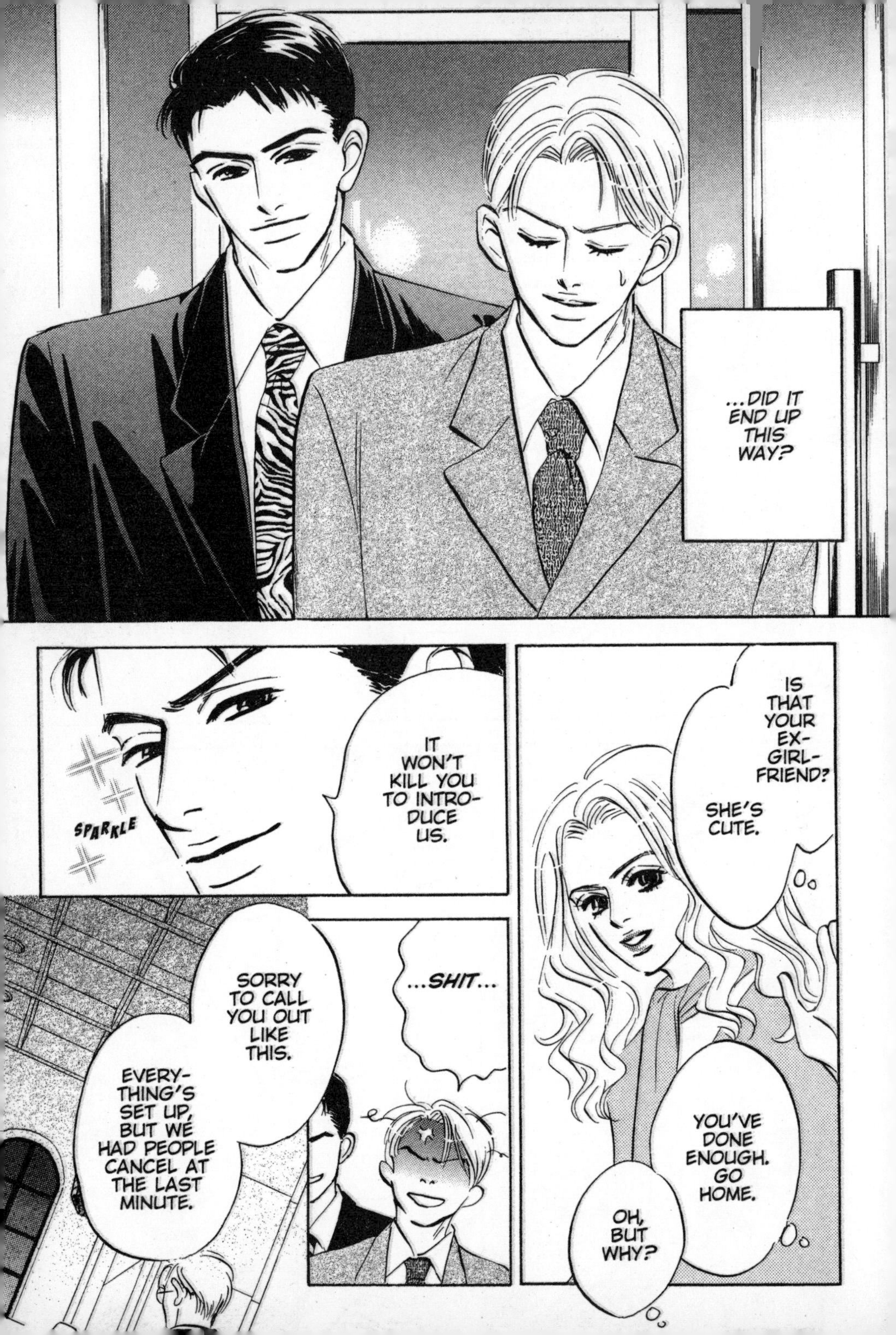
...DID IT END UP THIS WAY?
IS THAT YOUR EX-GIRLFRIEND?
SHE'S CUTE.
YOU'VE DONE ENOUGH. GO HOME.
OH, BUT WHY?
IT WON'T KILL YOU TO INTRODUCE US.
SPARKLE
...SHIT...
SORRY TO CALL YOU OUT LIKE THIS.
EVERYTHING'S SET UP, BUT WE HAD PEOPLE CANCEL AT THE LAST MINUTE.

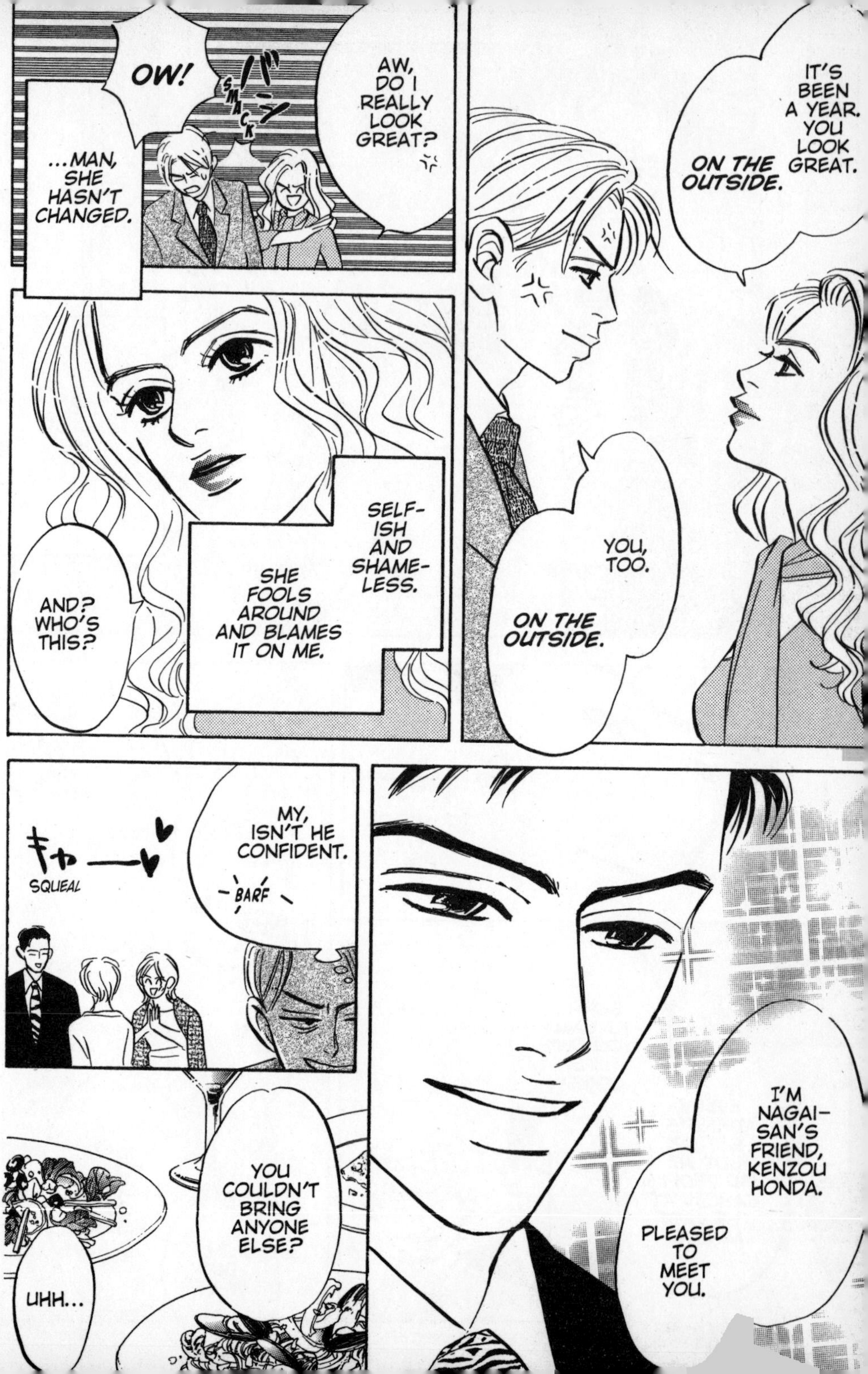
IT'S BEEN A YEAR. YOU LOOK GREAT.
ON THE OUTSIDE.
YOU, TOO.
ON THE OUTSIDE.
AW, DO I REALLY LOOK GREAT?
バーン SMACK
OW!
...MAN, SHE HASN'T CHANGED.
SELF-ISH AND SHAME-LESS.
SHE FOOLS AROUND AND BLAMES IT ON ME.
AND? WHO'S THIS?
I'M NAGAI-SAN'S FRIEND, KENZOU HONDA.
PLEASED TO MEET YOU.
MY, ISN'T HE CONFIDENT.
キャー SQUEAL
BARF
YOU COULDN'T BRING ANYONE ELSE?
UHH...

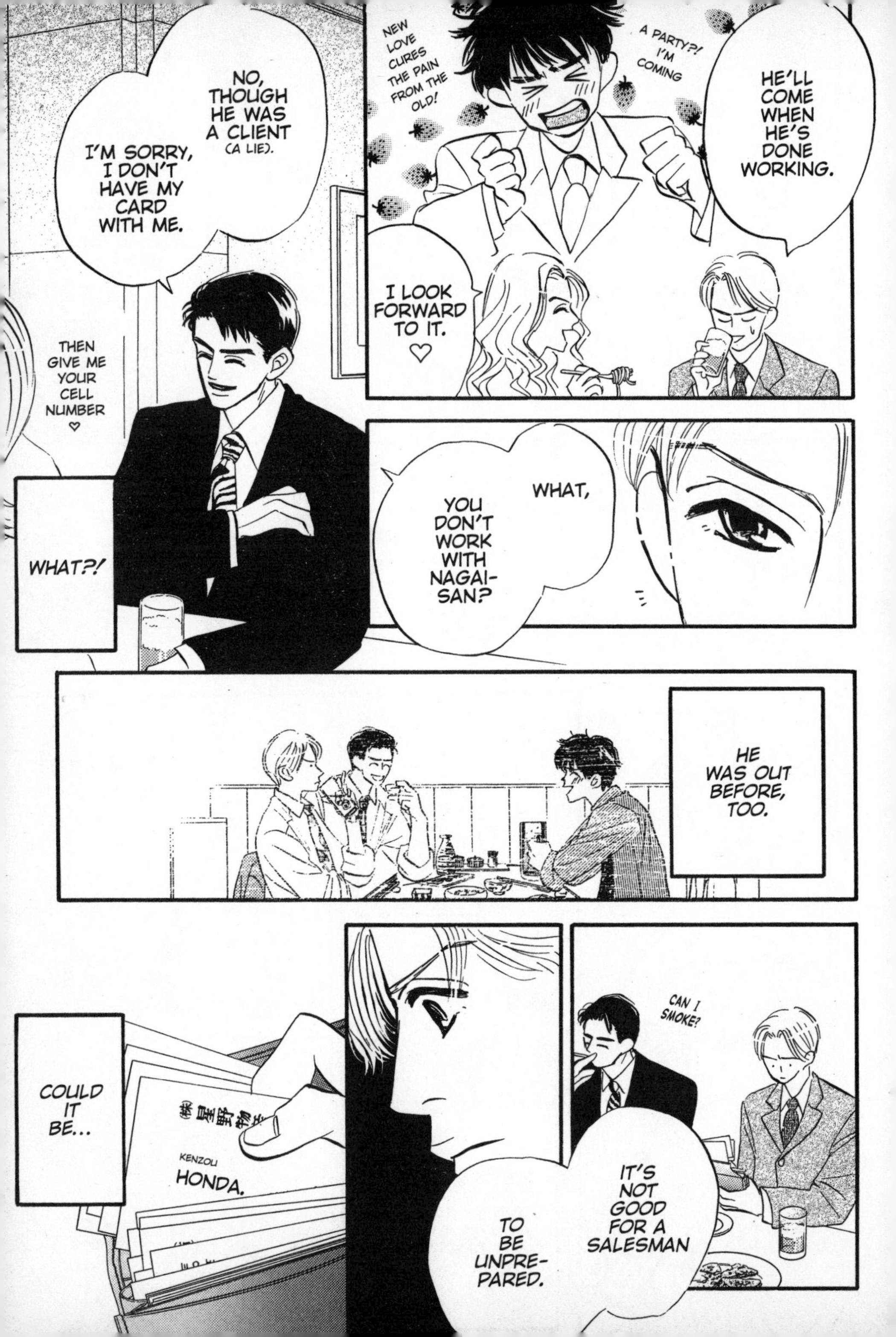
HE'LL COME WHEN HE'S DONE WORKING.
A PARTY?! I'M COMING
NEW LOVE CURES THE PAIN FROM THE OLD!
I LOOK FORWARD TO IT. ♡
WHAT,
YOU DON'T WORK WITH NAGAI-SAN?
NO, THOUGH HE WAS A CLIENT (A LIE).
I'M SORRY, I DON'T HAVE MY CARD WITH ME.
THEN GIVE ME YOUR CELL NUMBER ♡
WHAT?!
HE WAS OUT BEFORE, TOO.
CAN I SMOKE?
IT'S NOT GOOD FOR A SALESMAN
TO BE UNPREPARED.
COULD IT BE...
KENZOU
HONDA.

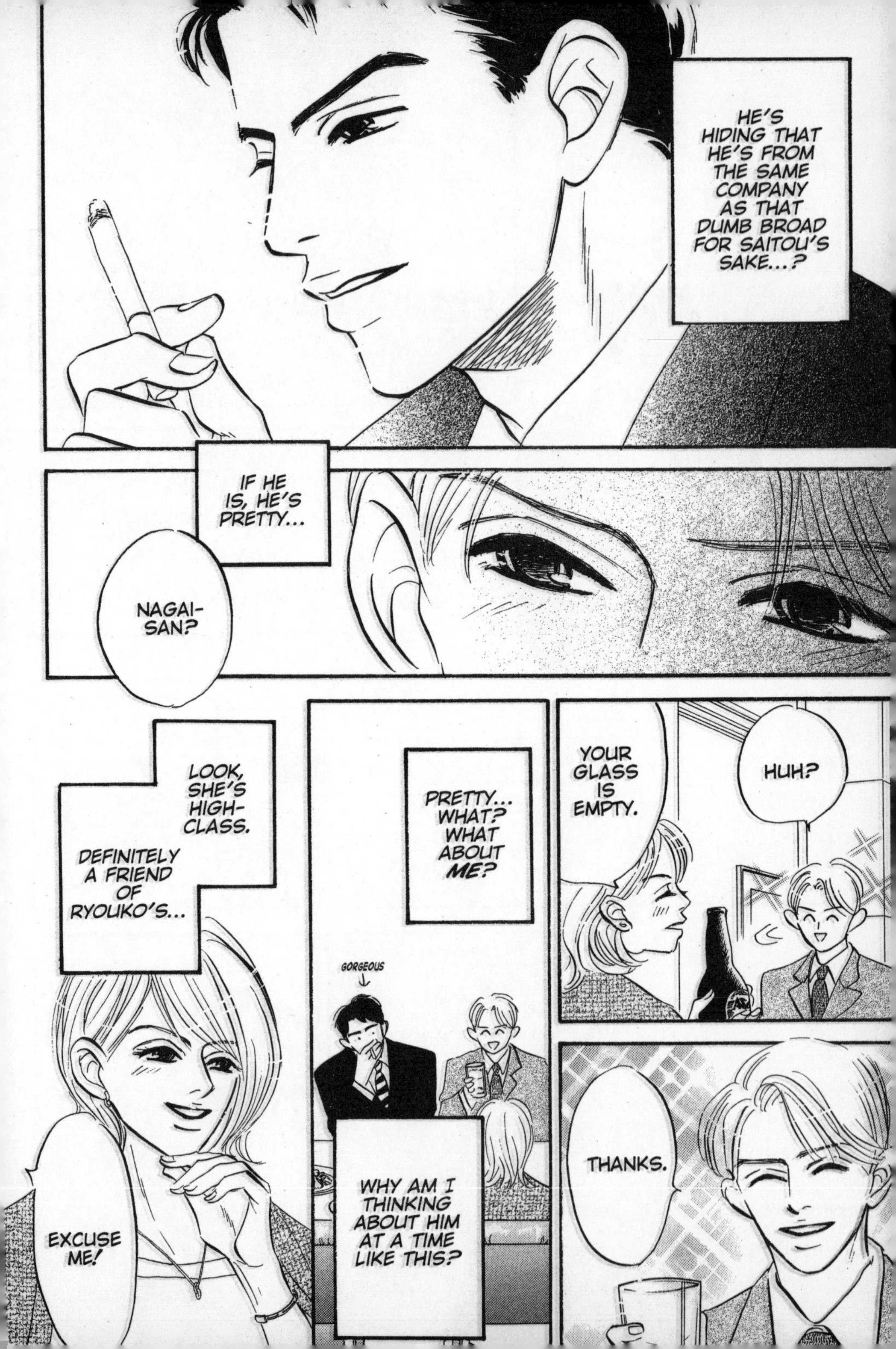

HE'S HIDING THAT HE'S FROM THE SAME COMPANY AS THAT DUMB BROAD FOR SAITOU'S SAKE...?
IF HE IS, HE'S PRETTY...
NAGAI-SAN?
HUH?
YOUR GLASS IS EMPTY.
THANKS.
PRETTY... WHAT? WHAT ABOUT *ME?*
GORGEOUS
WHY AM I THINKING ABOUT HIM AT A TIME LIKE THIS?
LOOK, SHE'S HIGH-CLASS.
DEFINITELY A FRIEND OF RYOUKO'S...
EXCUSE ME!

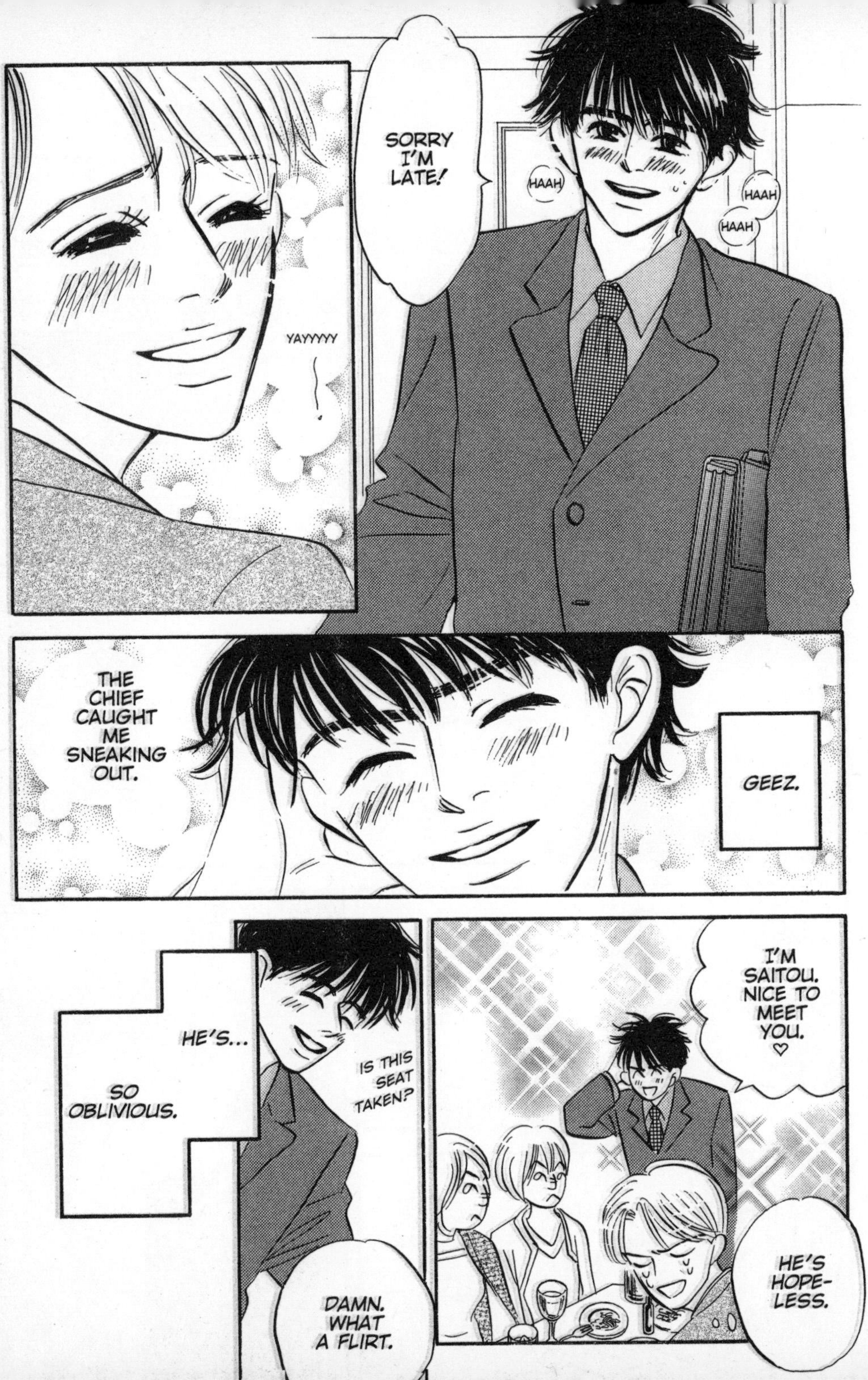
SORRY I'M LATE!
HAAH
HAAH
HAAH
YAYYYY
THE CHIEF CAUGHT ME SNEAKING OUT.
GEEZ.
I'M SAITOU. NICE TO MEET YOU. ♡
HE'S HOPE-LESS.
IS THIS SEAT TAKEN?
HE'S...
SO OBLIVIOUS.
DAMN. WHAT A FLIRT.

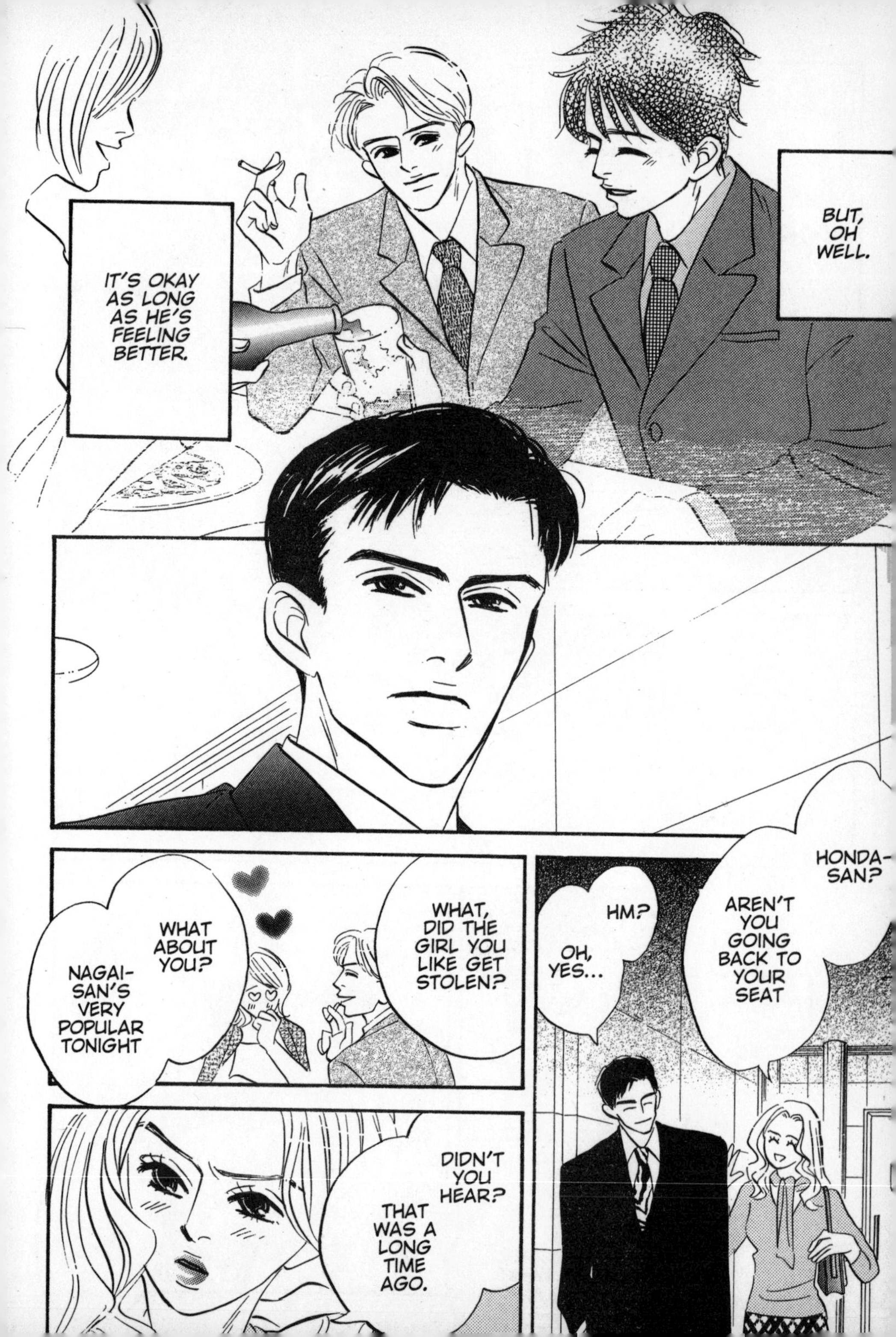
BUT, OH WELL.
IT'S OKAY AS LONG AS HE'S FEELING BETTER.
HONDA-SAN?
AREN'T YOU GOING BACK TO YOUR SEAT
HM?
OH, YES...
WHAT, DID THE GIRL YOU LIKE GET STOLEN?
WHAT ABOUT YOU?
NAGAI-SAN'S VERY POPULAR TONIGHT
DIDN'T YOU HEAR?
THAT WAS A LONG TIME AGO.

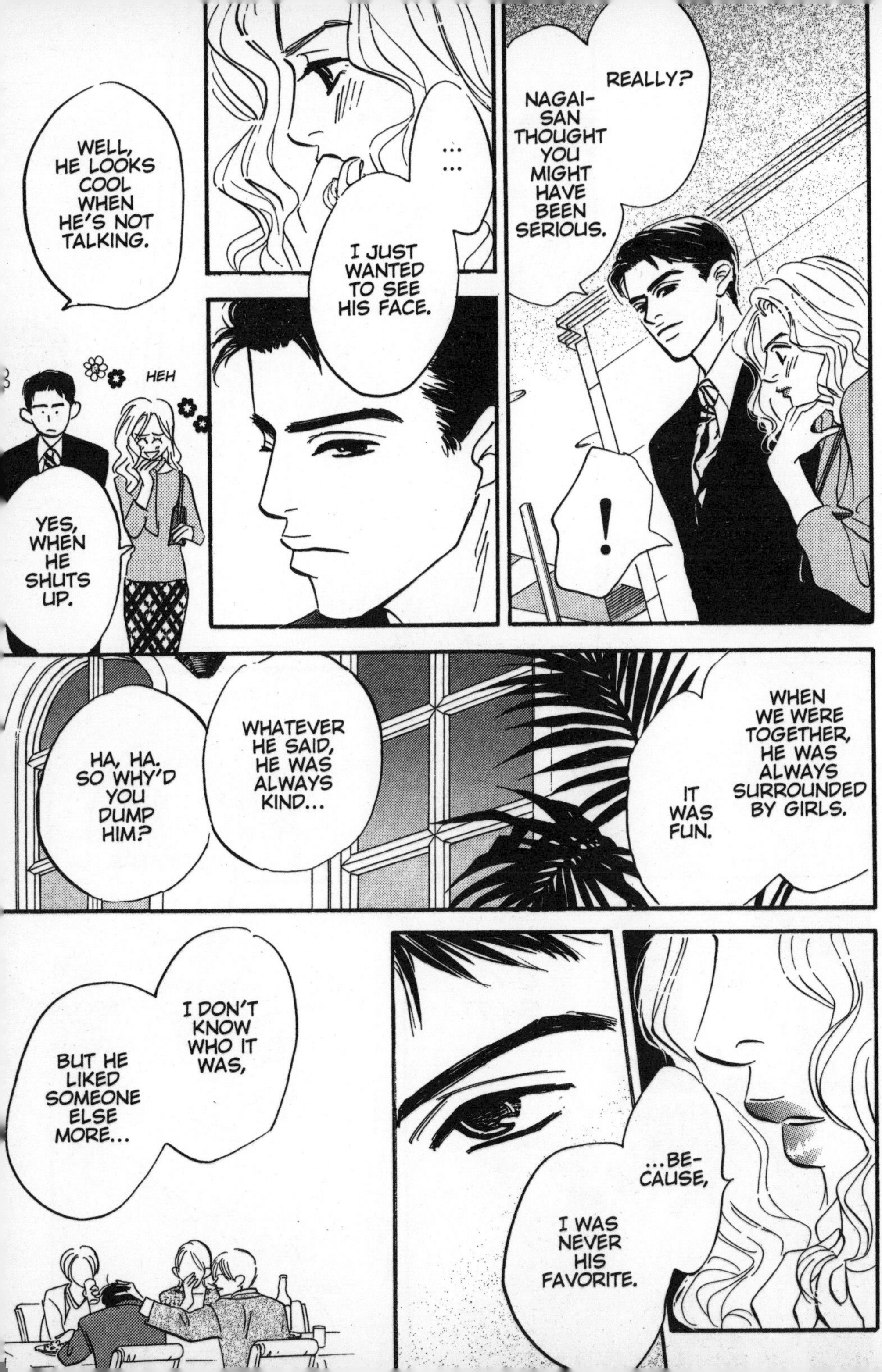
REALLY?
NAGAI-SAN THOUGHT YOU MIGHT HAVE BEEN SERIOUS.
!
… …
I JUST WANTED TO SEE HIS FACE.
WELL, HE LOOKS COOL WHEN HE'S NOT TALKING.
HEH
YES, WHEN HE SHUTS UP.
WHEN WE WERE TOGETHER, HE WAS ALWAYS SURROUNDED BY GIRLS.
IT WAS FUN.
WHATEVER HE SAID, HE WAS ALWAYS KIND…
HA, HA. SO WHY'D YOU DUMP HIM?
…BE-CAUSE,
I WAS NEVER HIS FAVORITE.
I DON'T KNOW WHO IT WAS,
BUT HE LIKED SOMEONE ELSE MORE…

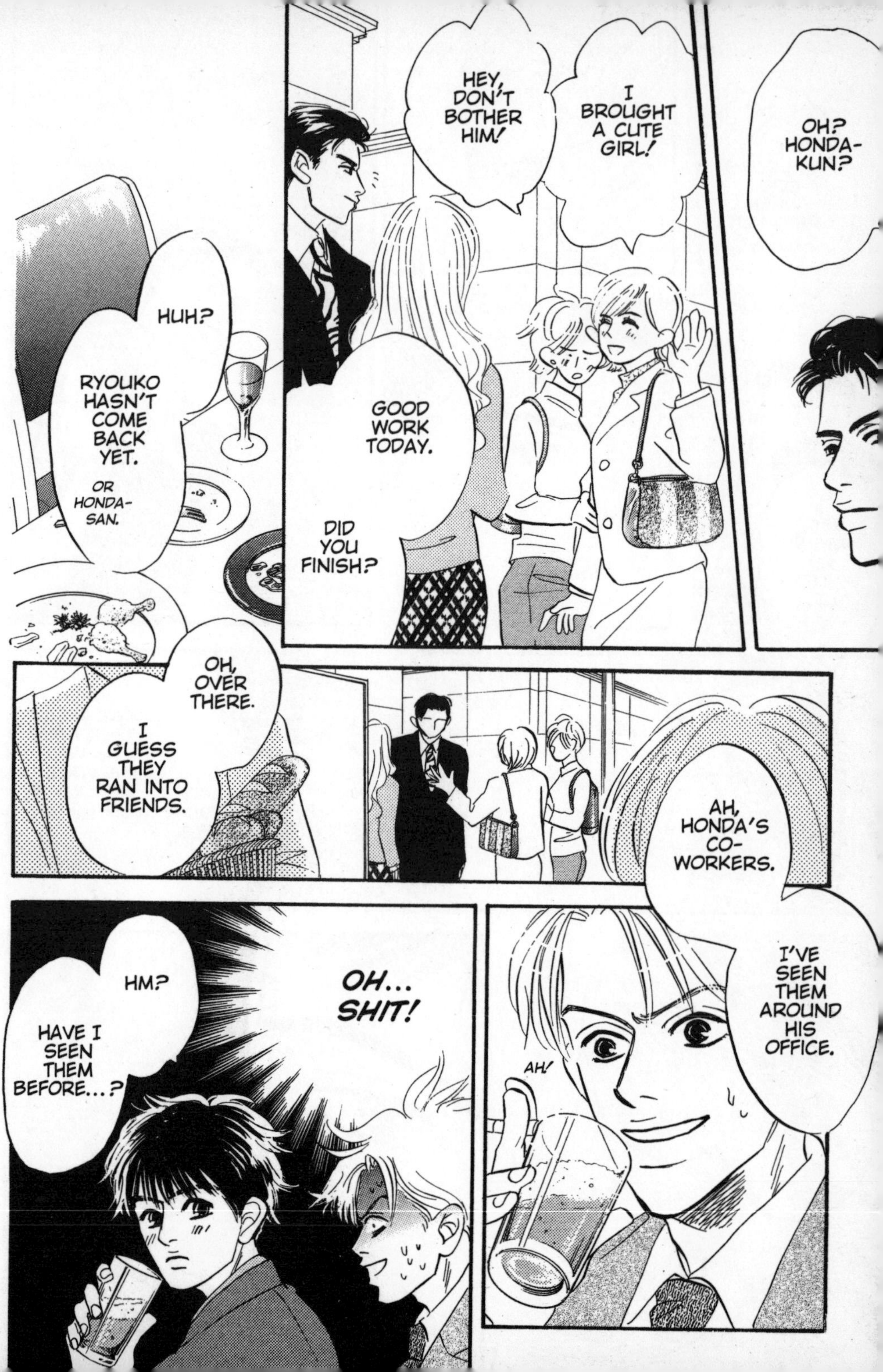
OH? HONDA-KUN?
I BROUGHT A CUTE GIRL!
HEY, DON'T BOTHER HIM!
GOOD WORK TODAY.
DID YOU FINISH?
HUH?
RYOUKO HASN'T COME BACK YET.
OR HONDA-SAN.
OH, OVER THERE.
I GUESS THEY RAN INTO FRIENDS.
AH, HONDA'S CO-WORKERS.
I'VE SEEN THEM AROUND HIS OFFICE.
AH!
OH... SHIT!
HM?
HAVE I SEEN THEM BEFORE...?

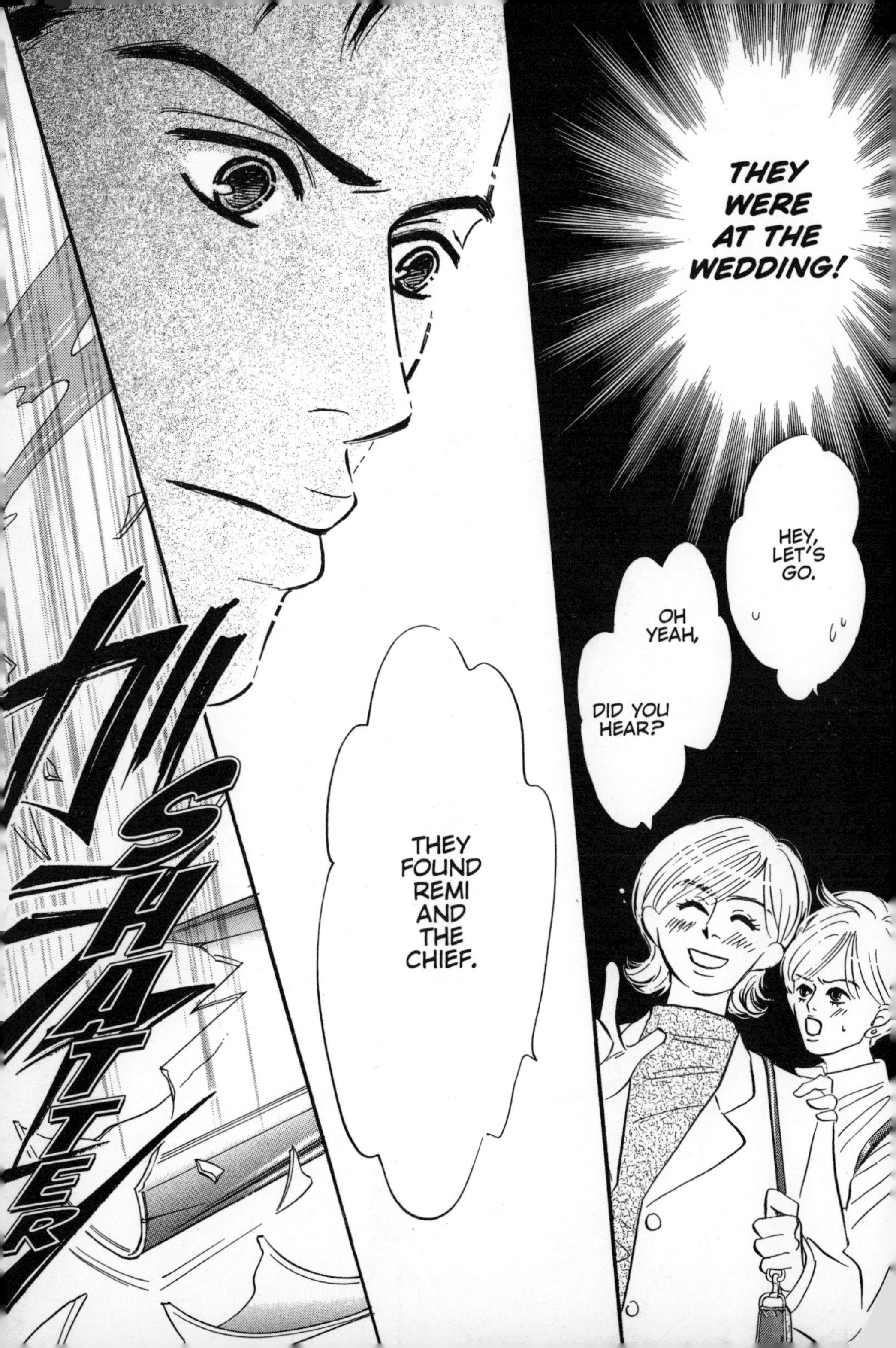
THEY WERE AT THE WEDDING!
HEY, LET'S GO.
OH YEAH, DID YOU HEAR?
THEY FOUND REMI AND THE CHIEF.
SHATTER

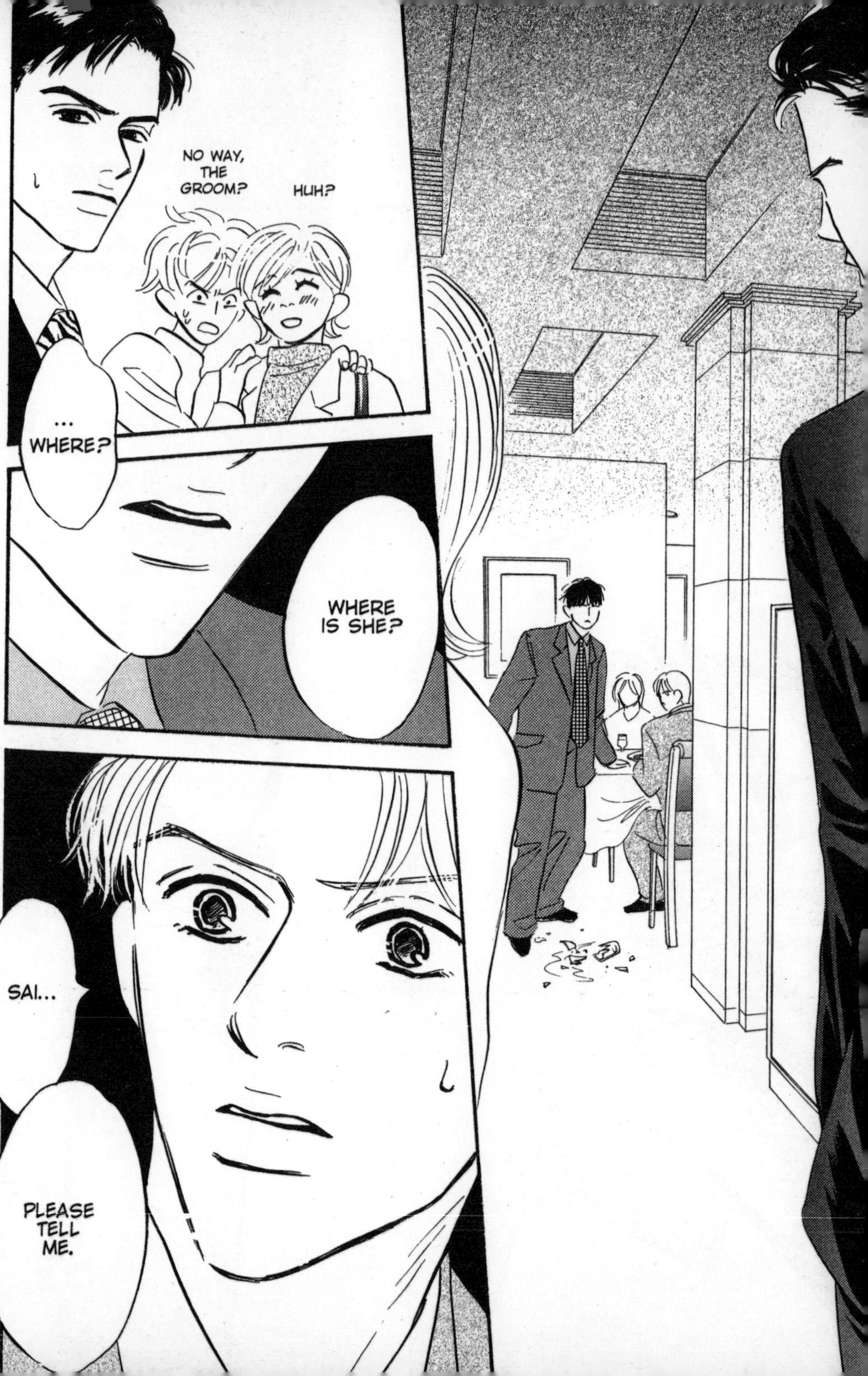
HUH?
NO WAY, THE GROOM?
... WHERE?
WHERE IS SHE?
SAI...
PLEASE TELL ME.

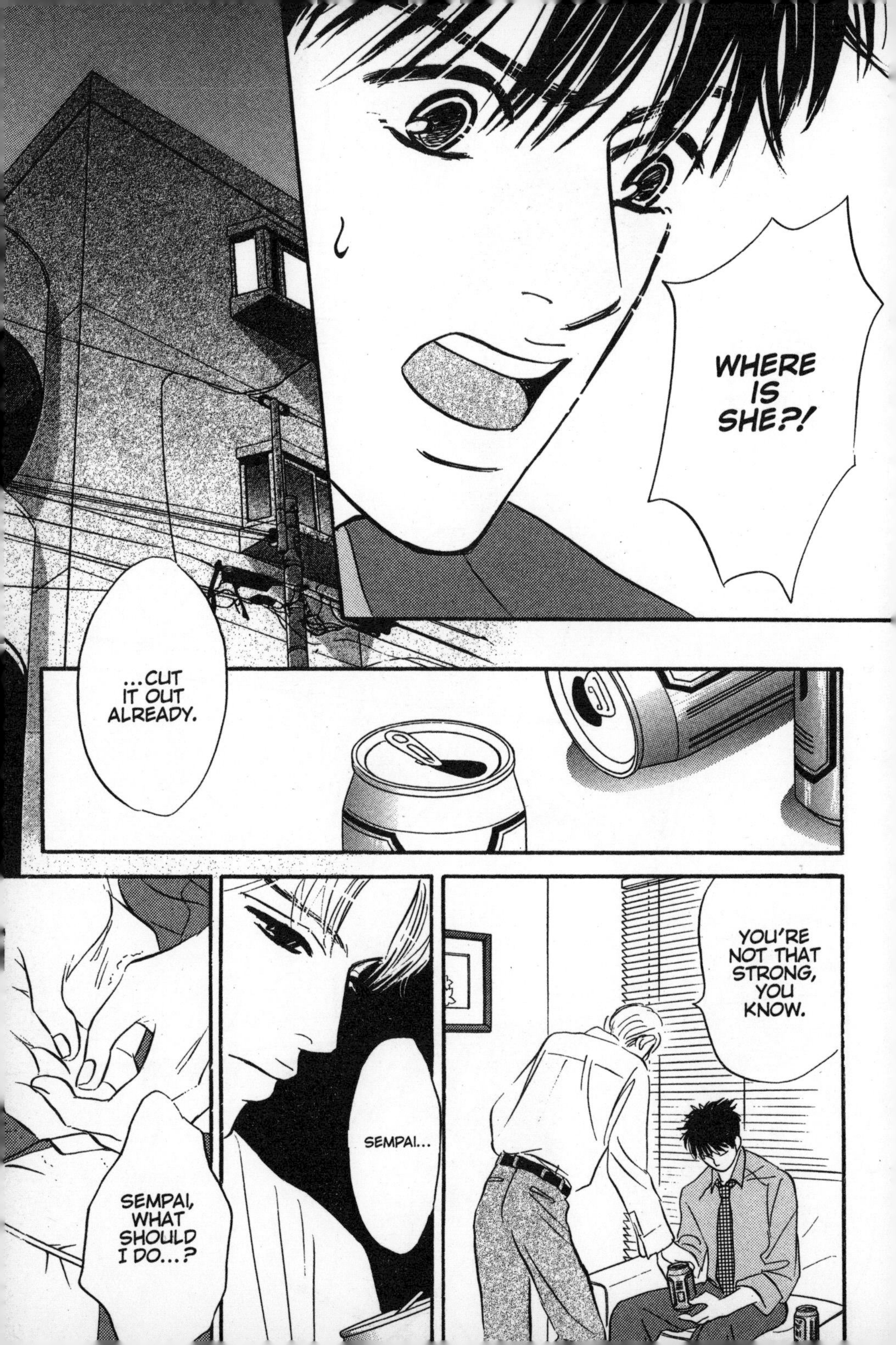
WHERE IS SHE?!
...CUT IT OUT ALREADY.
YOU'RE NOT THAT STRONG, YOU KNOW.
SEMPAI...
SEMPAI, WHAT SHOULD I DO...?

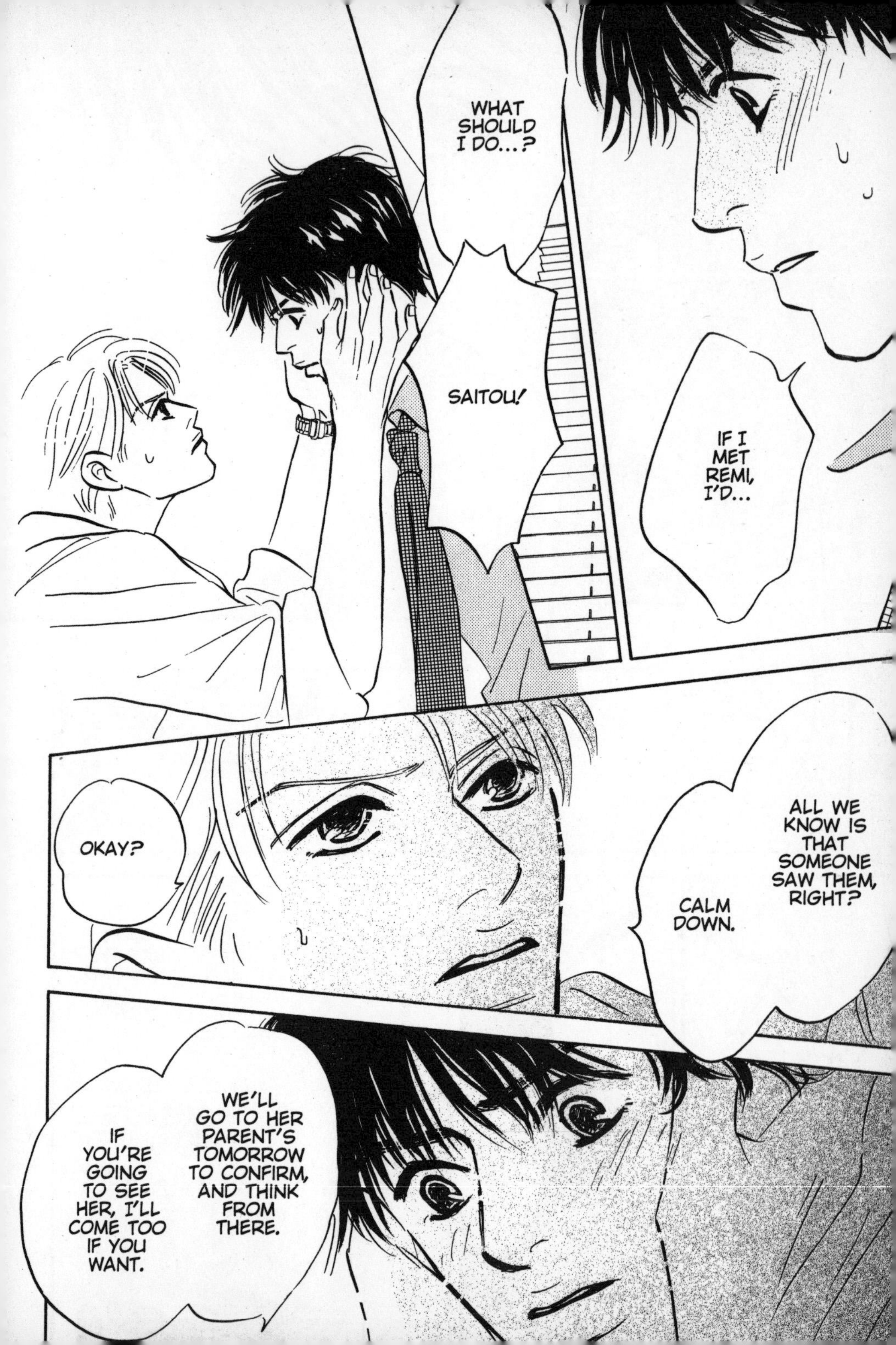

WHAT SHOULD I DO...?
IF I MET REMI, I'D...
SAITOU!
ALL WE KNOW IS THAT SOMEONE SAW THEM, RIGHT?
CALM DOWN.
OKAY?
WE'LL GO TO HER PARENT'S TOMORROW TO CONFIRM, AND THINK FROM THERE.
IF YOU'RE GOING TO SEE HER, I'LL COME TOO IF YOU WANT.

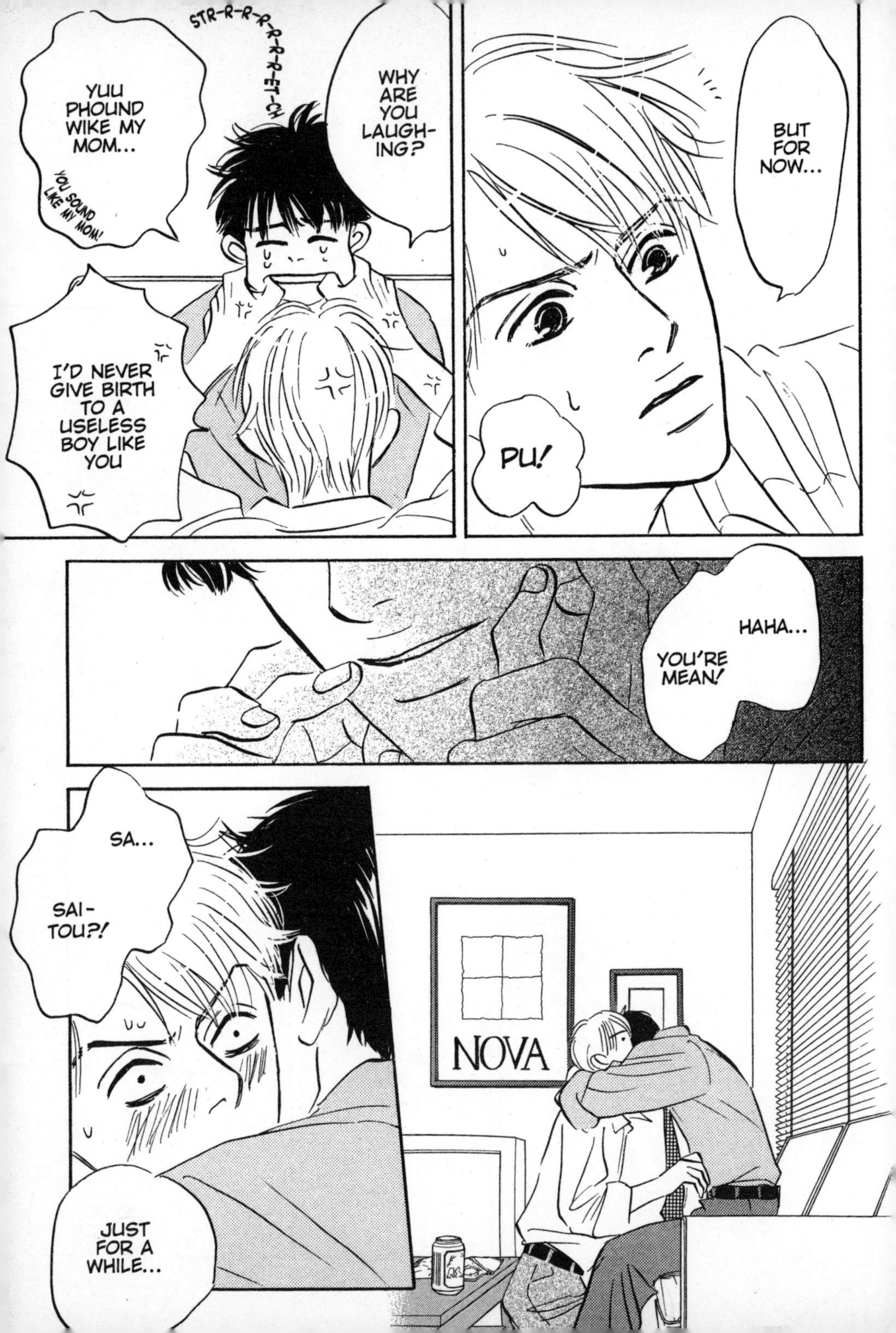
BUT FOR NOW...
PU!
WHY ARE YOU LAUGHING?
STR-R-R-R-R-R-ET-CH
YUU PHOUND WIKE MY MOM...
YOU SOUND LIKE MY MOM!
I'D NEVER GIVE BIRTH TO A USELESS BOY LIKE YOU
HAHA...
YOU'RE MEAN!
NOVA
SA...
SAI-TOU?!
JUST FOR A WHILE...

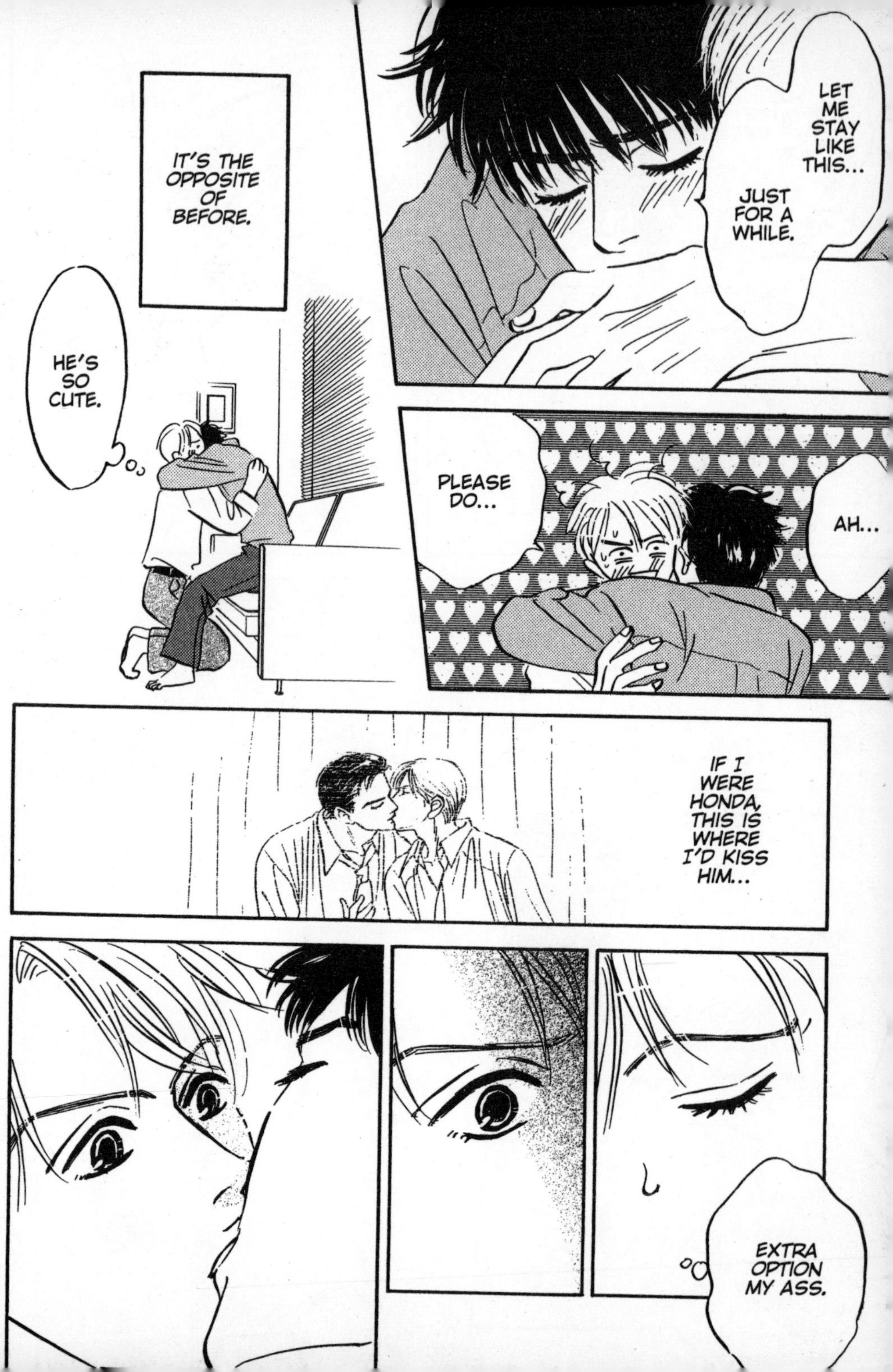
LET ME STAY LIKE THIS...
JUST FOR A WHILE.
AH...
PLEASE DO...
IT'S THE OPPOSITE OF BEFORE.
HE'S SO CUTE.
IF I WERE HONDA, THIS IS WHERE I'D KISS HIM...
EXTRA OPTION MY ASS.

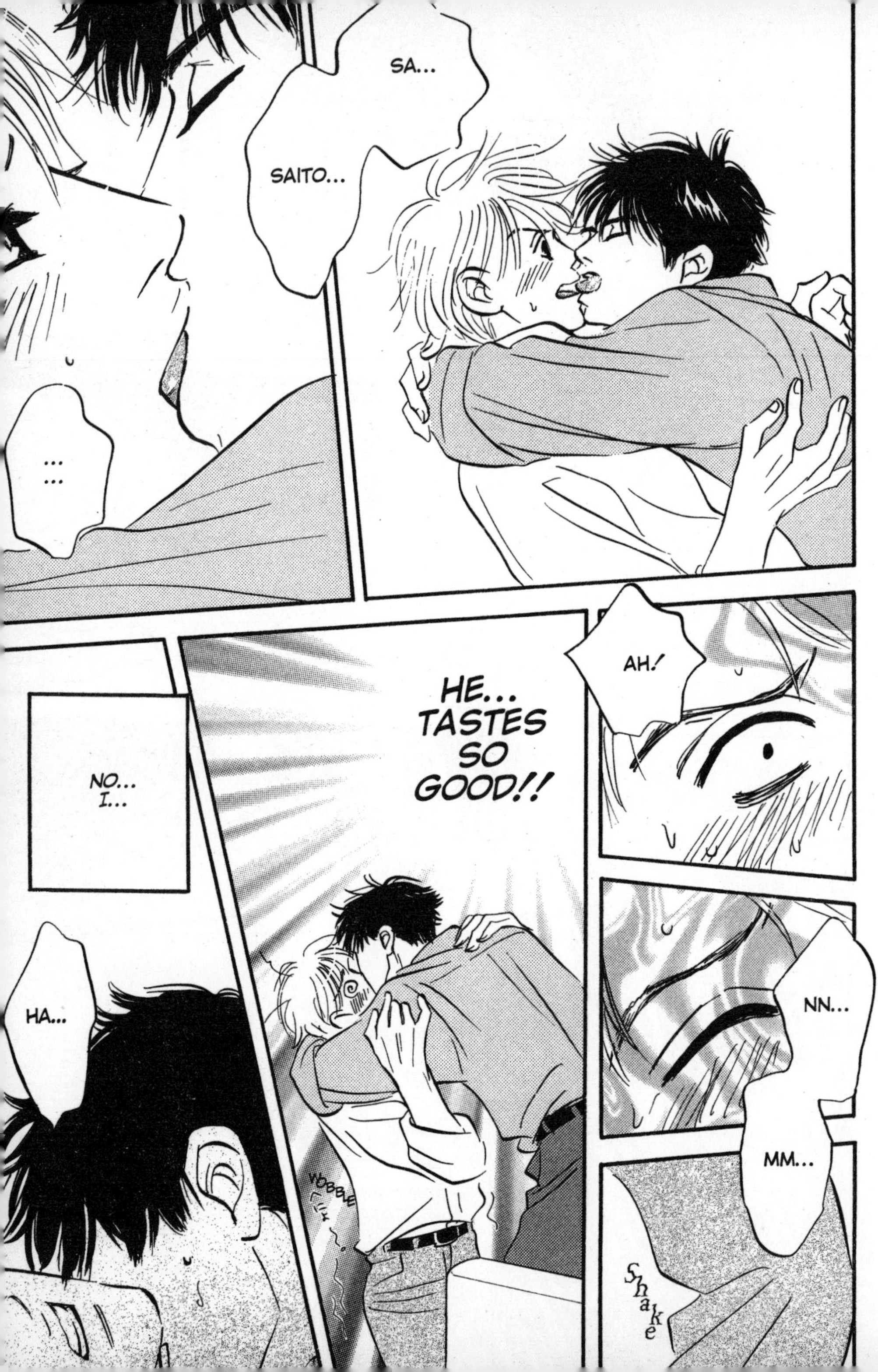
SA...
SAITO...
......
AH!
NN...
MM...
Shake
HE... TASTES SO GOOD!!
WOBBLE
NO... I...
HA...

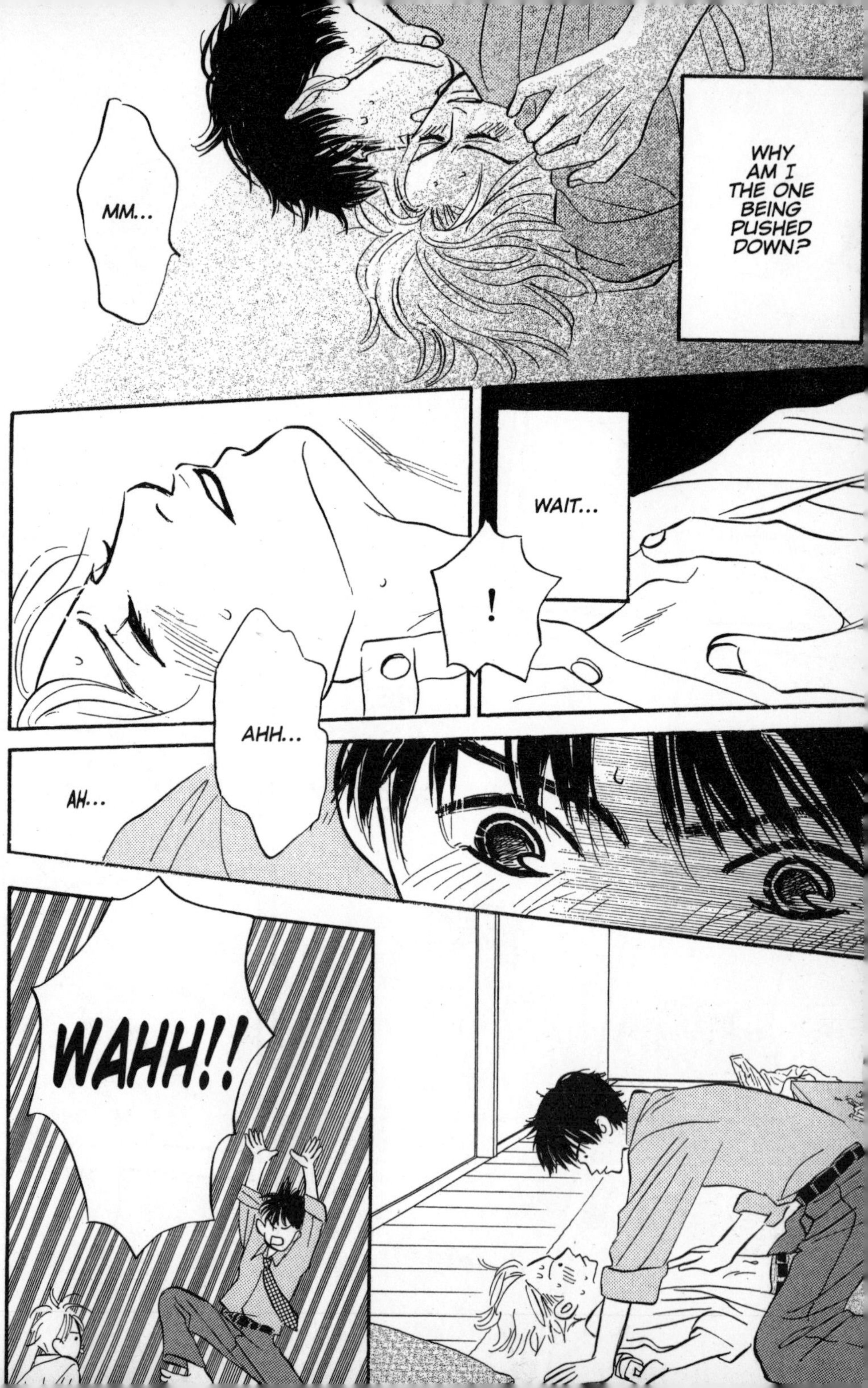
WHY AM I THE ONE BEING PUSHED DOWN?
MM...
WAIT...
!
AHH...
AH...
WAHH!!

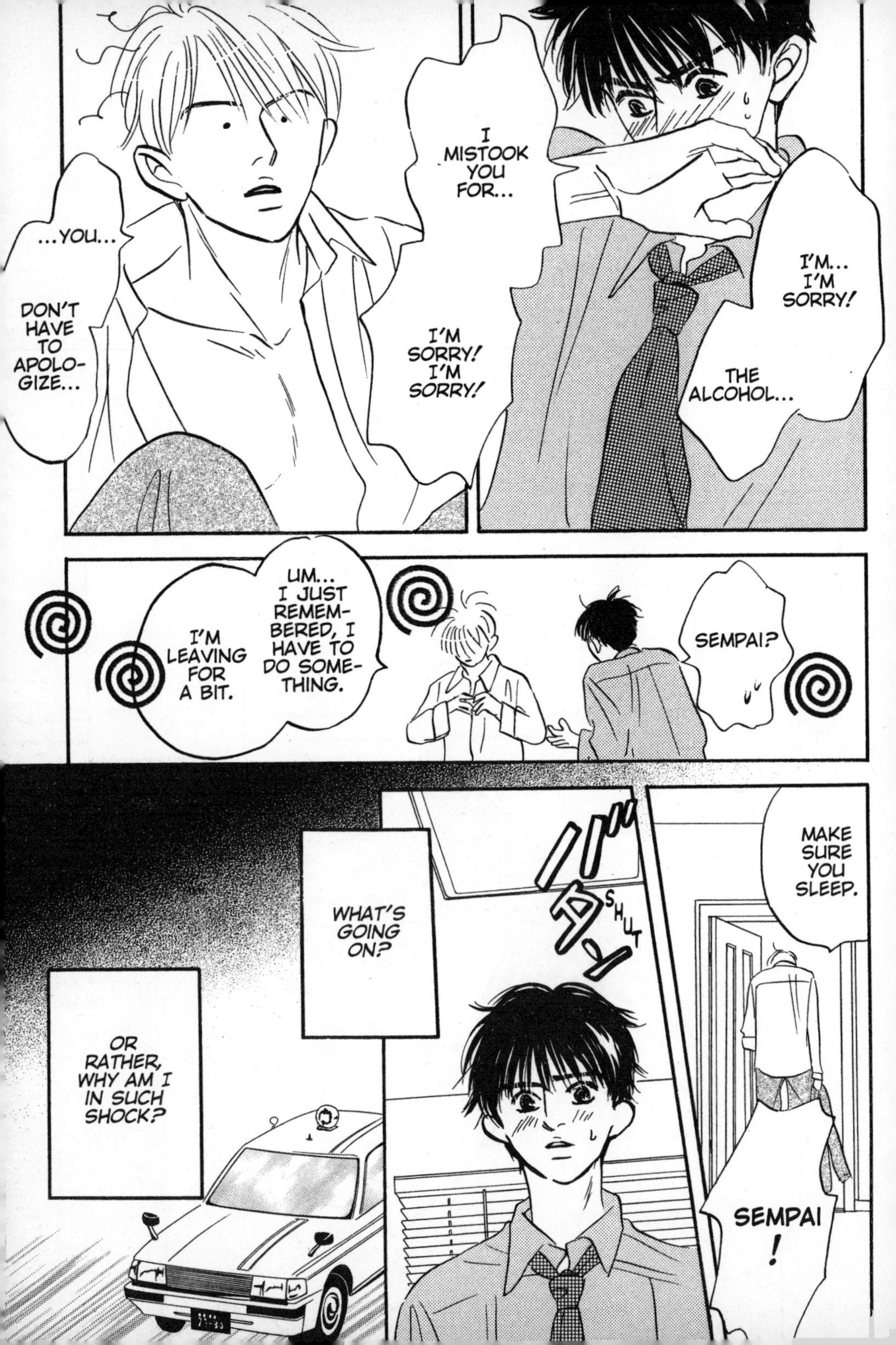
I'M... I'M SORRY!
THE ALCOHOL...
I MISTOOK YOU FOR...
I'M SORRY! I'M SORRY!
...YOU...
DON'T HAVE TO APOLOGIZE...
SEMPAI?
UM... I JUST REMEMBERED, I HAVE TO DO SOMETHING.
I'M LEAVING FOR A BIT.
MAKE SURE YOU SLEEP.
SEMPAI!
SHUT
WHAT'S GOING ON?
OR RATHER, WHY AM I IN SUCH SHOCK?

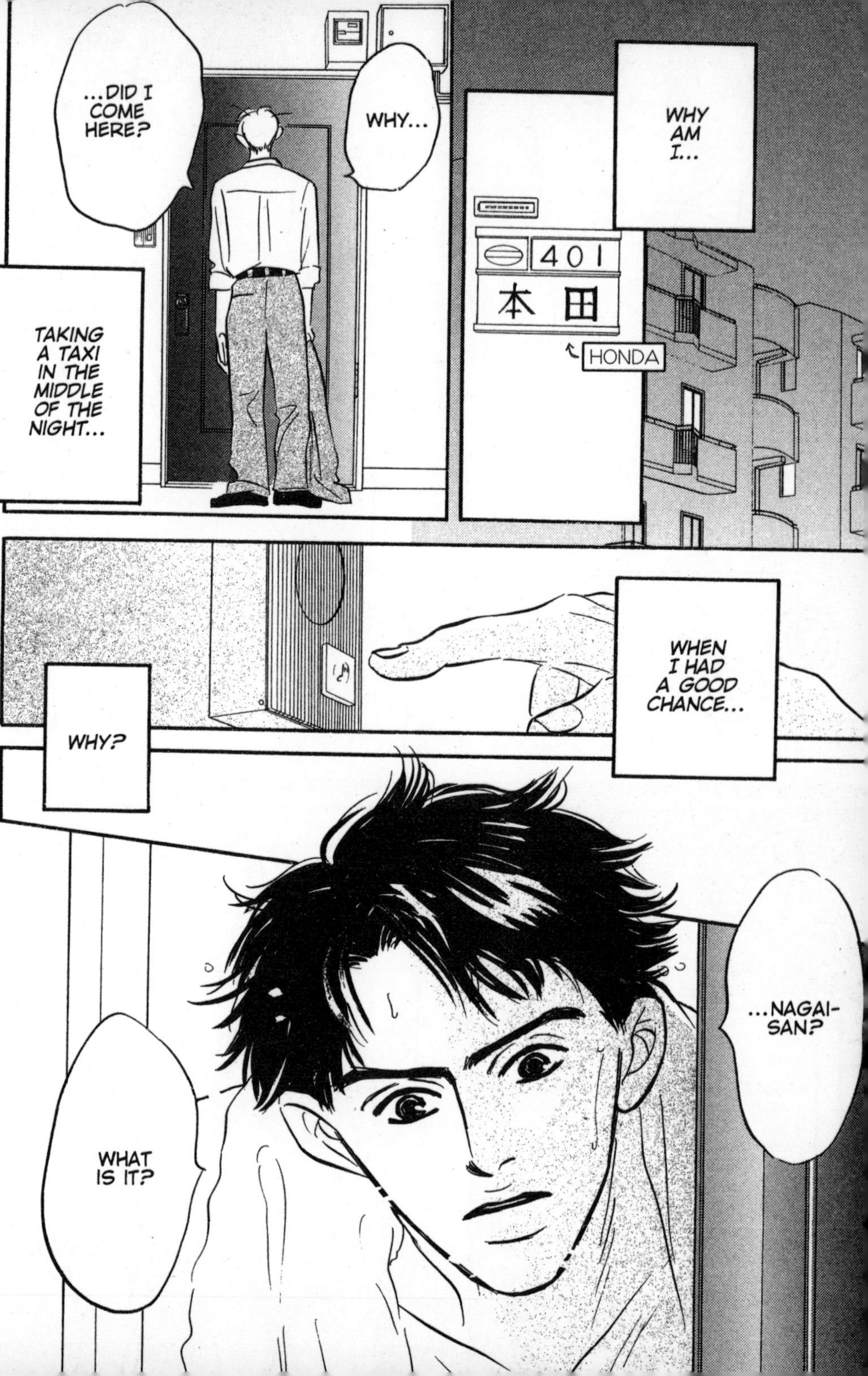
WHY AM I...
401
本田
HONDA
WHY...
...DID I COME HERE?
TAKING A TAXI IN THE MIDDLE OF THE NIGHT...
WHEN I HAD A GOOD CHANCE...
WHY?
...NAGAI-SAN?
WHAT IS IT?

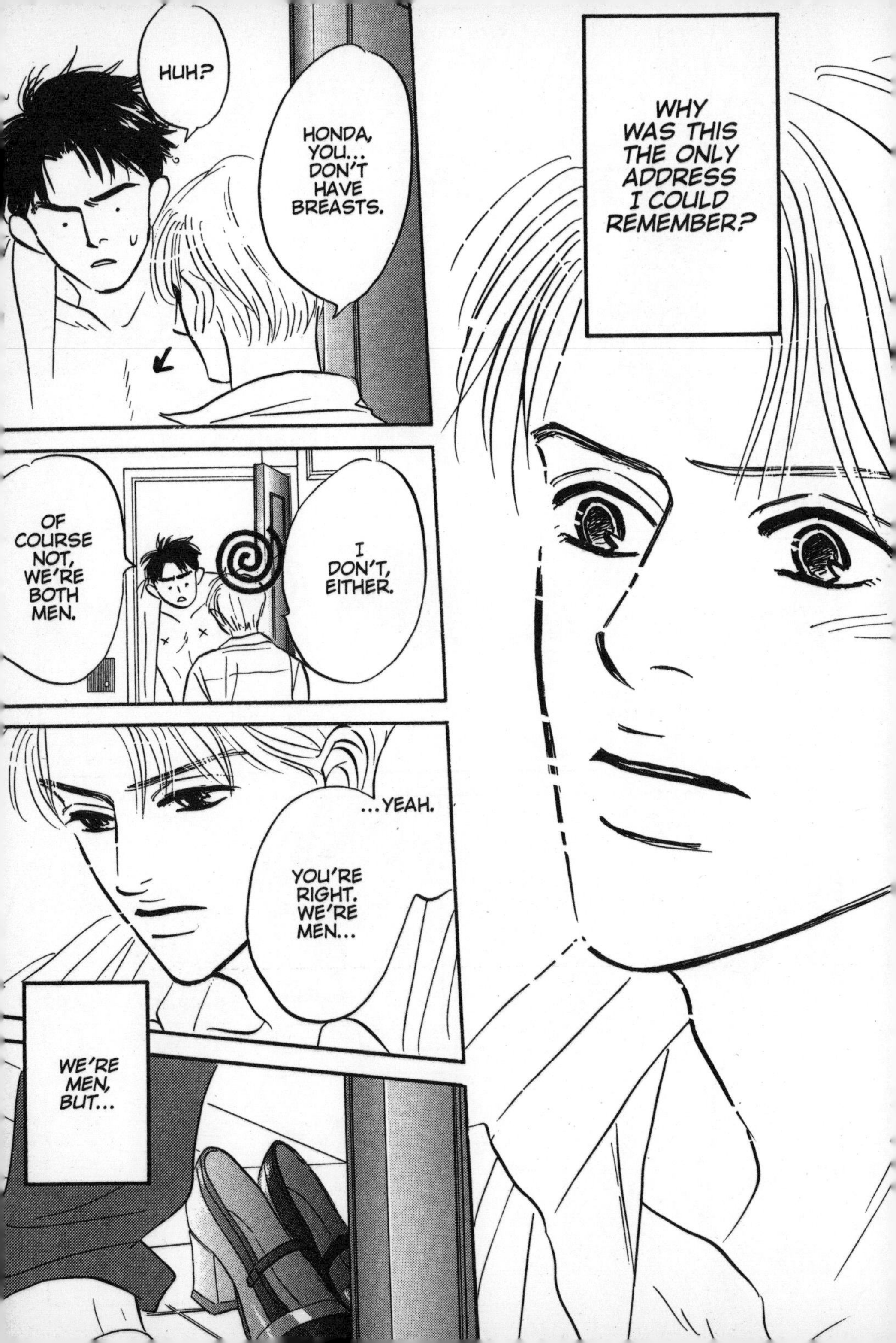
WHY WAS THIS THE ONLY ADDRESS I COULD REMEMBER?
HONDA, YOU... DON'T HAVE BREASTS.
HUH?
I DON'T, EITHER.
OF COURSE NOT, WE'RE BOTH MEN.
...YEAH.
YOU'RE RIGHT. WE'RE MEN...
WE'RE MEN, BUT...

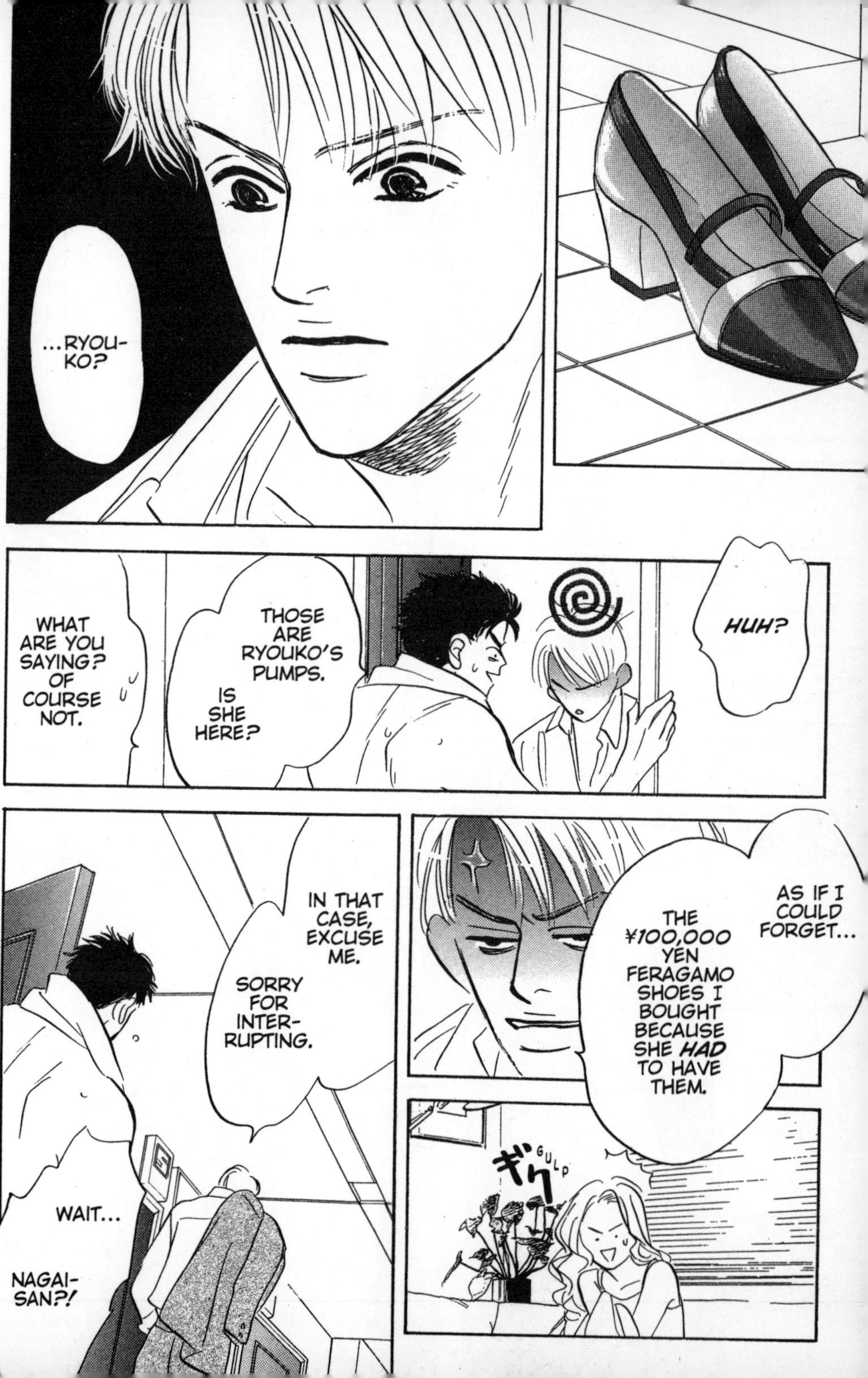
...RYOUKO?
HUH?
THOSE ARE RYOUKO'S PUMPS.
IS SHE HERE?
WHAT ARE YOU SAYING? OF COURSE NOT.
AS IF I COULD FORGET...
THE ¥100,000 YEN FERAGAMO SHOES I BOUGHT BECAUSE SHE *HAD* TO HAVE THEM.
ギク
GULP
IN THAT CASE, EXCUSE ME.
SORRY FOR INTERRUPTING.
WAIT...
NAGAI-SAN?!

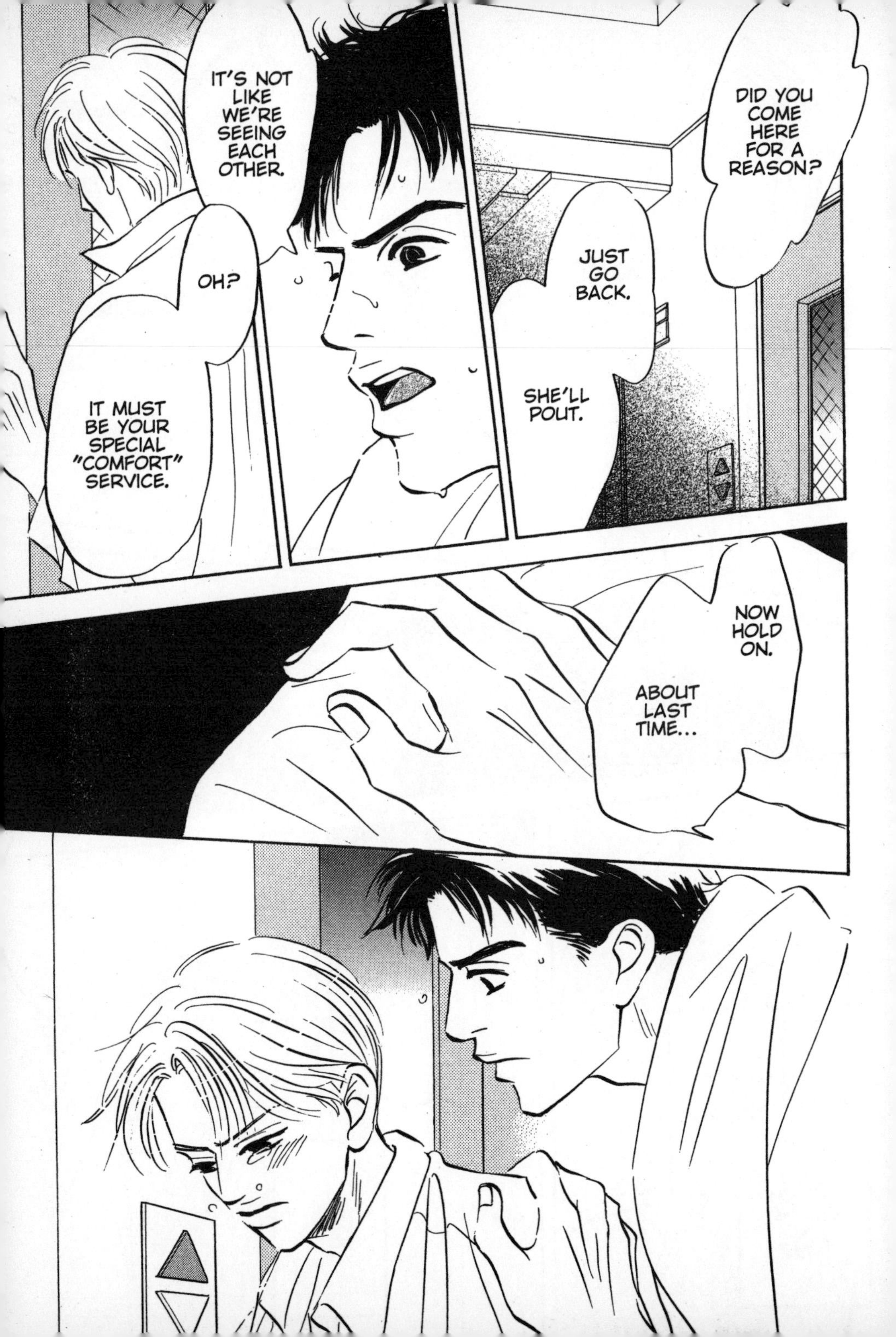
DID YOU COME HERE FOR A REASON?
JUST GO BACK.
SHE'LL POUT.
IT'S NOT LIKE WE'RE SEEING EACH OTHER.
OH?
IT MUST BE YOUR SPECIAL "COMFORT" SERVICE.
NOW HOLD ON.
ABOUT LAST TIME...

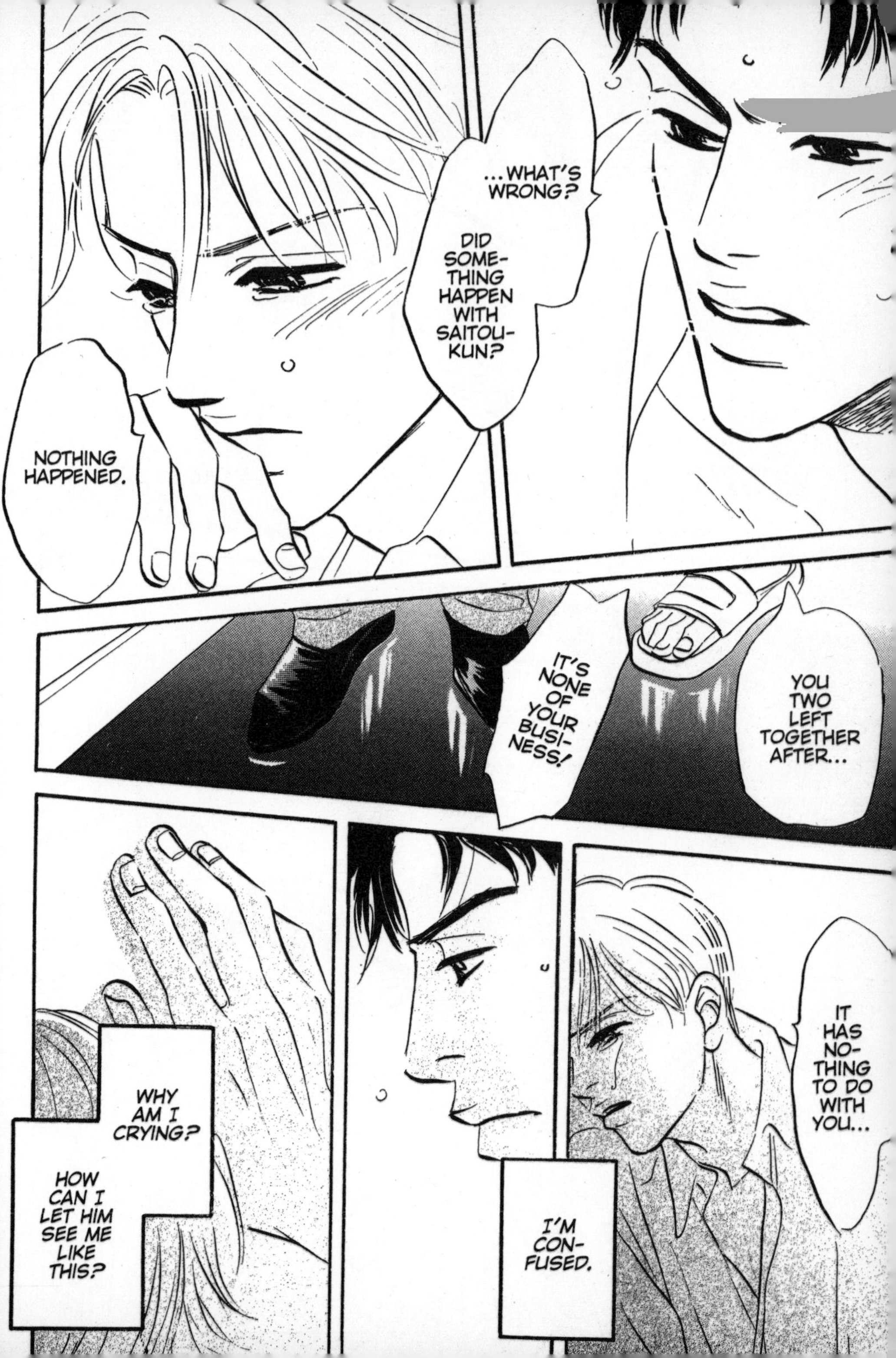
...WHAT'S WRONG?
DID SOMETHING HAPPEN WITH SAITOU-KUN?
NOTHING HAPPENED.
YOU TWO LEFT TOGETHER AFTER...
IT'S NONE OF YOUR BUSINESS!
IT HAS NOTHING TO DO WITH YOU...
I'M CONFUSED.
WHY AM I CRYING?
HOW CAN I LET HIM SEE ME LIKE THIS?

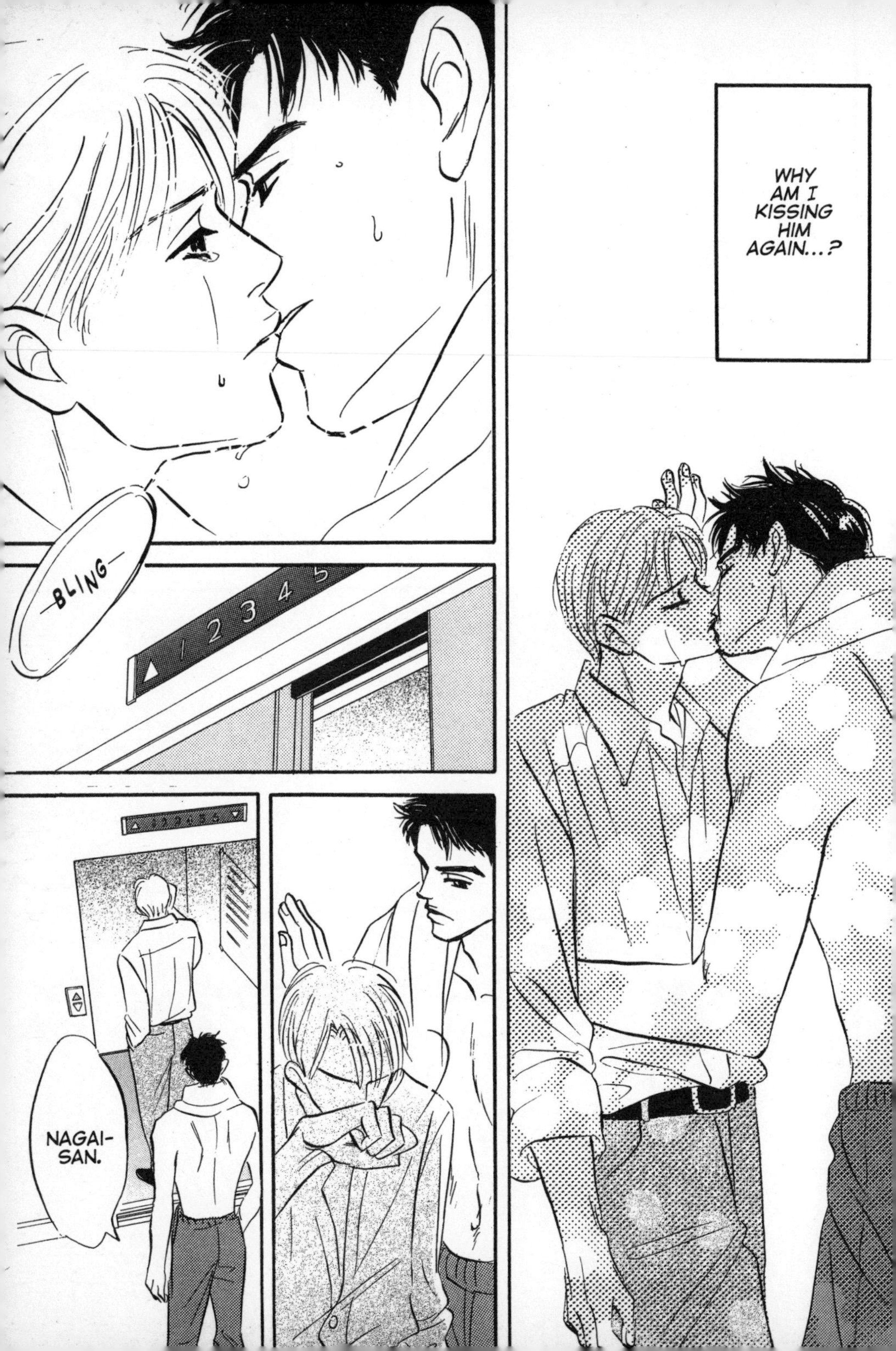
WHY AM I KISSING HIM AGAIN...?
BLING
NAGAI-SAN.

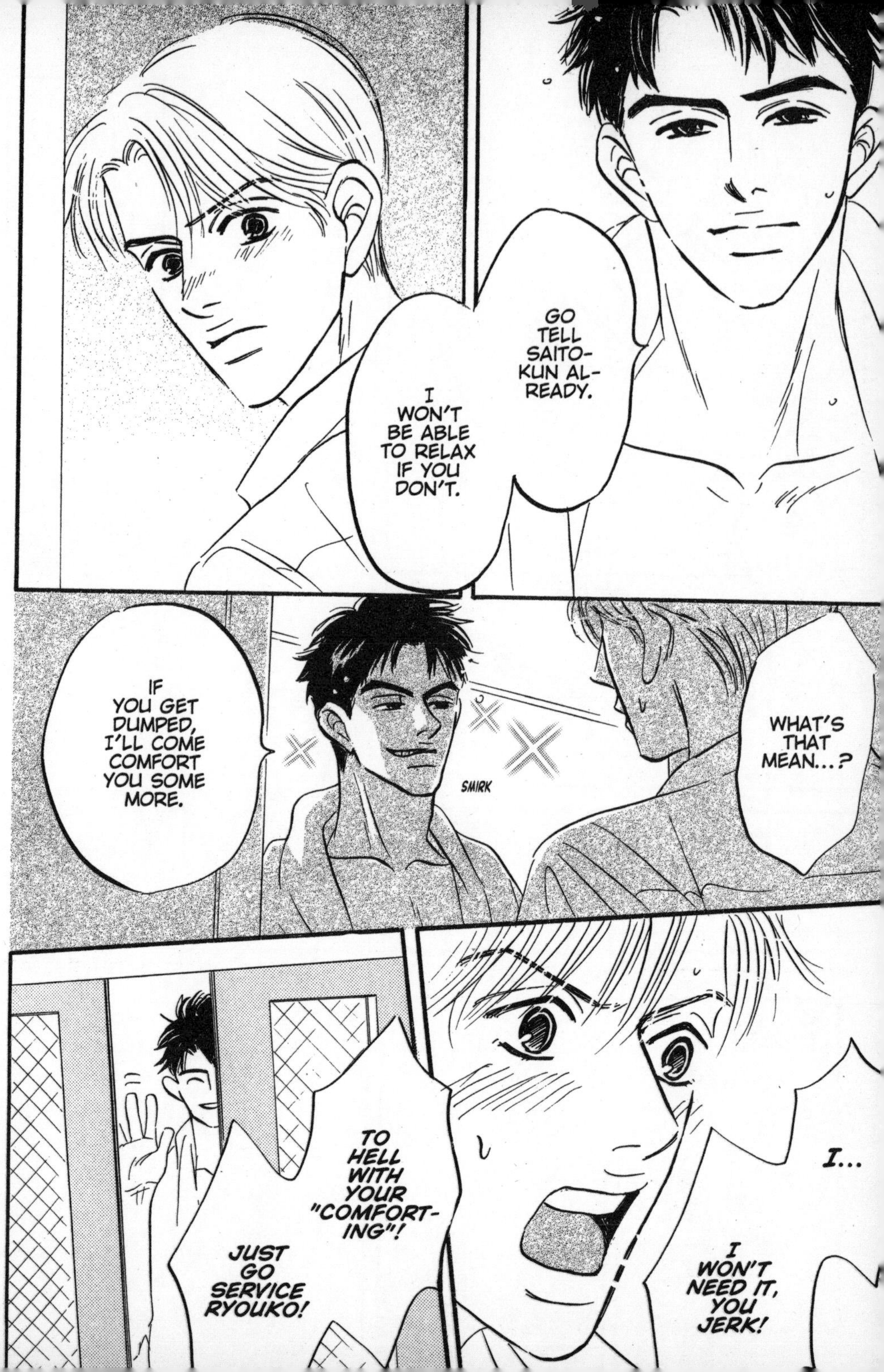
GO TELL SAITO-KUN AL-READY.
I WON'T BE ABLE TO RELAX IF YOU DON'T.
WHAT'S THAT MEAN...?
SMIRK
IF YOU GET DUMPED, I'LL COME COMFORT YOU SOME MORE.
I...
I WON'T NEED IT, YOU JERK!
TO HELL WITH YOUR "COMFORT-ING"!
JUST GO SERVICE RYOUKO!

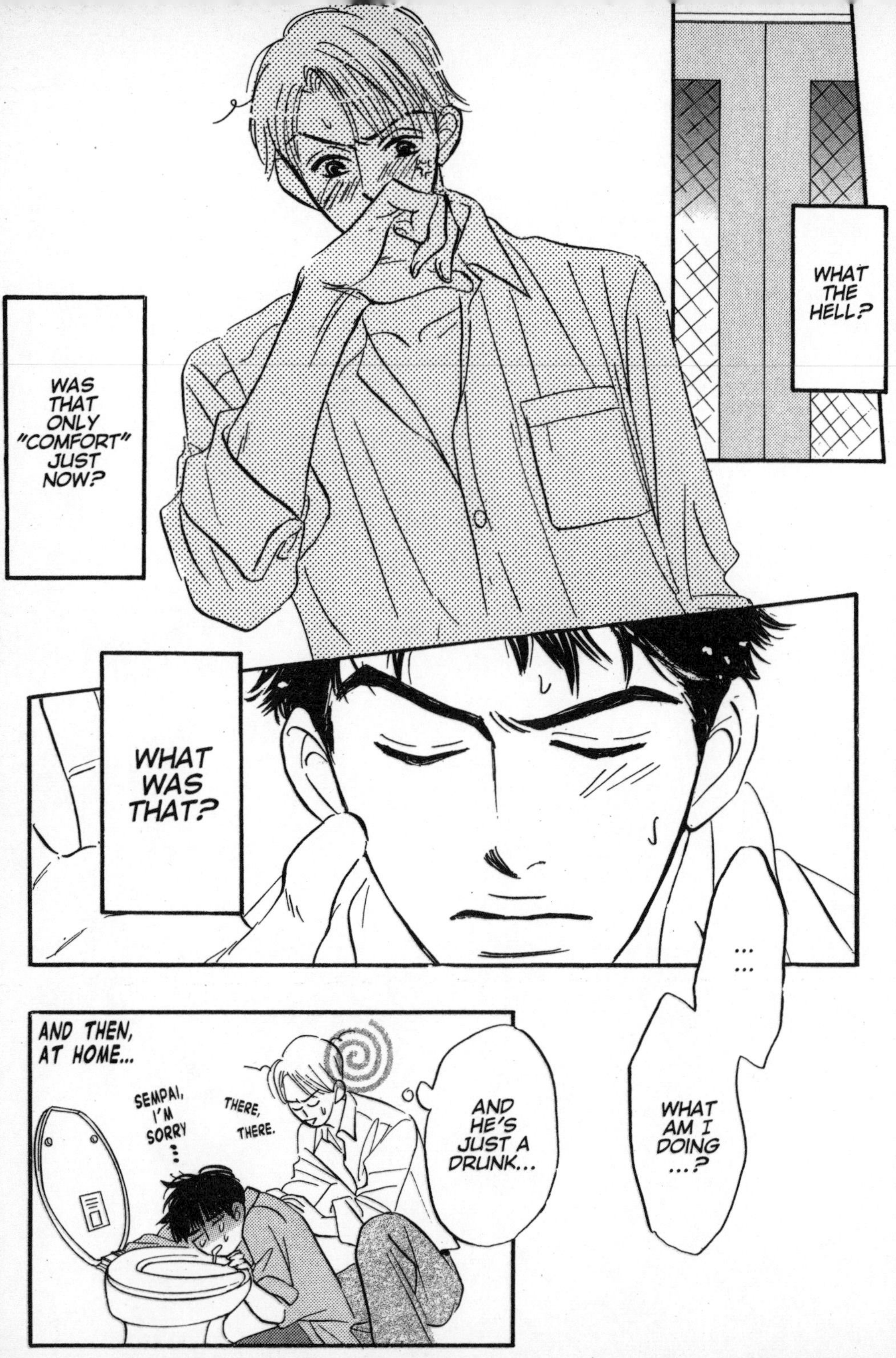
WHAT THE HELL?
WAS THAT ONLY "COMFORT" JUST NOW?
WHAT WAS THAT?
......
WHAT AM I DOING ...?
AND THEN, AT HOME...
AND HE'S JUST A DRUNK...
THERE, THERE.
SEMPAI, I'M SORRY ...

YUGI YAMADA PRESENTS COMICS / CLOSE THE LAST DOOR
ATSUSHI NAGAI/KENZOU HONDA/TOSHIHISA SAITOH

CLOSE
THE
LAST
DOOR

LOVE

ACT.3

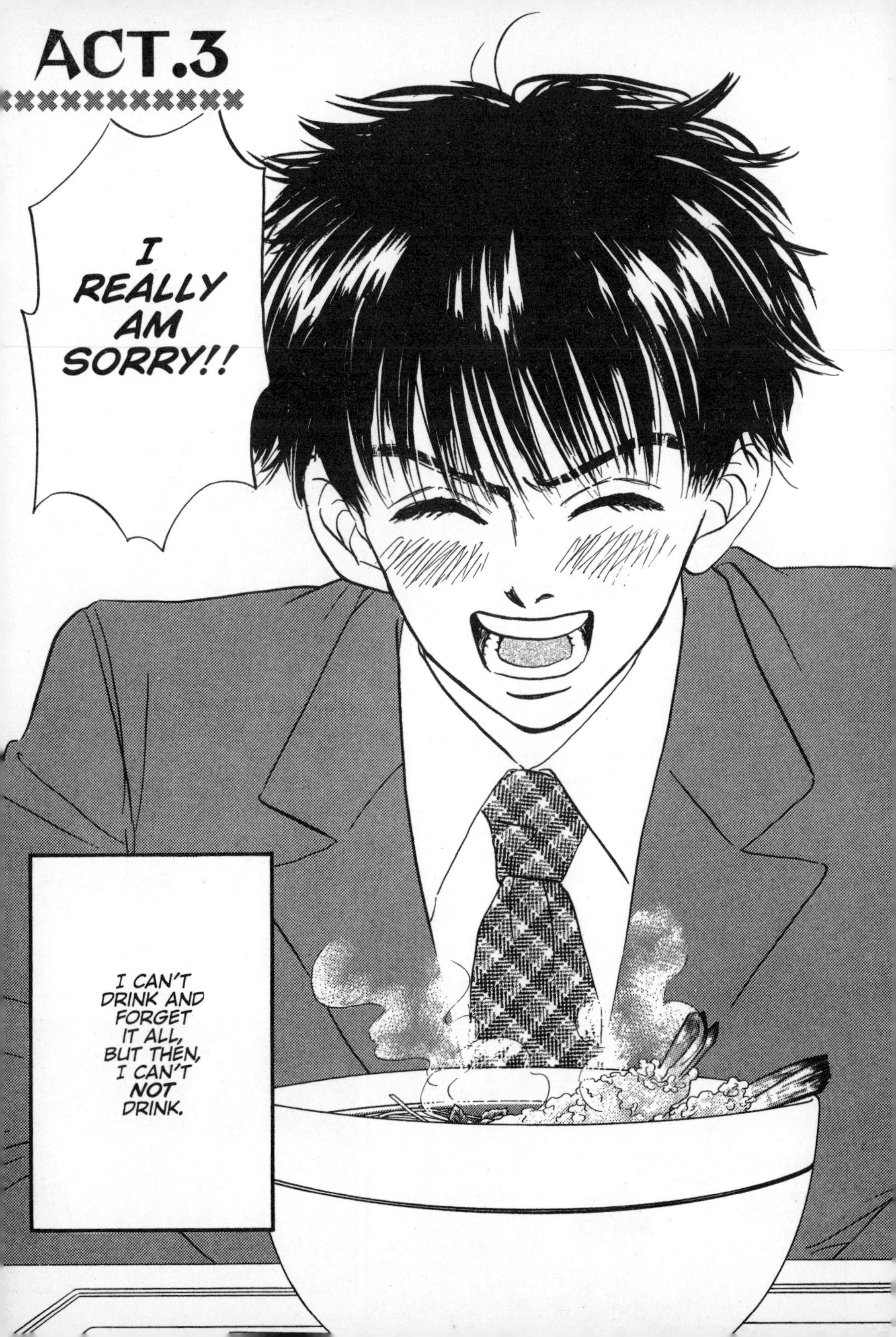
I REALLY AM SORRY!!
I CAN'T DRINK AND FORGET IT ALL, BUT THEN, I CAN'T NOT DRINK.

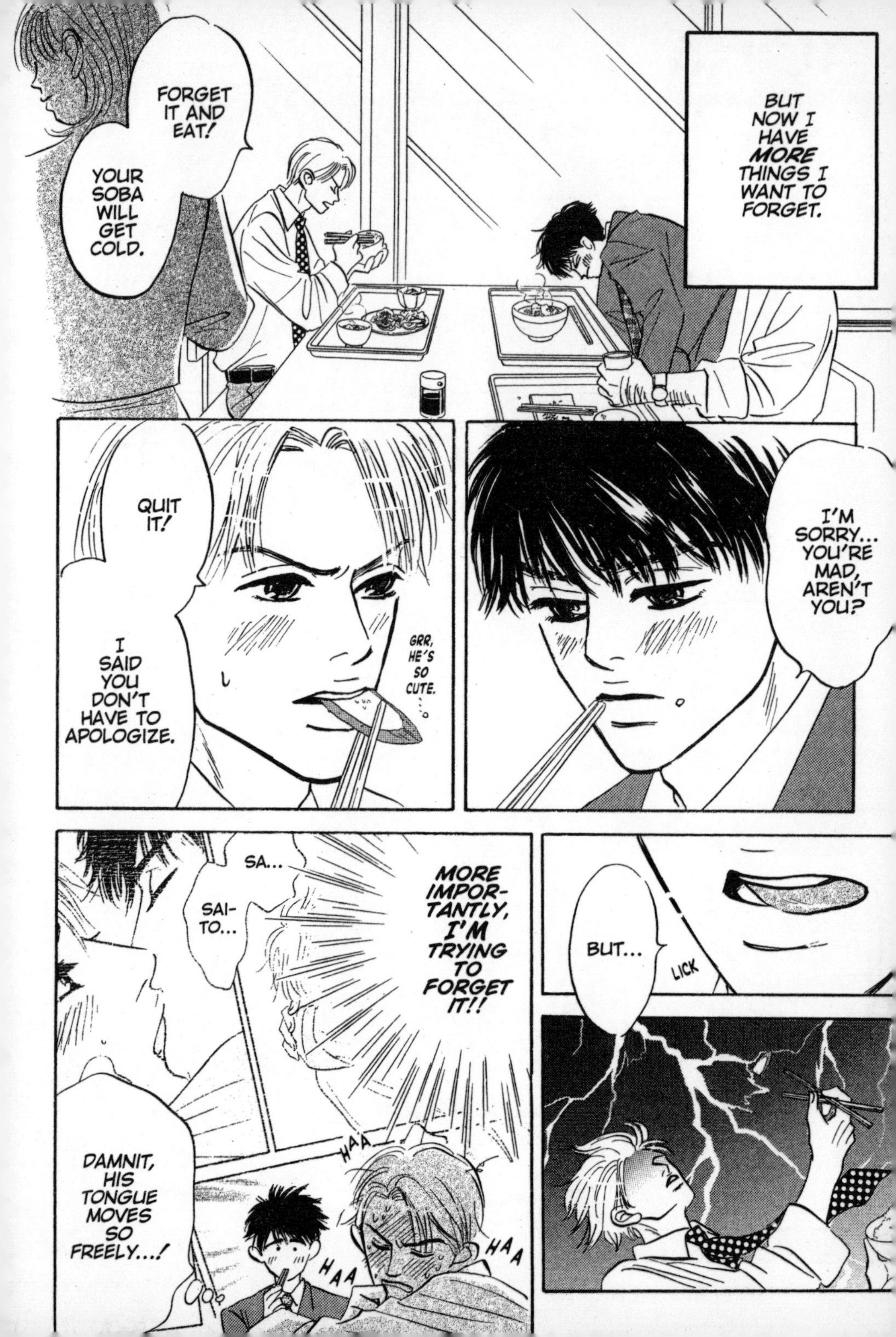

BUT NOW I HAVE MORE THINGS I WANT TO FORGET.
FORGET IT AND EAT!
YOUR SOBA WILL GET COLD.
I'M SORRY... YOU'RE MAD, AREN'T YOU?
QUIT IT!
I SAID YOU DON'T HAVE TO APOLOGIZE.
GRR, HE'S SO CUTE.
BUT...
LICK
MORE IMPORTANTLY, I'M TRYING TO FORGET IT!!
SA...
SAI-TO...
HAA
HAA
DAMNIT, HIS TONGUE MOVES SO FREELY...!
HAA

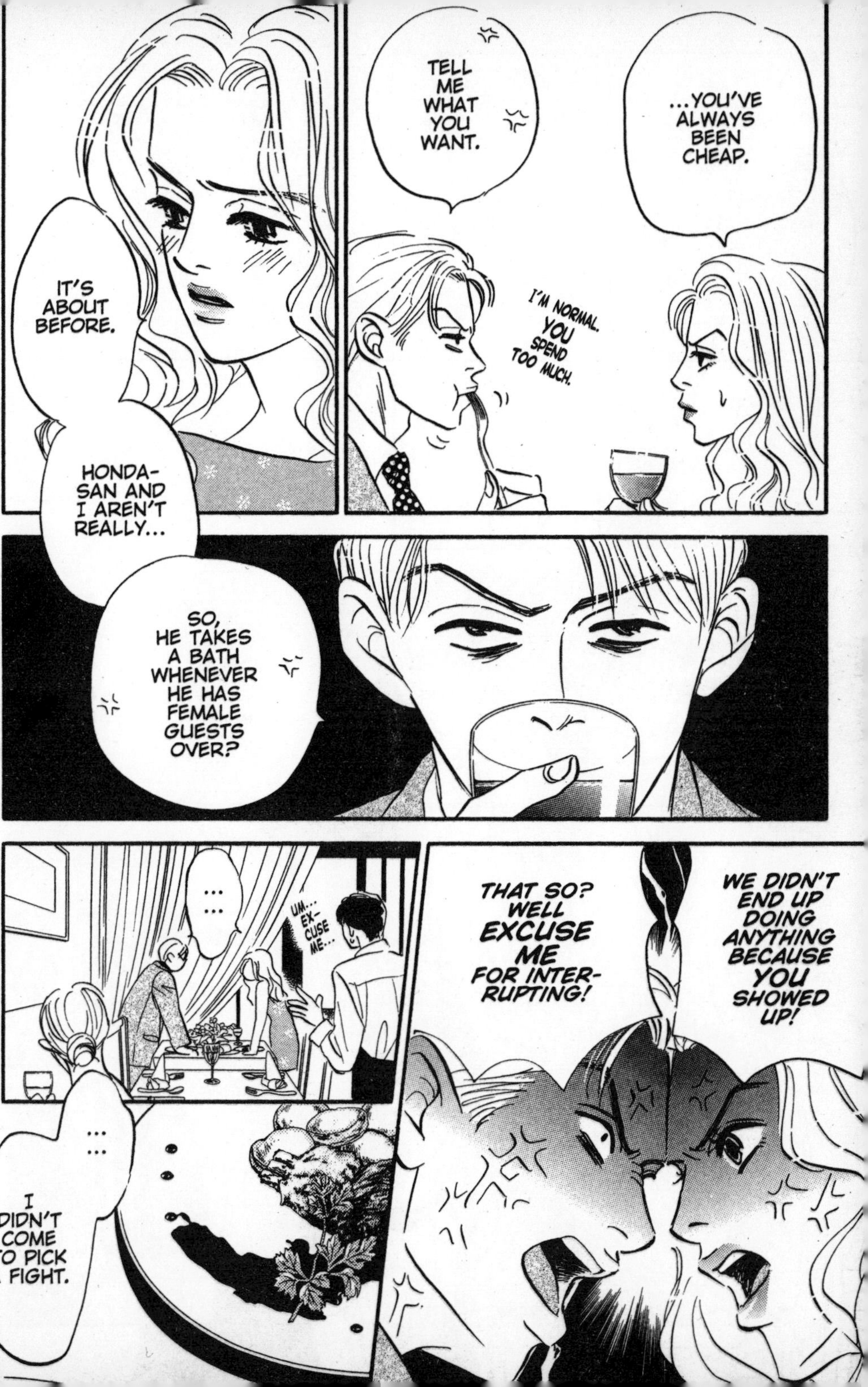

...YOU'VE ALWAYS BEEN CHEAP.
TELL ME WHAT YOU WANT.
I'M NORMAL. YOU SPEND TOO MUCH.
IT'S ABOUT BEFORE.
HONDA-SAN AND I AREN'T REALLY...
SO, HE TAKES A BATH WHENEVER HE HAS FEMALE GUESTS OVER?
WE DIDN'T END UP DOING ANYTHING BECAUSE YOU SHOWED UP!
THAT SO? WELL EXCUSE ME FOR INTERRUPTING!
UM... EX-CUSE ME...
......
......
I DIDN'T COME TO PICK A FIGHT.

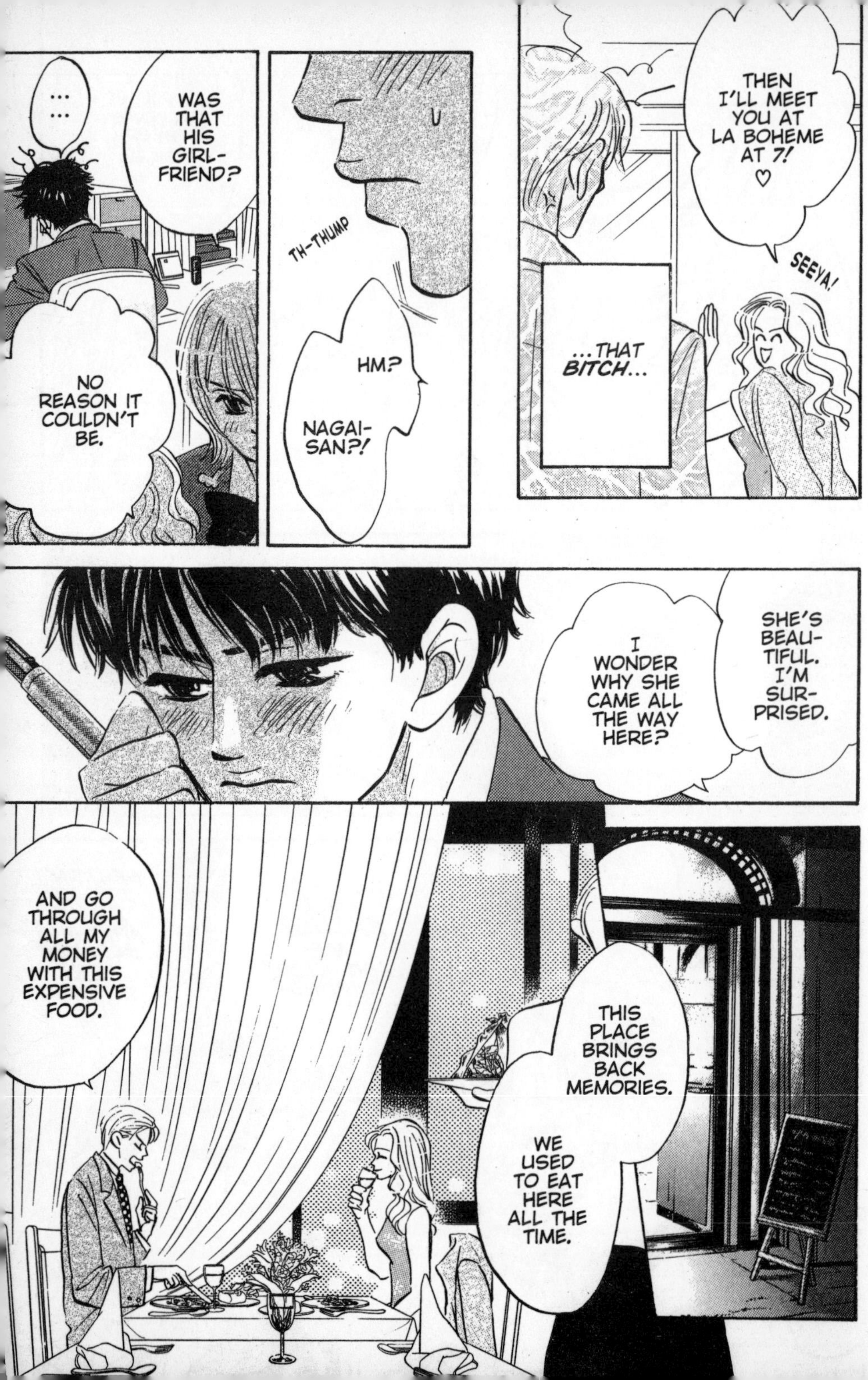
THEN I'LL MEET YOU AT LA BOHEME AT 7! ♡
SEEYA!
...THAT *BITCH*...
TH-THUMP
HM?
NAGAI-SAN?!
WAS THAT HIS GIRLFRIEND?
... ...
NO REASON IT COULDN'T BE.
SHE'S BEAUTIFUL. I'M SURPRISED.
I WONDER WHY SHE CAME ALL THE WAY HERE?
THIS PLACE BRINGS BACK MEMORIES.
WE USED TO EAT HERE ALL THE TIME.
AND GO THROUGH ALL MY MONEY WITH THIS EXPENSIVE FOOD.

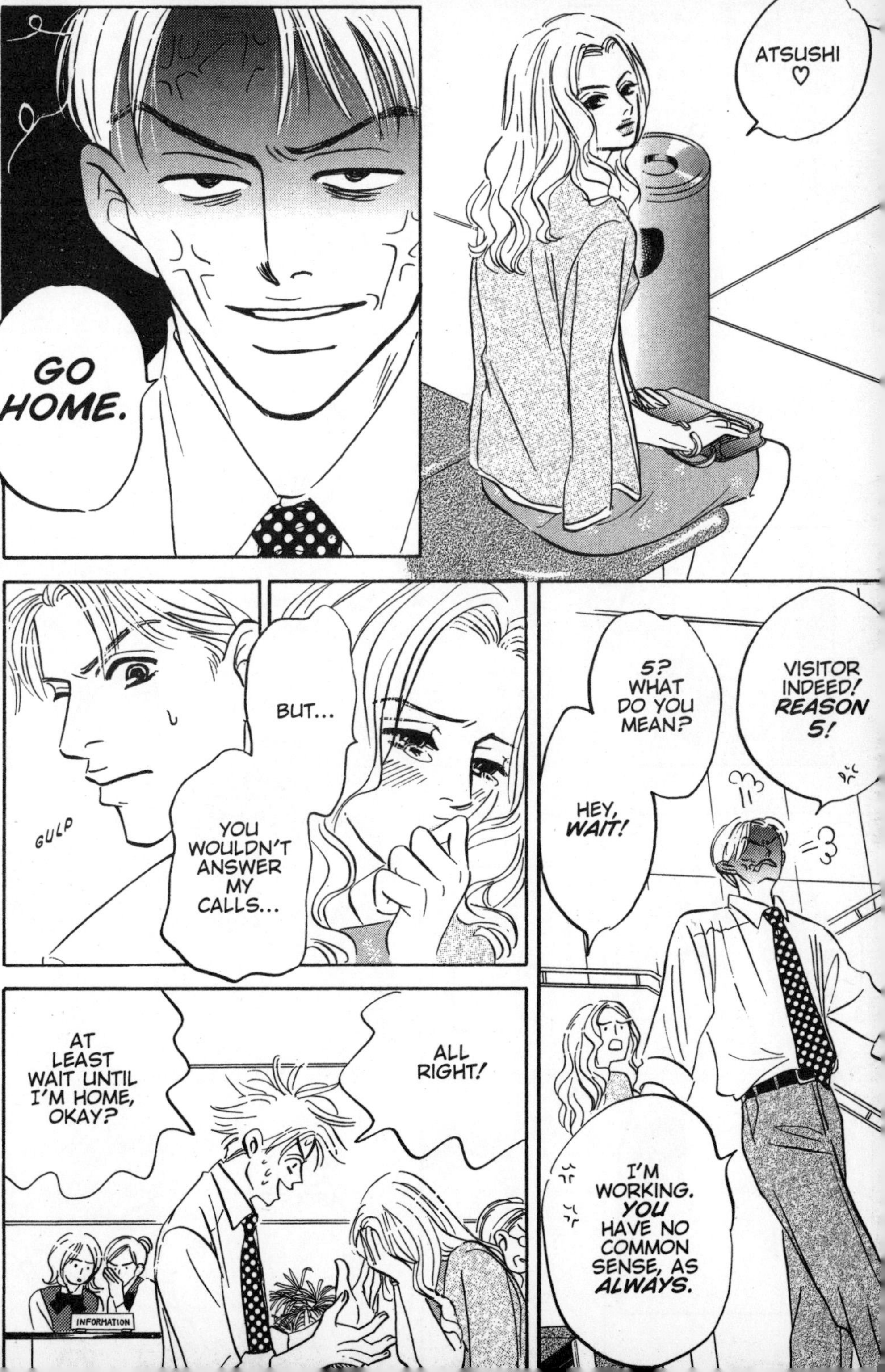
ATSUSHI ♡
GO HOME.
VISITOR INDEED! REASON 5!
5? WHAT DO YOU MEAN?
HEY, WAIT!
I'M WORKING. YOU HAVE NO COMMON SENSE, AS ALWAYS.
BUT...
YOU WOULDN'T ANSWER MY CALLS...
GULP
AT LEAST WAIT UNTIL I'M HOME, OKAY?
ALL RIGHT!
INFORMATION

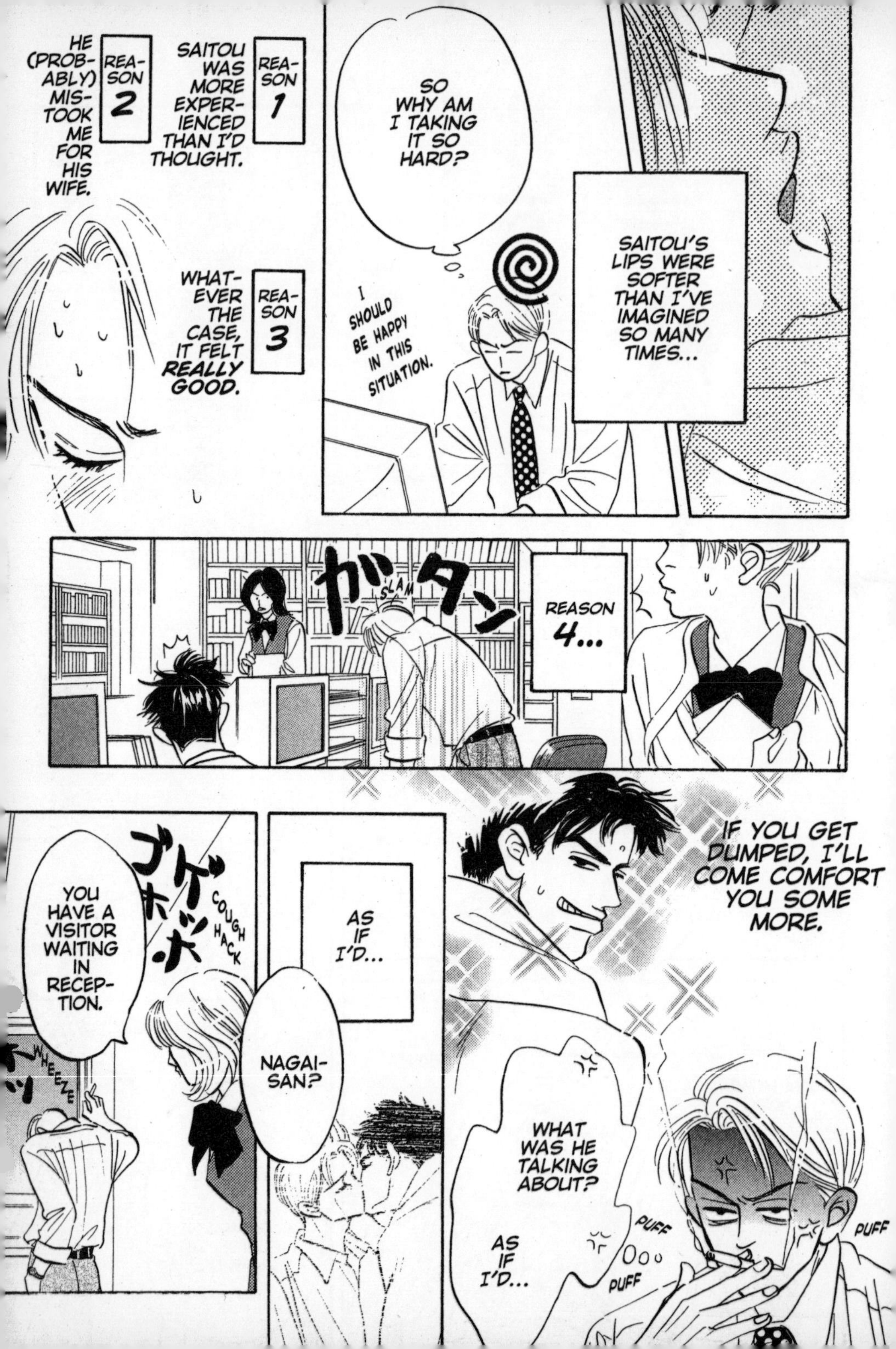
SAITOU'S LIPS WERE SOFTER THAN I'VE IMAGINED SO MANY TIMES...
SO WHY AM I TAKING IT SO HARD?
I SHOULD BE HAPPY IN THIS SITUATION.
REASON 1
SAITOU WAS MORE EXPERIENCED THAN I'D THOUGHT.
REASON 2
HE (PROBABLY) MISTOOK ME FOR HIS WIFE.
REASON 3
WHATEVER THE CASE, IT FELT REALLY GOOD.
REASON 4...
ガタン
SLAM
IF YOU GET DUMPED, I'LL COME COMFORT YOU SOME MORE.
WHAT WAS HE TALKING ABOUT?
AS IF I'D...
PUFF
PUFF
PUFF
AS IF I'D...
NAGAI-SAN?
YOU HAVE A VISITOR WAITING IN RECEPTION.
ゲホゴホ
COUGH HACK
WHEEZE

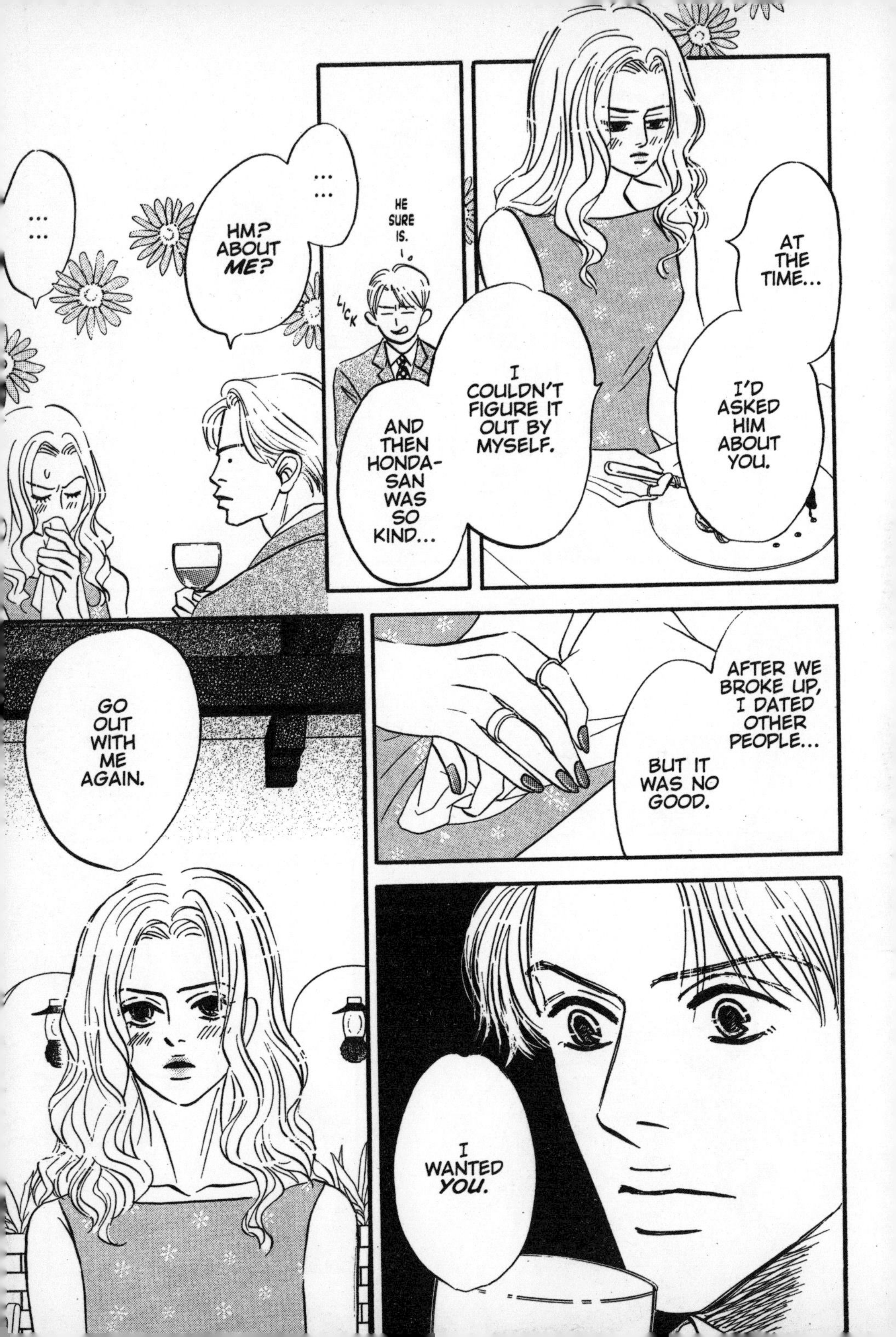
AT THE TIME...
I'D ASKED HIM ABOUT YOU.
I COULDN'T FIGURE IT OUT BY MYSELF.
AND THEN HONDA-SAN WAS SO KIND...
HE SURE IS.
LICK
......
HM? ABOUT ME?
......
AFTER WE BROKE UP, I DATED OTHER PEOPLE...
BUT IT WAS NO GOOD.
GO OUT WITH ME AGAIN.
I WANTED YOU.

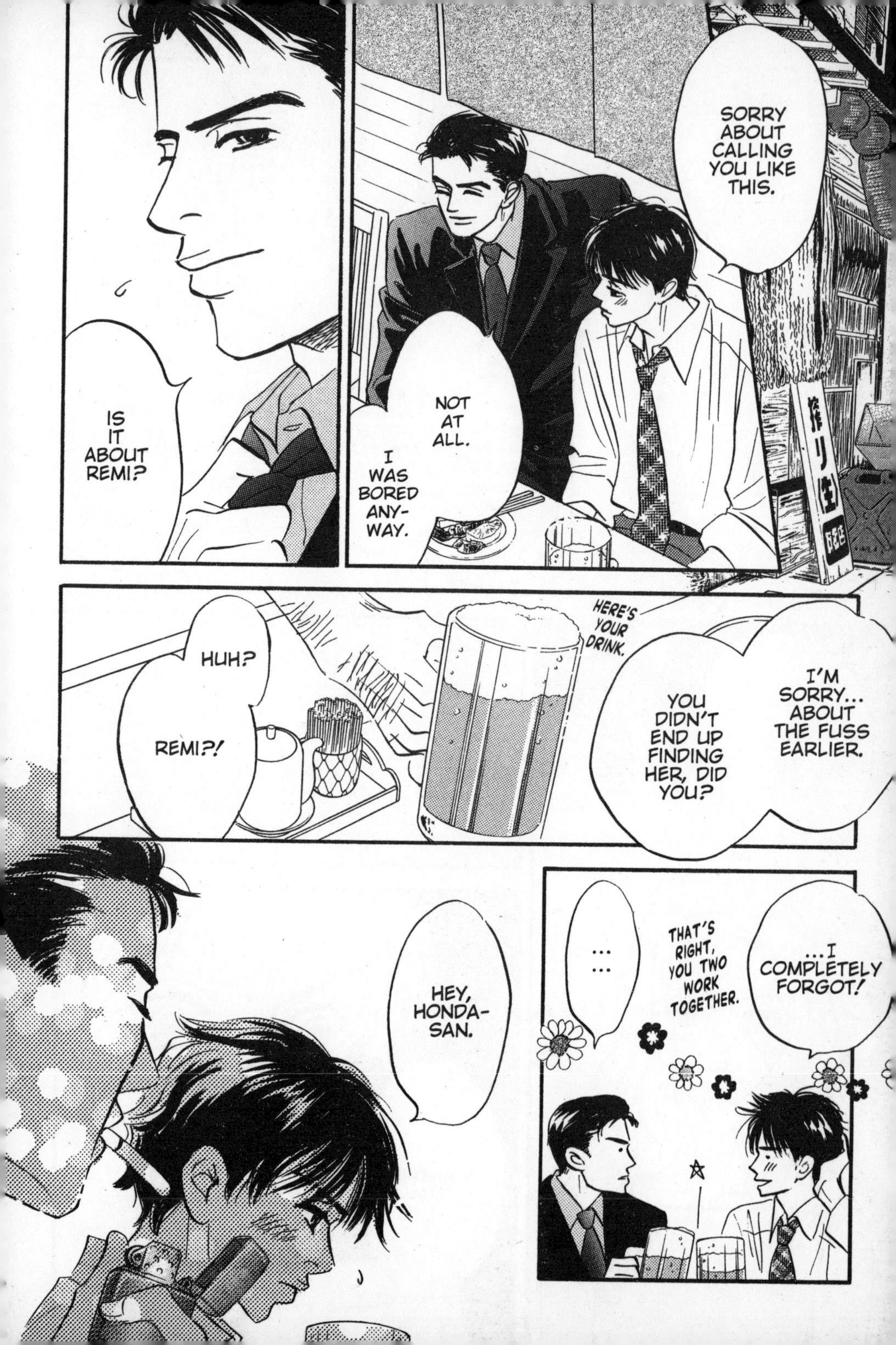
SORRY ABOUT CALLING YOU LIKE THIS.
NOT AT ALL.
I WAS BORED ANY-WAY.
IS IT ABOUT REMI?
I'M SORRY... ABOUT THE FUSS EARLIER.
YOU DIDN'T END UP FINDING HER, DID YOU?
HERE'S YOUR DRINK.
HUH?
REMI?!
...I COMPLETELY FORGOT!
THAT'S RIGHT, YOU TWO WORK TOGETHER.
... ...
HEY, HONDA-SAN.

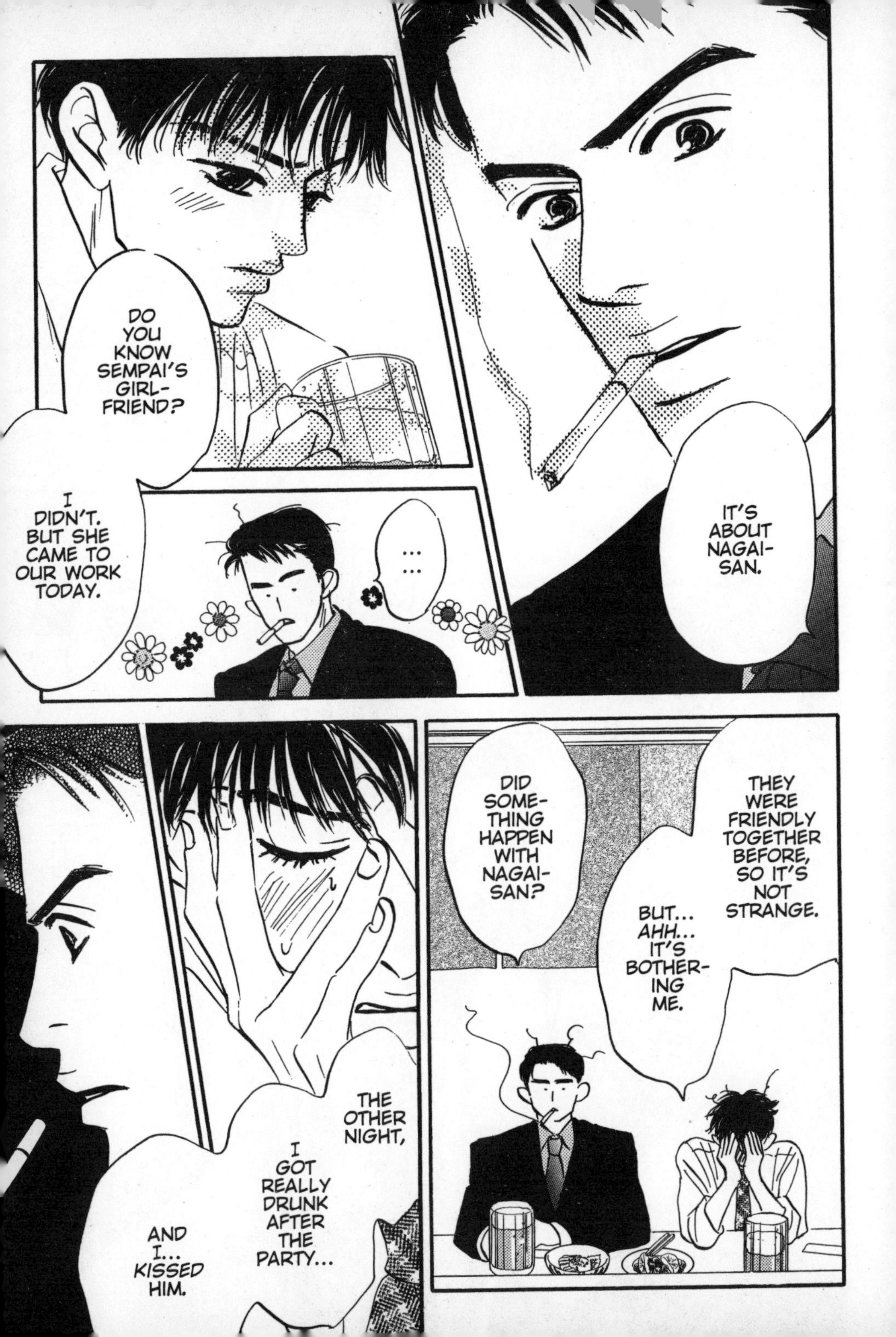
IT'S ABOUT NAGAI-SAN.
DO YOU KNOW SEMPAI'S GIRL-FRIEND?
... ...
I DIDN'T. BUT SHE CAME TO OUR WORK TODAY.
THEY WERE FRIENDLY TOGETHER BEFORE, SO IT'S NOT STRANGE.
BUT... AHH... IT'S BOTHER-ING ME.
DID SOME-THING HAPPEN WITH NAGAI-SAN?
THE OTHER NIGHT,
I GOT REALLY DRUNK AFTER THE PARTY...
AND I... KISSED HIM.

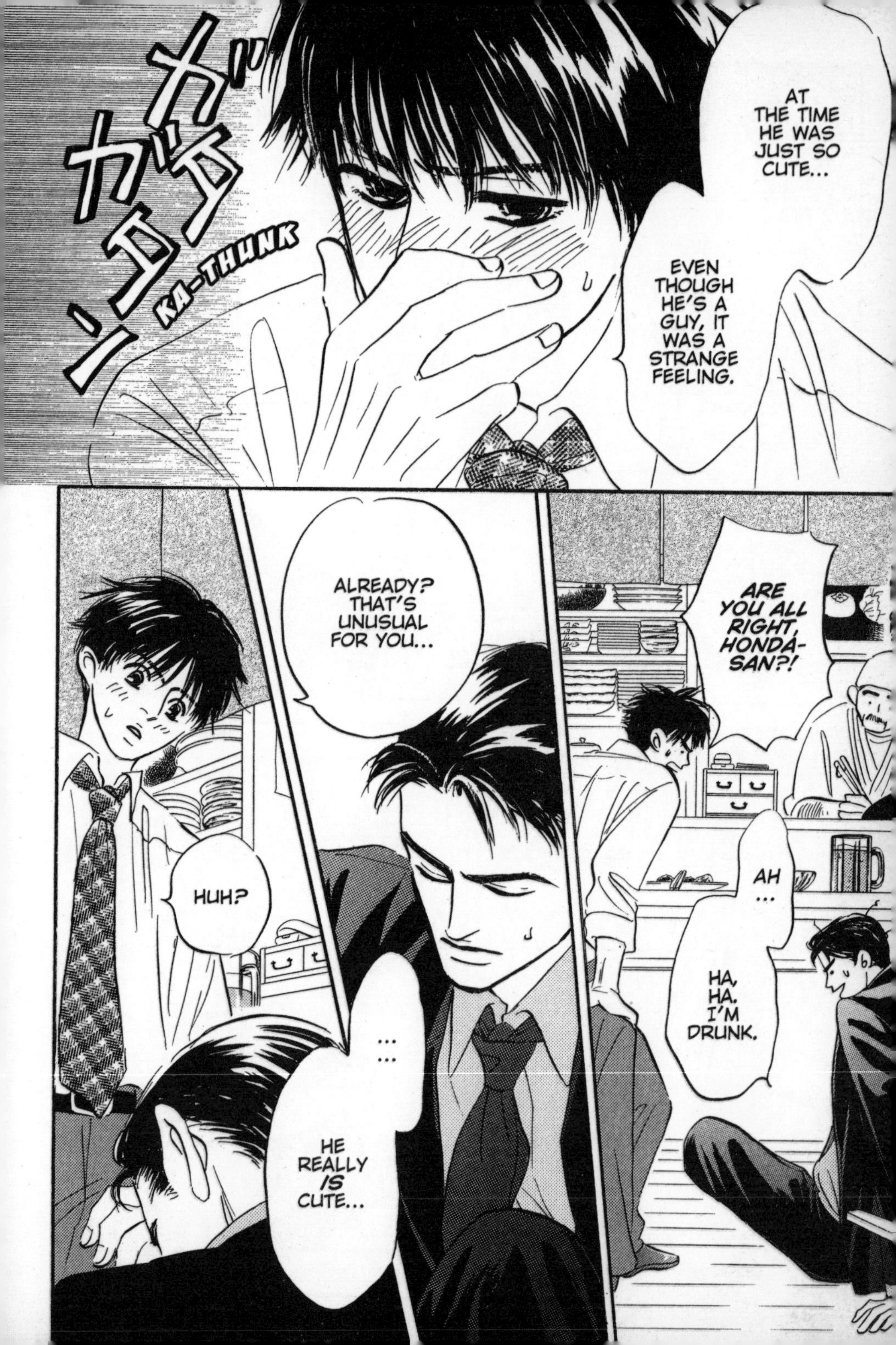
AT THE TIME HE WAS JUST SO CUTE...
EVEN THOUGH HE'S A GUY, IT WAS A STRANGE FEELING.
KA-THUNK
ARE YOU ALL RIGHT, HONDA-SAN?!
AH...
HA, HA. I'M DRUNK.
ALREADY? THAT'S UNUSUAL FOR YOU...
......
HE REALLY *IS* CUTE...
HUH?

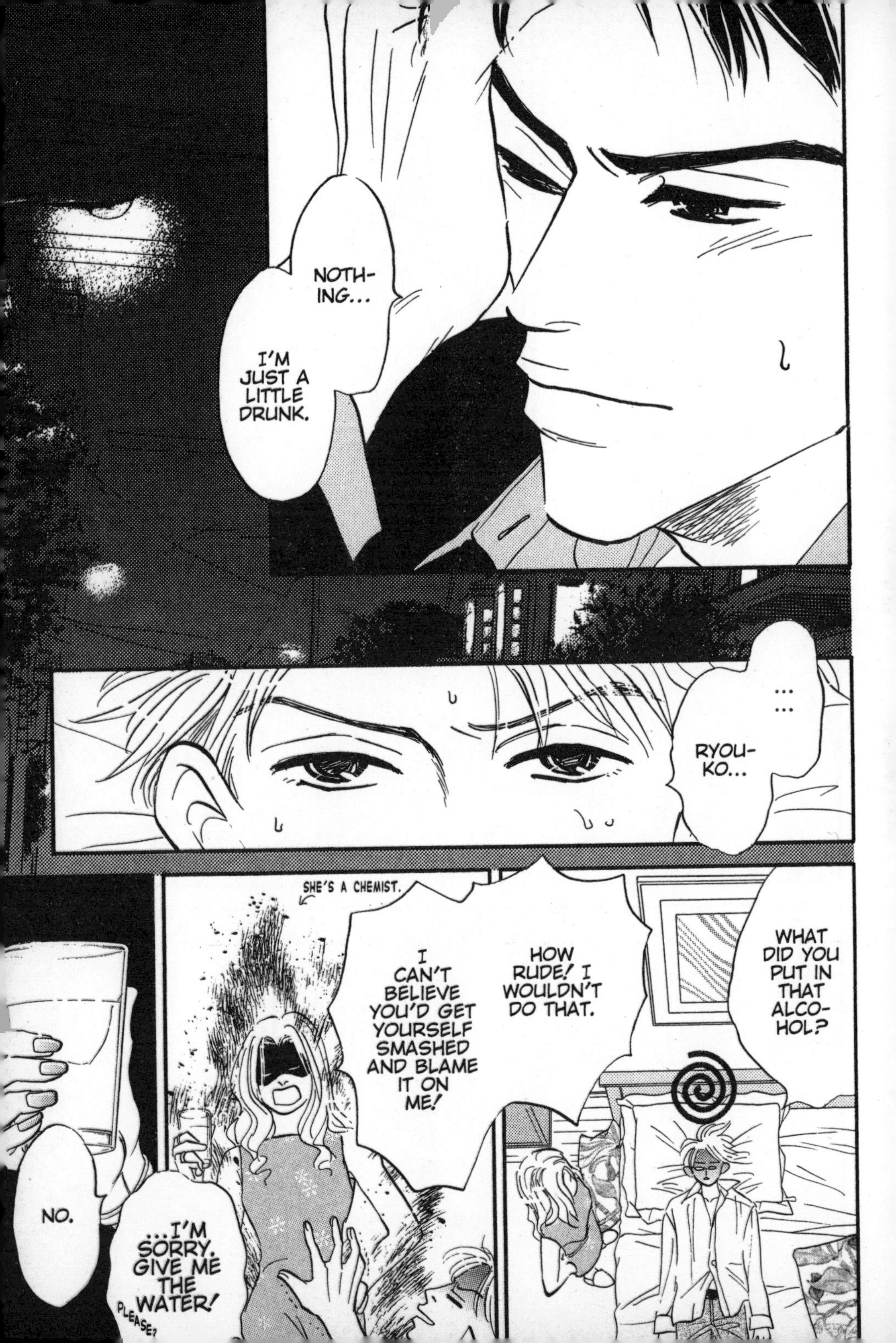
NOTH-ING...
I'M JUST A LITTLE DRUNK.
... ...
RYOU-KO...
WHAT DID YOU PUT IN THAT ALCO-HOL?
HOW RUDE! I WOULDN'T DO THAT.
I CAN'T BELIEVE YOU'D GET YOURSELF SMASHED AND BLAME IT ON ME!
SHE'S A CHEMIST.
NO.
...I'M SORRY. GIVE ME THE WATER!
PLEASE?

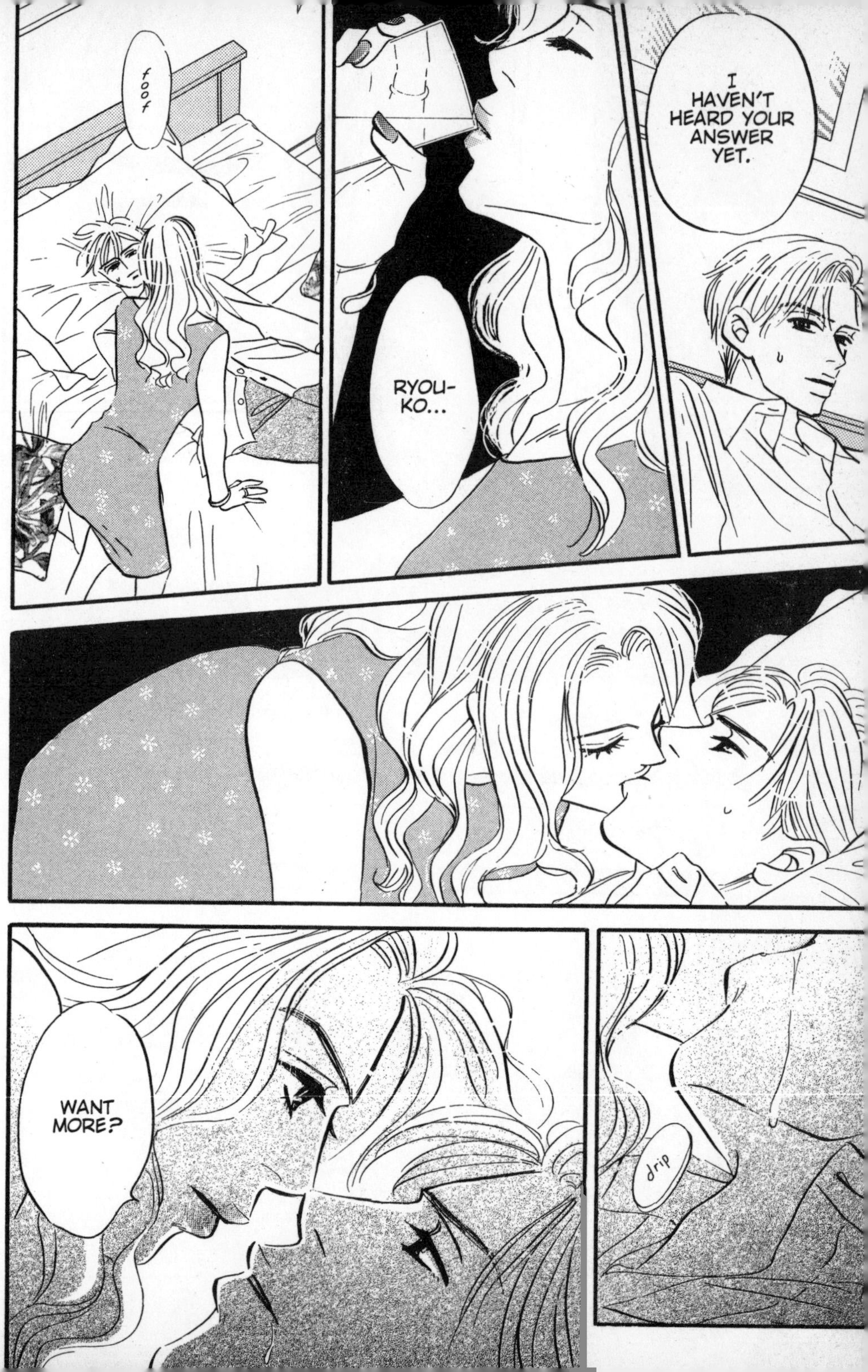
I HAVEN'T HEARD YOUR ANSWER YET.
RYOU-KO...
foof
drip
WANT MORE?

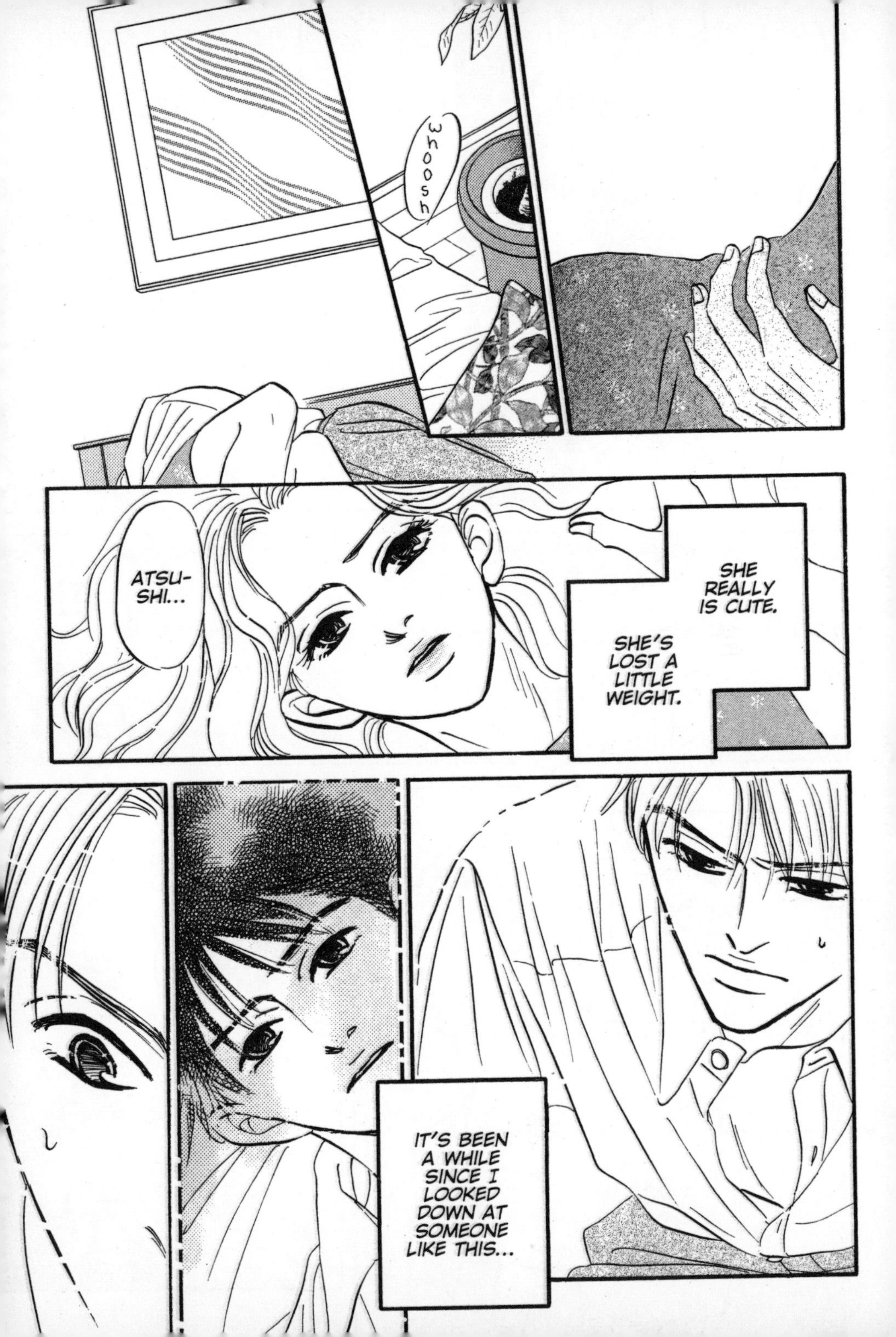
whoosh
SHE REALLY IS CUTE.
SHE'S LOST A LITTLE WEIGHT.
ATSU-SHI...
IT'S BEEN A WHILE SINCE I LOOKED DOWN AT SOMEONE LIKE THIS...

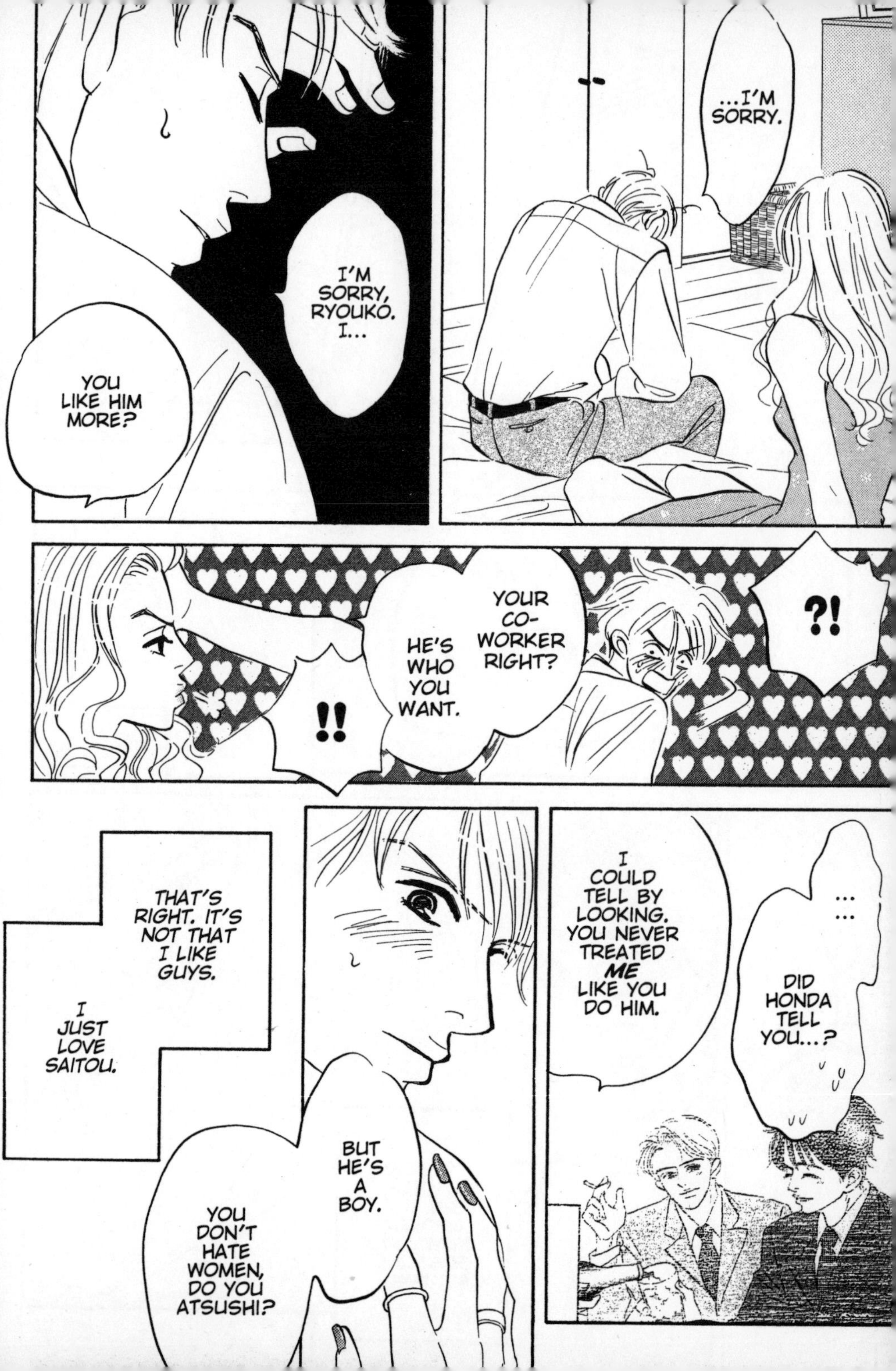
...I'M SORRY.
I'M SORRY, RYOUKO. I...
YOU LIKE HIM MORE?
?!
YOUR CO-WORKER RIGHT?
HE'S WHO YOU WANT.
!!
......
DID HONDA TELL YOU...?
I COULD TELL BY LOOKING. YOU NEVER TREATED *ME* LIKE YOU DO HIM.
BUT HE'S A BOY.
YOU DON'T HATE WOMEN, DO YOU ATSUSHI?
THAT'S RIGHT. IT'S NOT THAT I LIKE GUYS.
I JUST LOVE SAITOU.

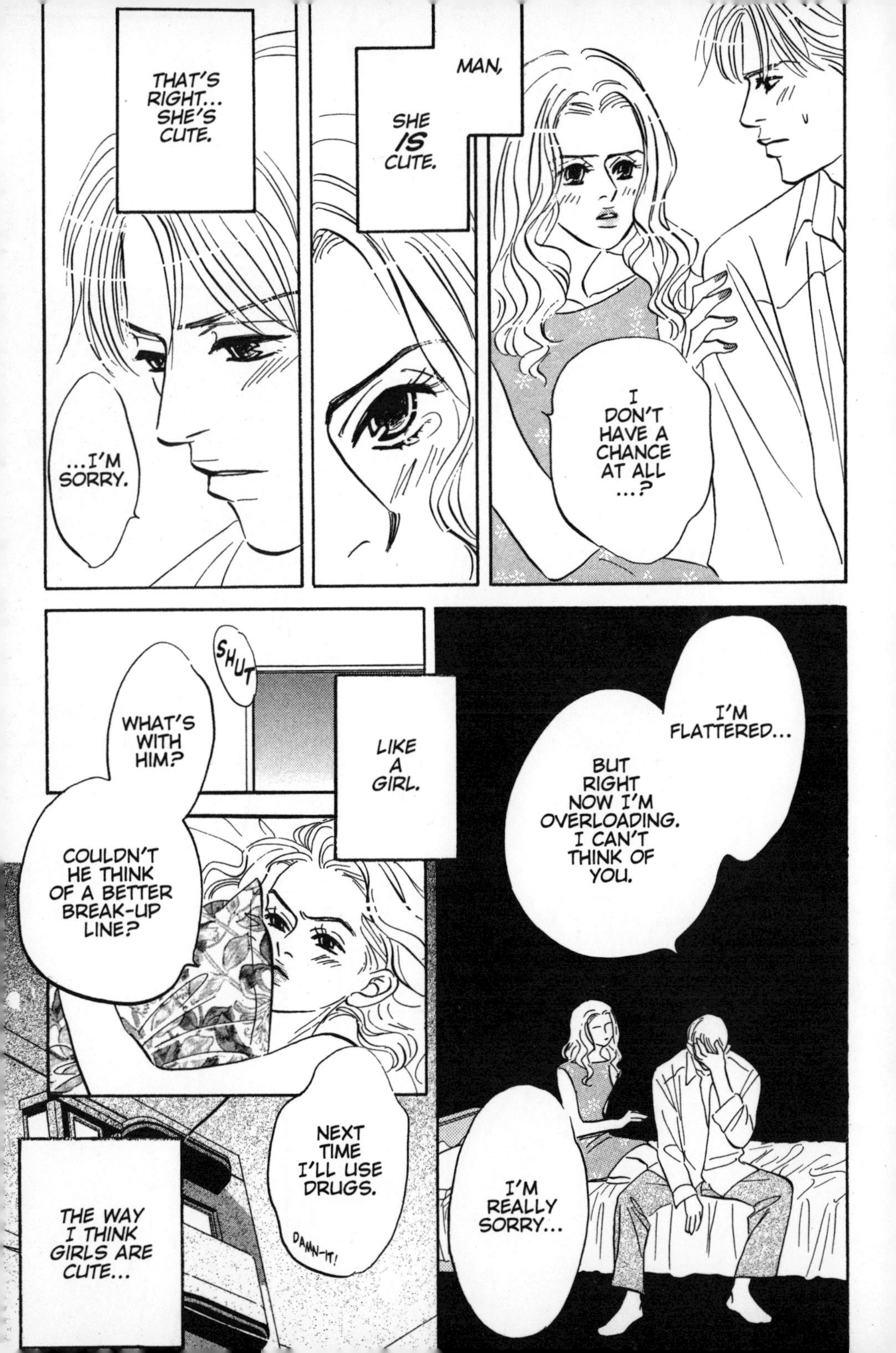
I DON'T HAVE A CHANCE AT ALL ...?
MAN,
SHE *IS* CUTE.
THAT'S RIGHT... SHE'S CUTE.
...I'M SORRY.
I'M FLATTERED...
BUT RIGHT NOW I'M OVERLOADING. I CAN'T THINK OF YOU.
I'M REALLY SORRY...
SHUT
WHAT'S WITH HIM?
LIKE A GIRL.
COULDN'T HE THINK OF A BETTER BREAK-UP LINE?
NEXT TIME I'LL USE DRUGS.
DAMN-IT!
THE WAY I THINK GIRLS ARE CUTE...

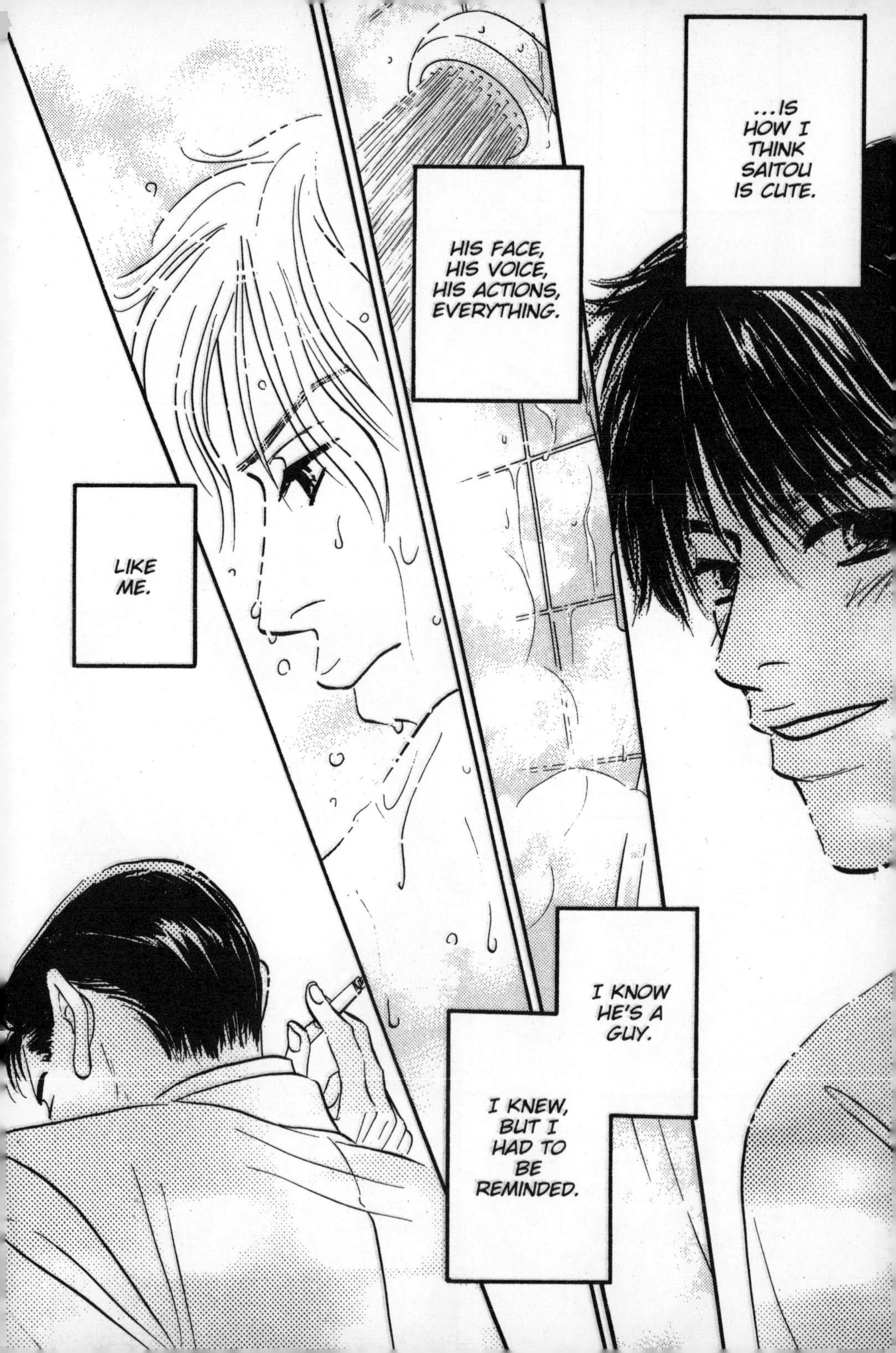
...IS HOW I THINK SAITOU IS CUTE.
HIS FACE, HIS VOICE, HIS ACTIONS, EVERYTHING.
LIKE ME.
I KNOW HE'S A GUY.
I KNEW, BUT I HAD TO BE REMINDED.

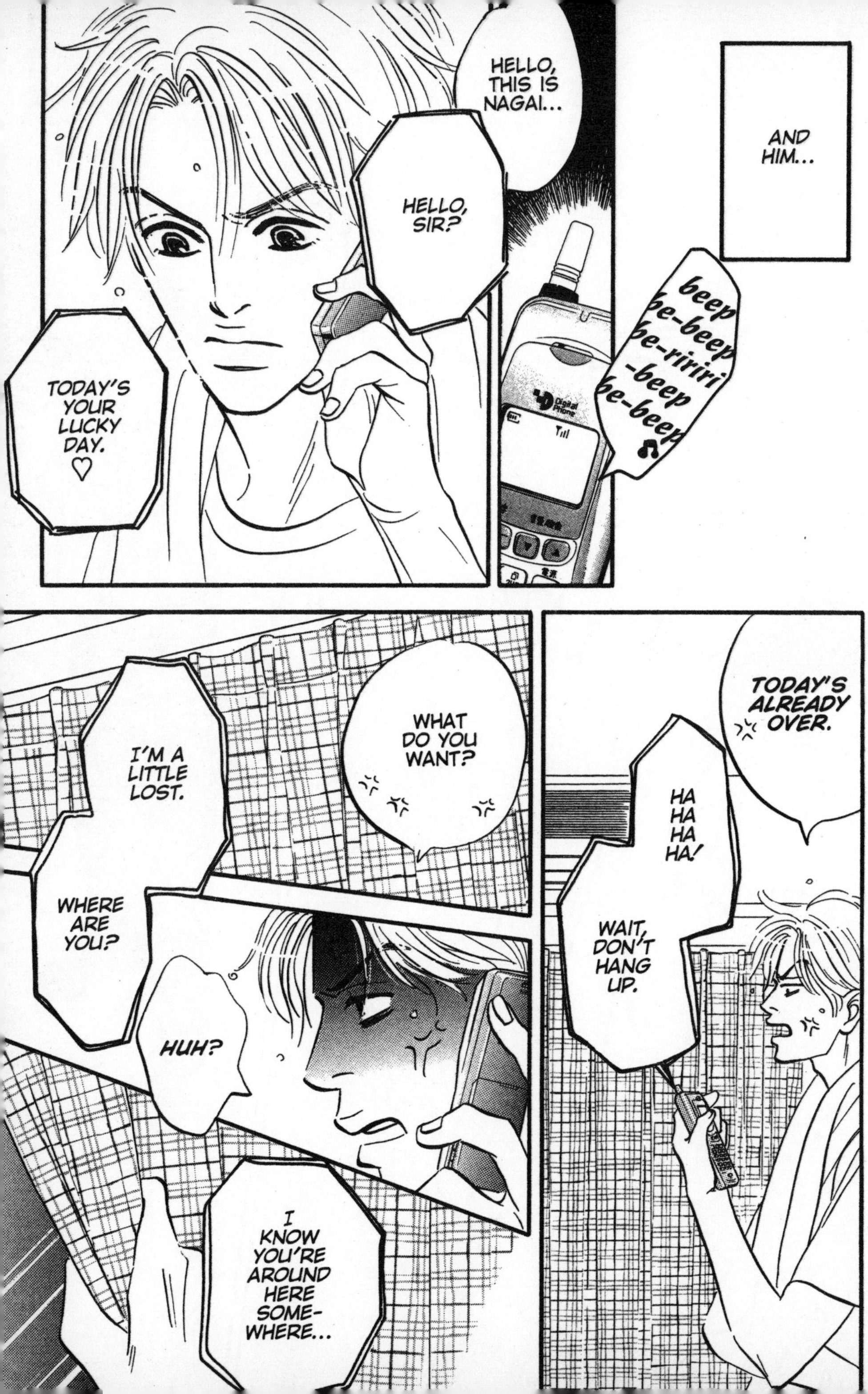
AND HIM...
beep be-beep be-ririri -beep be-beep ♫
HELLO, THIS IS NAGAI...
HELLO, SIR?
TODAY'S YOUR LUCKY DAY. ♡
TODAY'S ALREADY OVER.
HA HA HA HA!
WAIT, DON'T HANG UP.
WHAT DO YOU WANT?
I'M A LITTLE LOST.
WHERE ARE YOU?
HUH?
I KNOW YOU'RE AROUND HERE SOMEWHERE...

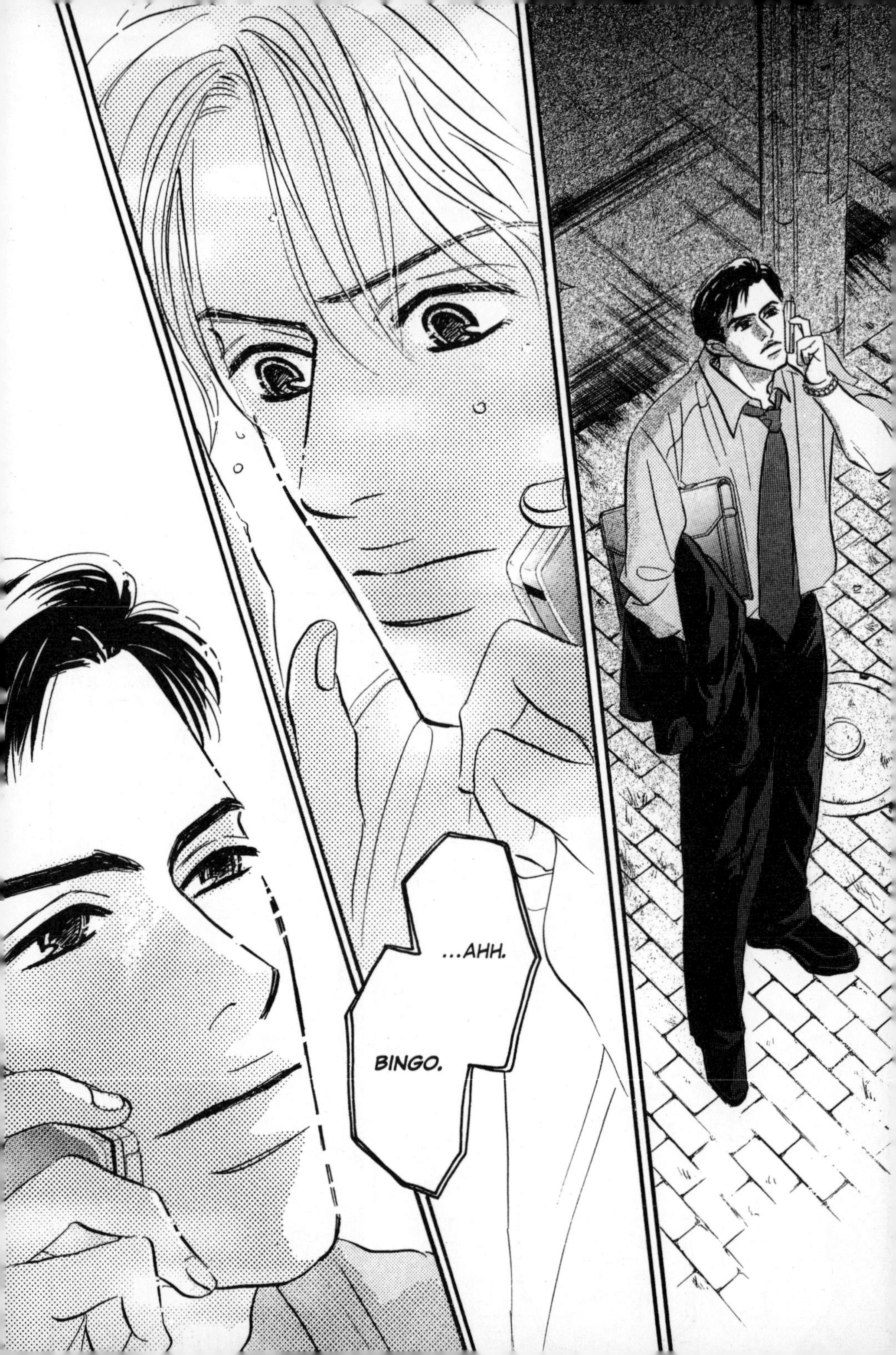
...AHH.
BINGO.

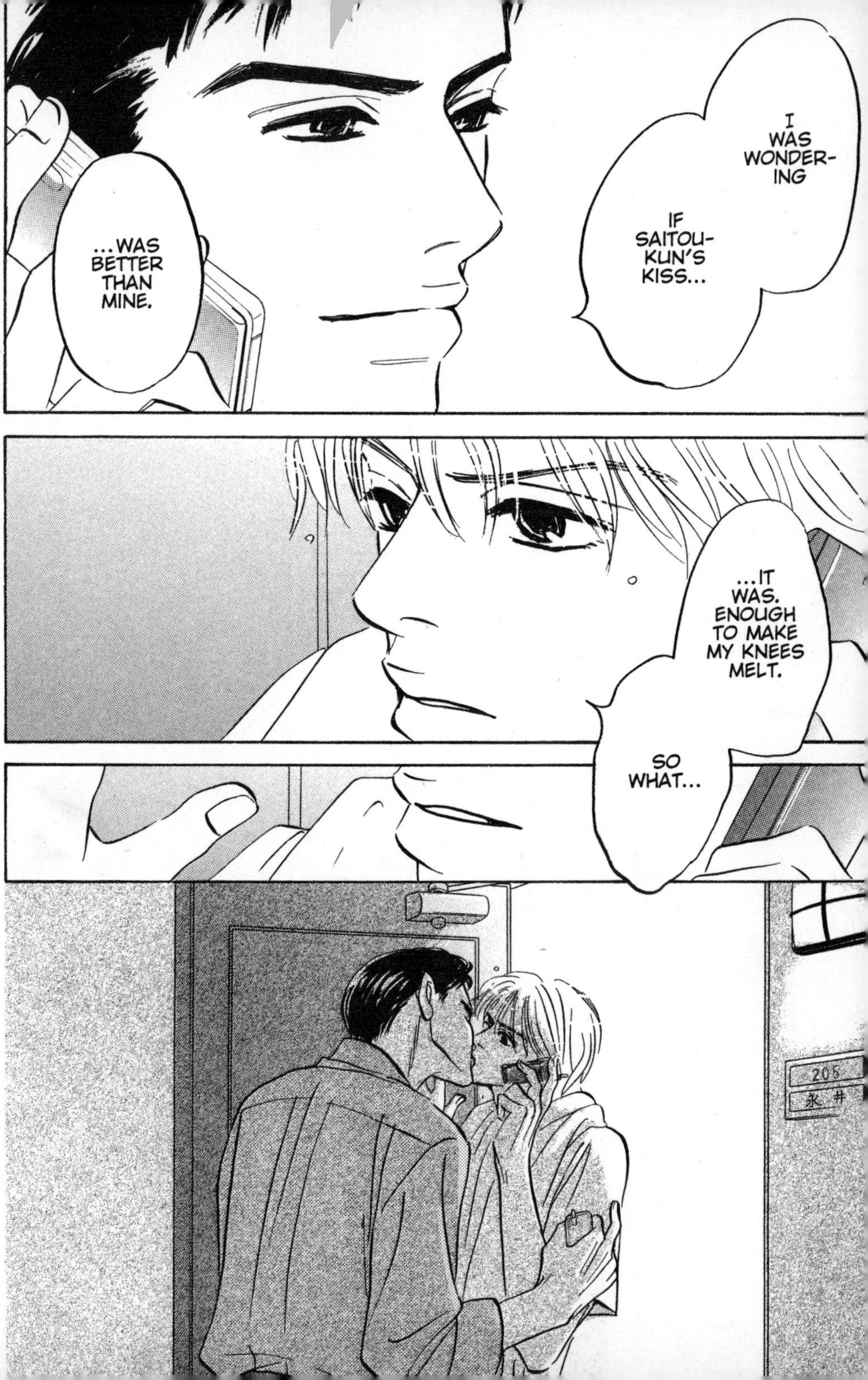
I WAS WONDERING-ING
IF SAITOU-KUN'S KISS...
...WAS BETTER THAN MINE.
...IT WAS. ENOUGH TO MAKE MY KNEES MELT.
SO WHAT...
205
永井

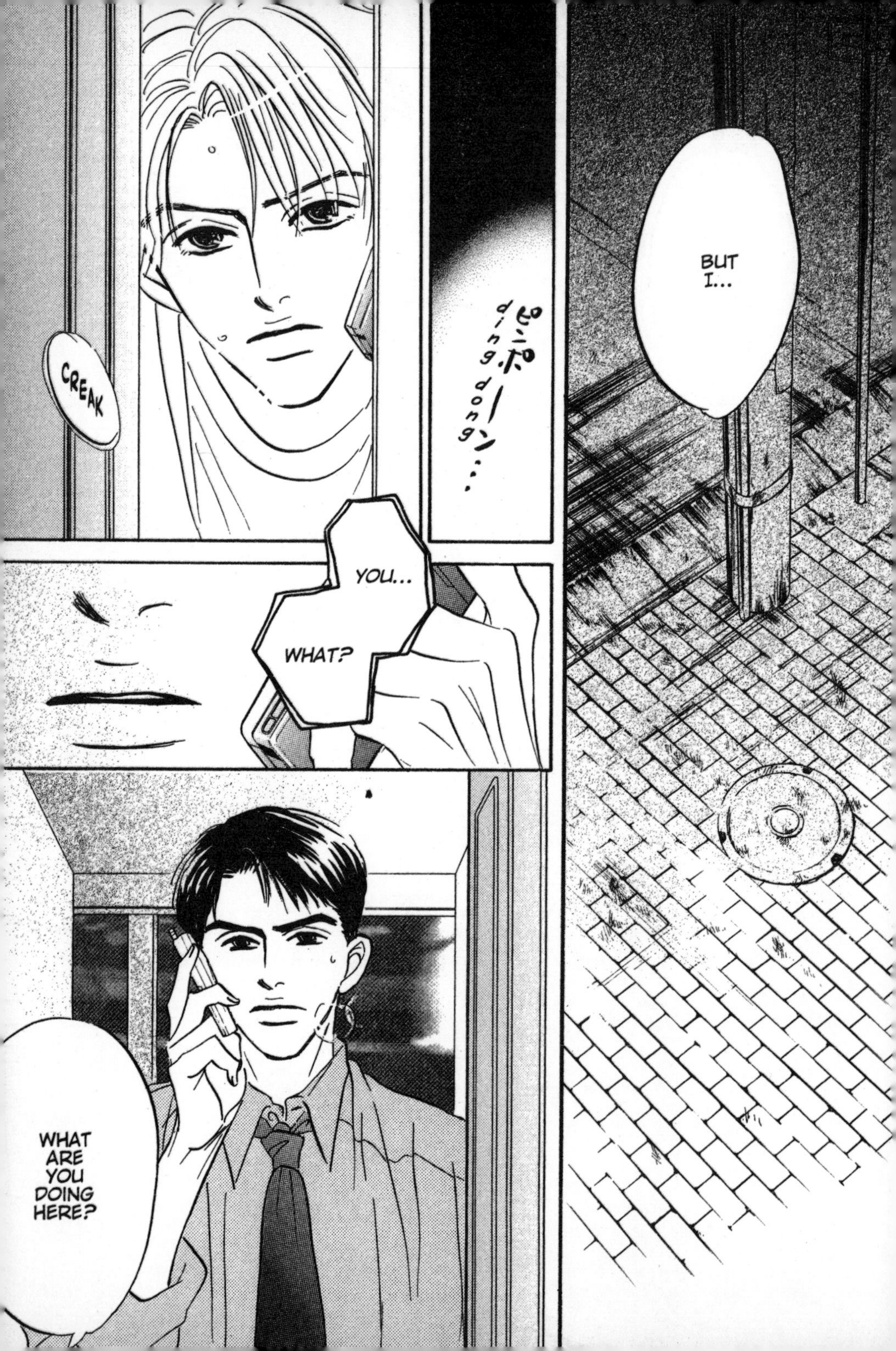
BUT I...
ピンポーン
ding dong...
CREAK
YOU...
WHAT?
WHAT ARE YOU DOING HERE?

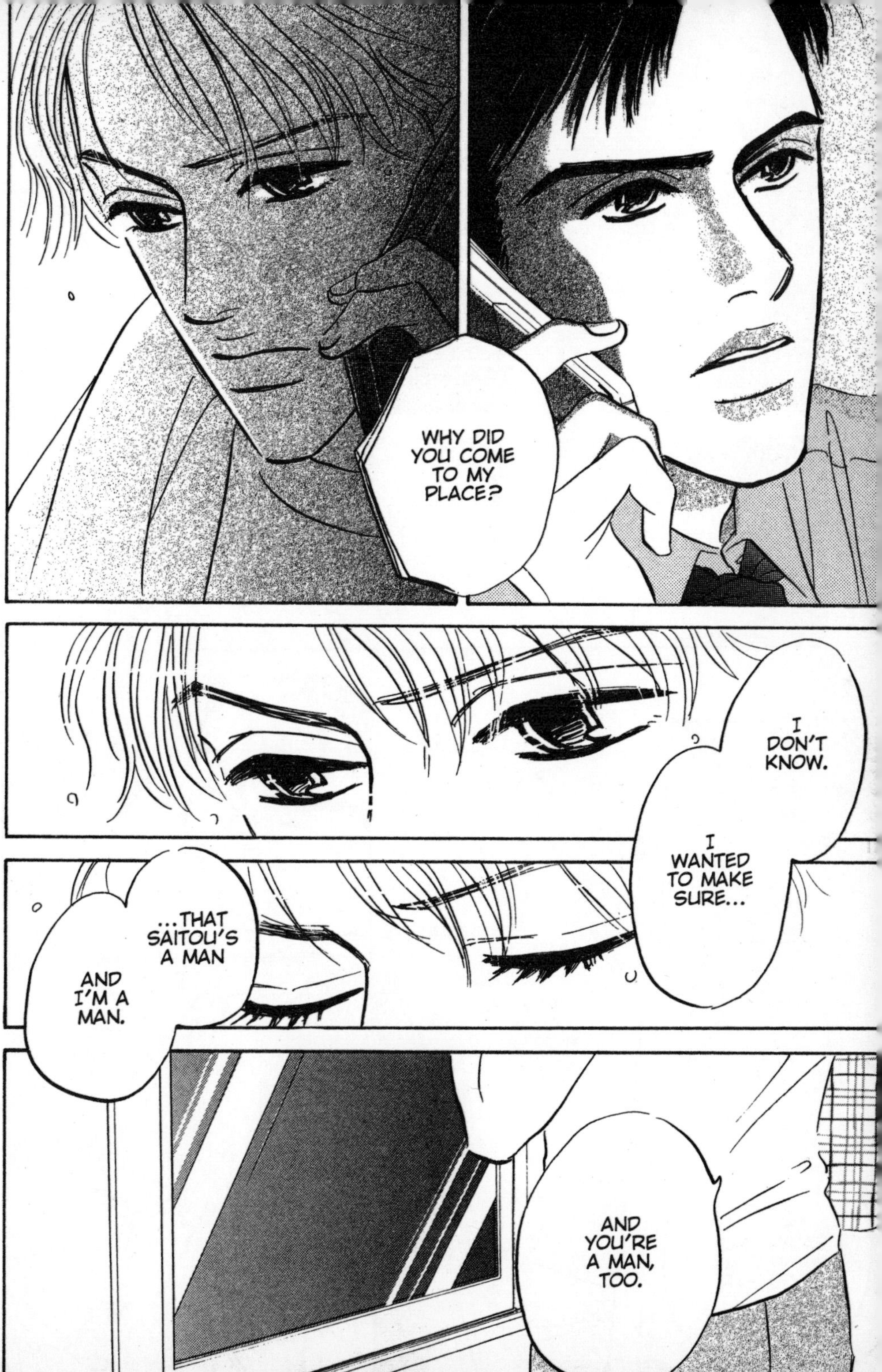
WHY DID YOU COME TO MY PLACE?
I DON'T KNOW.
I WANTED TO MAKE SURE...
...THAT SAITOU'S A MAN
AND I'M A MAN.
AND YOU'RE A MAN, TOO.

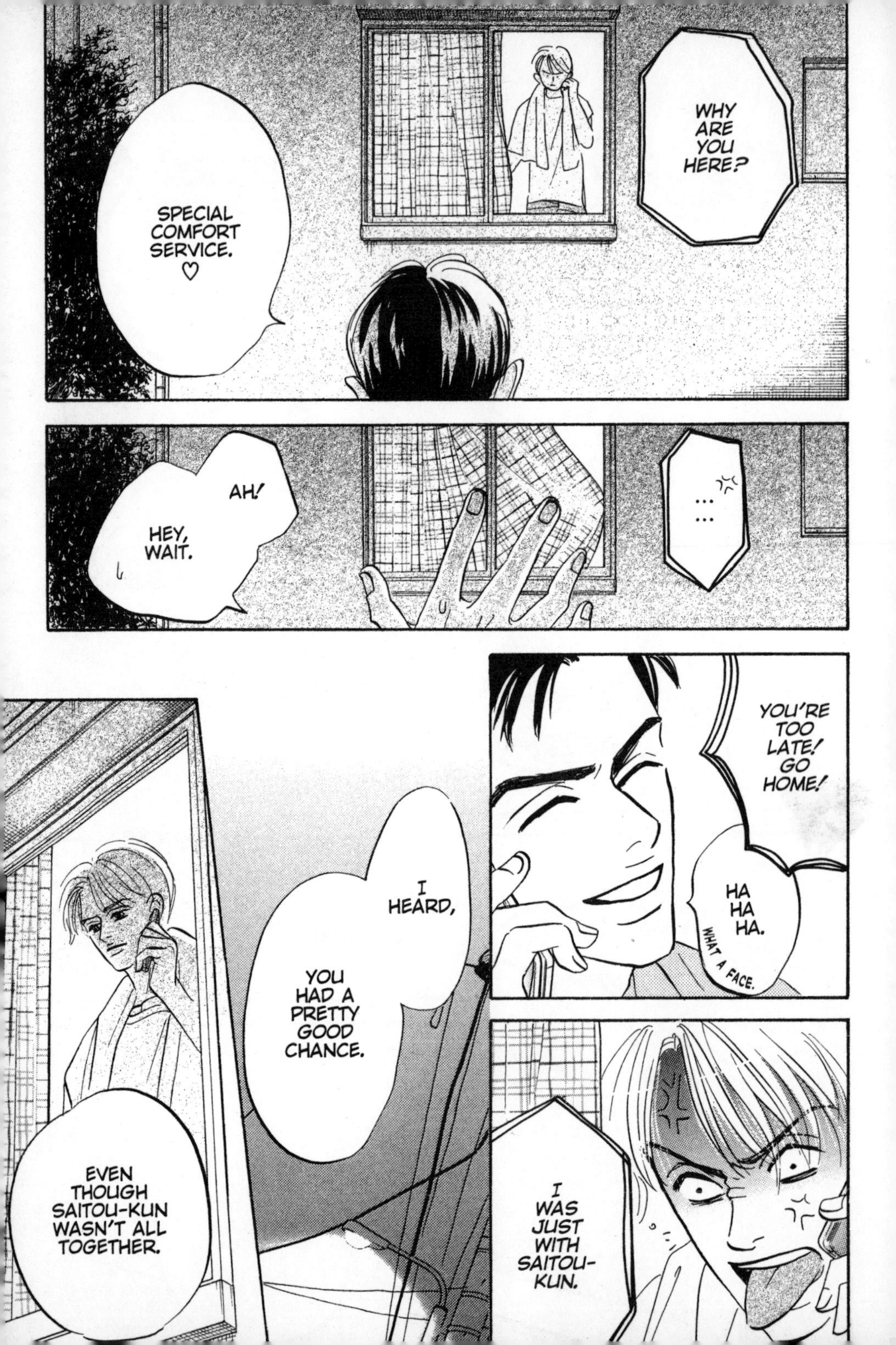
WHY ARE YOU HERE?
SPECIAL COMFORT SERVICE. ♡
... ...
AH!
HEY, WAIT.
YOU'RE TOO LATE! GO HOME!
HA HA HA.
WHAT A FACE.
I WAS JUST WITH SAITOU-KUN.
I HEARD,
YOU HAD A PRETTY GOOD CHANCE.
EVEN THOUGH SAITOU-KUN WASN'T ALL TOGETHER.

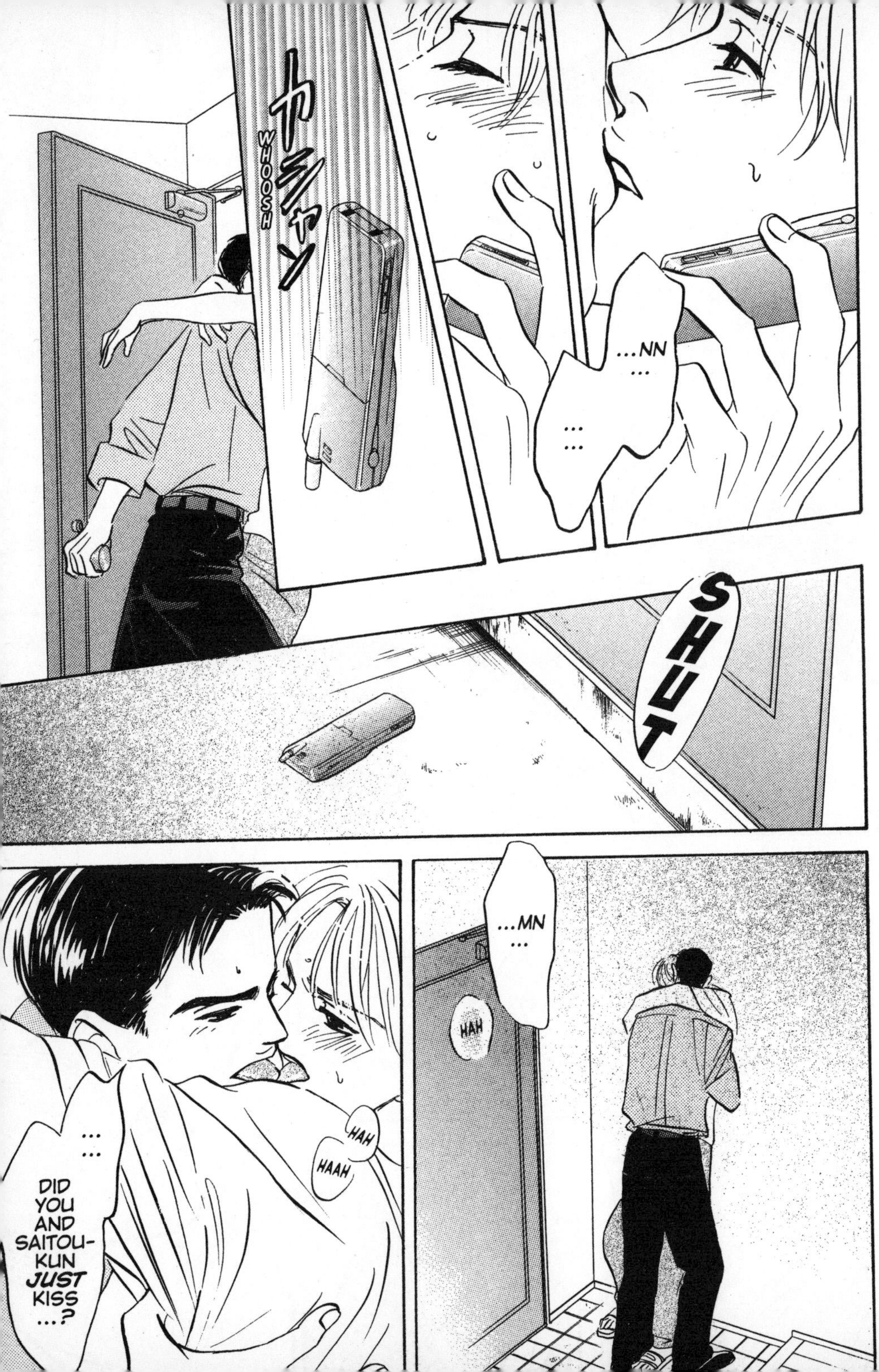
...NN ...
... ...
カシャン
WHOOSH
SHUT
...MN ...
HAH
... ...
HAH
HAAH
DID YOU AND SAITOU-KUN *JUST* KISS ...?

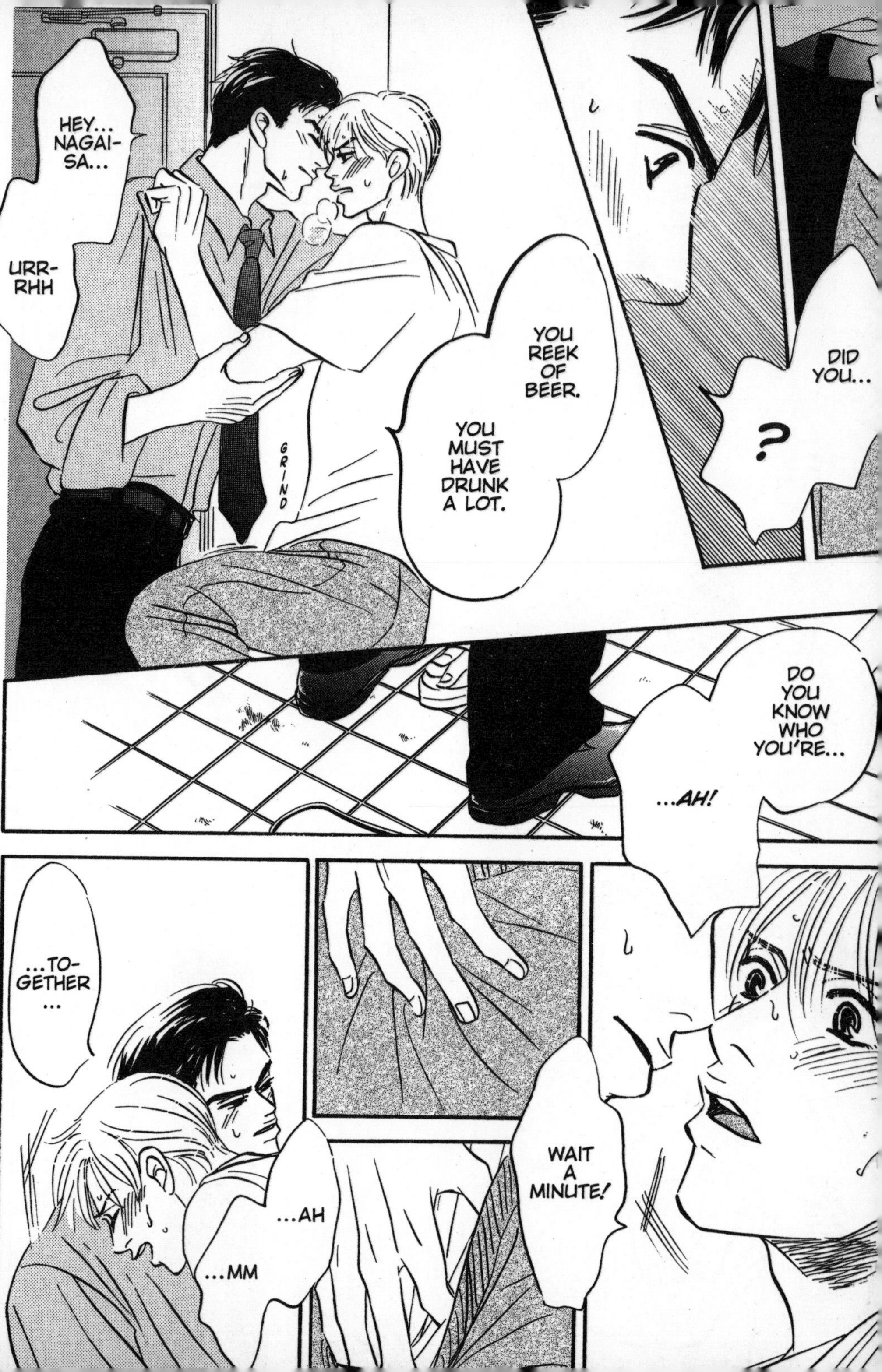
DID YOU...
?
HEY... NAGAI-SA...
URR-RHH
YOU REEK OF BEER.
YOU MUST HAVE DRUNK A LOT.
GRIND
DO YOU KNOW WHO YOU'RE...
...AH!
WAIT A MINUTE!
...TO-GETHER...
...AH
...MM

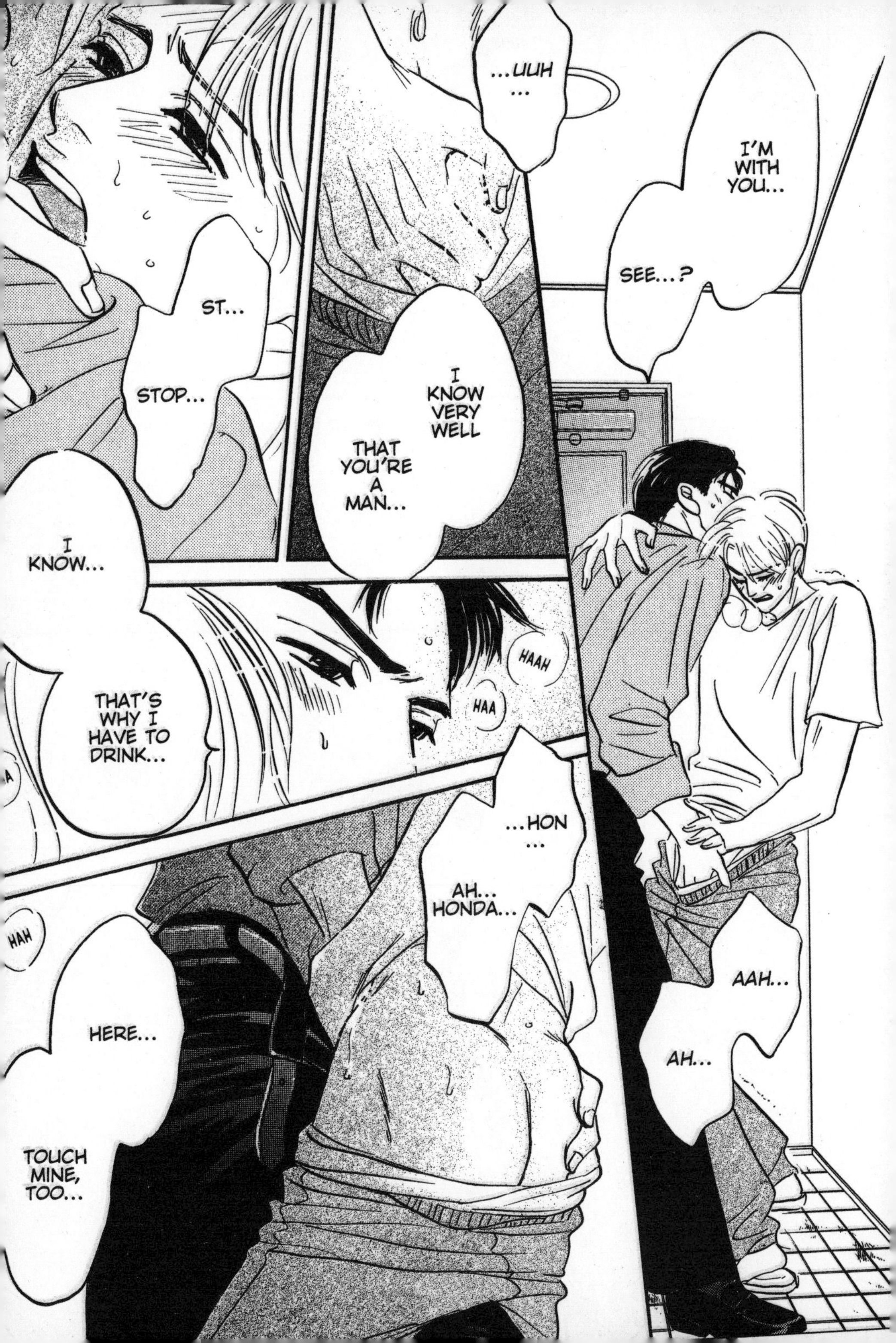
I'M WITH YOU...
SEE...?
AAH...
AH...
...UUH...
I KNOW VERY WELL
THAT YOU'RE A MAN...
ST...
STOP...
HAAH
HAA
I KNOW...
THAT'S WHY I HAVE TO DRINK...
...HON...
AH... HONDA...
HAH
HERE...
TOUCH MINE, TOO...

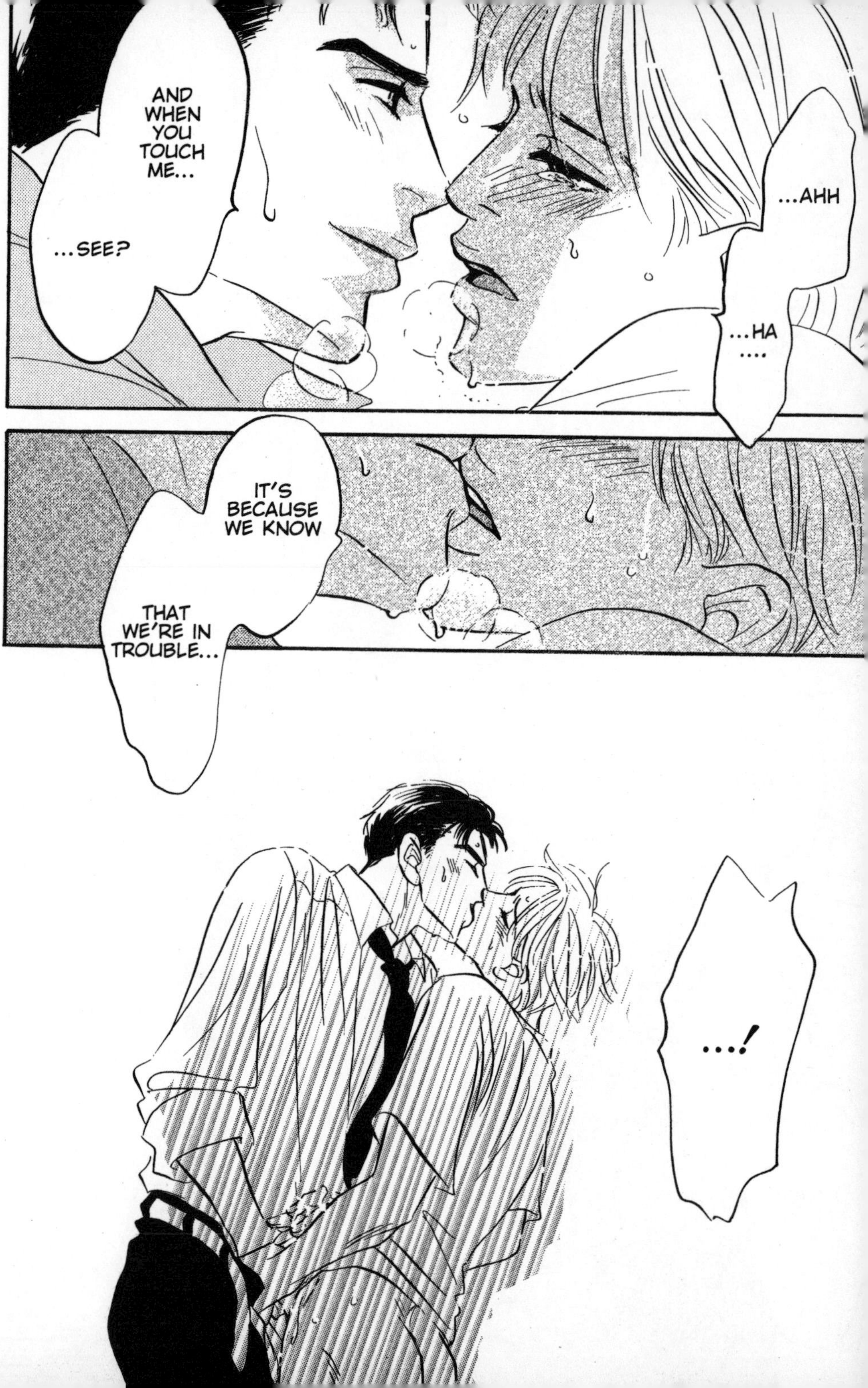
...AHH
...HA ....
AND WHEN YOU TOUCH ME...
...SEE?
IT'S BECAUSE WE KNOW
THAT WE'RE IN TROUBLE...
...!

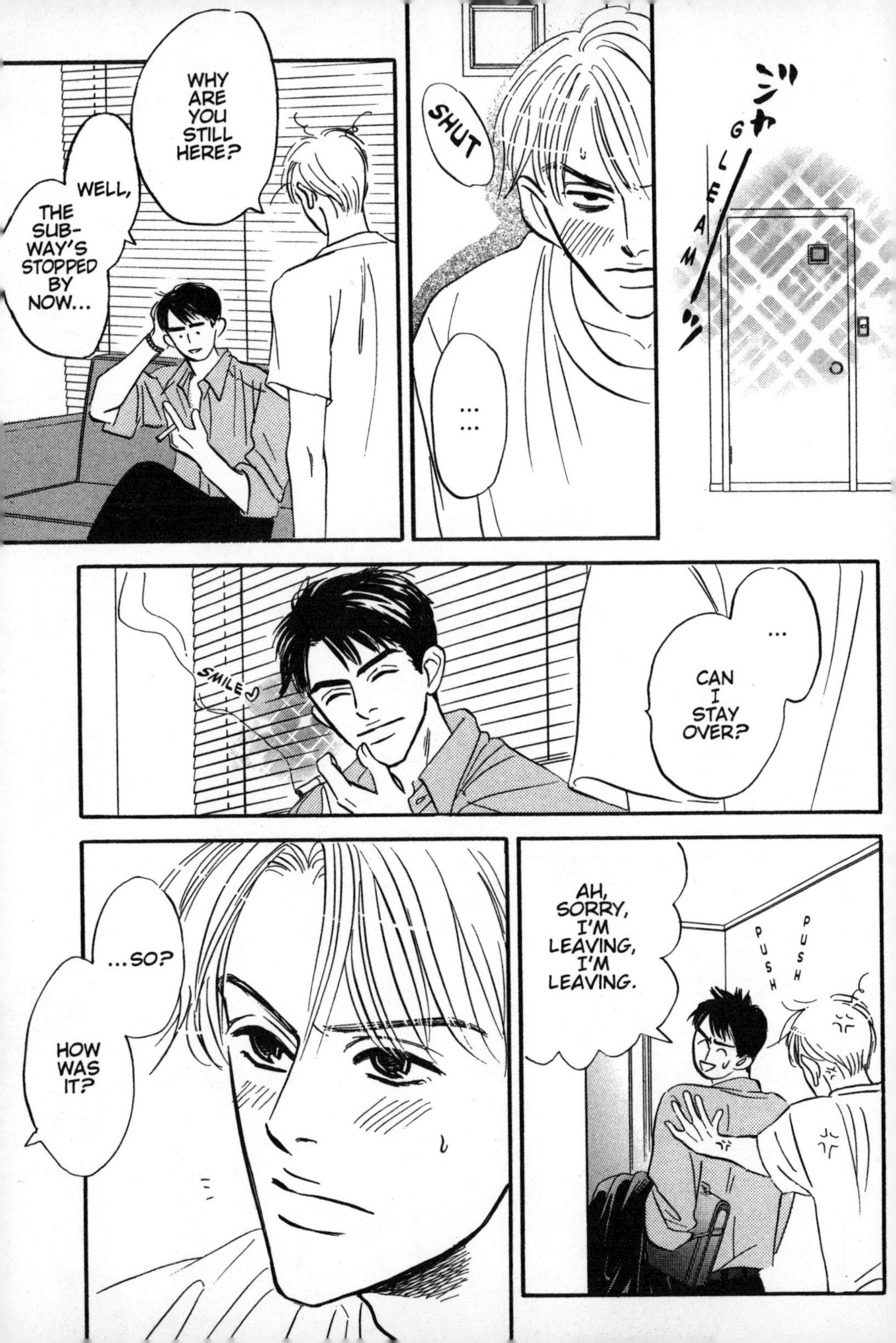
ジャ
GLEAM
ッ
SHUT
......
WHY ARE YOU STILL HERE?
WELL, THE SUB-WAY'S STOPPED BY NOW...
... CAN I STAY OVER?
SMILE♡
AH, SORRY, I'M LEAVING, I'M LEAVING.
PUSH PUSH
...SO? HOW WAS IT?

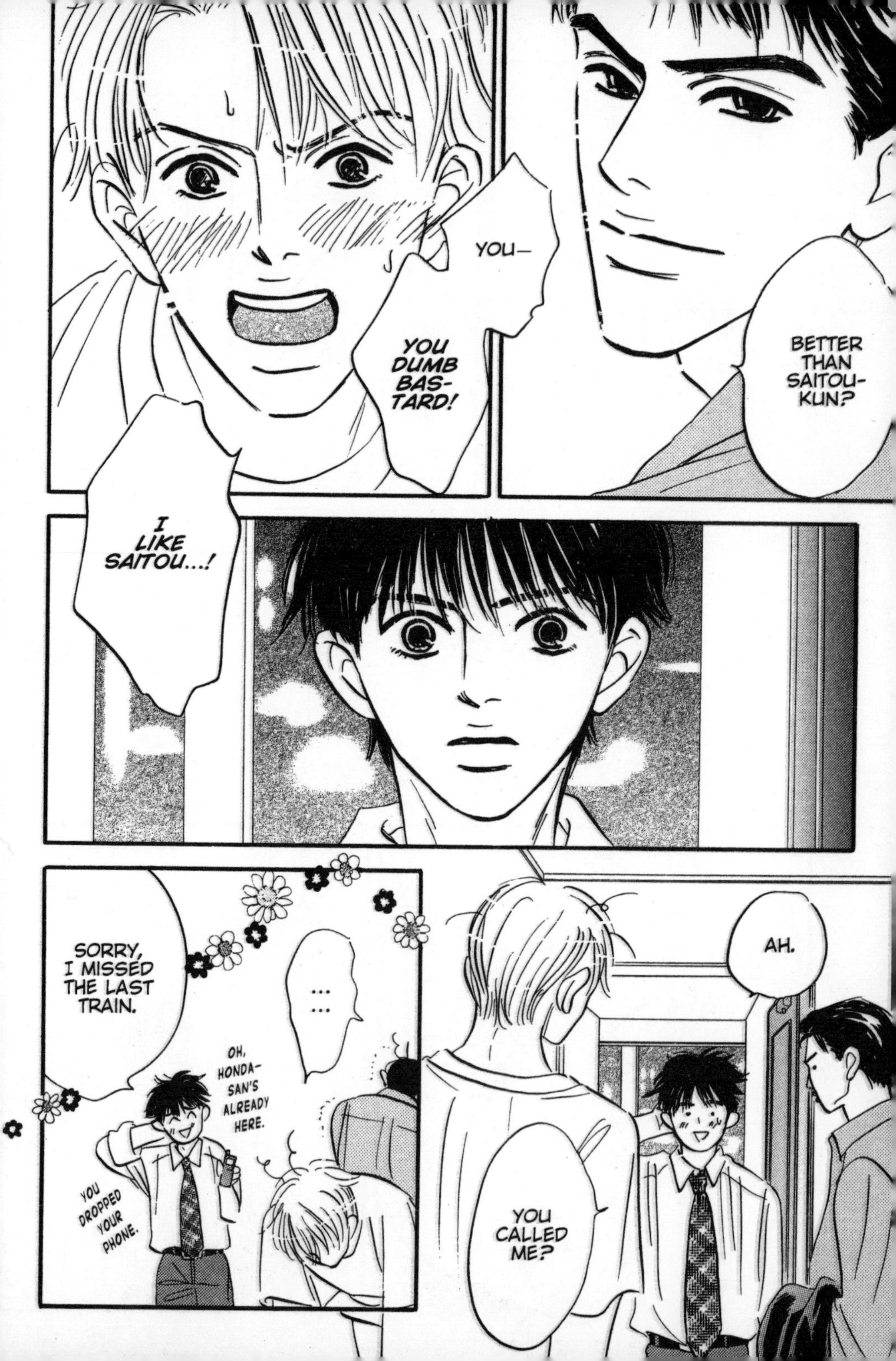

BETTER THAN SAITOU-KUN?
YOU—
YOU DUMB BAS-TARD!
I LIKE SAITOU...!
AH.
YOU CALLED ME?
SORRY, I MISSED THE LAST TRAIN.
......
OH, HONDA-SAN'S ALREADY HERE.
YOU DROPPED YOUR PHONE.

ACT.4

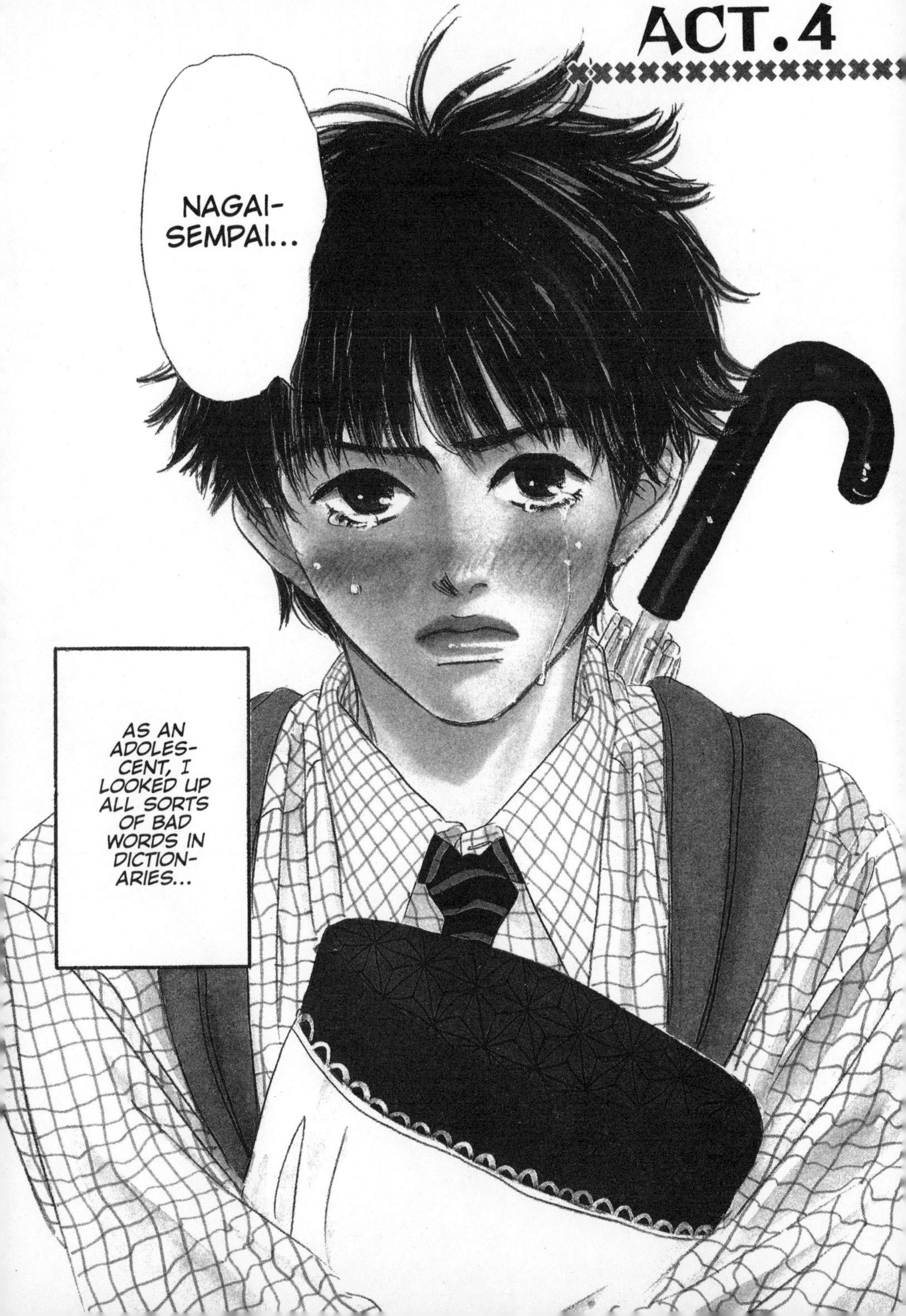
NAGAI-SEMPAI...
AS AN ADOLESCENT, I LOOKED UP ALL SORTS OF BAD WORDS IN DICTIONARIES...

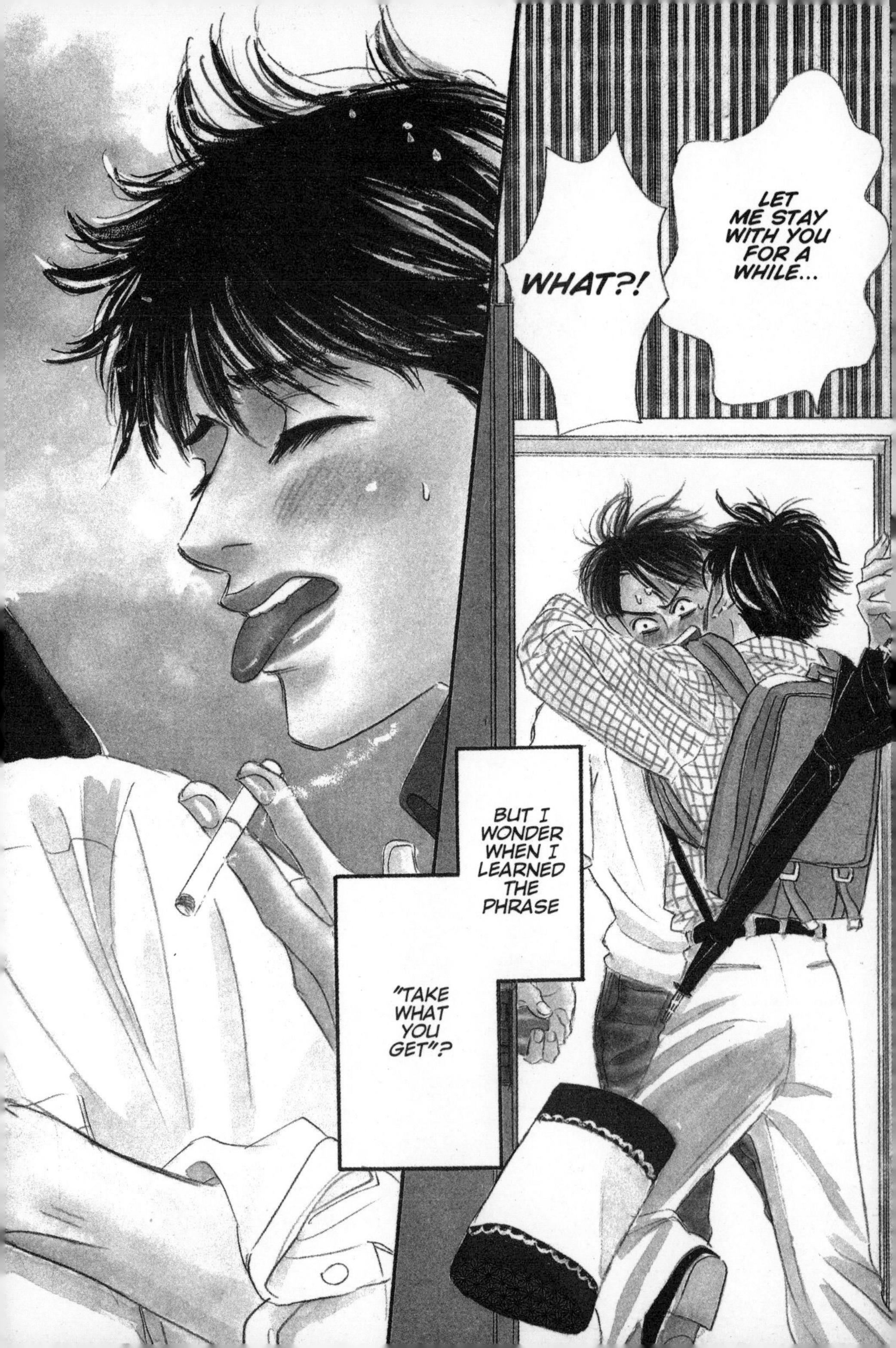
LET ME STAY WITH YOU FOR A WHILE...
WHAT?!
BUT I WONDER WHEN I LEARNED THE PHRASE
"TAKE WHAT YOU GET"?

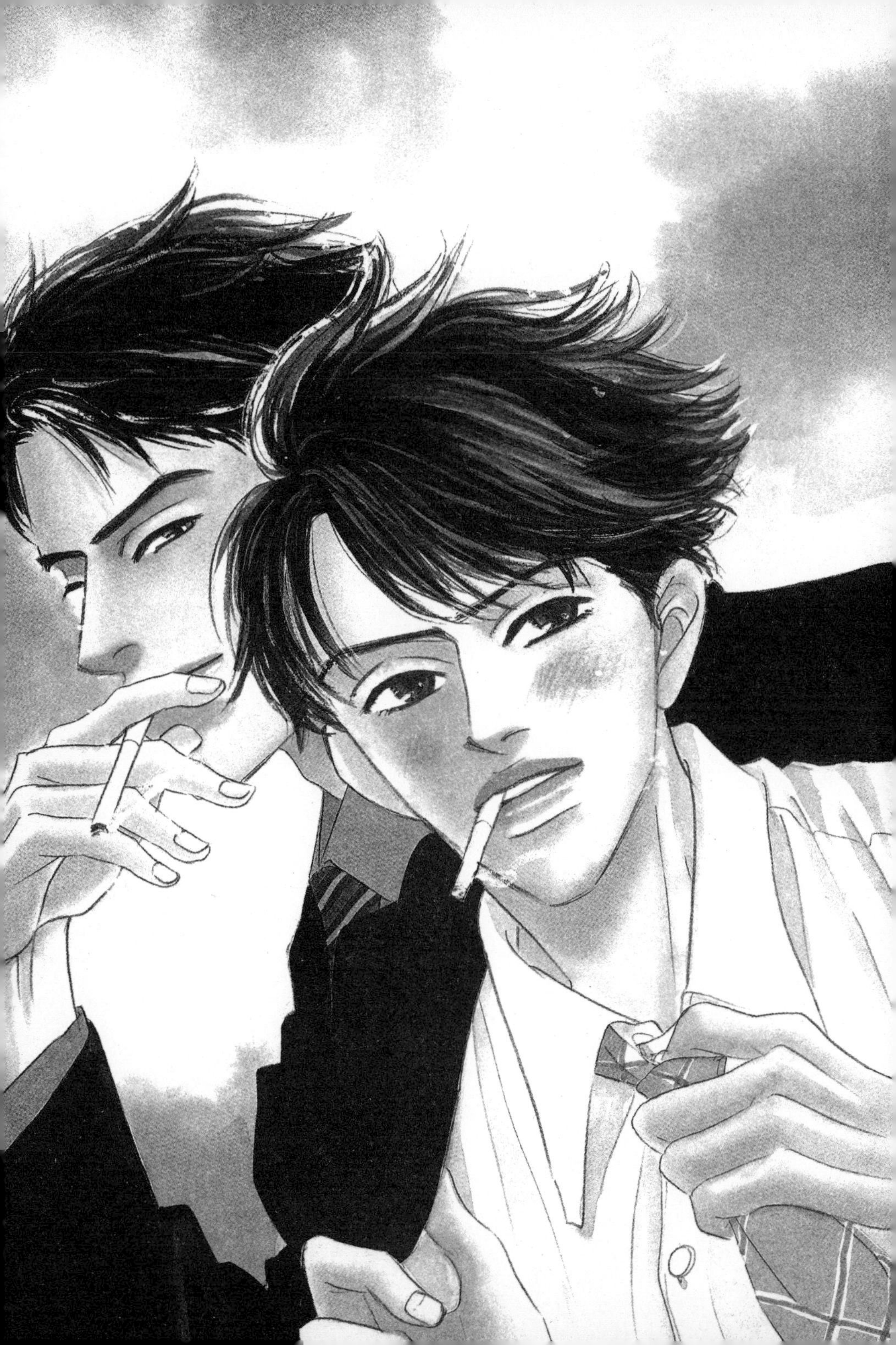

YUGI YAMADA PRESENTS COMICS / CLOSE THE LAST DOOR
ATSUSHI NAGAI/KENZOU HONDA/TOSHIHISA SAITOH

CLOSE
THE
LAST
DOOR

LOVE

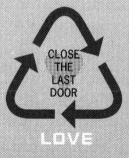

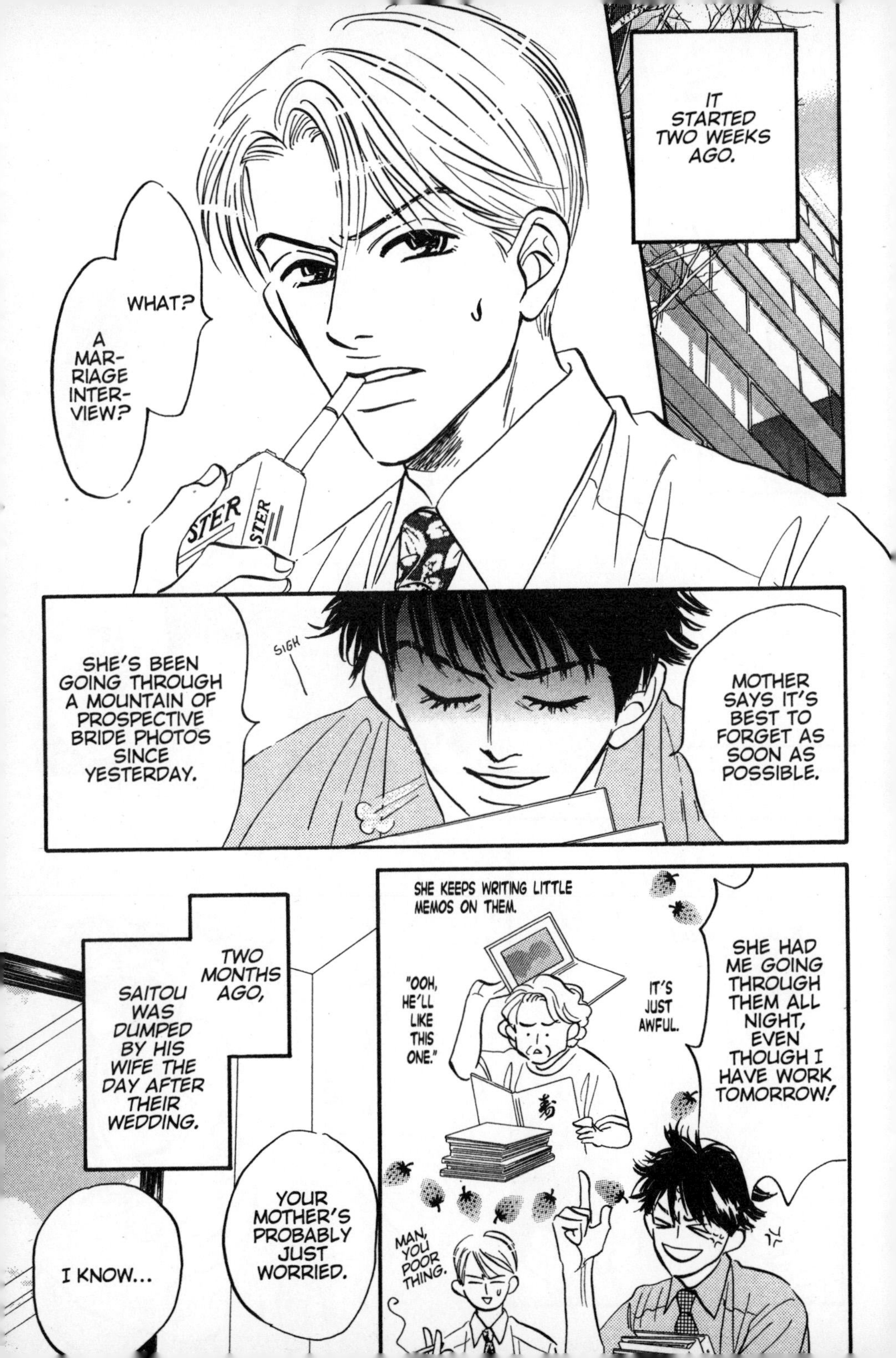
IT STARTED TWO WEEKS AGO.
WHAT? A MARRIAGE INTERVIEW?
STER
MOTHER SAYS IT'S BEST TO FORGET AS SOON AS POSSIBLE.
SIGH
SHE'S BEEN GOING THROUGH A MOUNTAIN OF PROSPECTIVE BRIDE PHOTOS SINCE YESTERDAY.
SHE HAD ME GOING THROUGH THEM ALL NIGHT, EVEN THOUGH I HAVE WORK TOMORROW!
SHE KEEPS WRITING LITTLE MEMOS ON THEM.
IT'S JUST AWFUL.
"OOH, HE'LL LIKE THIS ONE."
MAN, YOU POOR THING.
TWO MONTHS AGO, SAITOU WAS DUMPED BY HIS WIFE THE DAY AFTER THEIR WEDDING.
YOUR MOTHER'S PROBABLY JUST WORRIED.
I KNOW...

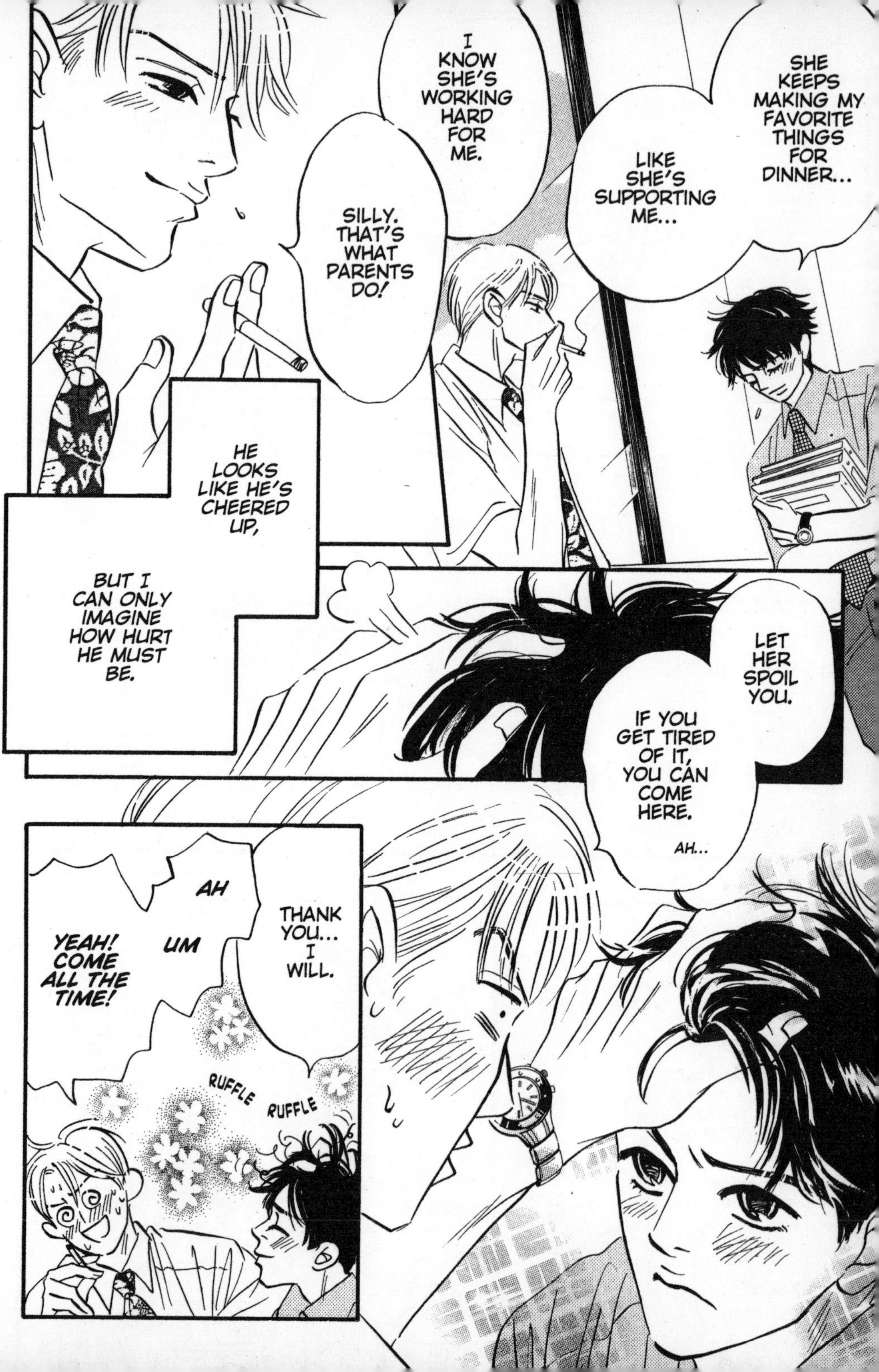

SHE KEEPS MAKING MY FAVORITE THINGS FOR DINNER...
LIKE SHE'S SUPPORTING ME...
I KNOW SHE'S WORKING HARD FOR ME.
SILLY. THAT'S WHAT PARENTS DO!
HE LOOKS LIKE HE'S CHEERED UP,
BUT I CAN ONLY IMAGINE HOW HURT HE MUST BE.
LET HER SPOIL YOU.
IF YOU GET TIRED OF IT, YOU CAN COME HERE.
AH...
THANK YOU... I WILL.
AH
UM
YEAH! COME ALL THE TIME!
RUFFLE RUFFLE

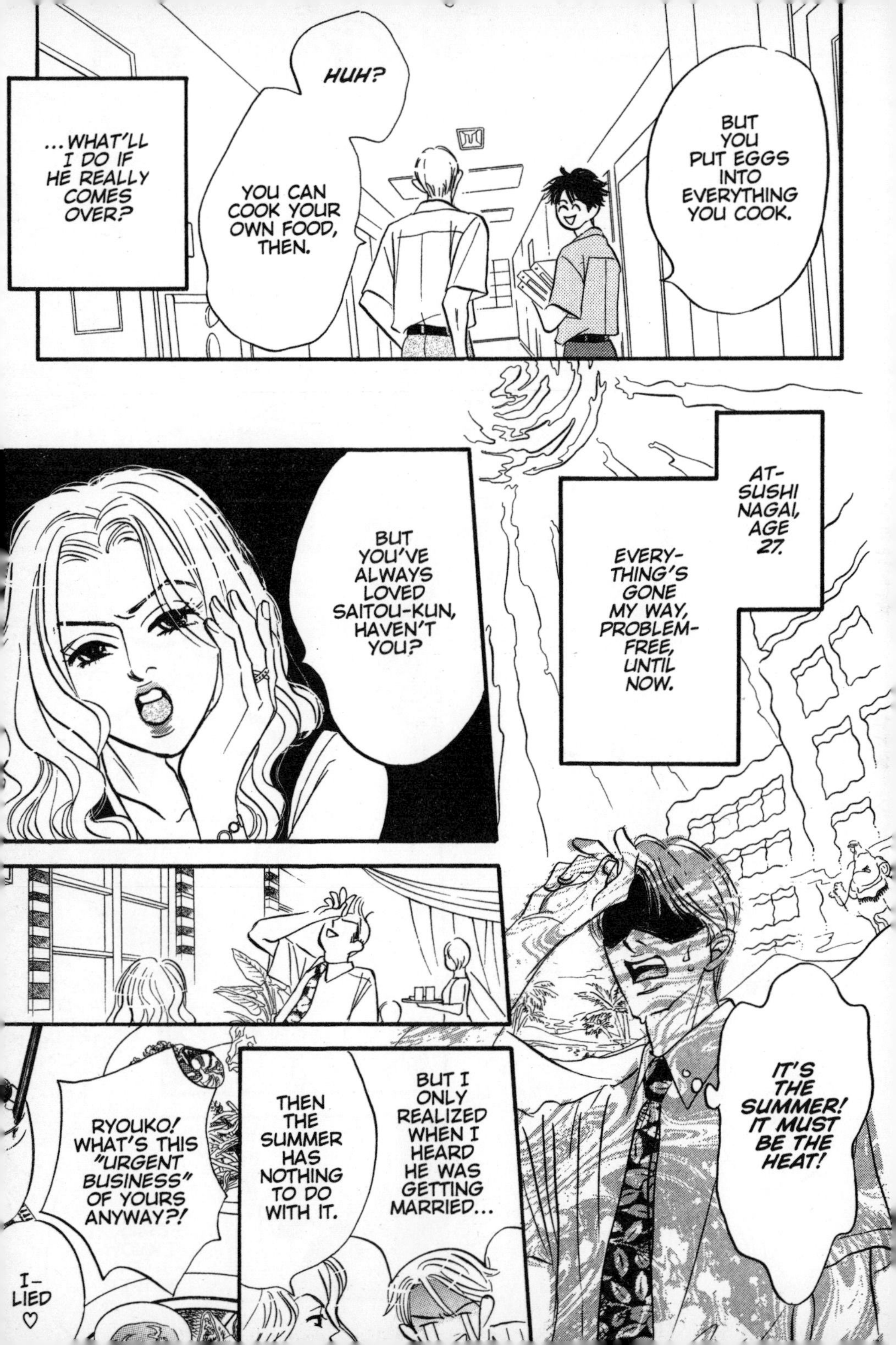
BUT YOU PUT EGGS INTO EVERYTHING YOU COOK.
HUH?
YOU CAN COOK YOUR OWN FOOD, THEN.
...WHAT'LL I DO IF HE REALLY COMES OVER?
ATSUSHI NAGAI, AGE 27.
EVERYTHING'S GONE MY WAY, PROBLEM-FREE, UNTIL NOW.
BUT YOU'VE ALWAYS LOVED SAITOU-KUN, HAVEN'T YOU?
IT'S THE SUMMER! IT MUST BE THE HEAT!
BUT I ONLY REALIZED WHEN I HEARD HE WAS GETTING MARRIED...
THEN THE SUMMER HAS NOTHING TO DO WITH IT.
RYOUKO! WHAT'S THIS "URGENT BUSINESS" OF YOURS ANYWAY?!
I-LIED ♡

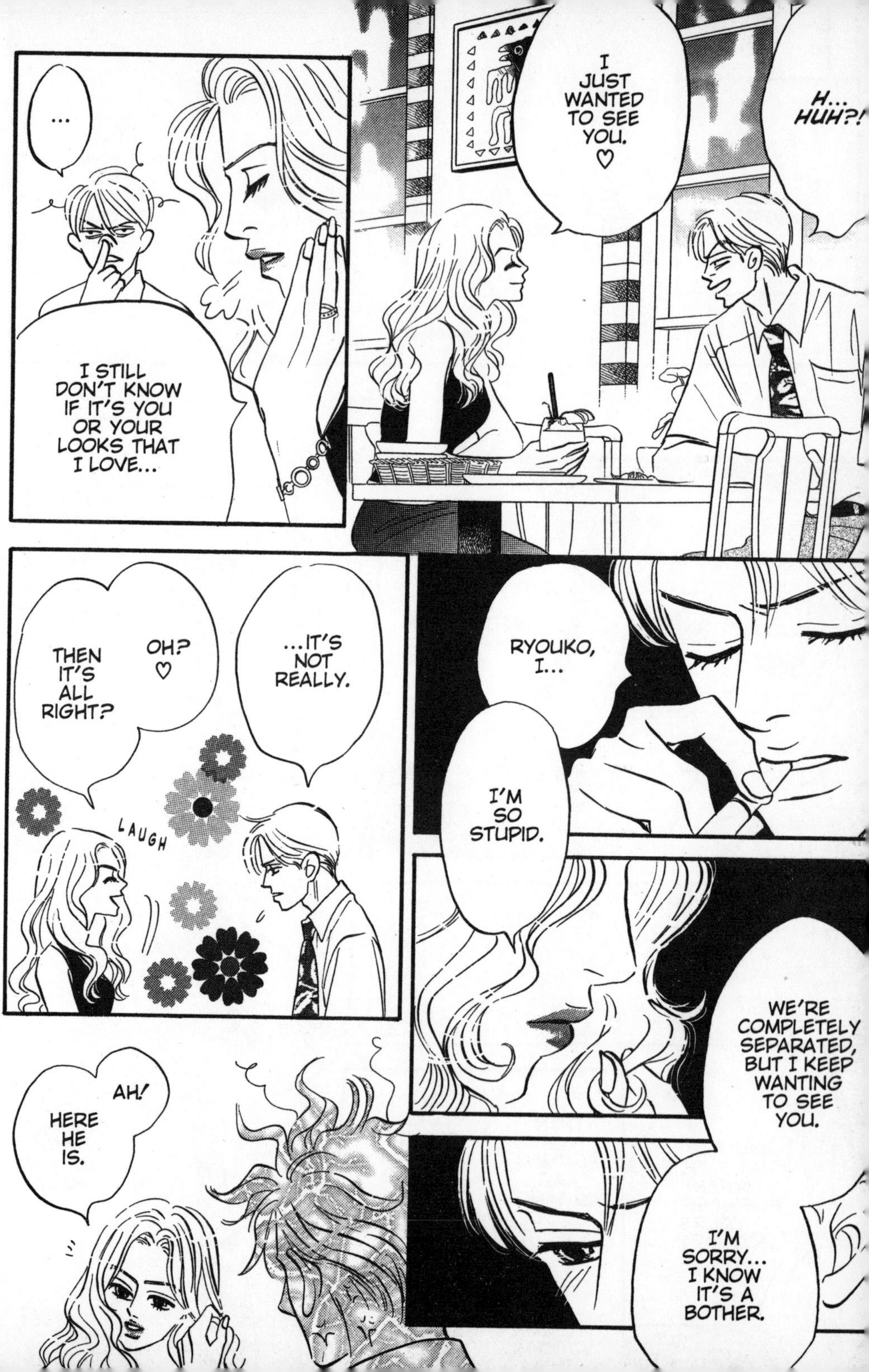
H... HUH?!
I JUST WANTED TO SEE YOU. ♡
...
I STILL DON'T KNOW IF IT'S YOU OR YOUR LOOKS THAT I LOVE...
RYOUKO, I...
I'M SO STUPID.
WE'RE COMPLETELY SEPARATED, BUT I KEEP WANTING TO SEE YOU.
I'M SORRY... I KNOW IT'S A BOTHER.
...IT'S NOT REALLY.
OH? ♡
THEN IT'S ALL RIGHT?
LAUGH
AH!
HERE HE IS.

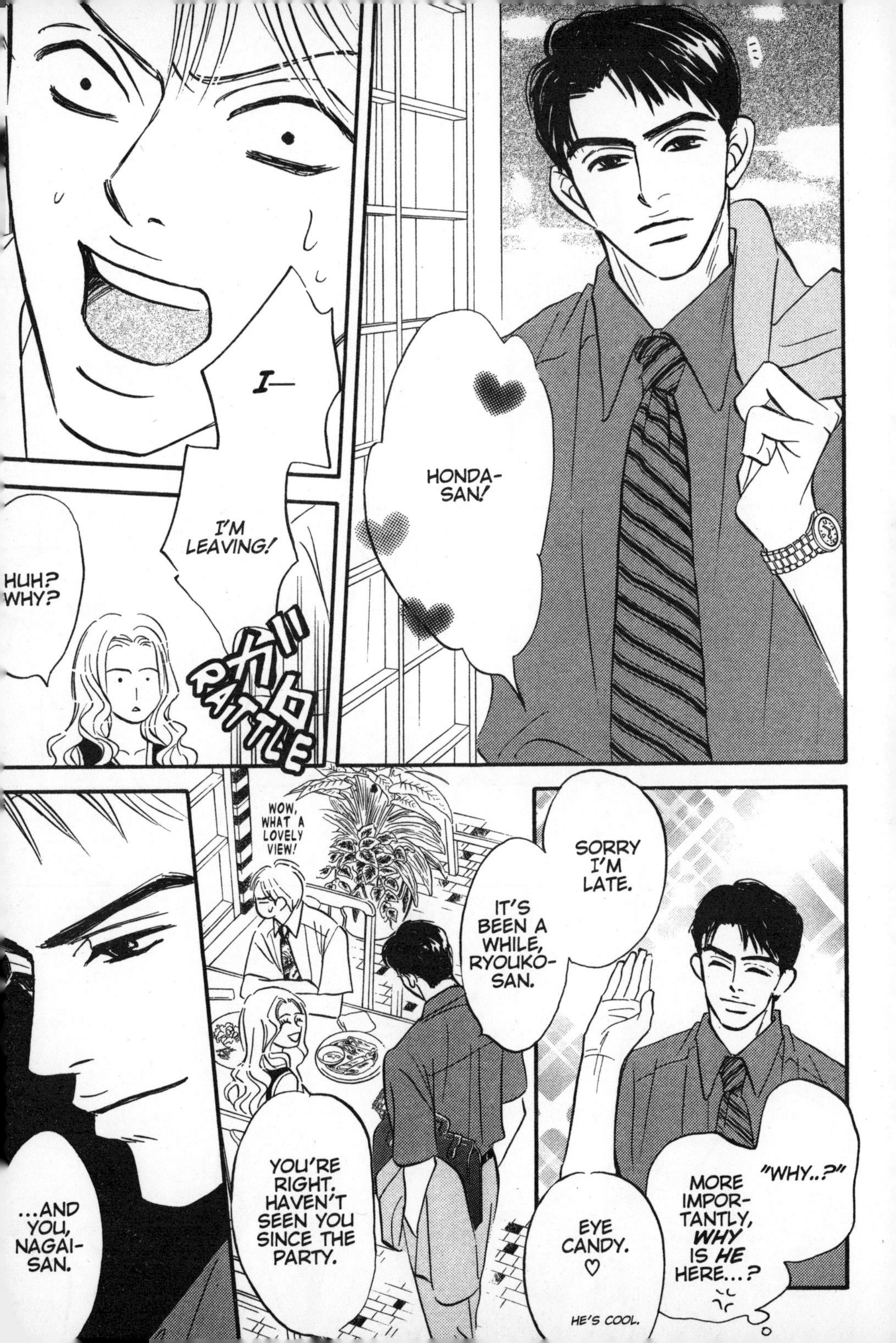
HONDA-SAN!
I—
I'M LEAVING!
HUH? WHY?
ガタ RATTLE
SORRY I'M LATE.
IT'S BEEN A WHILE, RYOUKO-SAN.
"WHY..?"
MORE IMPORTANTLY, ***WHY*** IS ***HE*** HERE...?
EYE CANDY. ♡
HE'S COOL.
WOW, WHAT A LOVELY VIEW!
YOU'RE RIGHT. HAVEN'T SEEN YOU SINCE THE PARTY.
...AND YOU, NAGAI-SAN.

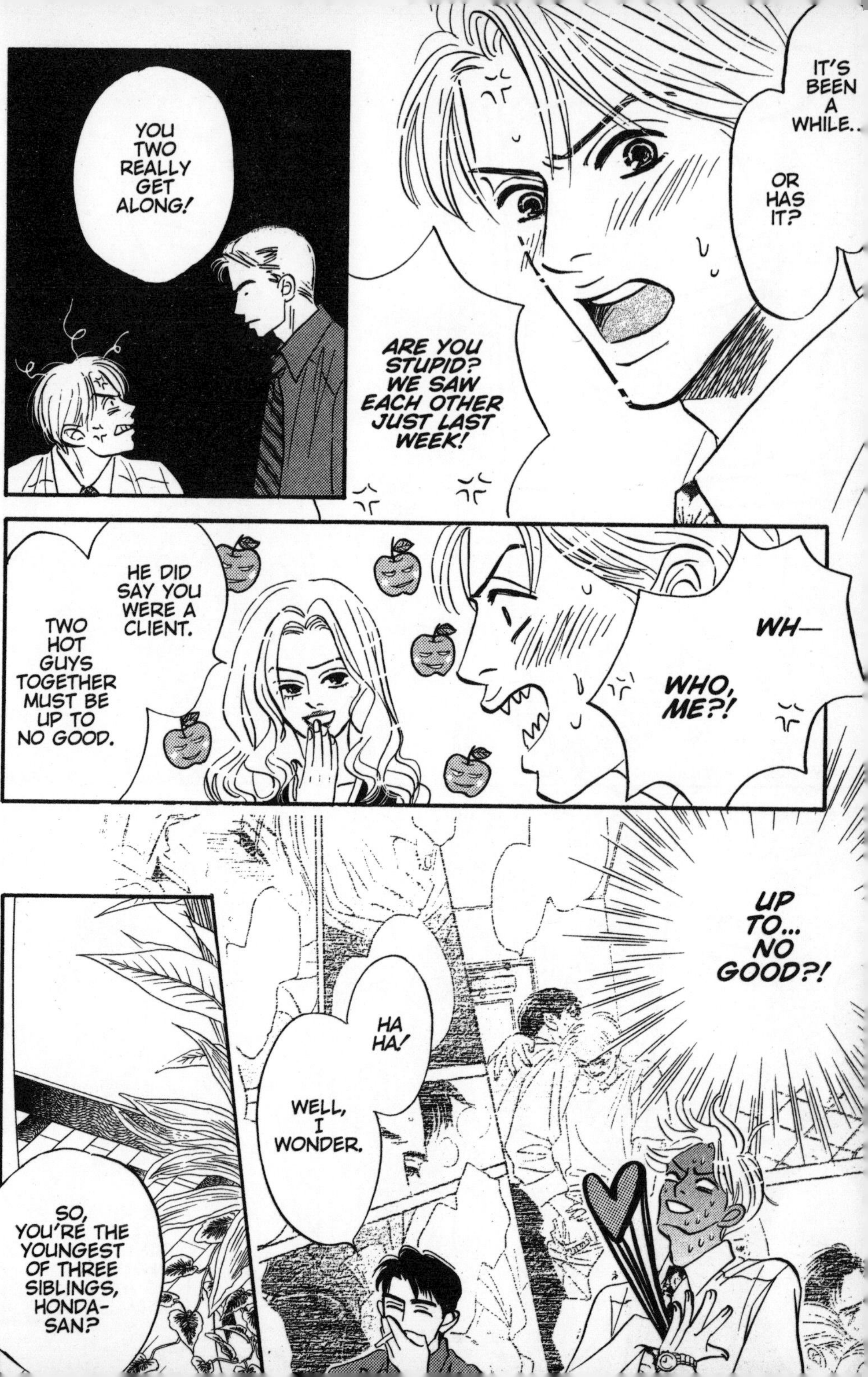
IT'S BEEN A WHILE..
OR HAS IT?
ARE YOU STUPID? WE SAW EACH OTHER JUST LAST WEEK!
YOU TWO REALLY GET ALONG!
WH—
WHO, ME?!
HE DID SAY YOU WERE A CLIENT.
TWO HOT GUYS TOGETHER MUST BE UP TO NO GOOD.
UP TO... NO GOOD?!
HA HA!
WELL, I WONDER.
SO, YOU'RE THE YOUNGEST OF THREE SIBLINGS, HONDA-SAN?

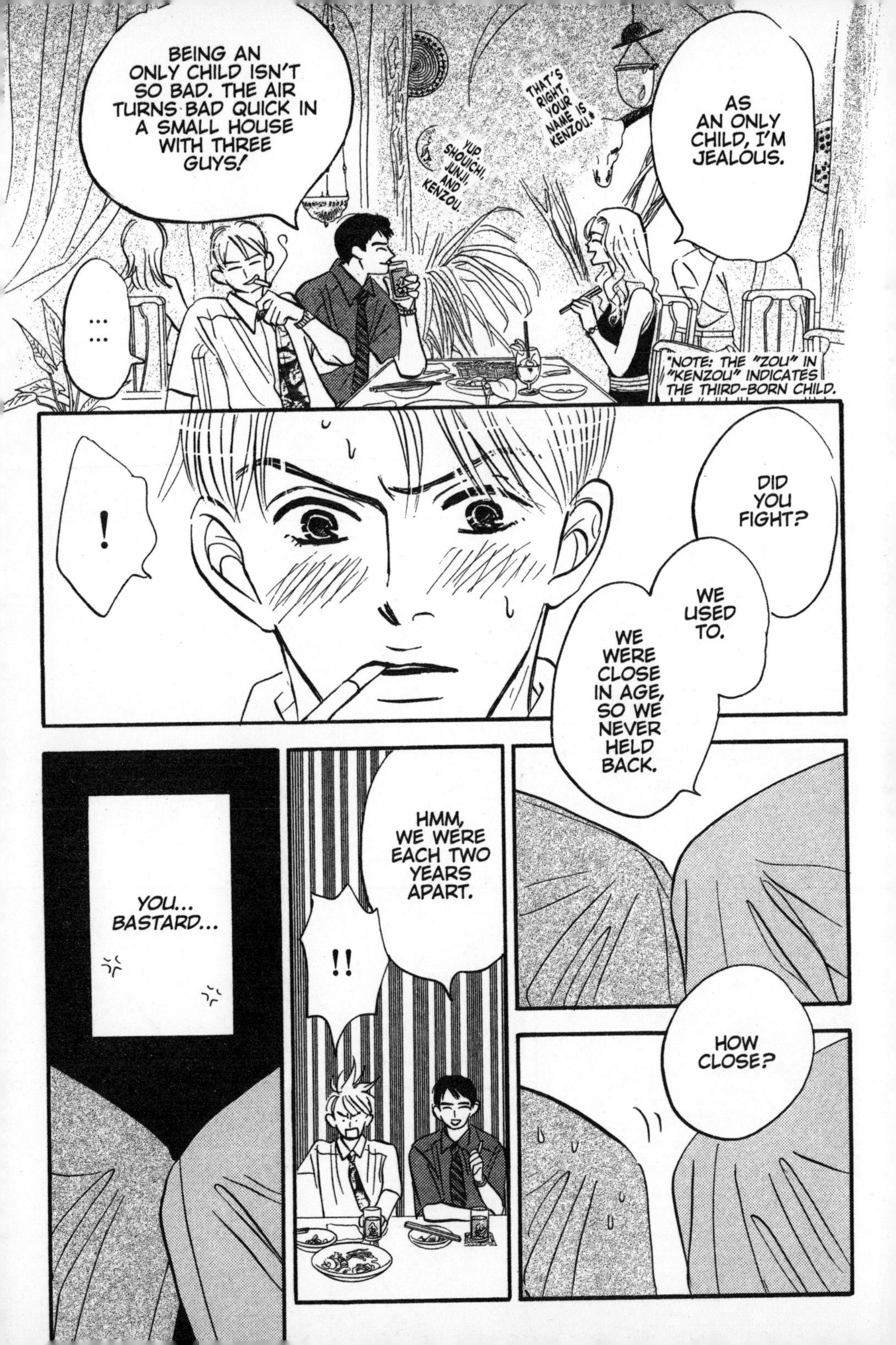
AS AN ONLY CHILD, I'M JEALOUS.
THAT'S RIGHT, YOUR NAME IS KENZOU.*
YUP. SHOUICHI, JUNJI, AND KENZOU.
BEING AN ONLY CHILD ISN'T SO BAD. THE AIR TURNS BAD QUICK IN A SMALL HOUSE WITH THREE GUYS!
……
*NOTE: THE "ZOU" IN "KENZOU" INDICATES THE THIRD-BORN CHILD.
DID YOU FIGHT?
WE USED TO.
WE WERE CLOSE IN AGE, SO WE NEVER HELD BACK.
!
HOW CLOSE?
HMM, WE WERE EACH TWO YEARS APART.
!!
YOU... BASTARD...

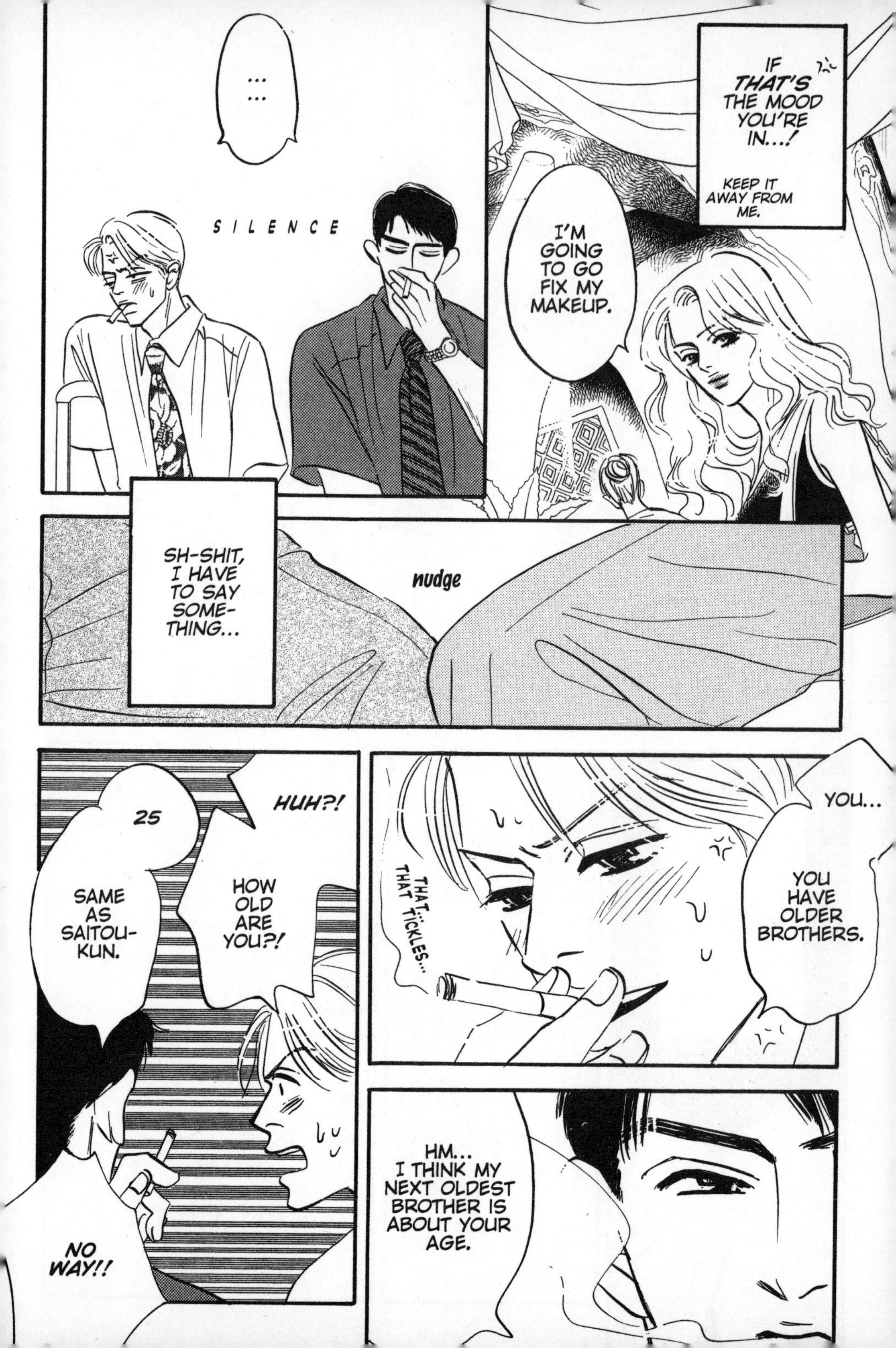
IF THAT'S THE MOOD YOU'RE IN...!
KEEP IT AWAY FROM ME.
I'M GOING TO GO FIX MY MAKEUP.
......
SILENCE
nudge
SH-SHIT, I HAVE TO SAY SOME-THING...
YOU...
YOU HAVE OLDER BROTHERS.
THAT... THAT TICKLES...
HM... I THINK MY NEXT OLDEST BROTHER IS ABOUT YOUR AGE.
HUH?!
HOW OLD ARE YOU?!
25
SAME AS SAITOU-KUN.
NO WAY!!

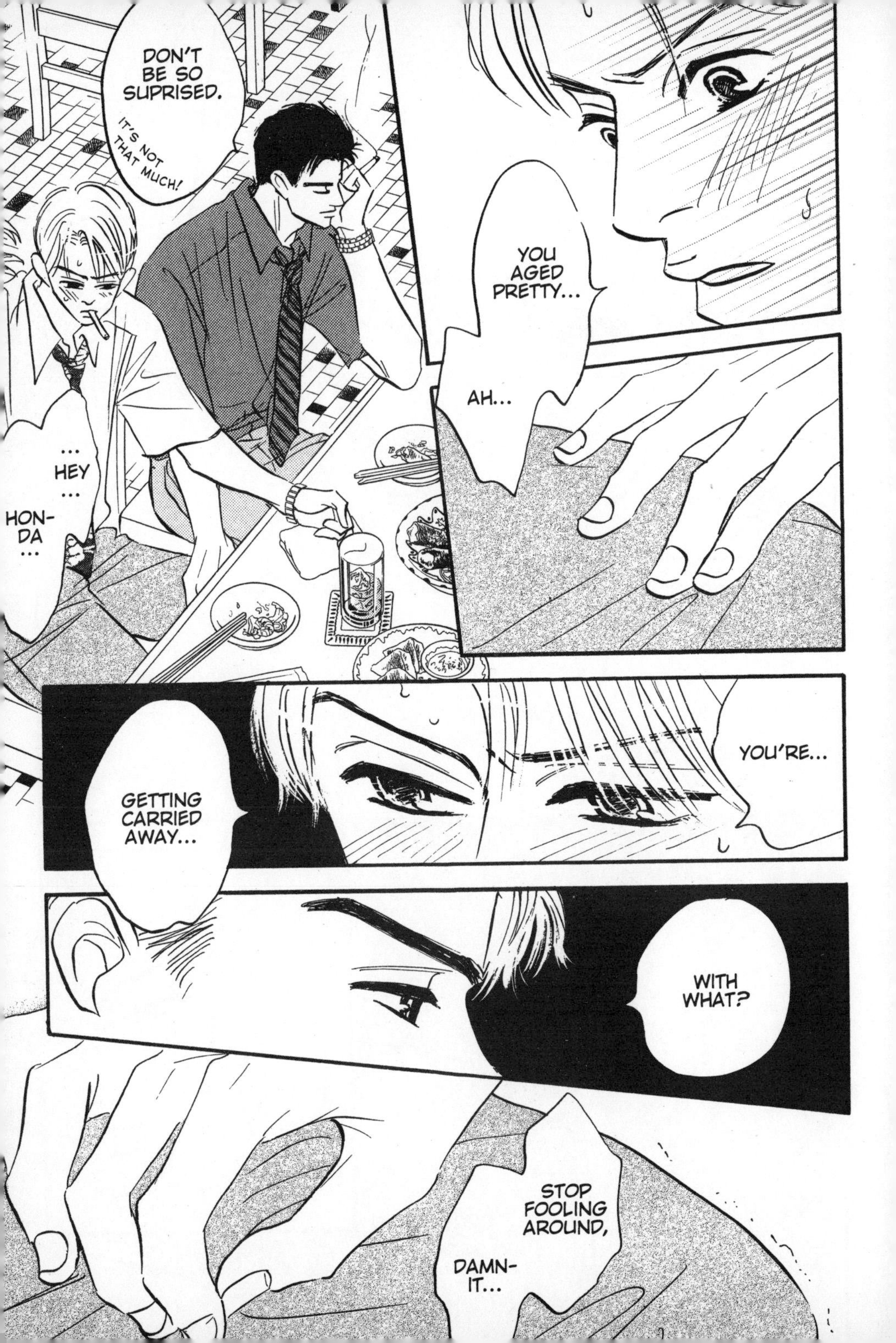
YOU AGED PRETTY...
AH...
DON'T BE SO SUPRISED.
IT'S NOT THAT MUCH!
...HEY...HON-DA...
YOU'RE...
GETTING CARRIED AWAY...
WITH WHAT?
STOP FOOLING AROUND,
DAMN-IT...

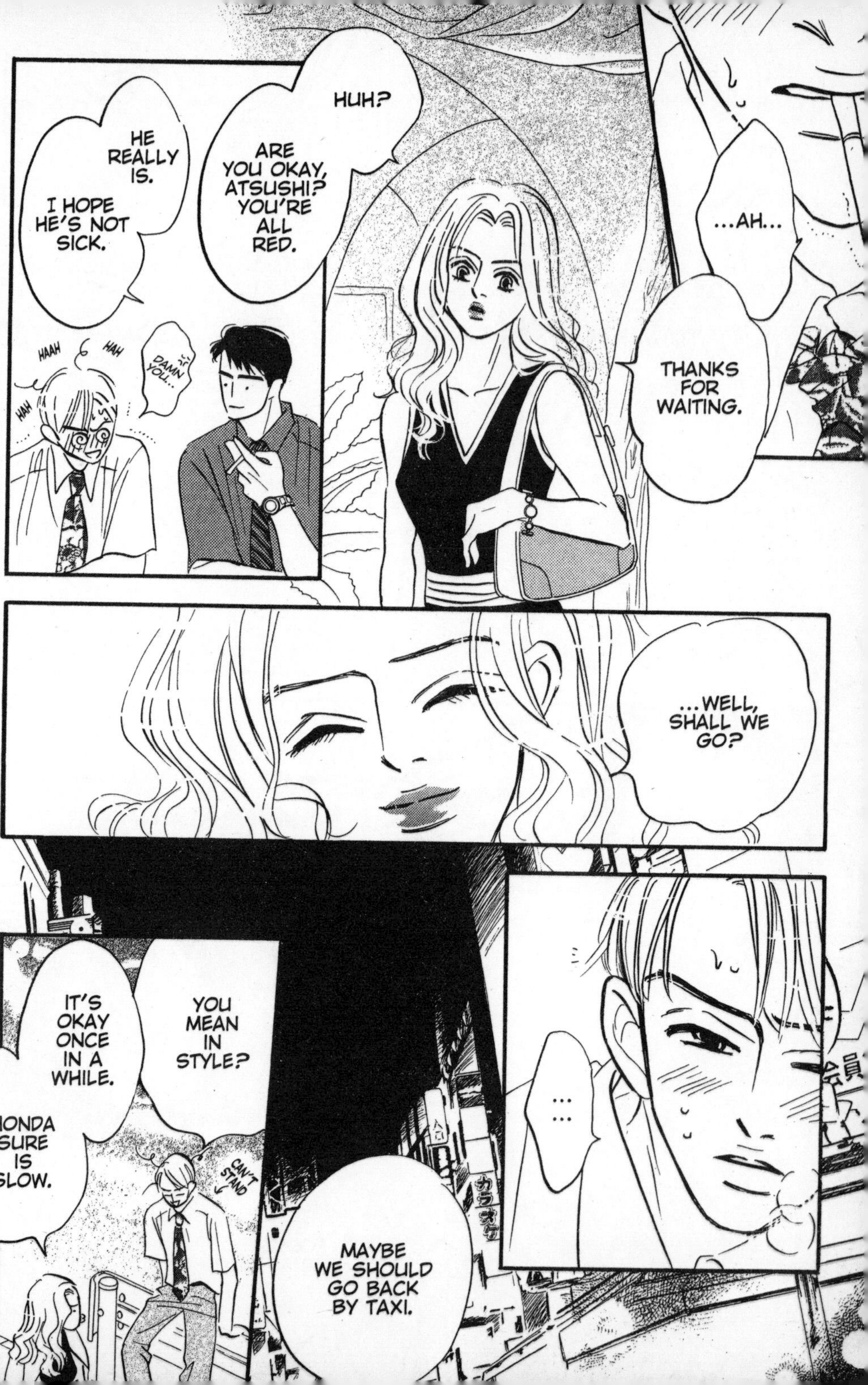
...AH...
THANKS FOR WAITING.
HUH?
ARE YOU OKAY, ATSUSHI? YOU'RE ALL RED.
HE REALLY IS.
I HOPE HE'S NOT SICK.
HAAH HAH HAH
DAMN YOU...
...WELL, SHALL WE GO?
...
...
会員
カラオケ
MAYBE WE SHOULD GO BACK BY TAXI.
YOU MEAN IN STYLE?
IT'S OKAY ONCE IN A WHILE.
HONDA SURE IS SLOW.
CAN'T STAND

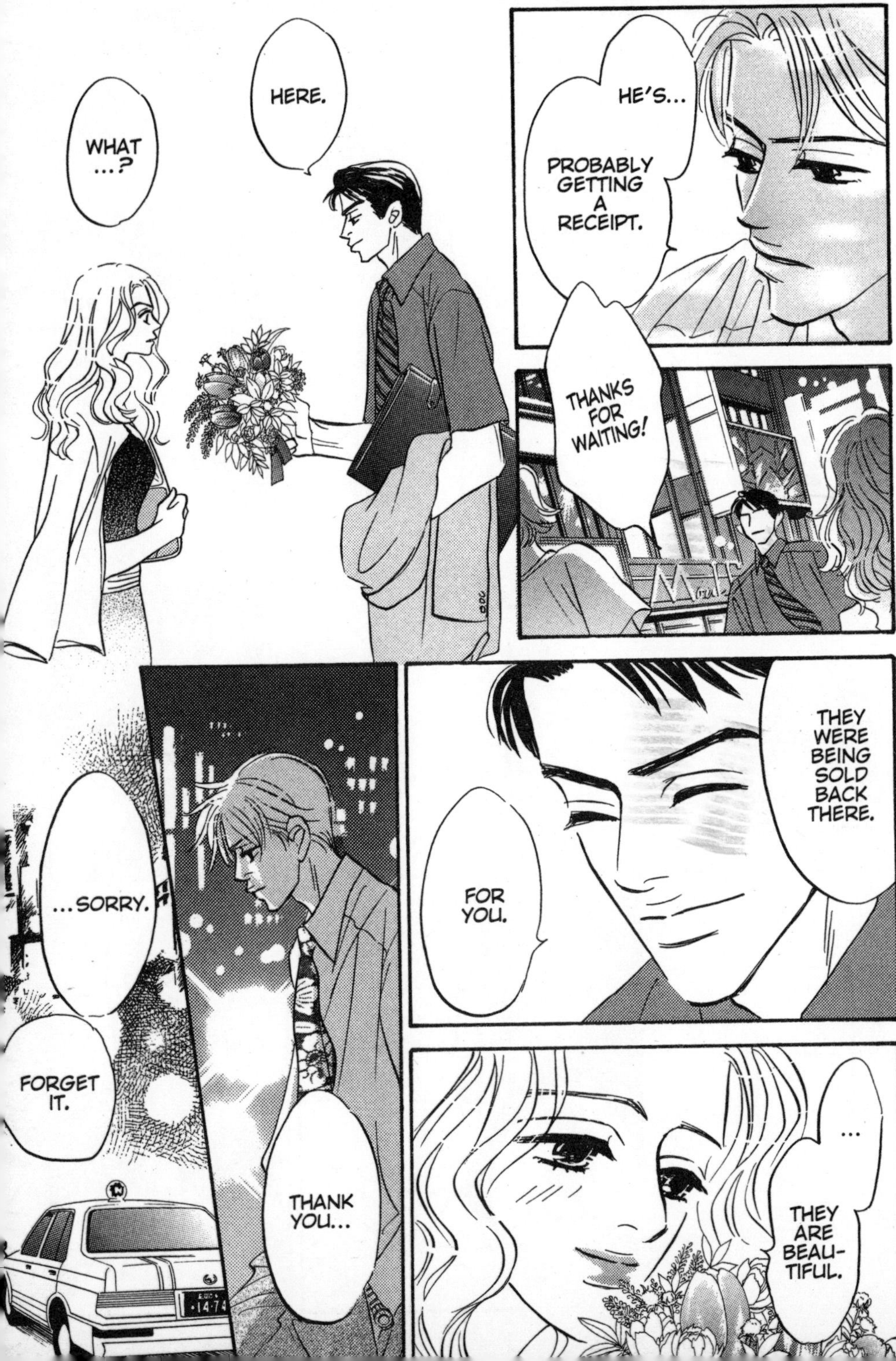
HE'S...
PROBABLY GETTING A RECEIPT.
THANKS FOR WAITING!
HERE.
WHAT ...?
THEY WERE BEING SOLD BACK THERE.
FOR YOU.
...
THEY ARE BEAU-TIFUL.
THANK YOU...
...SORRY.
FORGET IT.

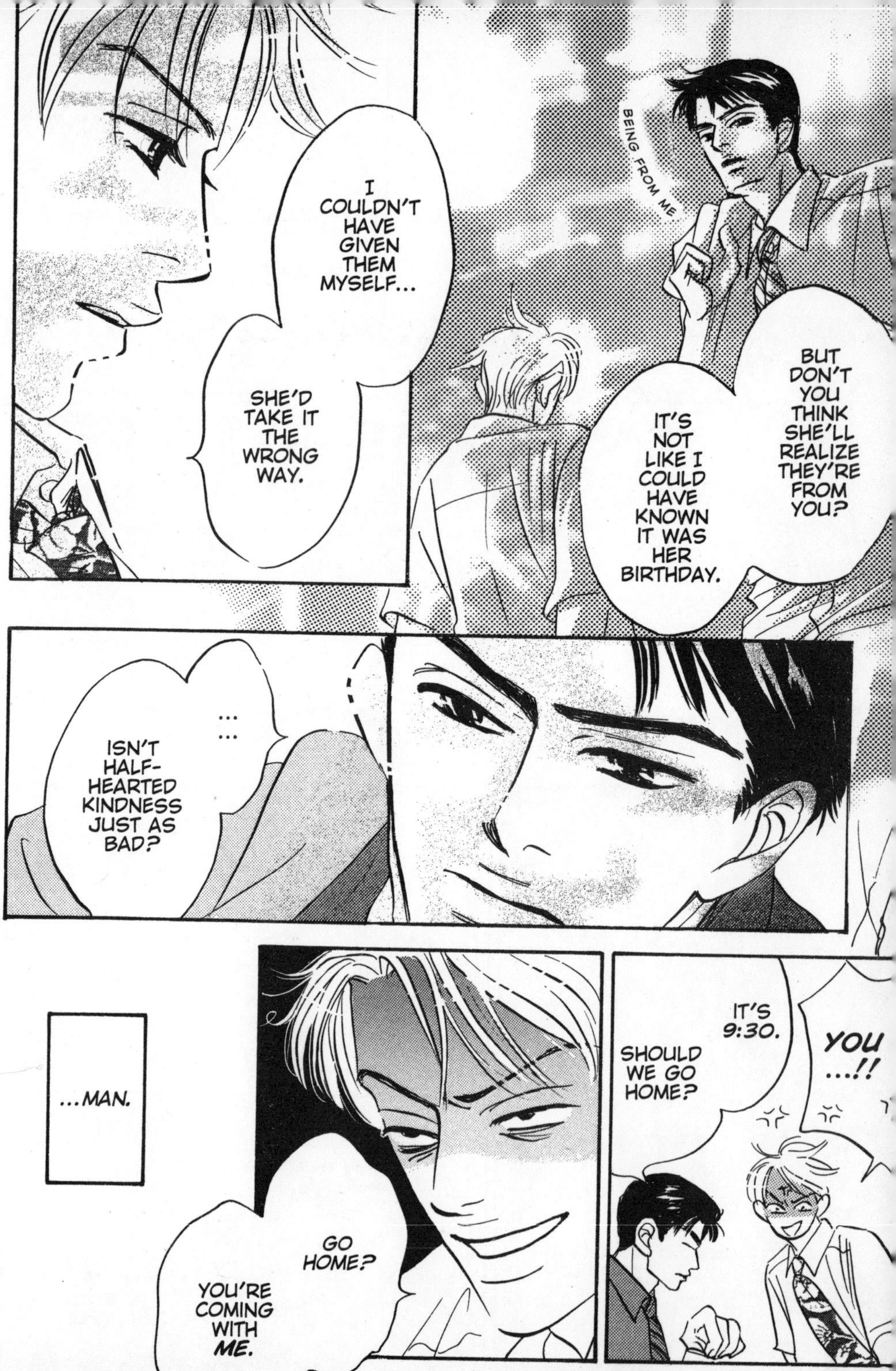
BUT DON'T YOU THINK SHE'LL REALIZE THEY'RE FROM YOU?
BEING FROM ME
IT'S NOT LIKE I COULD HAVE KNOWN IT WAS HER BIRTHDAY.
I COULDN'T HAVE GIVEN THEM MYSELF...
SHE'D TAKE IT THE WRONG WAY.
......
ISN'T HALF-HEARTED KINDNESS JUST AS BAD?
YOU ...!!
IT'S 9:30.
SHOULD WE GO HOME?
GO HOME?
YOU'RE COMING WITH ME.
...MAN.

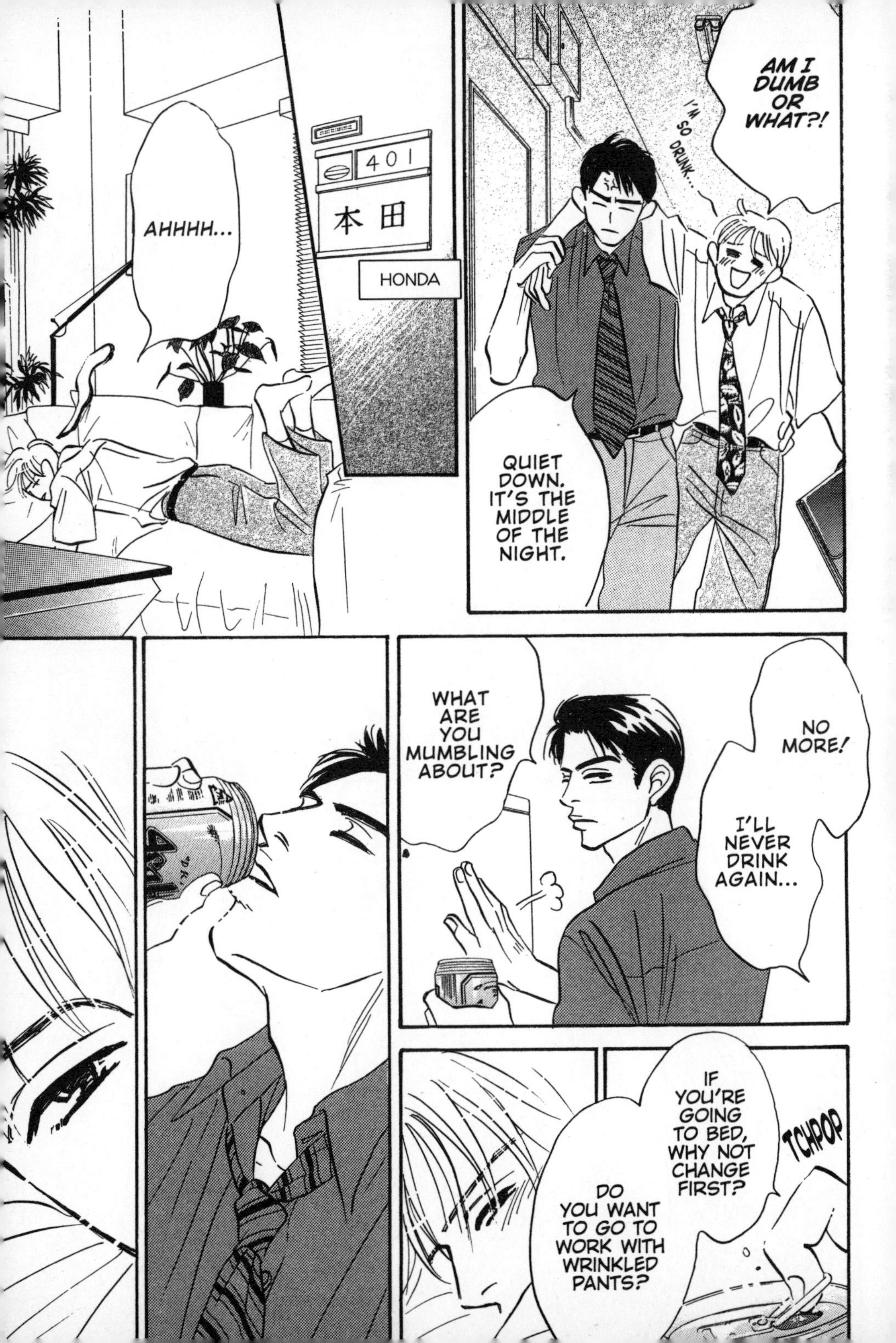
AM I DUMB OR WHAT?!
I'M SO DRUNK...
QUIET DOWN. IT'S THE MIDDLE OF THE NIGHT.
401
本田
HONDA
AHHHH...
NO MORE!
I'LL NEVER DRINK AGAIN...
WHAT ARE YOU MUMBLING ABOUT?
TCHPOP
IF YOU'RE GOING TO BED, WHY NOT CHANGE FIRST?
DO YOU WANT TO GO TO WORK WITH WRINKLED PANTS?

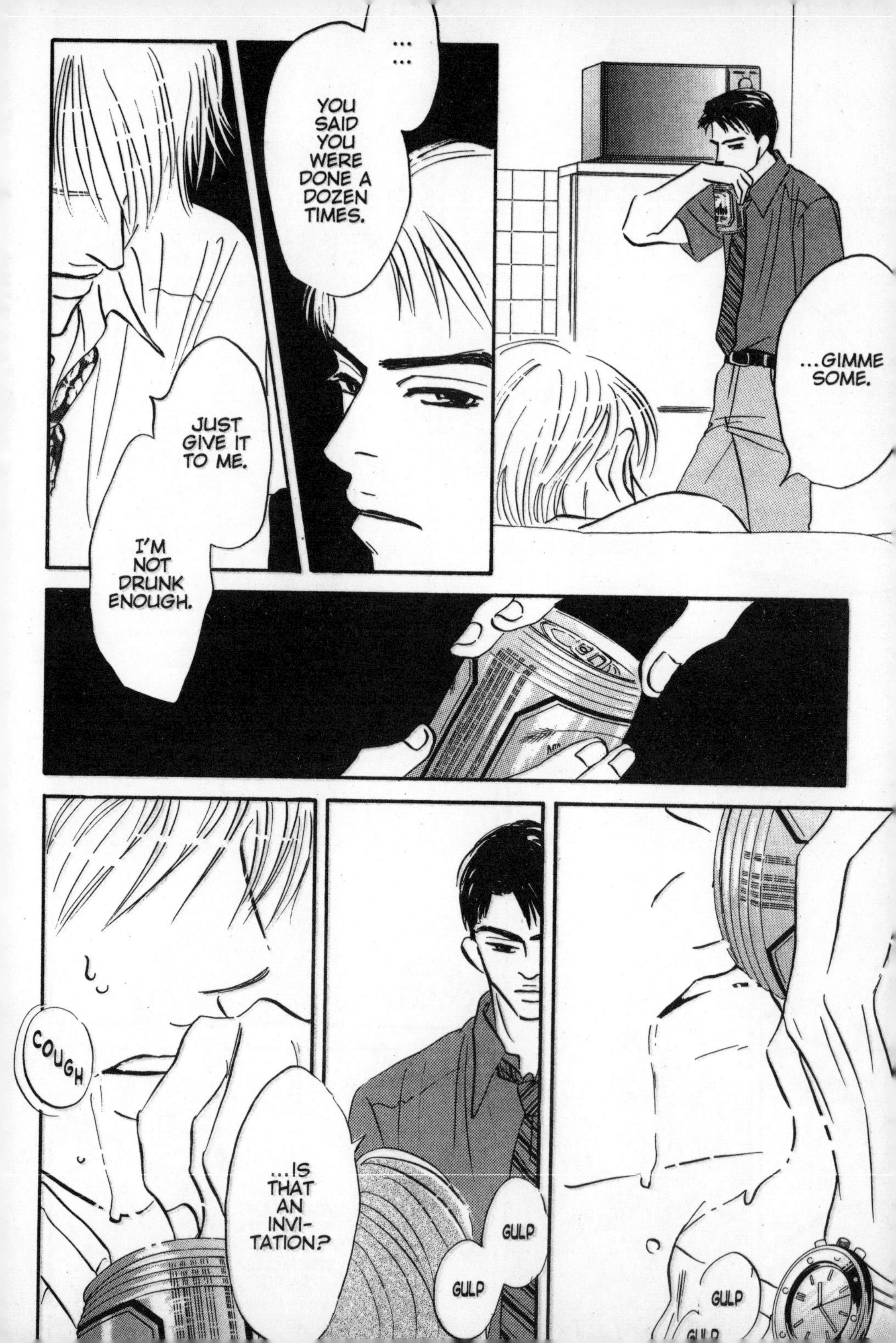

...GIMME SOME.
...
...
YOU SAID YOU WERE DONE A DOZEN TIMES.
JUST GIVE IT TO ME.
I'M NOT DRUNK ENOUGH.
GULP
...IS THAT AN INVITATION?
GULP
GULP
COUGH

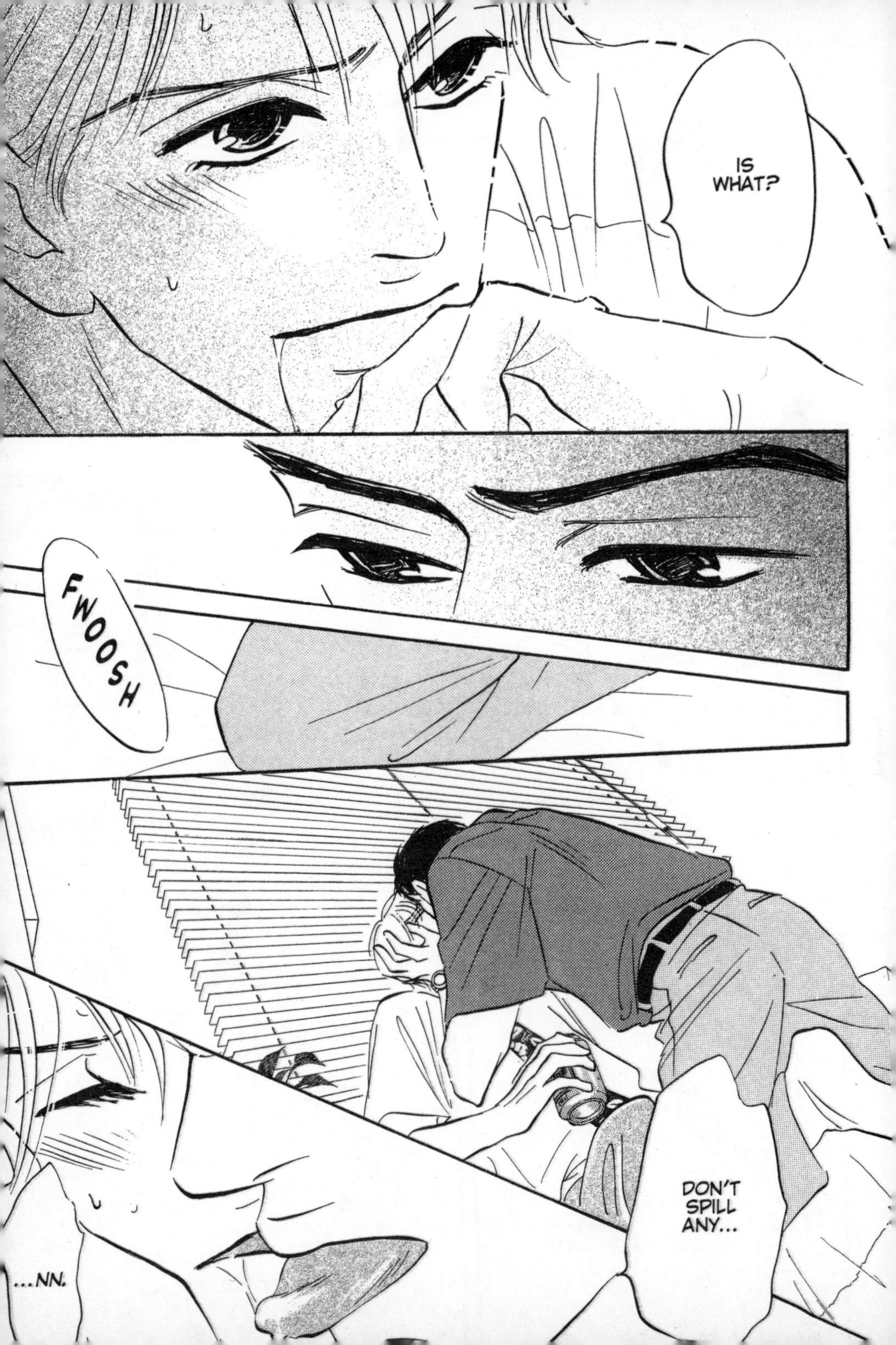
IS WHAT?
FWOOSH
DON'T SPILL ANY...
...NN.

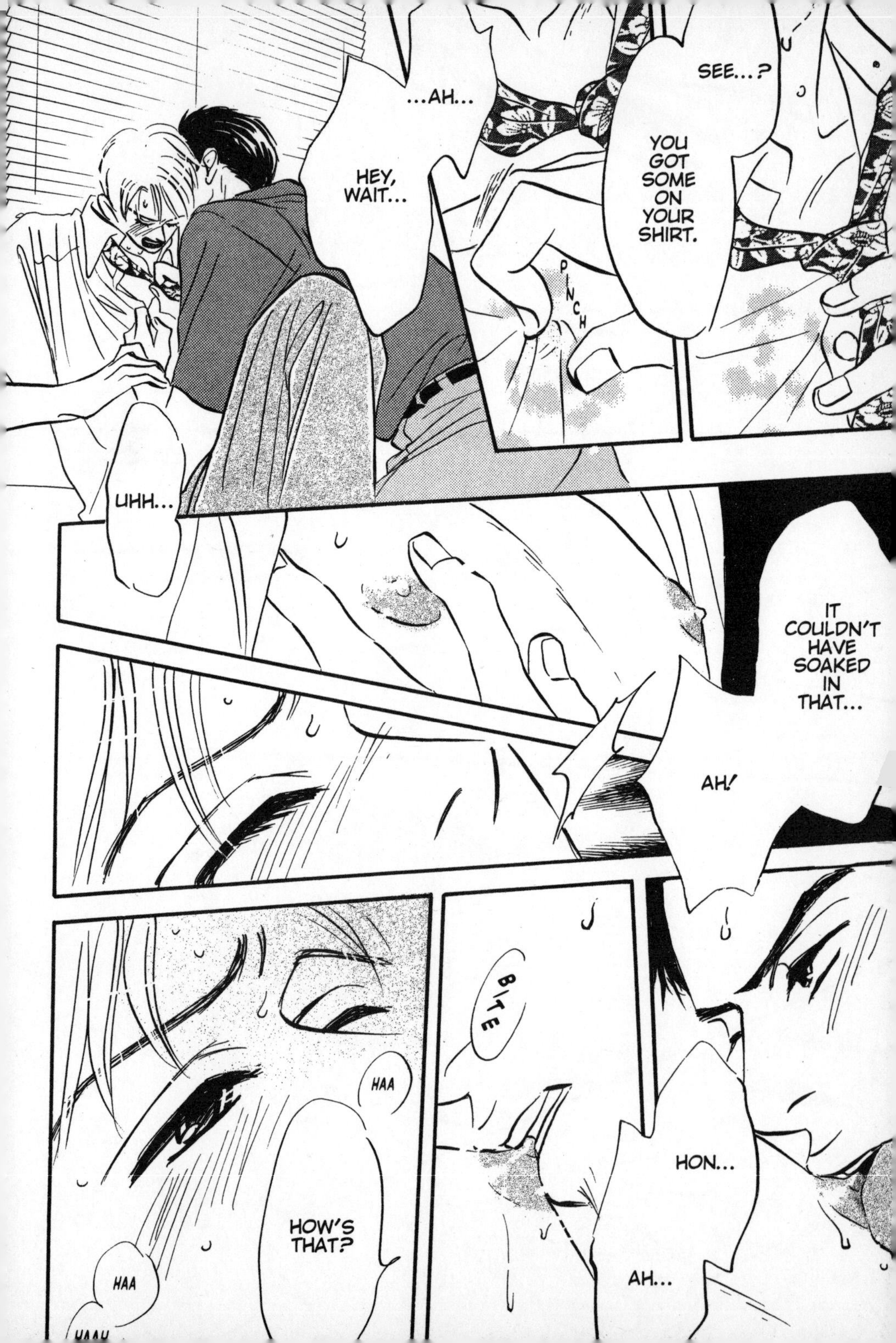
SEE...?
YOU GOT SOME ON YOUR SHIRT.
PINCH
...AH...
HEY, WAIT...
UHH...
IT COULDN'T HAVE SOAKED IN THAT...
AH!
BITE
HON...
AH...
HAA
HOW'S THAT?
HAA

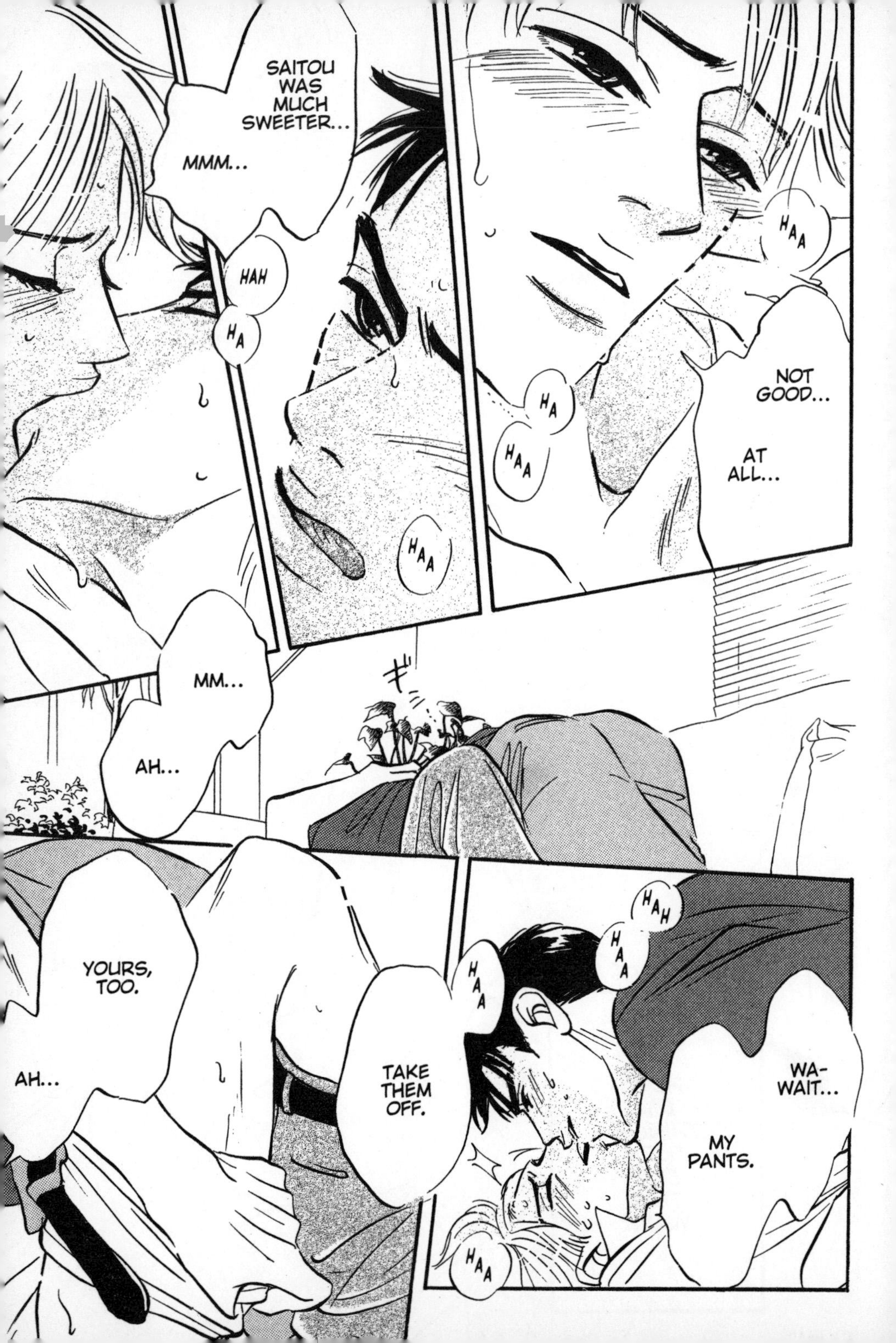
HAA
NOT GOOD...
AT ALL...
HA
HAA
SAITOU WAS MUCH SWEETER...
HAH
HA
HAA
MMM...
ギ
MM...
AH...
HAH
HAA
HAA
WA-WAIT...
MY PANTS.
HAA
TAKE THEM OFF.
YOURS, TOO.
AH...

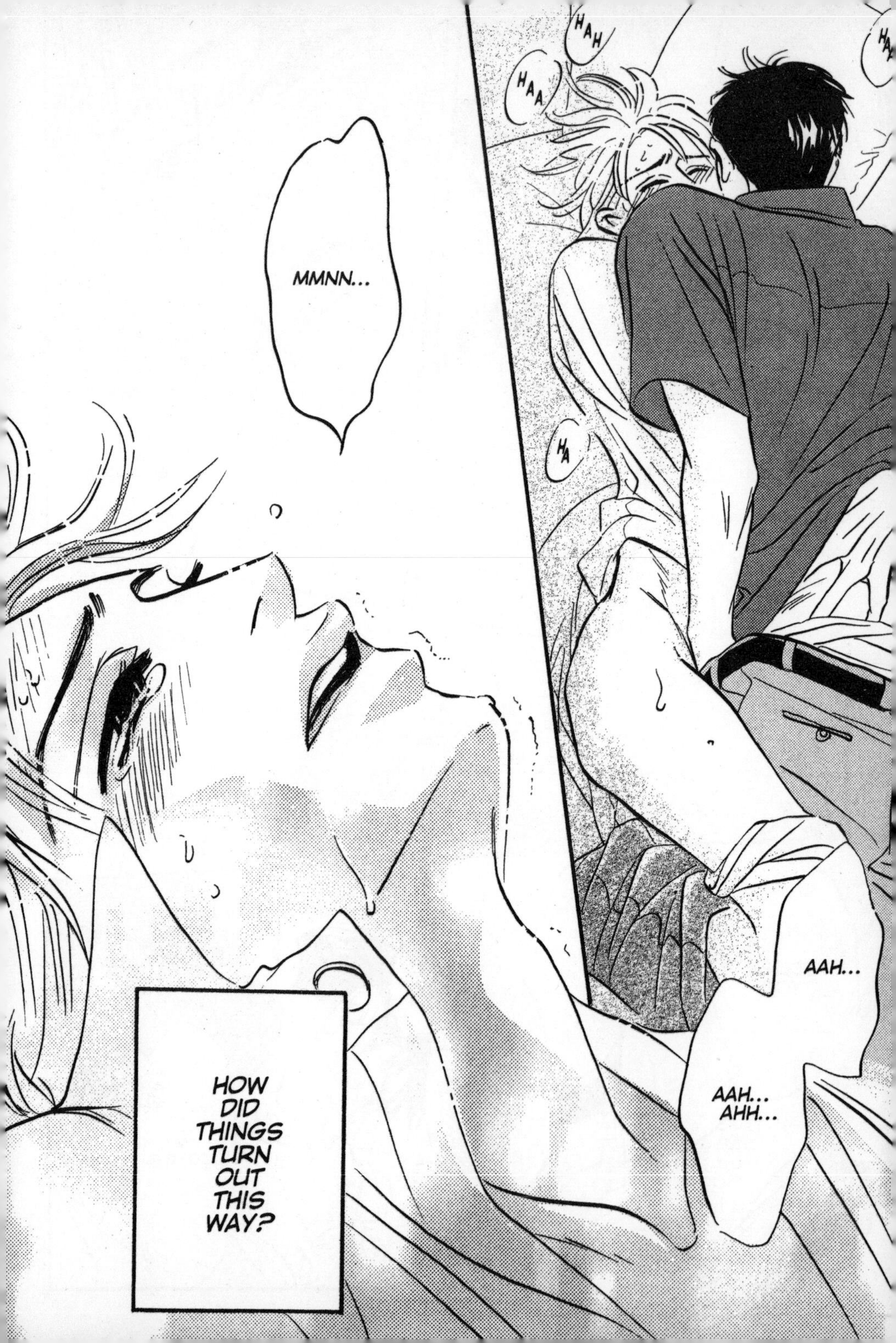

HAH
HAA
HA
AAH...
AAH... AHH...
MMNN...
HOW DID THINGS TURN OUT THIS WAY?

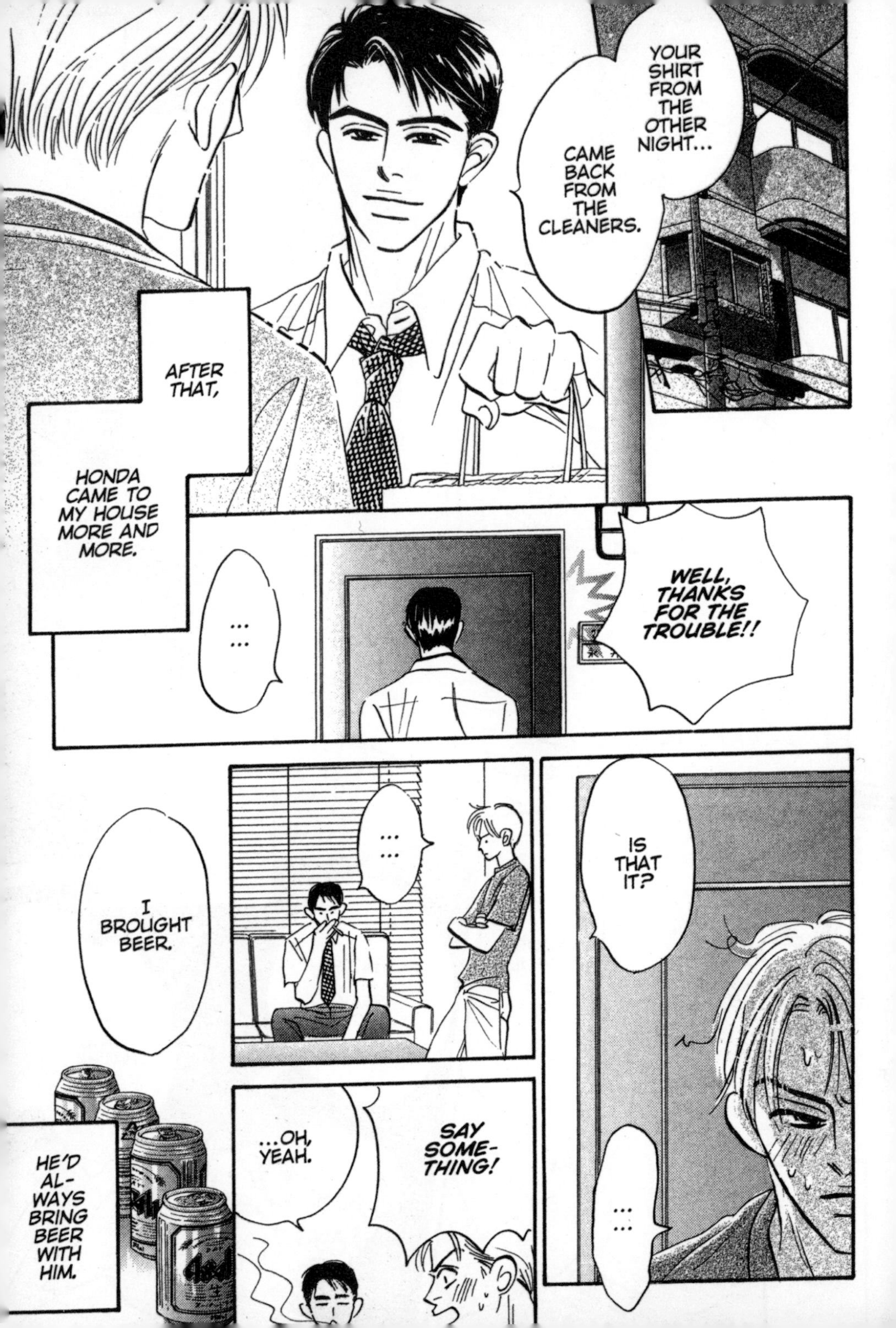
YOUR SHIRT FROM THE OTHER NIGHT...
CAME BACK FROM THE CLEANERS.
AFTER THAT,
HONDA CAME TO MY HOUSE MORE AND MORE.
WELL, THANKS FOR THE TROUBLE!!
......
IS THAT IT?
......
......
I BROUGHT BEER.
SAY SOME-THING!
...OH, YEAH.
HE'D AL-WAYS BRING BEER WITH HIM.

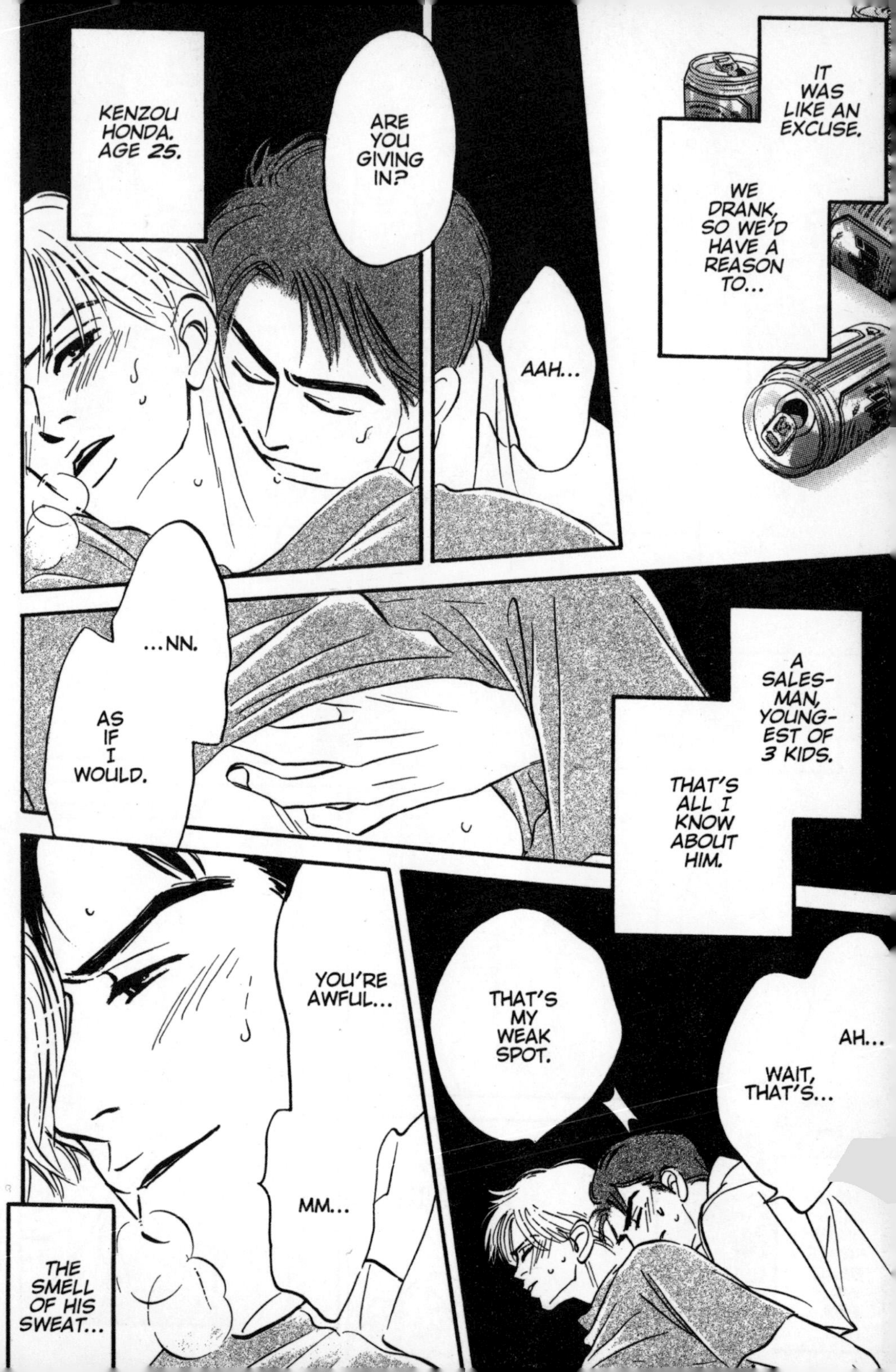
IT WAS LIKE AN EXCUSE.
WE DRANK, SO WE'D HAVE A REASON TO...
AAH...
ARE YOU GIVING IN?
KENZOU HONDA. AGE 25.
A SALES-MAN, YOUNG-EST OF 3 KIDS.
THAT'S ALL I KNOW ABOUT HIM.
...NN.
AS IF I WOULD.
AH...
WAIT, THAT'S...
THAT'S MY WEAK SPOT.
YOU'RE AWFUL...
MM...
THE SMELL OF HIS SWEAT...

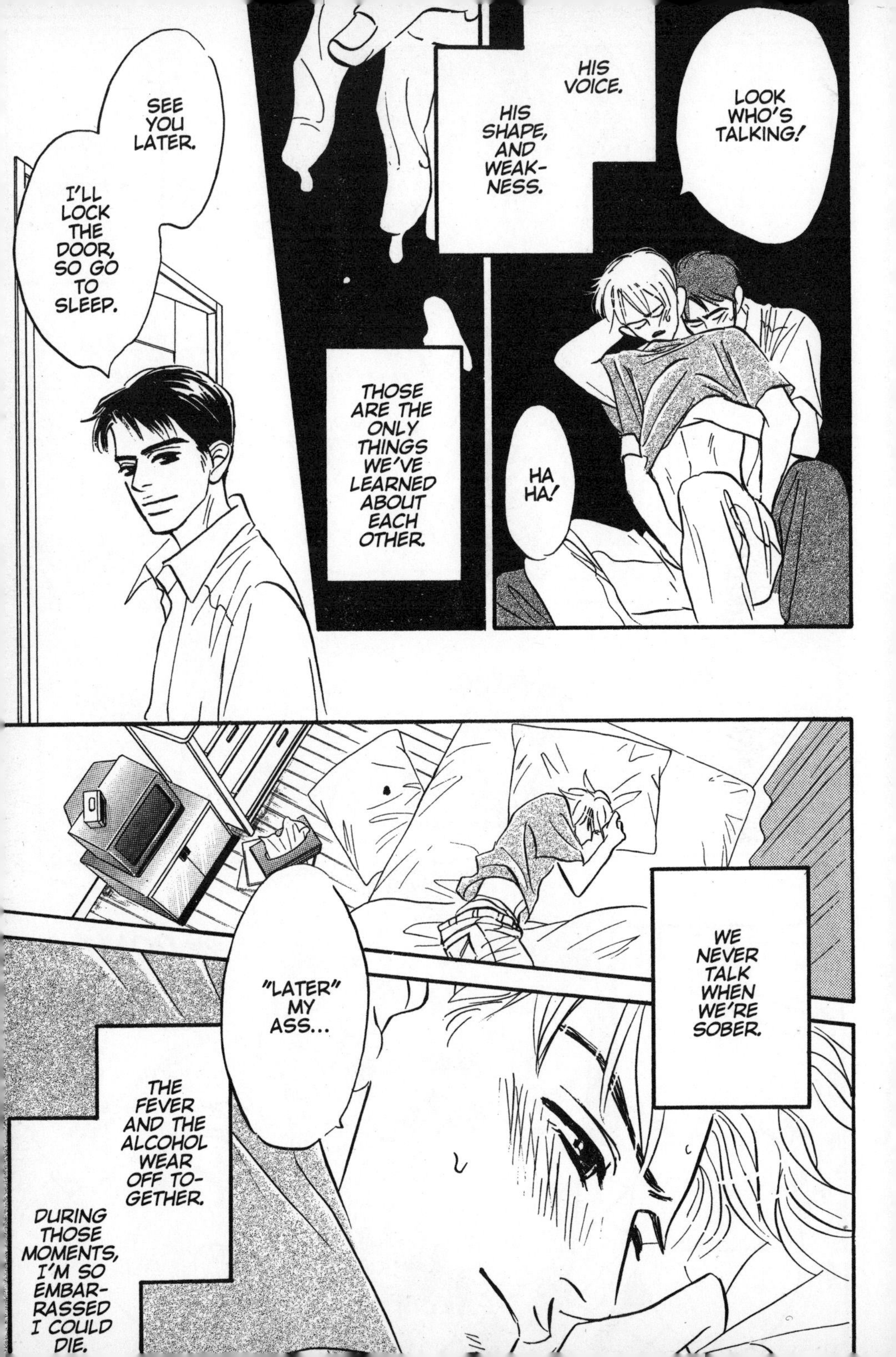
LOOK WHO'S TALKING!
HIS VOICE.
HIS SHAPE, AND WEAKNESS.
HA HA!
THOSE ARE THE ONLY THINGS WE'VE LEARNED ABOUT EACH OTHER.
SEE YOU LATER.
I'LL LOCK THE DOOR, SO GO TO SLEEP.
WE NEVER TALK WHEN WE'RE SOBER.
"LATER" MY ASS...
THE FEVER AND THE ALCOHOL WEAR OFF TOGETHER.
DURING THOSE MOMENTS, I'M SO EMBARRASSED I COULD DIE.

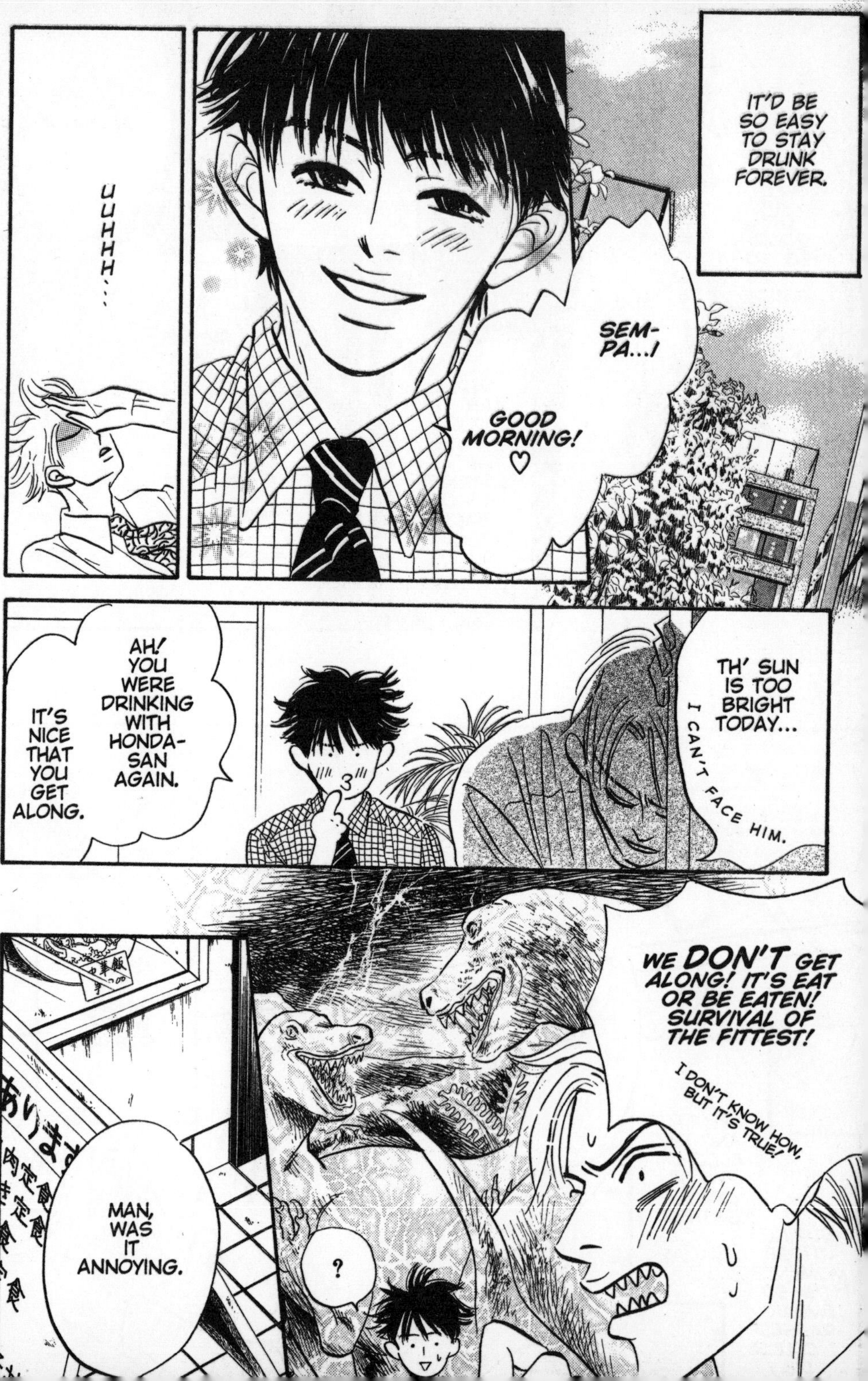
IT'D BE SO EASY TO STAY DRUNK FOREVER.
SEM-PA...!
GOOD MORNING! ♡
UUHHH...
TH' SUN IS TOO BRIGHT TODAY...
I CAN'T FACE HIM.
AH! YOU WERE DRINKING WITH HONDA-SAN AGAIN.
IT'S NICE THAT YOU GET ALONG.
WE DON'T GET ALONG! IT'S EAT OR BE EATEN! SURVIVAL OF THE FITTEST!
I DON'T KNOW HOW, BUT IT'S TRUE!
?
MAN, WAS IT ANNOYING.

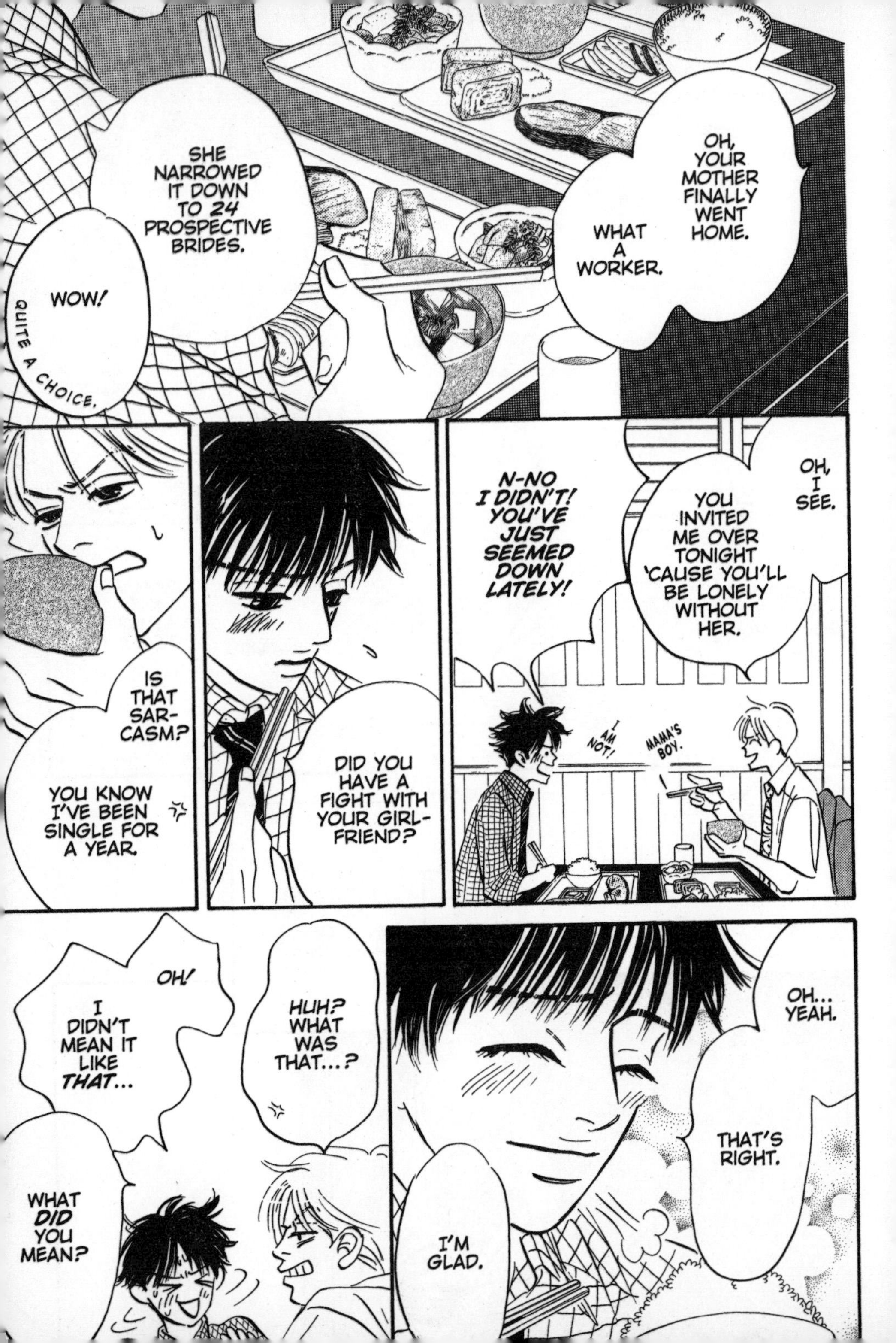
OH, YOUR MOTHER FINALLY WENT HOME.
WHAT A WORKER.
SHE NARROWED IT DOWN TO 24 PROSPECTIVE BRIDES.
WOW!
QUITE A CHOICE.
OH, I SEE.
YOU INVITED ME OVER TONIGHT 'CAUSE YOU'LL BE LONELY WITHOUT HER.
N-NO I DIDN'T! YOU'VE JUST SEEMED DOWN LATELY!
MAMA'S BOY.
I AM NOT!
DID YOU HAVE A FIGHT WITH YOUR GIRL-FRIEND?
IS THAT SAR-CASM?
YOU KNOW I'VE BEEN SINGLE FOR A YEAR.
OH... YEAH.
THAT'S RIGHT.
I'M GLAD.
HUH? WHAT WAS THAT...?
OH!
I DIDN'T MEAN IT LIKE THAT...
WHAT DID YOU MEAN?

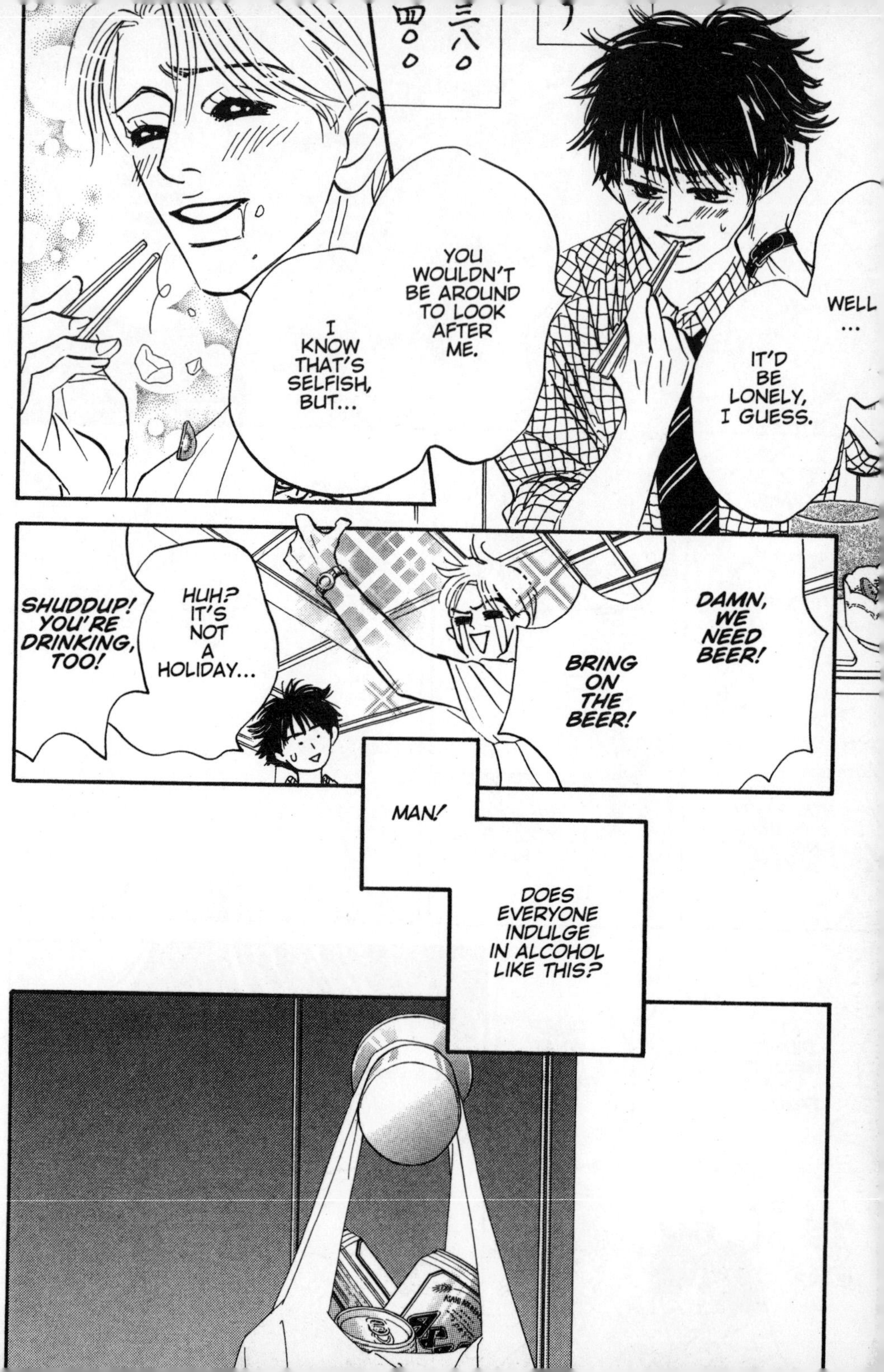
WELL ...
IT'D BE LONELY, I GUESS.
YOU WOULDN'T BE AROUND TO LOOK AFTER ME.
I KNOW THAT'S SELFISH, BUT...
DAMN, WE NEED BEER!
BRING ON THE BEER!
HUH? IT'S NOT A HOLIDAY...
SHUDDUP! YOU'RE DRINKING, TOO!
MAN!
DOES EVERYONE INDULGE IN ALCOHOL LIKE THIS?

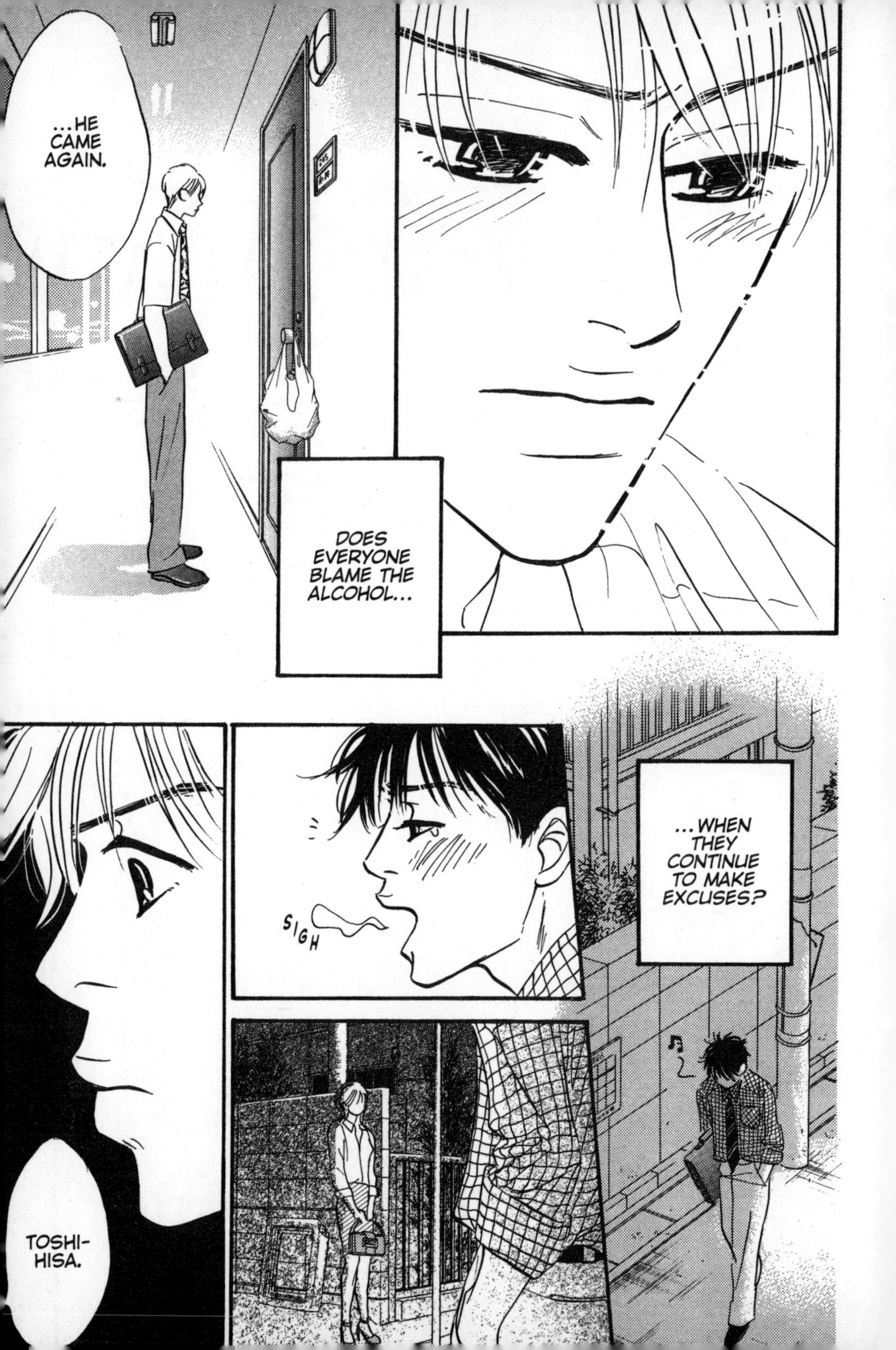
...HE CAME AGAIN.
DOES EVERYONE BLAME THE ALCOHOL...
...WHEN THEY CONTINUE TO MAKE EXCUSES?
SIGH
TOSHI-HISA.

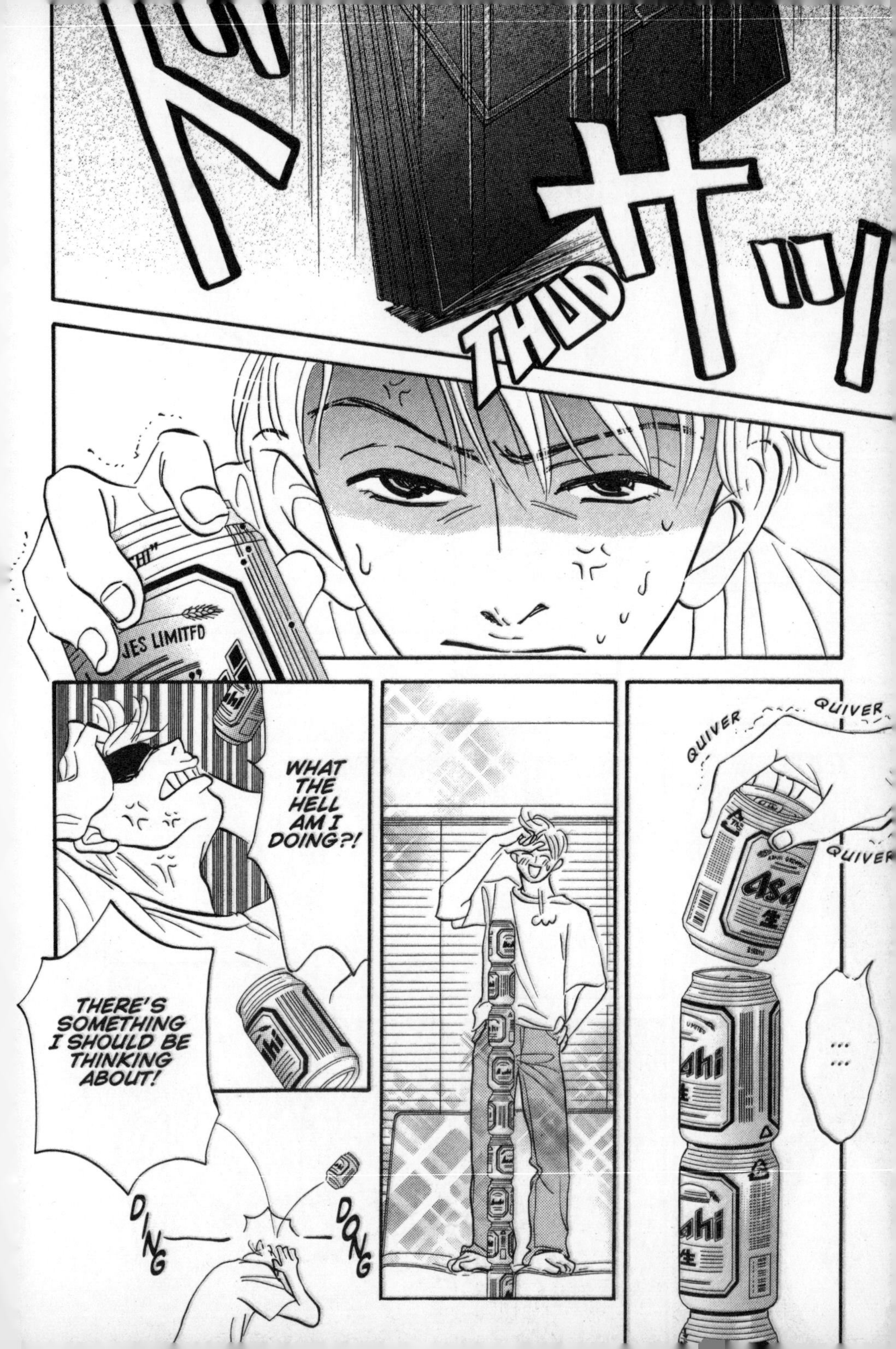
THUD
QUIVER
QUIVER
QUIVER
...
...
WHAT THE HELL AM I DOING?!
THERE'S SOMETHING I SHOULD BE THINKING ABOUT!
DING—
—DONG

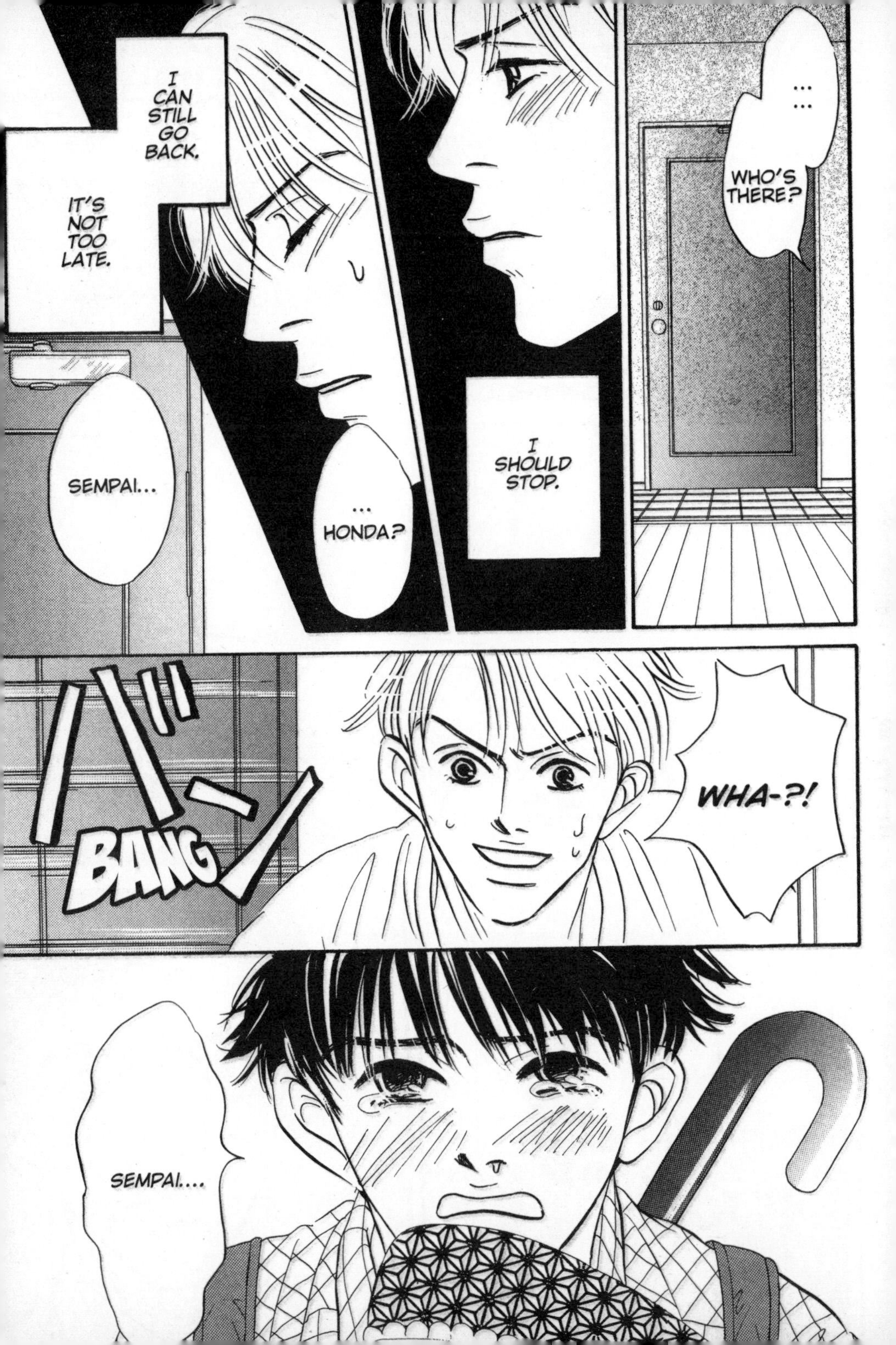

...
...
WHO'S THERE?
I SHOULD STOP.
I CAN STILL GO BACK.
IT'S NOT TOO LATE.
... HONDA?
SEMPAI...
WHA-?!
BANG
SEMPAI....

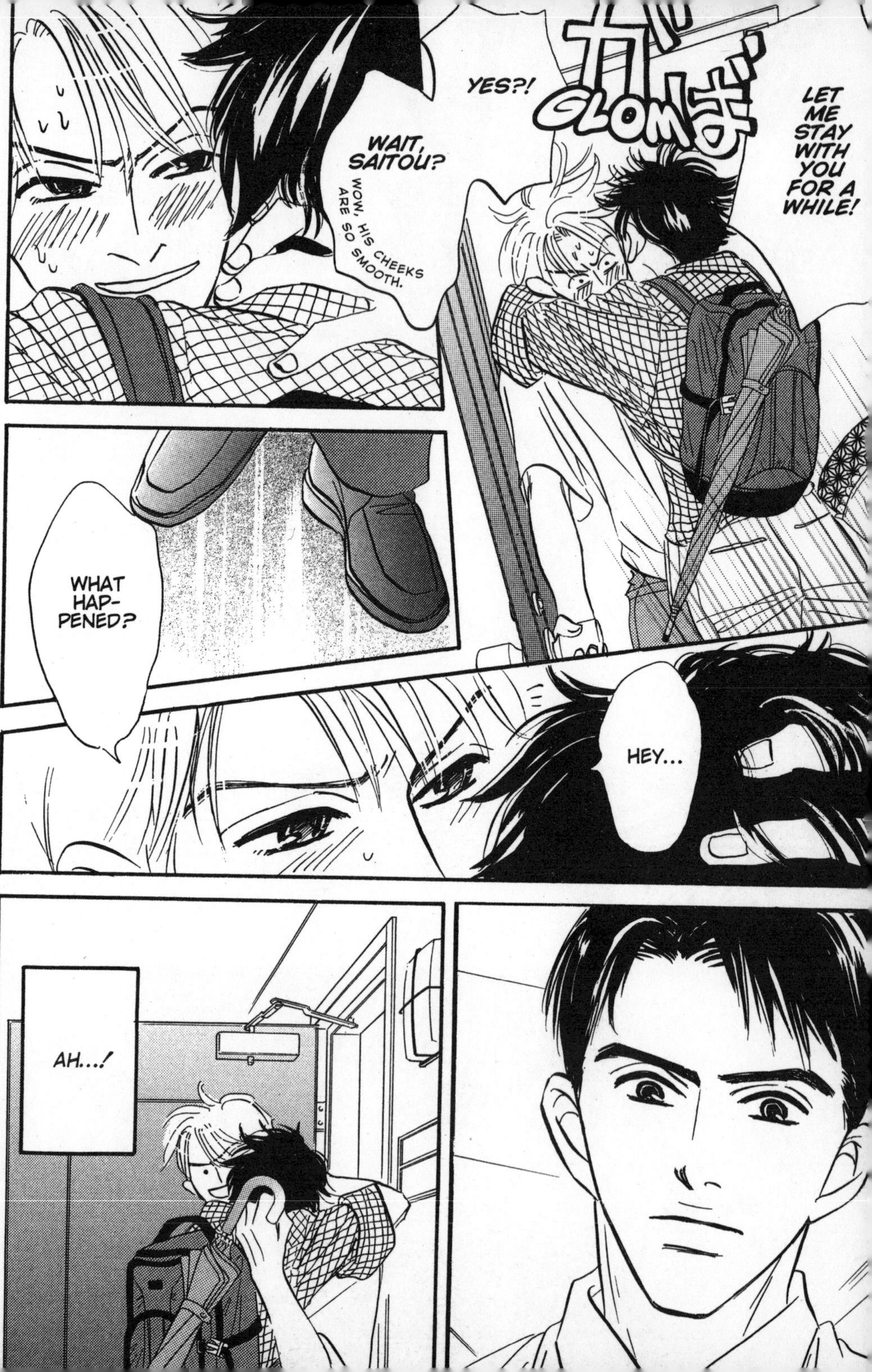
LET ME STAY WITH YOU FOR A WHILE!
GLOM
YES?!
WAIT, SAITOU?
WOW, HIS CHEEKS ARE SO SMOOTH.
WHAT HAP-PENED?
HEY...
AH...!

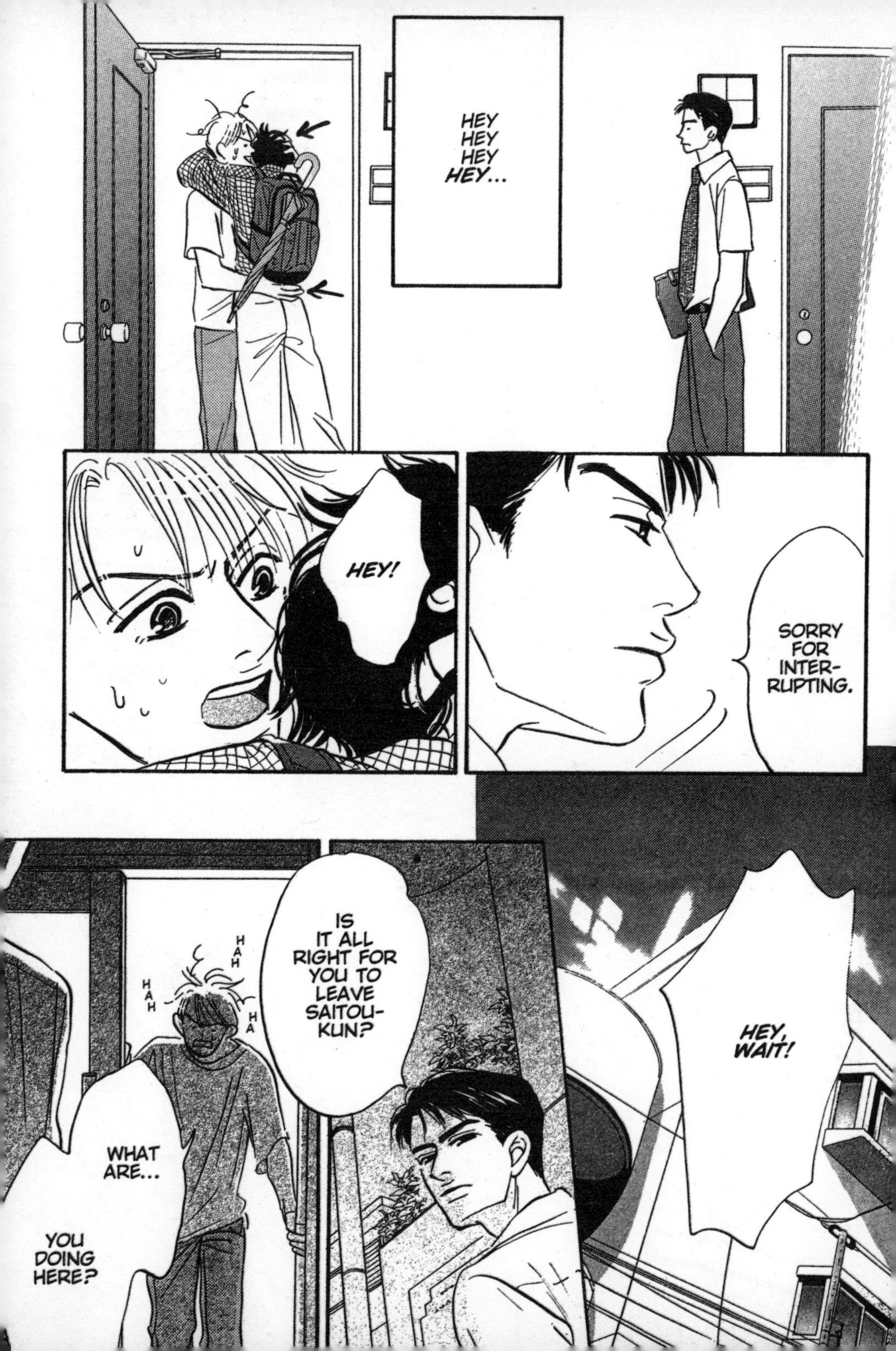
HEY HEY HEY HEY...
SORRY FOR INTER-RUPTING.
HEY!
HEY, WAIT!
IS IT ALL RIGHT FOR YOU TO LEAVE SAITOU-KUN?
HAH HAH HA
WHAT ARE...
YOU DOING HERE?

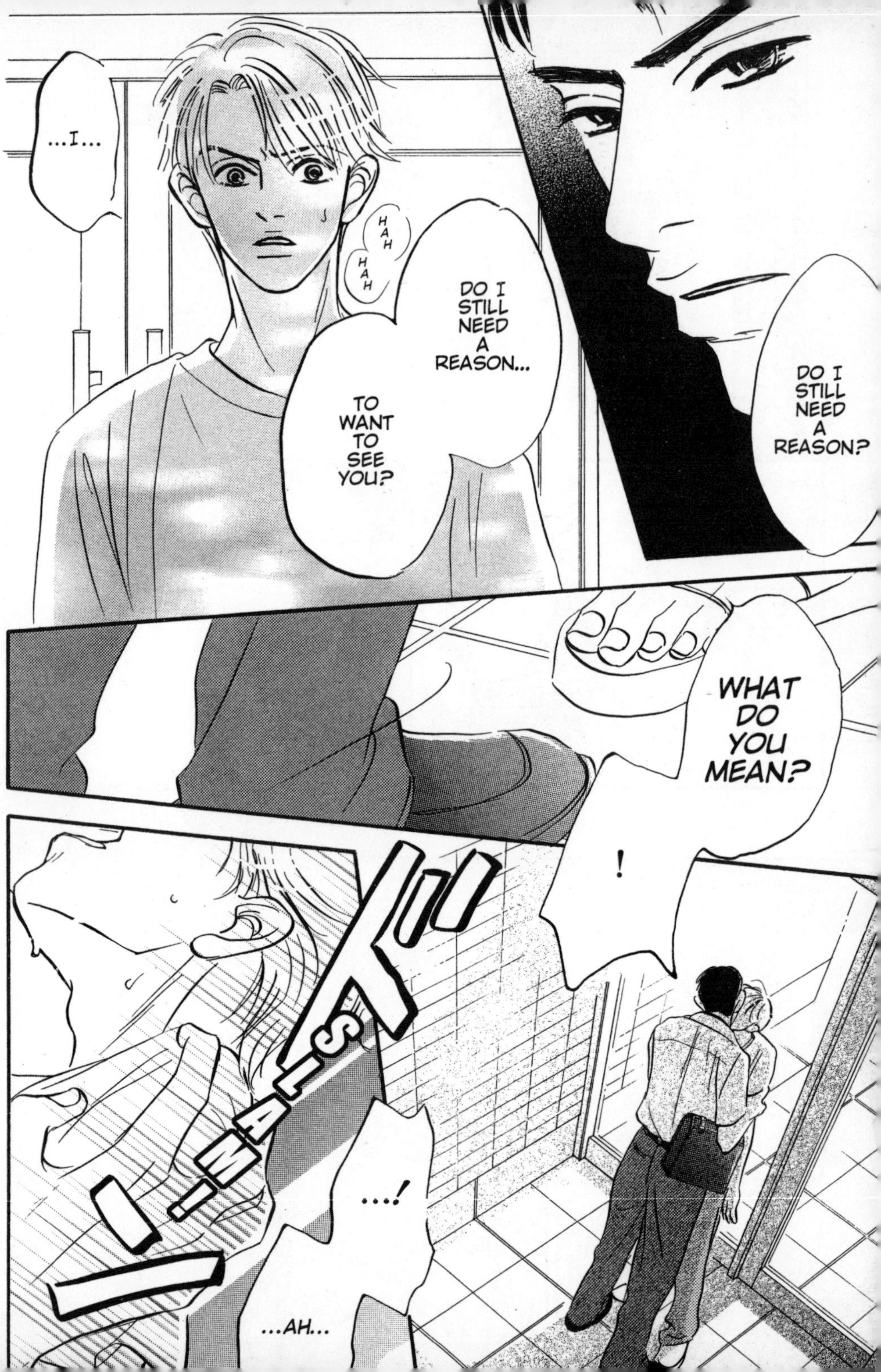
DO I STILL NEED A REASON?
DO I STILL NEED A REASON... TO WANT TO SEE YOU?
HAH HAH
...I...
WHAT DO YOU MEAN?
!
SLAM!
...!
...AH...

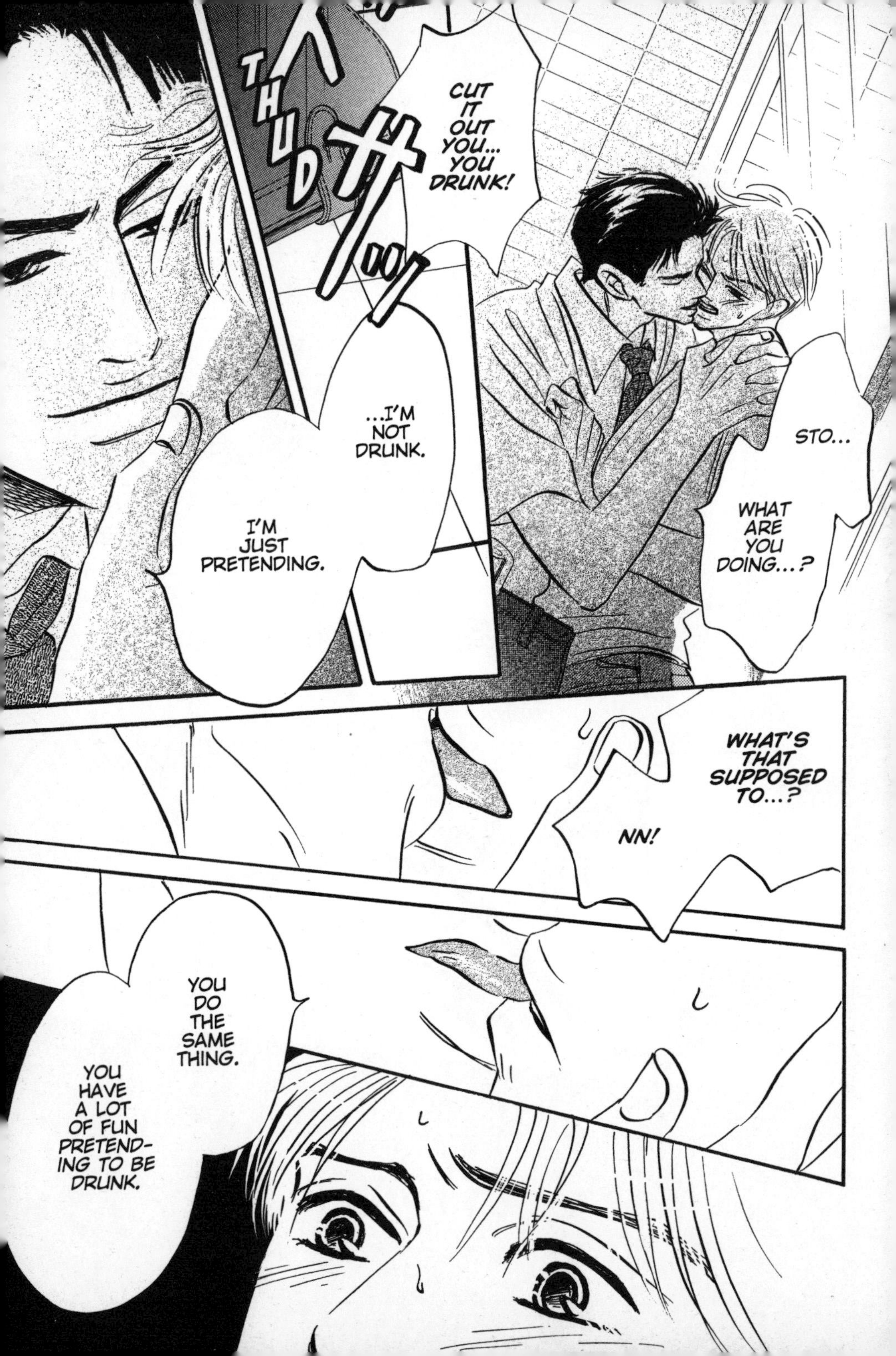
THUD
CUT IT OUT YOU... YOU DRUNK!
STO...
WHAT ARE YOU DOING...?
...I'M NOT DRUNK.
I'M JUST PRETENDING.
WHAT'S THAT SUPPOSED TO...?
NN!
YOU DO THE SAME THING.
YOU HAVE A LOT OF FUN PRETENDING TO BE DRUNK.

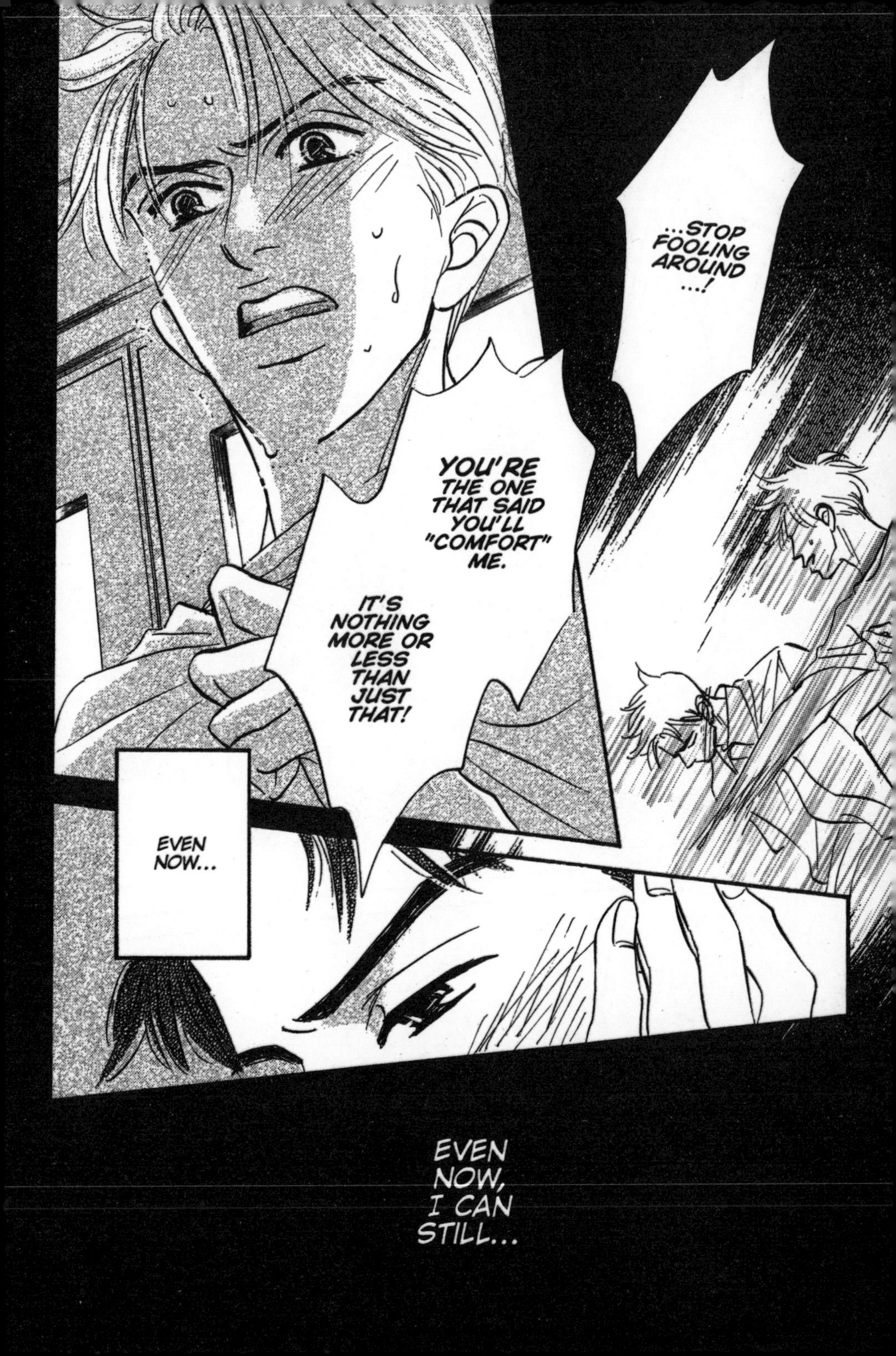
...STOP FOOLING AROUND...!
YOU'RE THE ONE THAT SAID YOU'LL "COMFORT" ME.
IT'S NOTHING MORE OR LESS THAN JUST THAT!
EVEN NOW...
EVEN NOW, I CAN STILL...

ACT.5

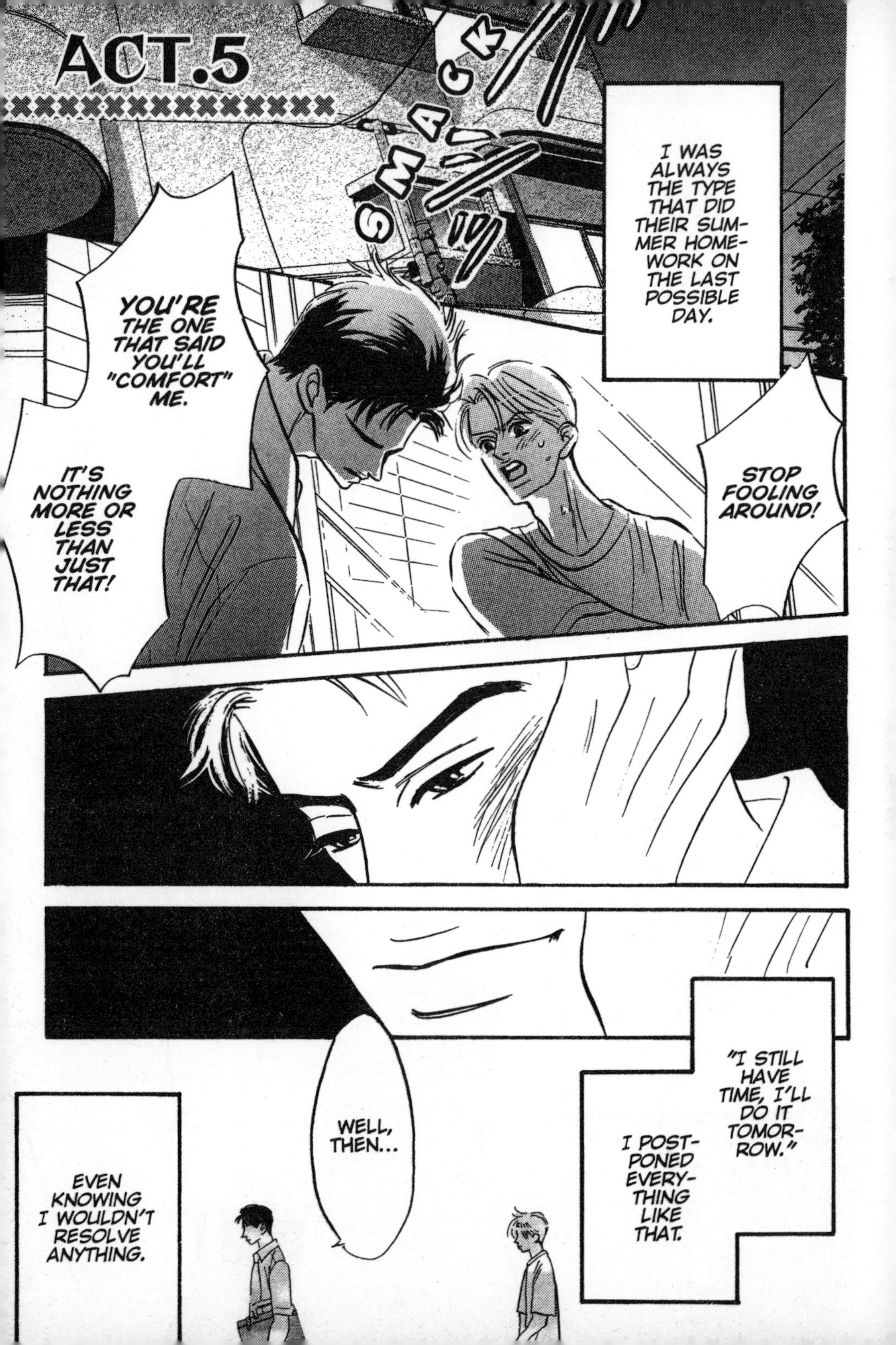
SMACK
I WAS ALWAYS THE TYPE THAT DID THEIR SUMMER HOMEWORK ON THE LAST POSSIBLE DAY.
STOP FOOLING AROUND!
YOU'RE THE ONE THAT SAID YOU'LL "COMFORT" ME.
IT'S NOTHING MORE OR LESS THAN JUST THAT!
"I STILL HAVE TIME, I'LL DO IT TOMORROW."
I POSTPONED EVERYTHING LIKE THAT.
WELL, THEN...
EVEN KNOWING I WOULDN'T RESOLVE ANYTHING.

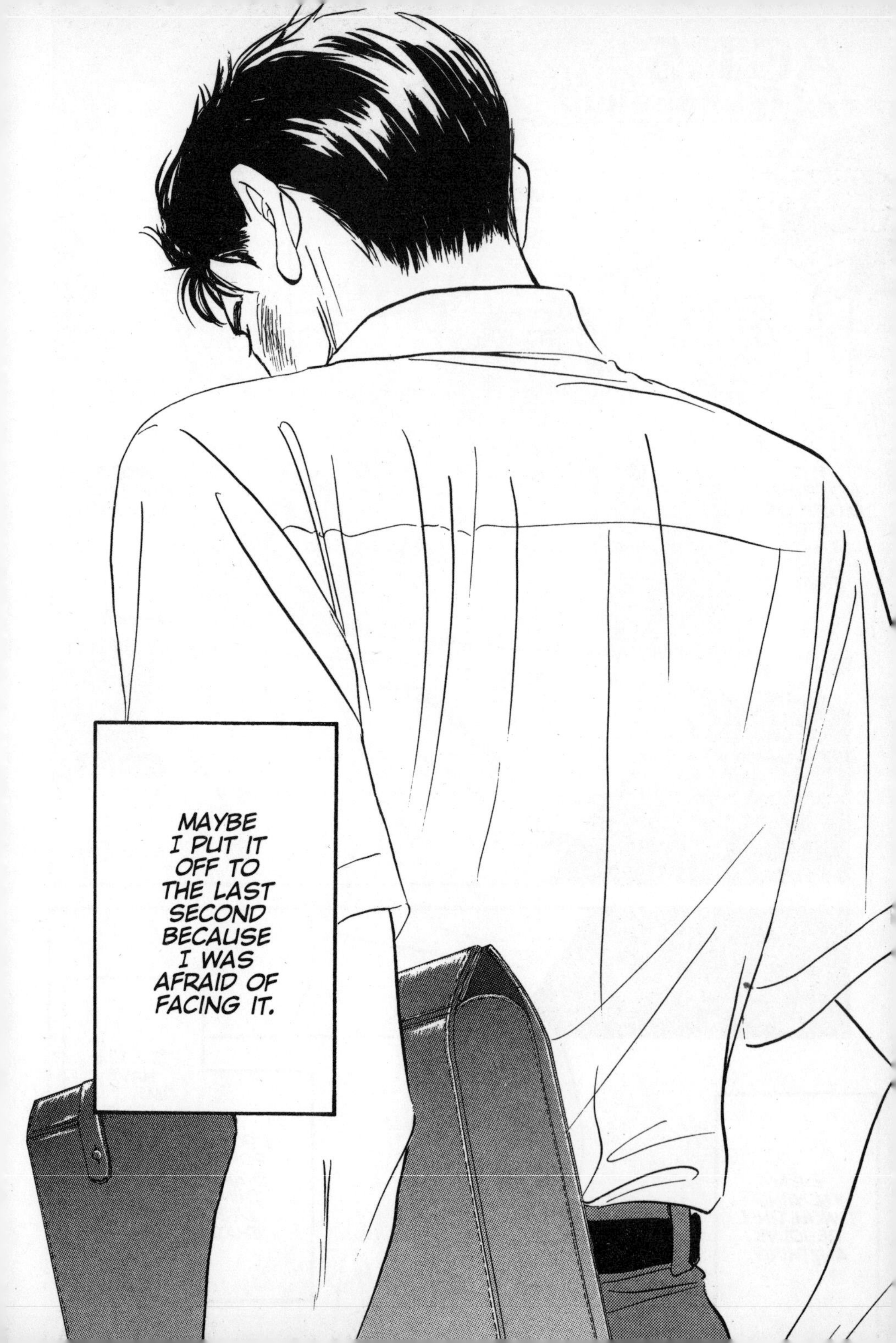
MAYBE I PUT IT OFF TO THE LAST SECOND BECAUSE I WAS AFRAID OF FACING IT.

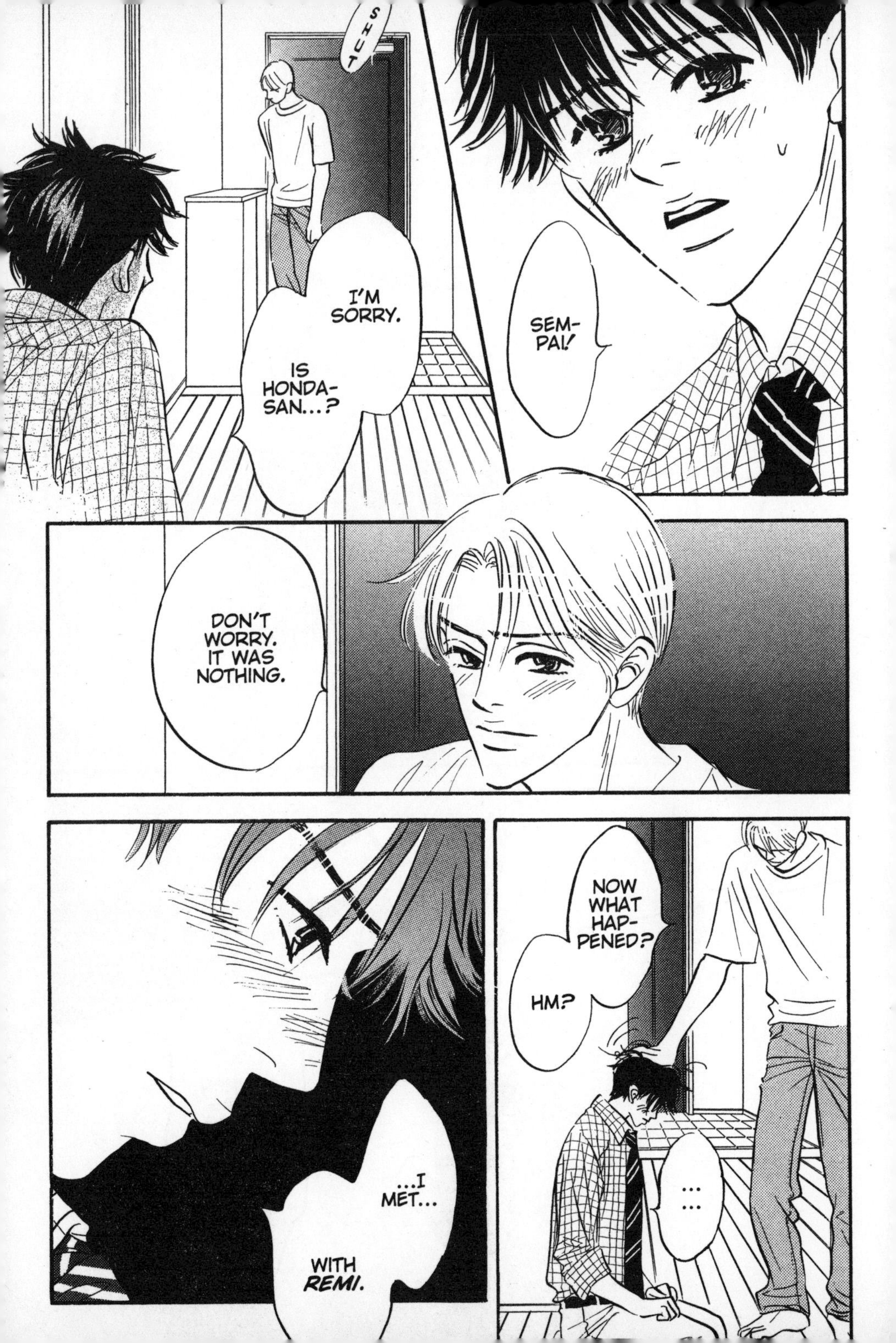
SEM-PAI!
SHUT
I'M SORRY.
IS HONDA-SAN...?
DON'T WORRY. IT WAS NOTHING.
NOW WHAT HAP-PENED?
HM?
... ...
...I MET...
WITH *REMI*.

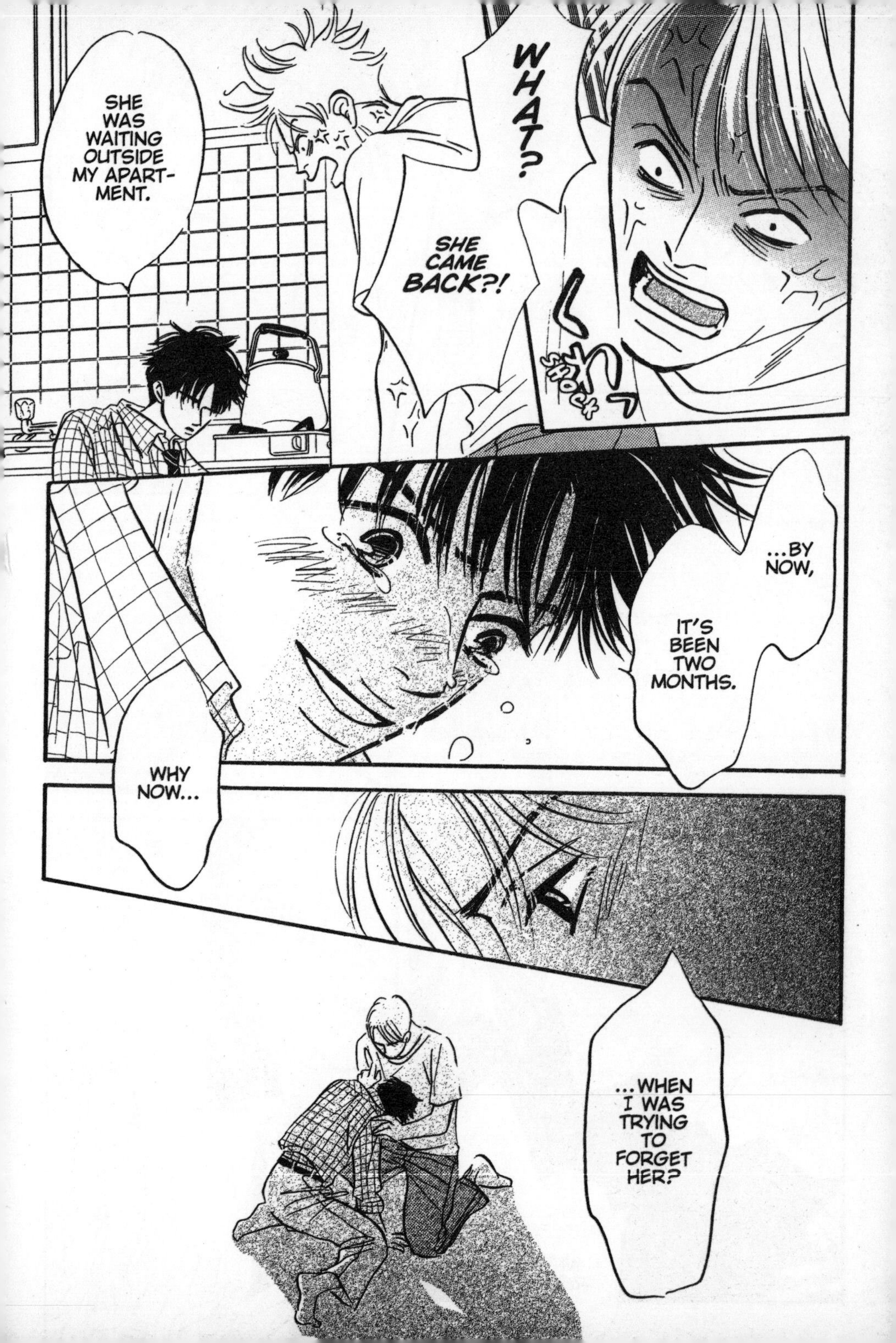
WHAT?
SHE CAME BACK?!
SHOCK
SHE WAS WAITING OUTSIDE MY APART-MENT.
...BY NOW,
IT'S BEEN TWO MONTHS.
WHY NOW...
...WHEN I WAS TRYING TO FORGET HER?

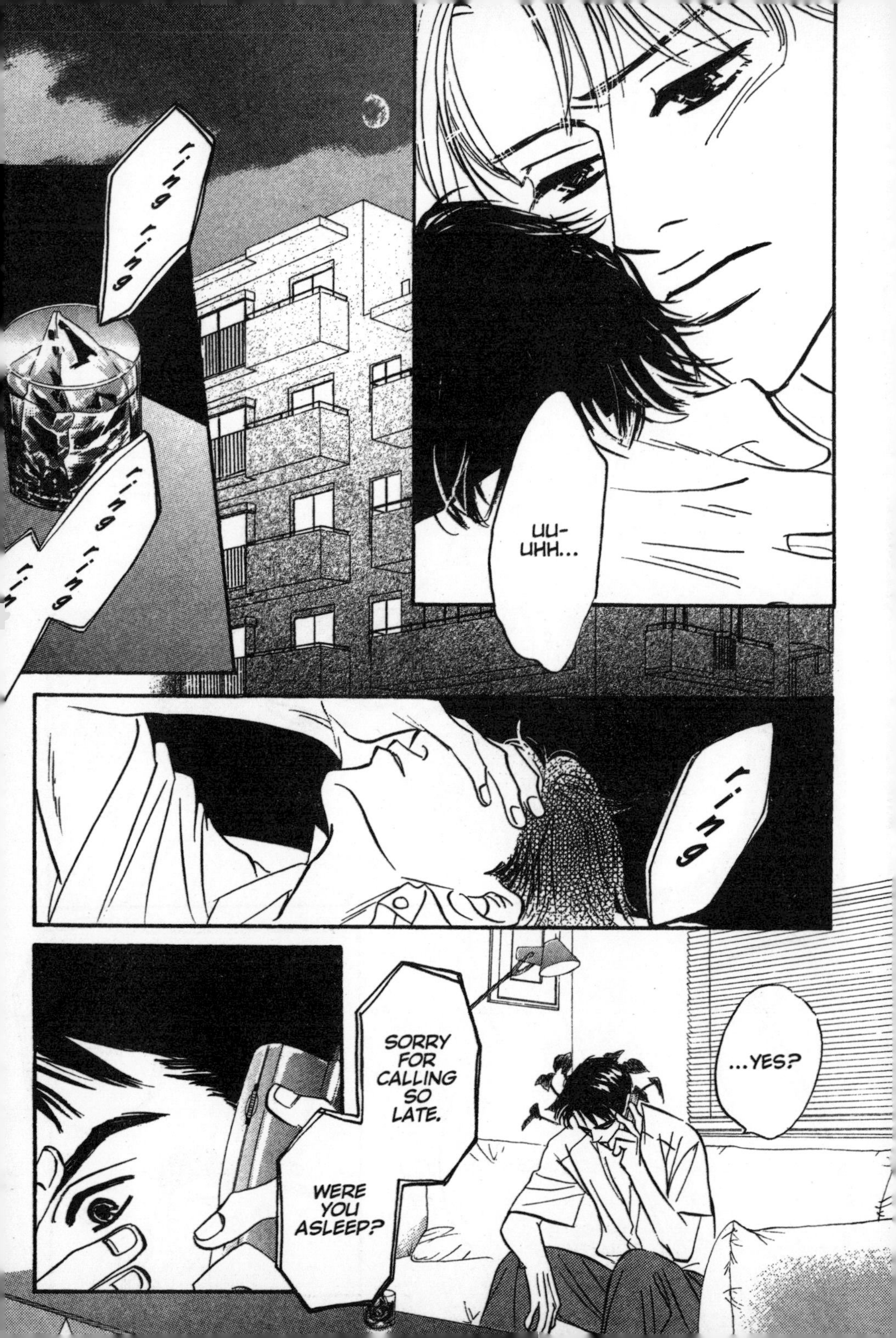

UU-UHH...
ring ring
ring ring
ring
...YES?
SORRY FOR CALLING SO LATE.
WERE YOU ASLEEP?

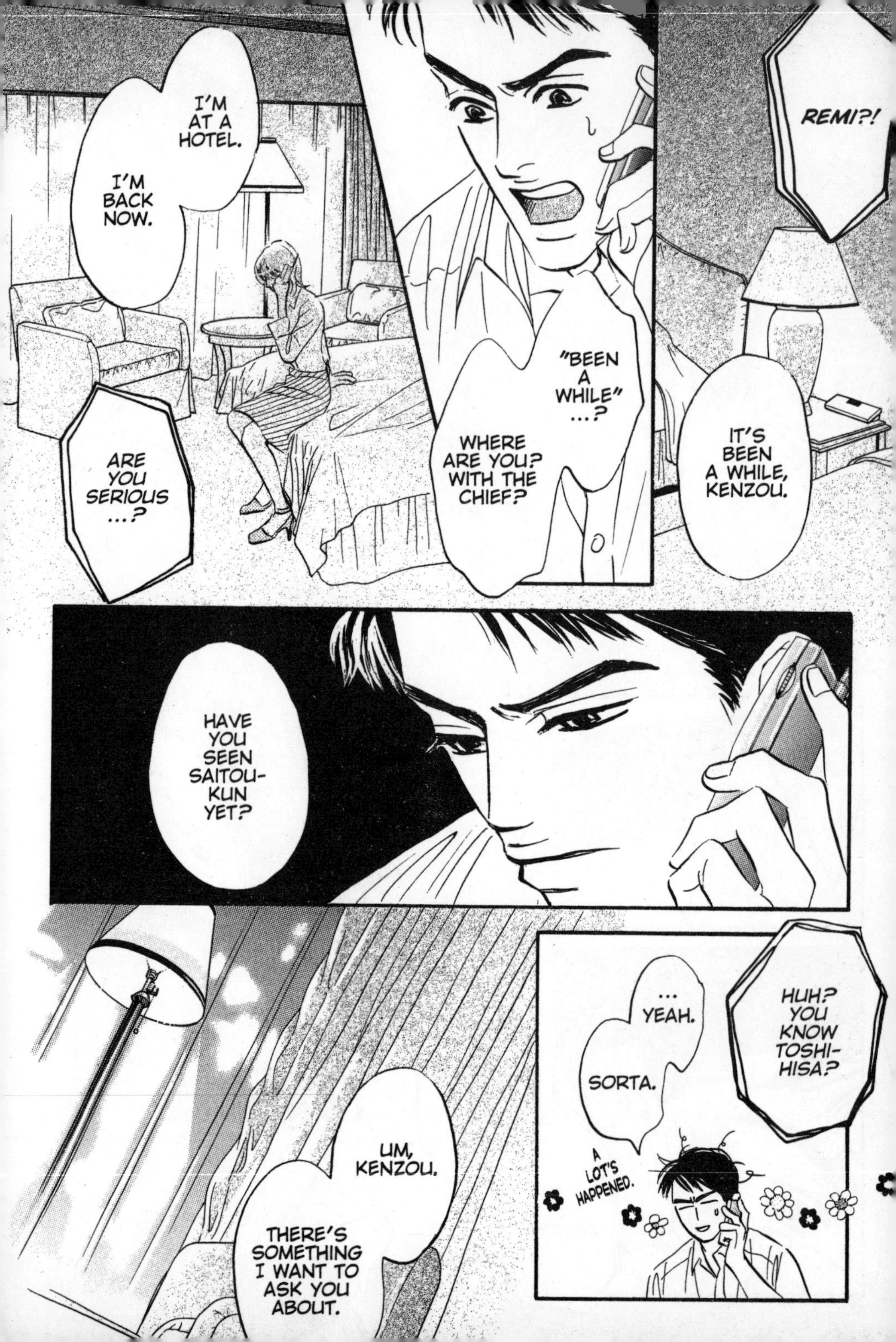
REMI?!
IT'S BEEN A WHILE, KENZOU.
"BEEN A WHILE"...?
WHERE ARE YOU? WITH THE CHIEF?
I'M AT A HOTEL.
I'M BACK NOW.
ARE YOU SERIOUS...?
HAVE YOU SEEN SAITOU-KUN YET?
HUH? YOU KNOW TOSHI-HISA?
...YEAH.
SORTA.
A LOT'S HAPPENED.
UM, KENZOU.
THERE'S SOMETHING I WANT TO ASK YOU ABOUT.

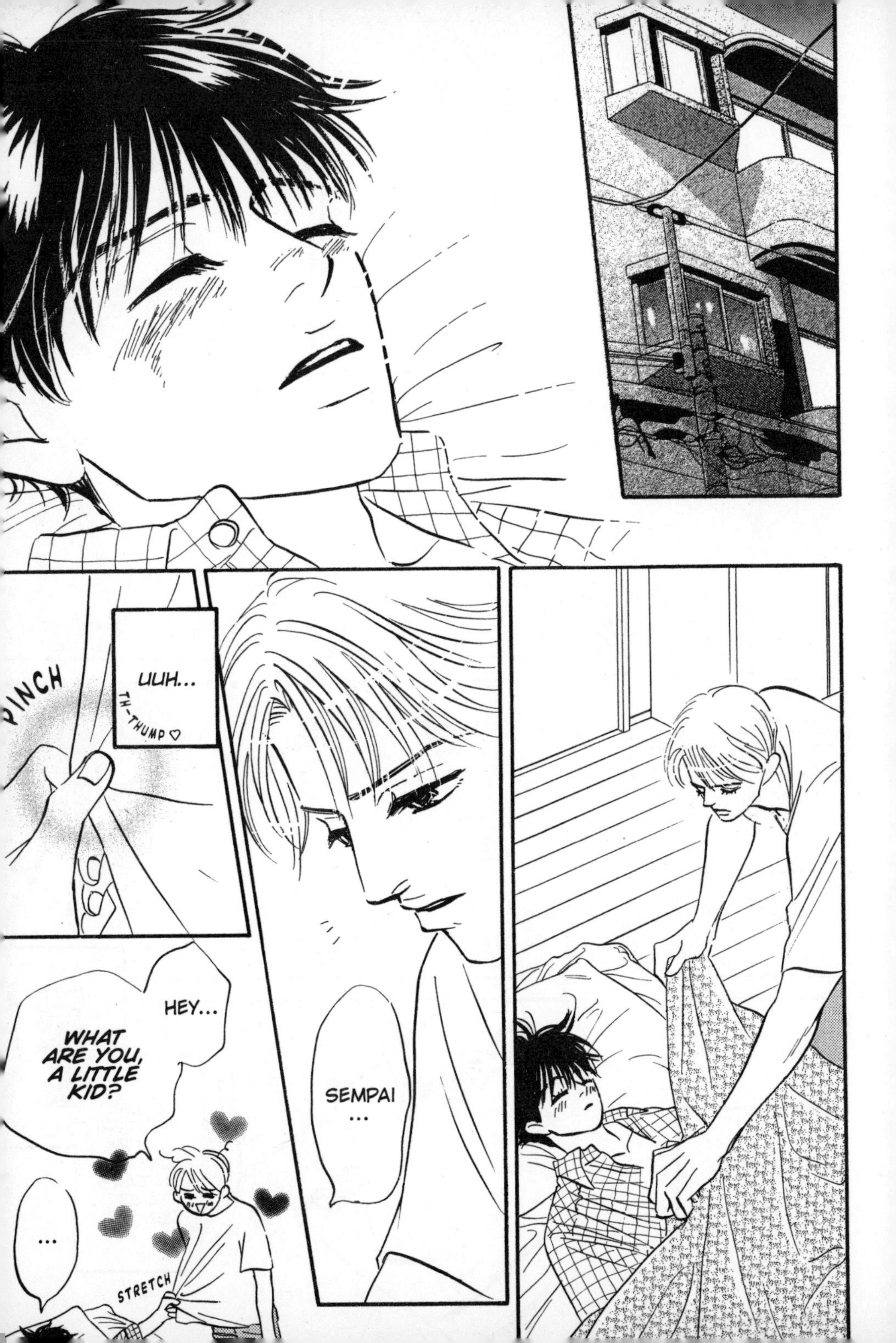
SEMPAI ...
UUH...
TH-THUMP ♡
PINCH
HEY...
WHAT ARE YOU, A LITTLE KID?
...
STRETCH

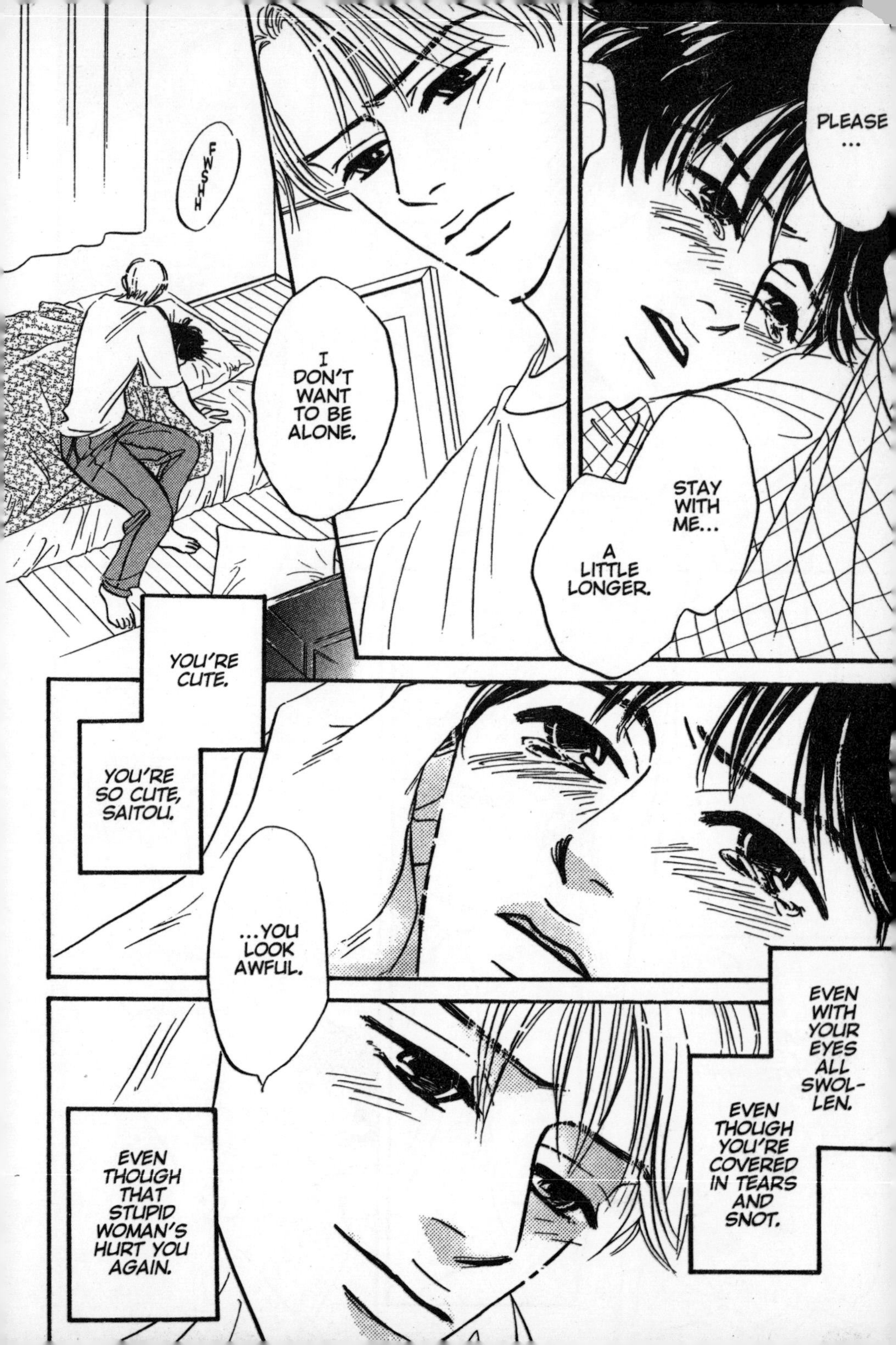

PLEASE ...
STAY WITH ME... A LITTLE LONGER.
I DON'T WANT TO BE ALONE.
FWSHH
...YOU LOOK AWFUL.
YOU'RE CUTE.
YOU'RE SO CUTE, SAITOU.
EVEN WITH YOUR EYES ALL SWOL-LEN.
EVEN THOUGH YOU'RE COVERED IN TEARS AND SNOT.
EVEN THOUGH THAT STUPID WOMAN'S HURT YOU AGAIN.

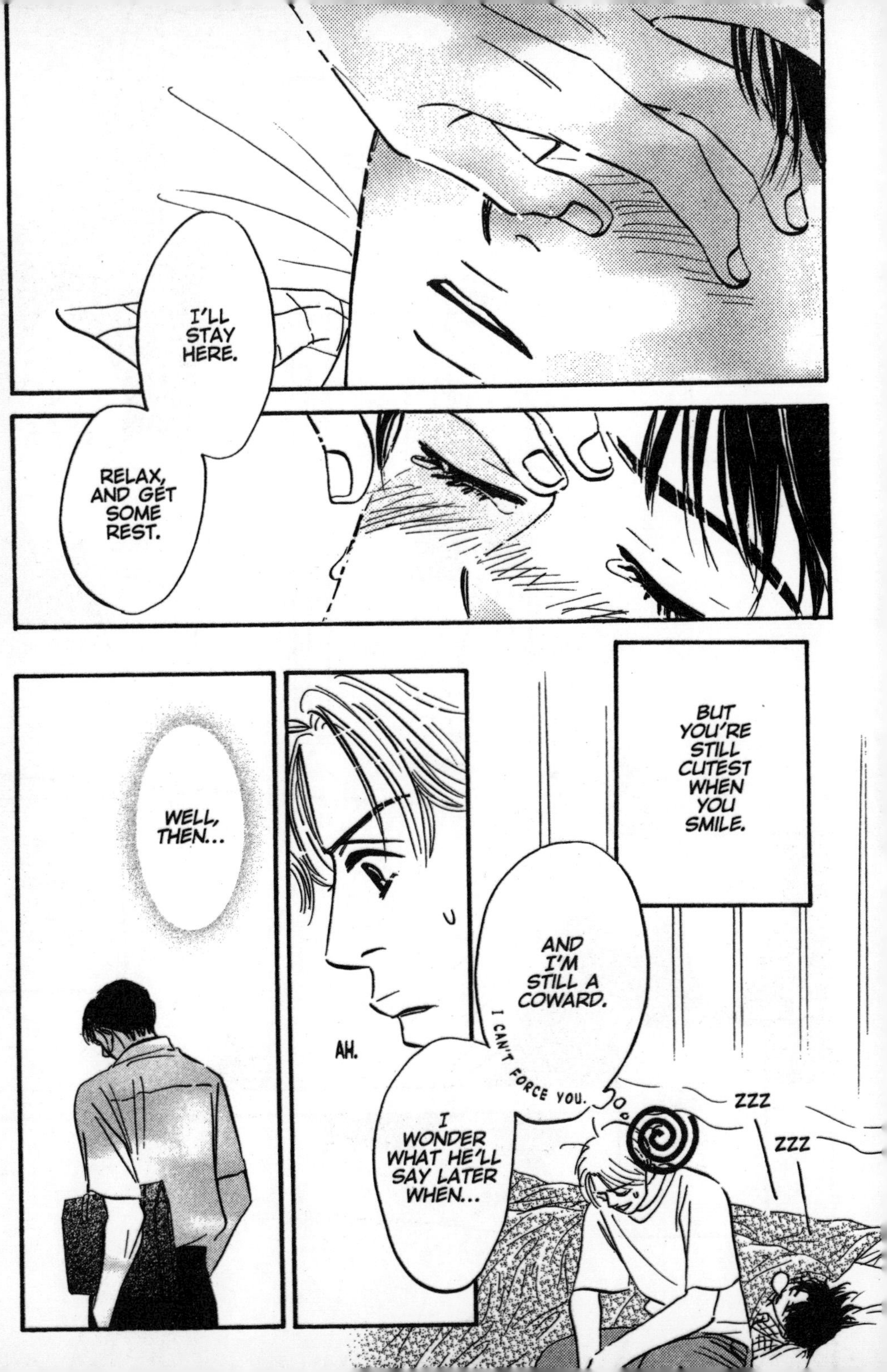
I'LL STAY HERE.
RELAX, AND GET SOME REST.
BUT YOU'RE STILL CUTEST WHEN YOU SMILE.
AND I'M STILL A COWARD.
I CAN'T FORCE YOU.
ZZZ
ZZZ
AH.
I WONDER WHAT HE'LL SAY LATER WHEN...
WELL, THEN...

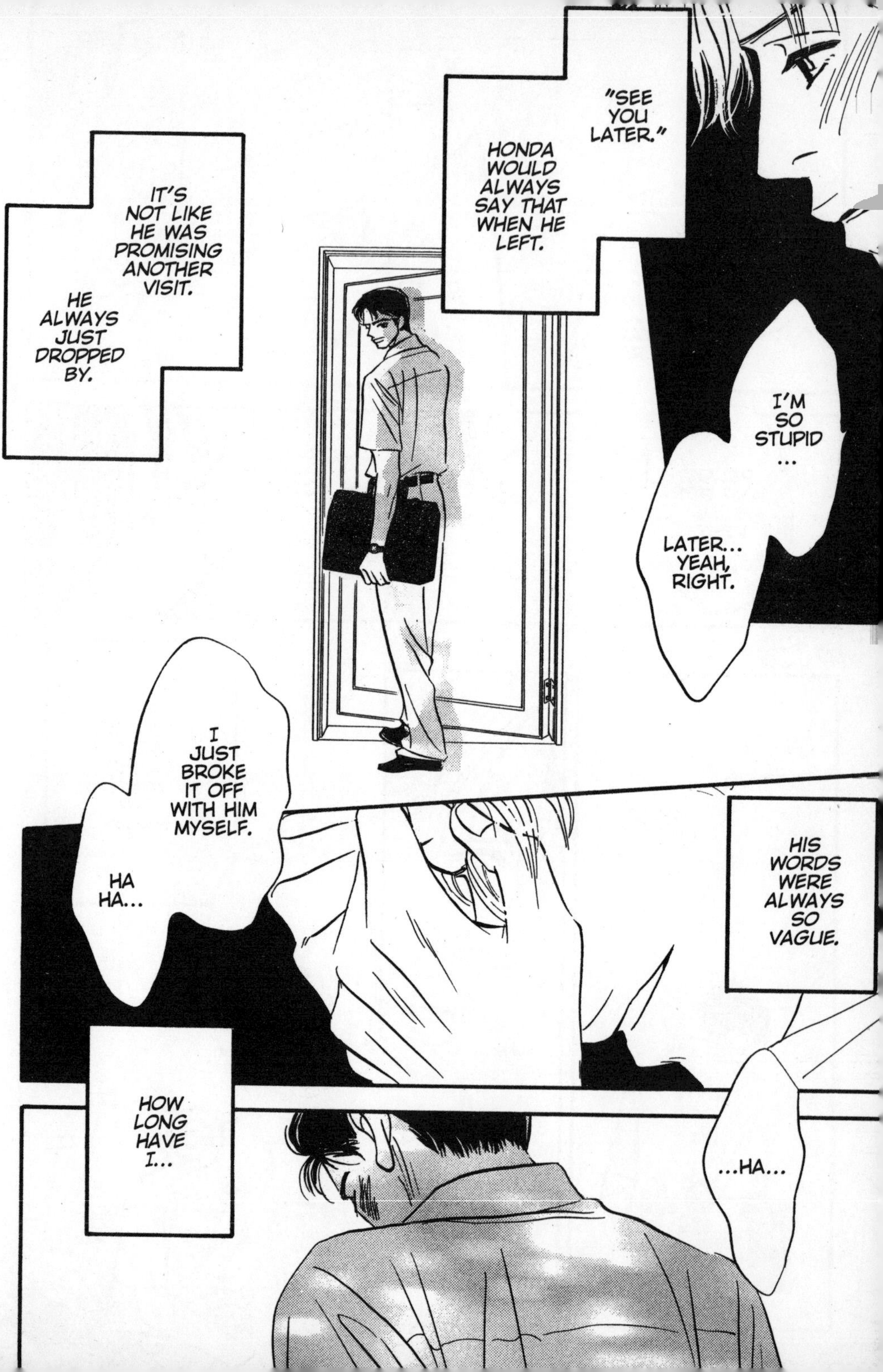
"SEE YOU LATER."
HONDA WOULD ALWAYS SAY THAT WHEN HE LEFT.
IT'S NOT LIKE HE WAS PROMISING ANOTHER VISIT.
HE ALWAYS JUST DROPPED BY.
I'M SO STUPID...
LATER... YEAH, RIGHT.
I JUST BROKE IT OFF WITH HIM MYSELF.
HA HA...
HIS WORDS WERE ALWAYS SO VAGUE.
...HA...
HOW LONG HAVE I...

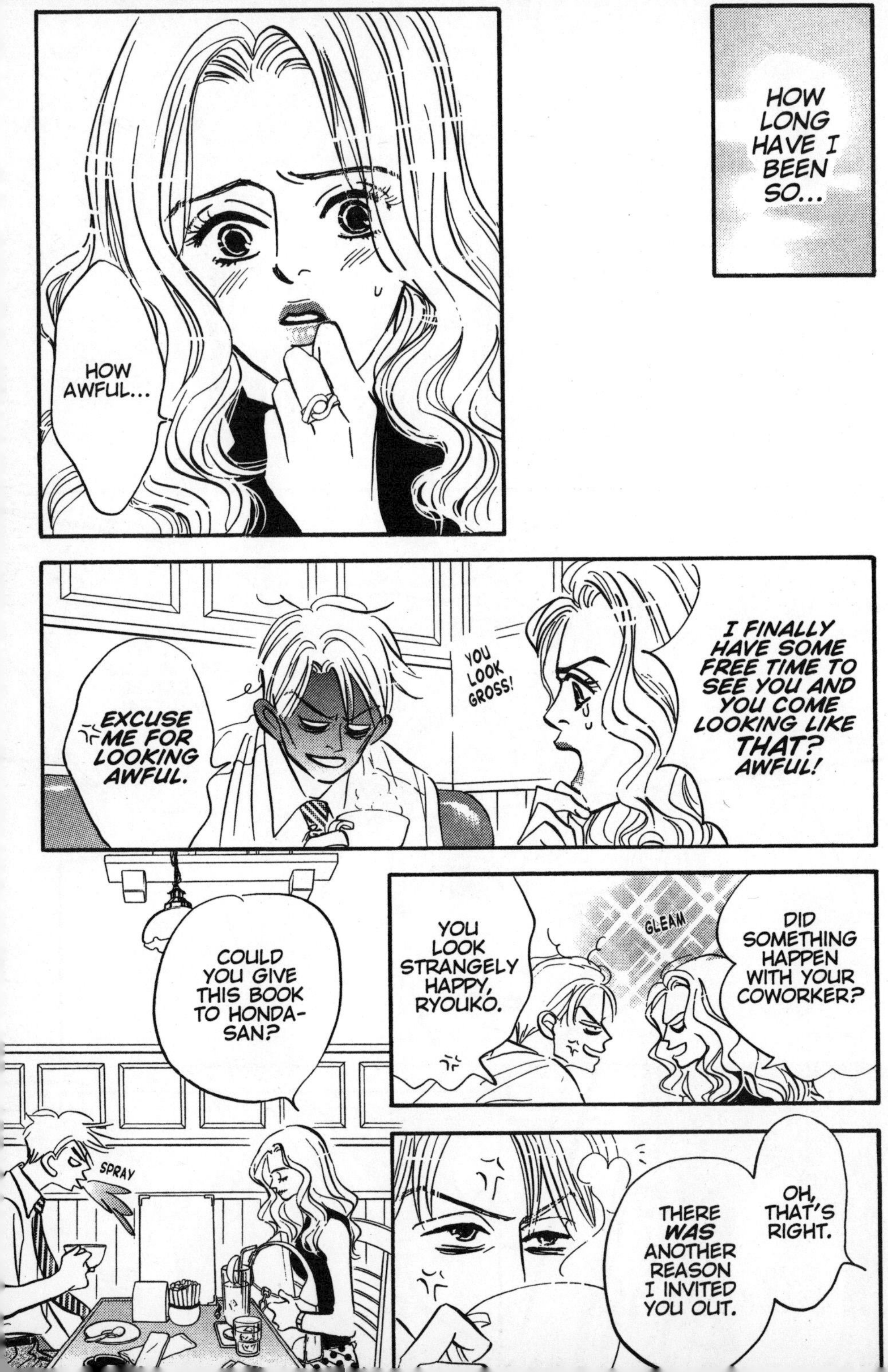
HOW LONG HAVE I BEEN SO...
HOW AWFUL...
I FINALLY HAVE SOME FREE TIME TO SEE YOU AND YOU COME LOOKING LIKE THAT? AWFUL!
YOU LOOK GROSS!
EXCUSE ME FOR LOOKING AWFUL.
DID SOMETHING HAPPEN WITH YOUR COWORKER?
GLEAM
YOU LOOK STRANGELY HAPPY, RYOUKO.
OH, THAT'S RIGHT.
THERE WAS ANOTHER REASON I INVITED YOU OUT.
COULD YOU GIVE THIS BOOK TO HONDA-SAN?
SPRAY

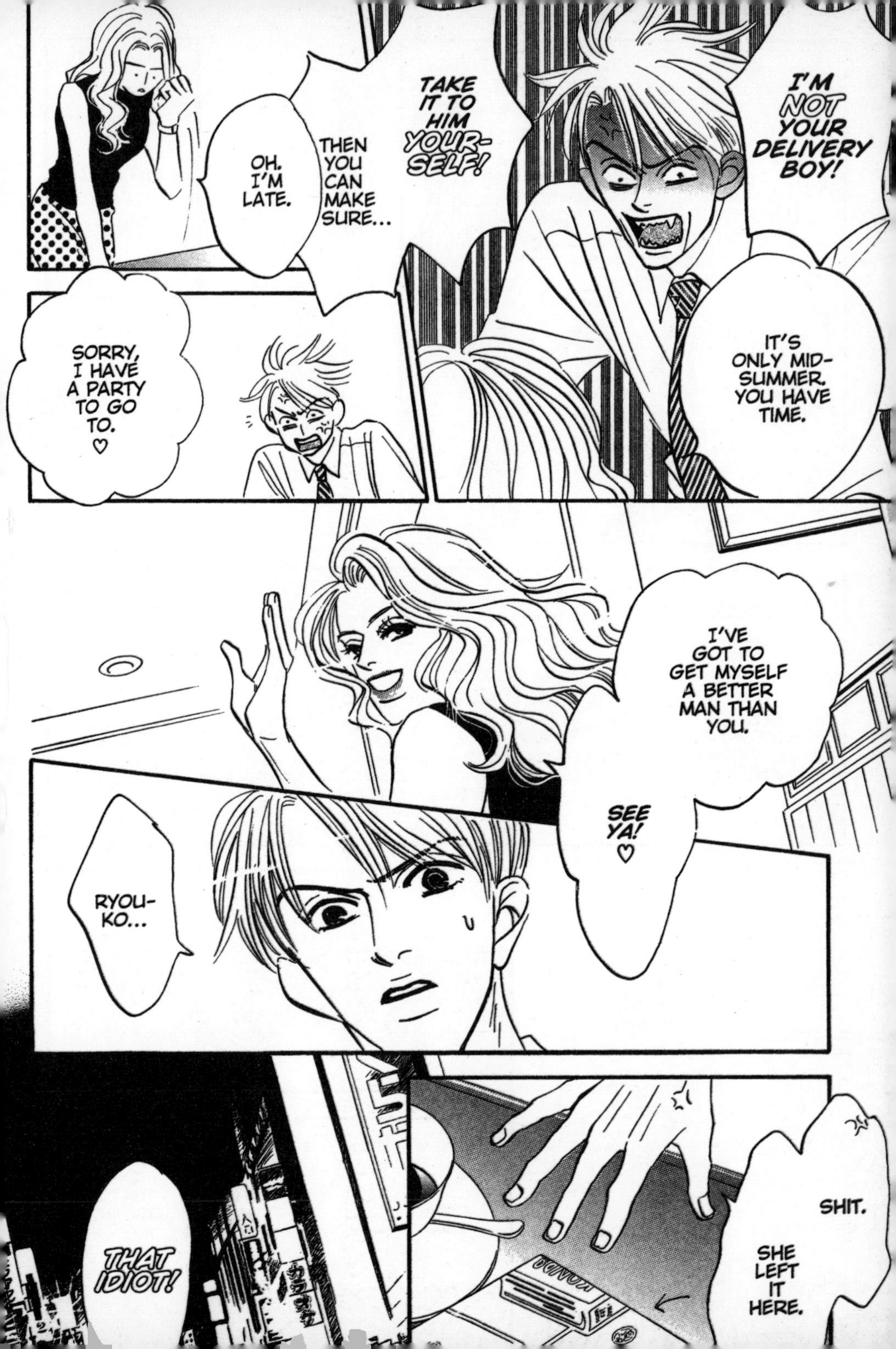
IT'S ONLY MID-SUMMER. YOU HAVE TIME.
THEN YOU CAN MAKE SURE...
OH. I'M LATE.
SORRY, I HAVE A PARTY TO GO TO. ♡
I'M NOT YOUR DELIVERY BOY!
TAKE IT TO HIM YOURSELF!
I'VE GOT TO GET MYSELF A BETTER MAN THAN YOU.
SEE YA! ♡
RYOU-KO...
SHIT.
SHE LEFT IT HERE.
THAT IDIOT!

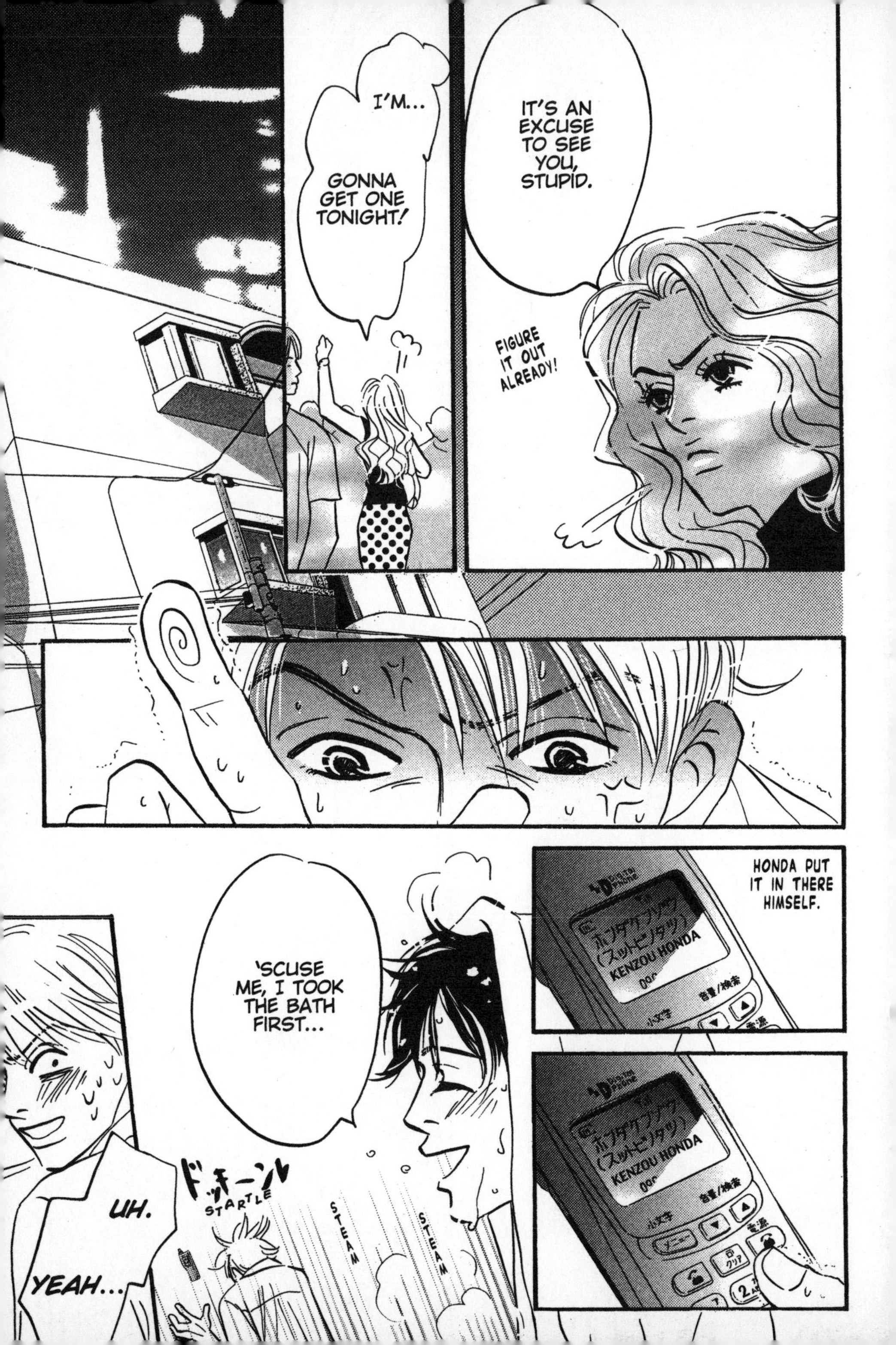

IT'S AN EXCUSE TO SEE YOU, STUPID.
FIGURE IT OUT ALREADY!
I'M...
GONNA GET ONE TONIGHT!
HONDA PUT IT IN THERE HIMSELF.
KENZOU HONDA
KENZOU HONDA
'SCUSE ME, I TOOK THE BATH FIRST...
ドッキーン
STARTLE
STEAM
STEAM
UH.
YEAH...

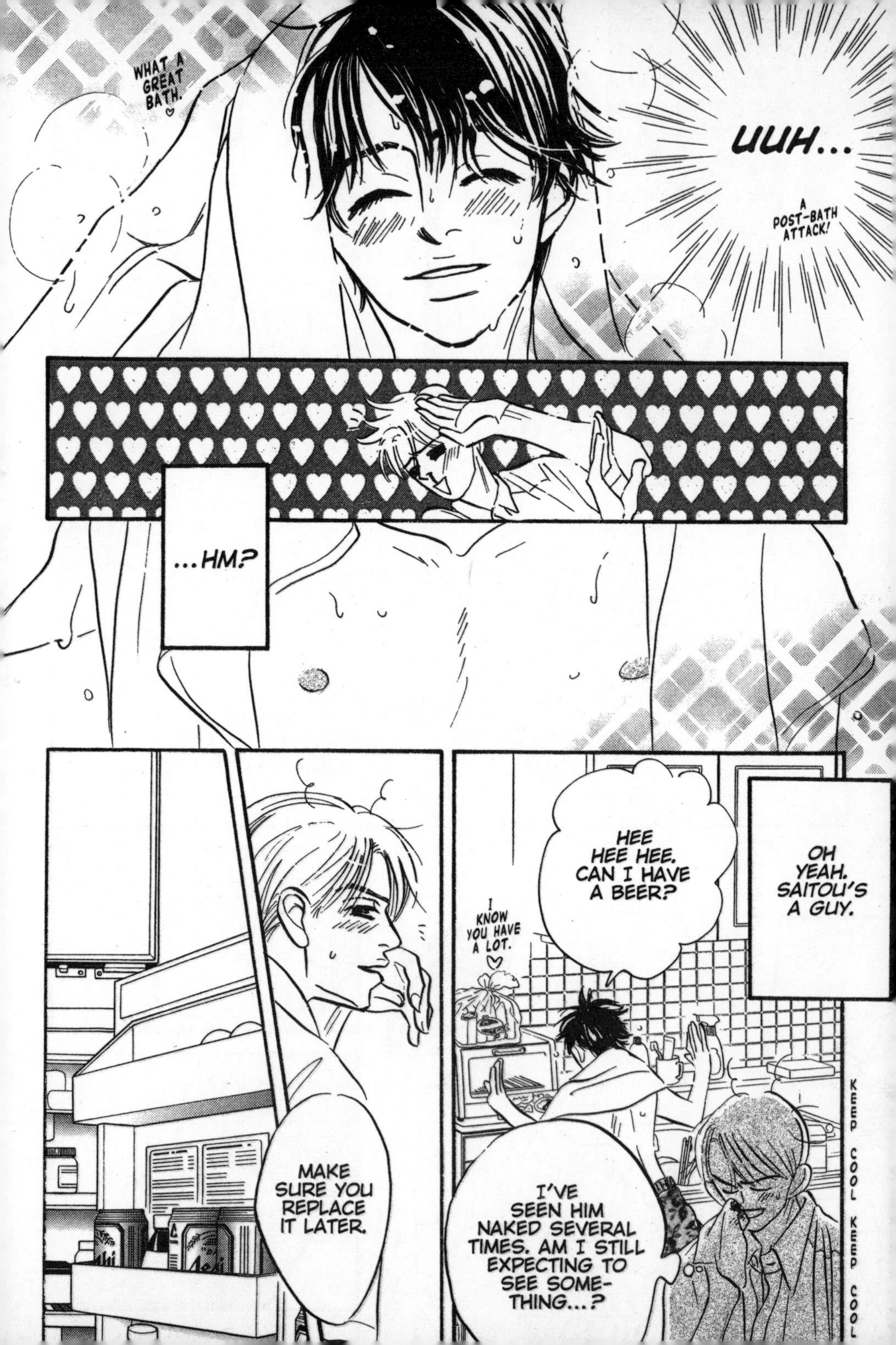
UUH...
A POST-BATH ATTACK!
WHAT A GREAT BATH. ♡
...HM?
OH YEAH. SAITOU'S A GUY.
HEE HEE HEE. CAN I HAVE A BEER?
I KNOW YOU HAVE A LOT. ♡
I'VE SEEN HIM NAKED SEVERAL TIMES. AM I STILL EXPECTING TO SEE SOME-THING...?
KEEP COOL KEEP COOL KEEP COOL
MAKE SURE YOU REPLACE IT LATER.

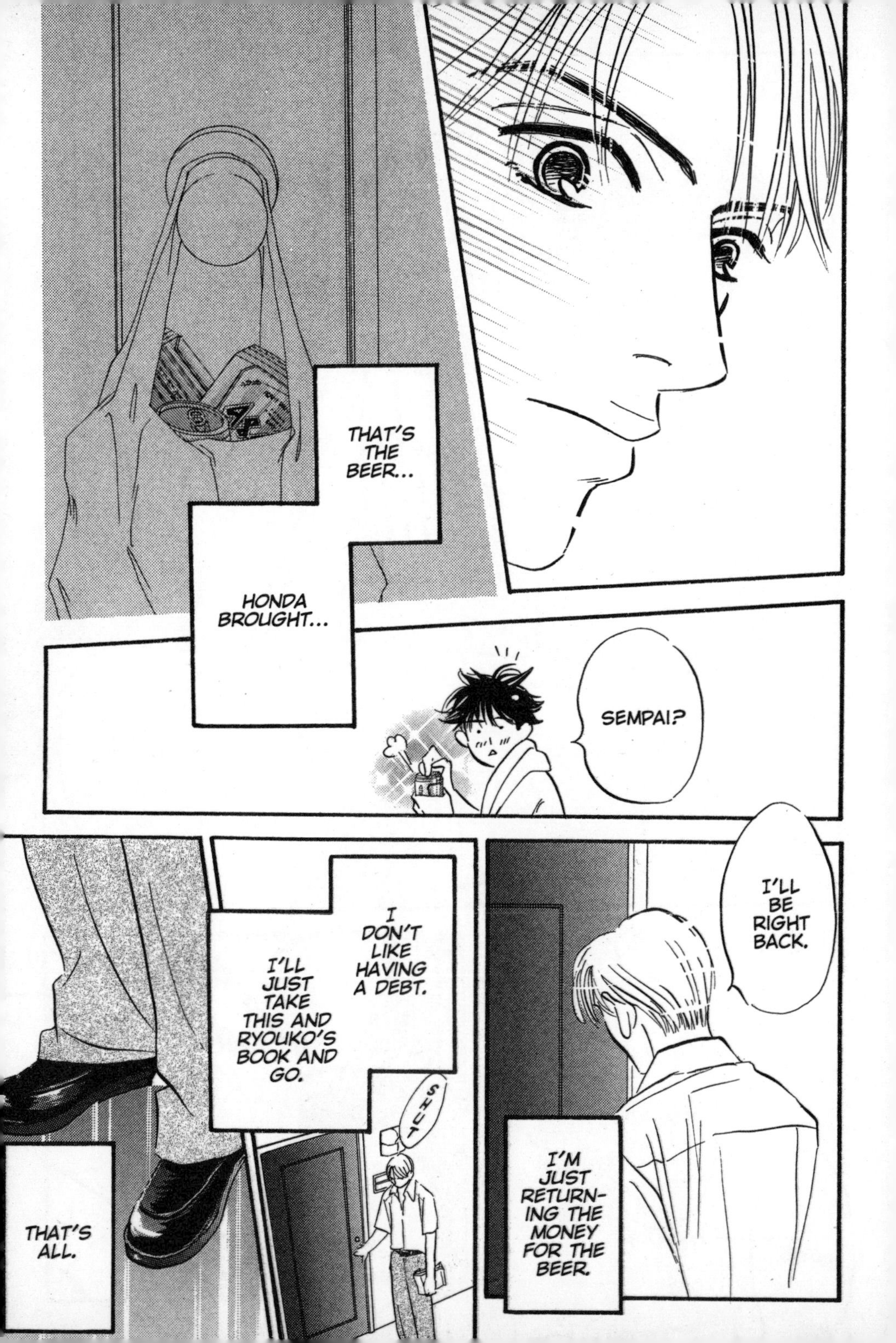
THAT'S THE BEER...
HONDA BROUGHT...
SEMPAI?
I'LL BE RIGHT BACK.
I'M JUST RETURNING THE MONEY FOR THE BEER.
I DON'T LIKE HAVING A DEBT.
I'LL JUST TAKE THIS AND RYOUKO'S BOOK AND GO.
SHUT
THAT'S ALL.

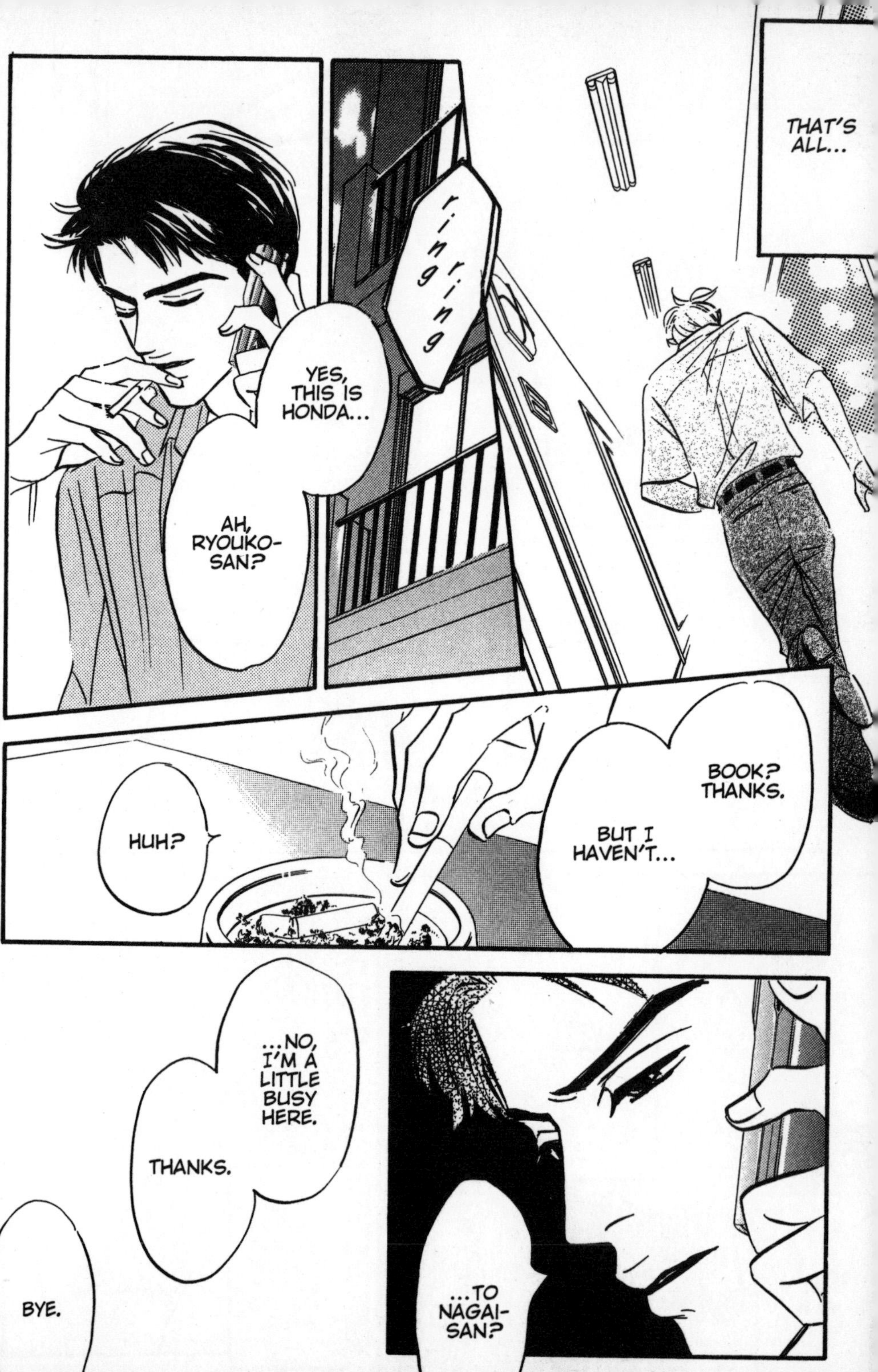
THAT'S ALL...
ringing ringing
YES, THIS IS HONDA...
AH, RYOUKO-SAN?
BOOK? THANKS.
BUT I HAVEN'T...
HUH?
...TO NAGAI-SAN?
...NO, I'M A LITTLE BUSY HERE.
THANKS.
BYE.

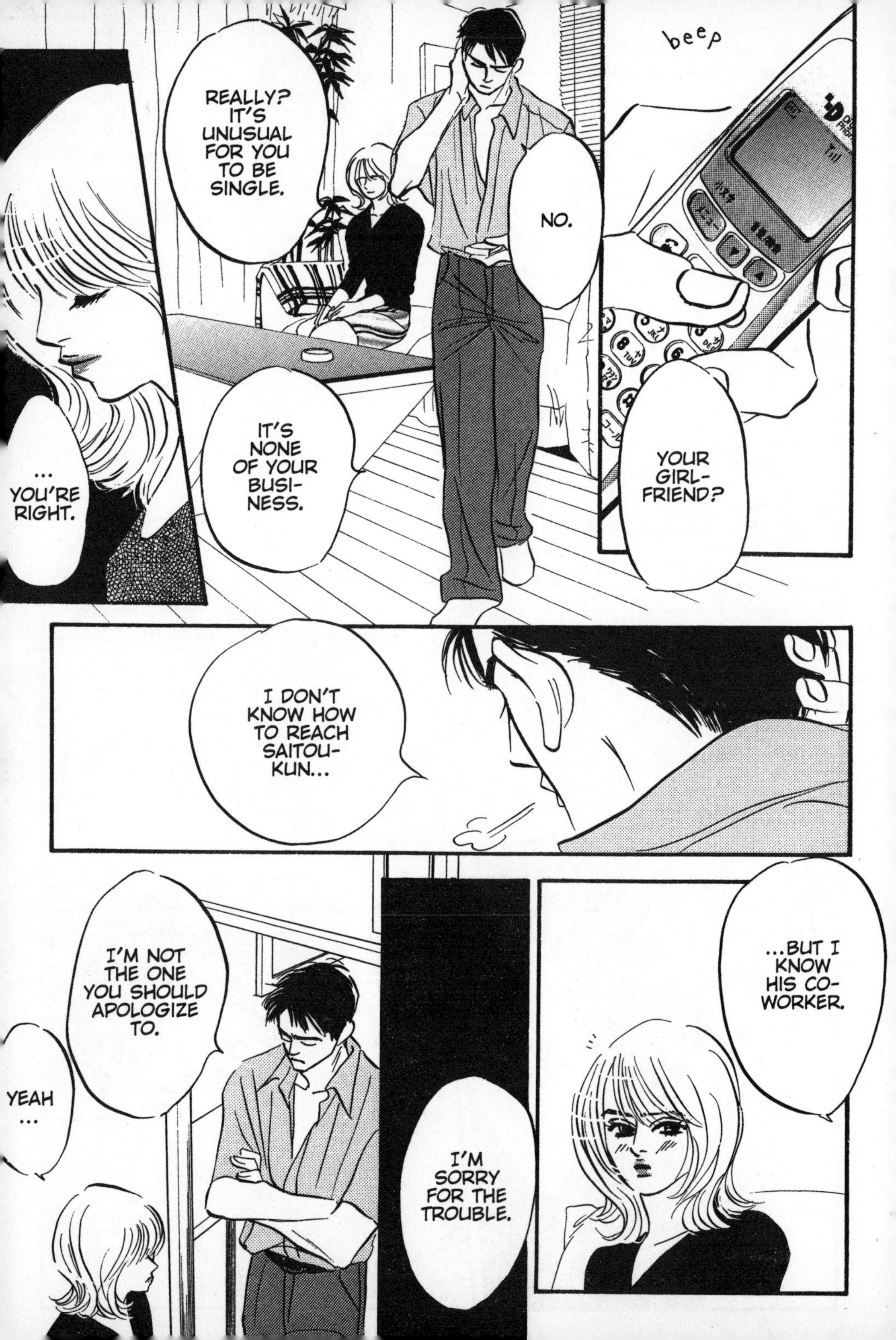
beep
YOUR GIRL-FRIEND?
NO.
REALLY? IT'S UNUSUAL FOR YOU TO BE SINGLE.
IT'S NONE OF YOUR BUSI-NESS.
... YOU'RE RIGHT.
I DON'T KNOW HOW TO REACH SAITOU-KUN...
...BUT I KNOW HIS CO-WORKER.
I'M SORRY FOR THE TROUBLE.
I'M NOT THE ONE YOU SHOULD APOLOGIZE TO.
YEAH ...

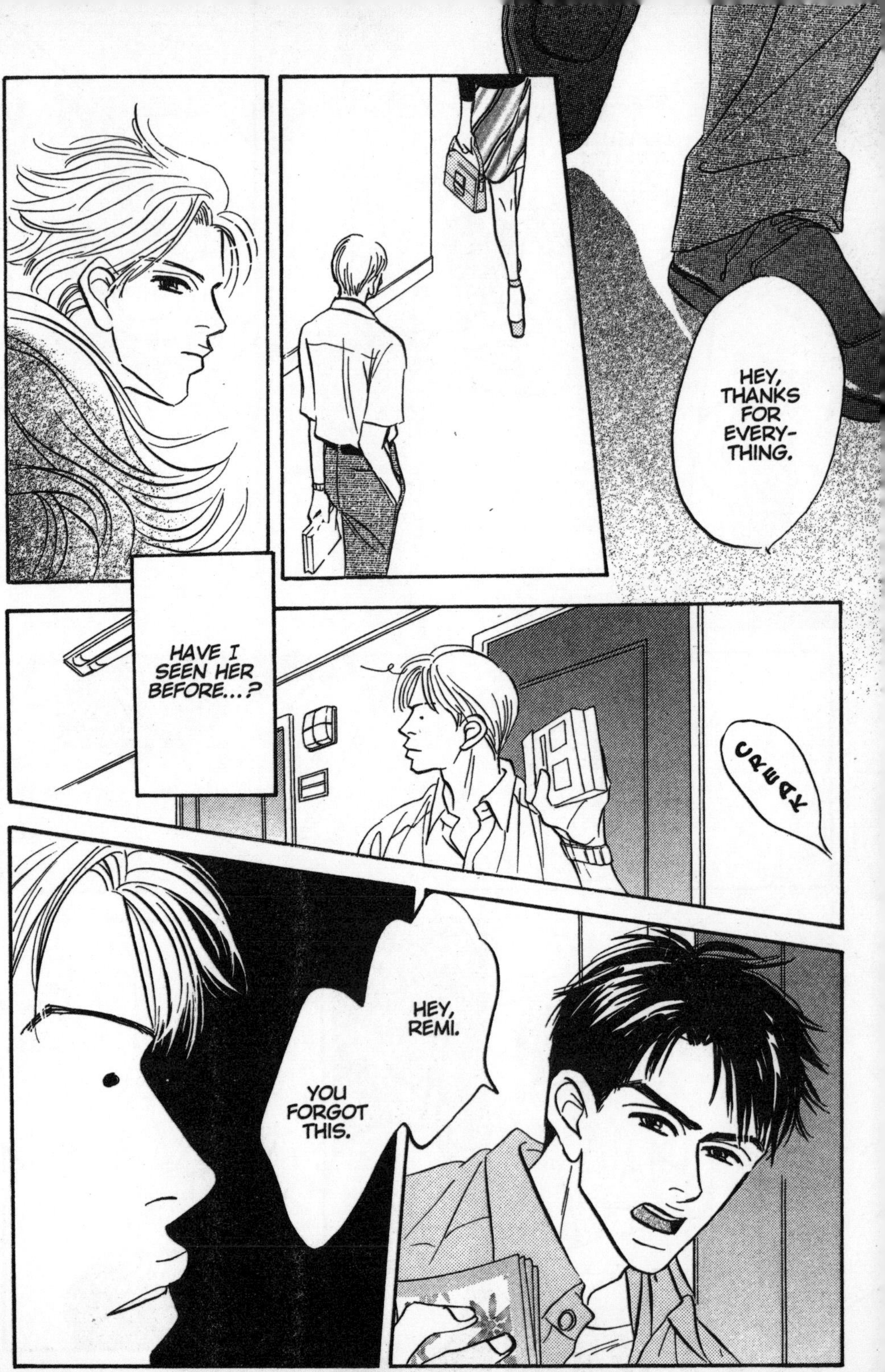
HEY, THANKS FOR EVERYTHING.
HAVE I SEEN HER BEFORE...?
CREAK
HEY, REMI.
YOU FORGOT THIS.

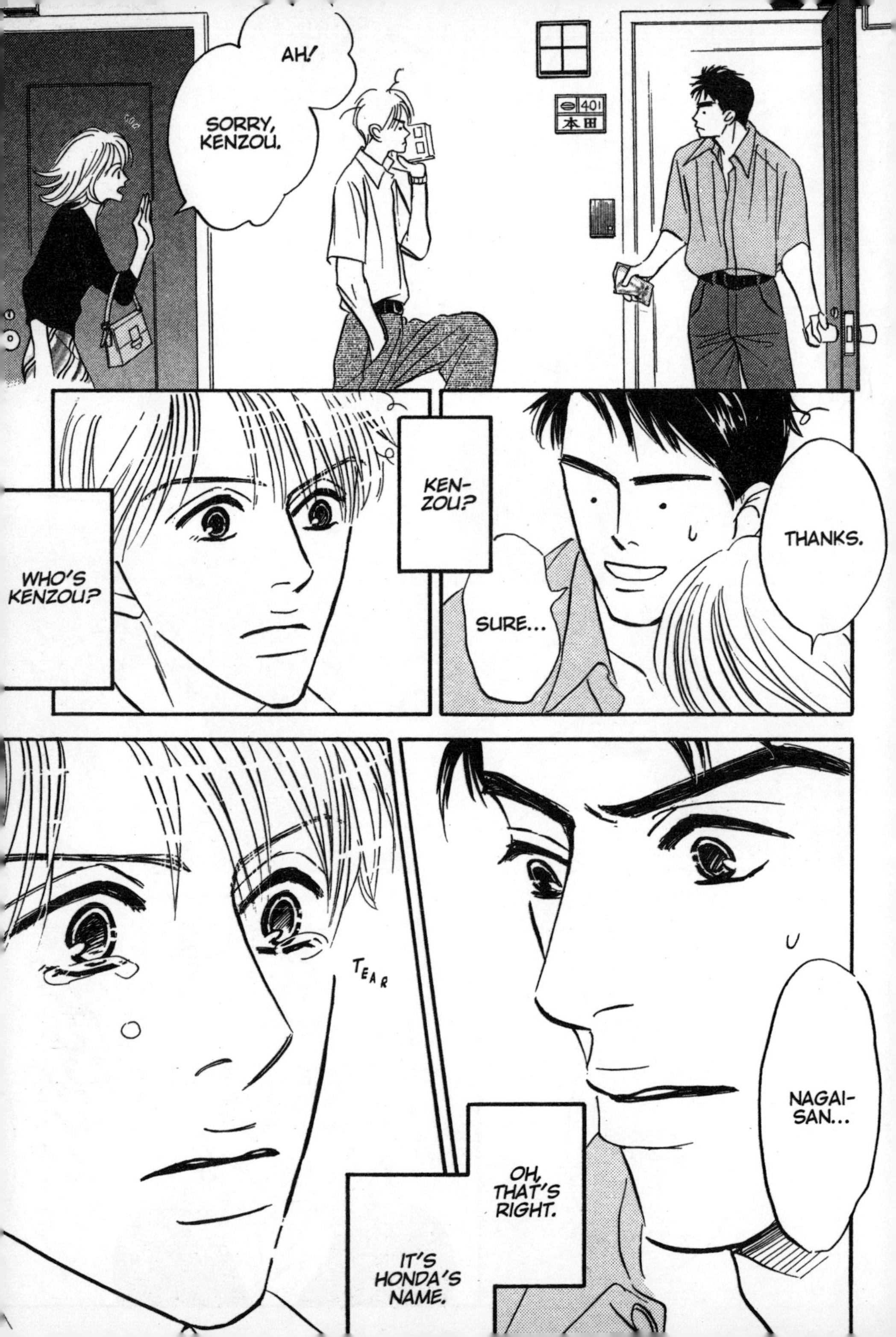
401
本田
AH!
SORRY, KENZOU.
THANKS.
SURE...
KEN-ZOU?
WHO'S KENZOU?
NAGAI-SAN...
OH, THAT'S RIGHT.
IT'S HONDA'S NAME.
TEAR

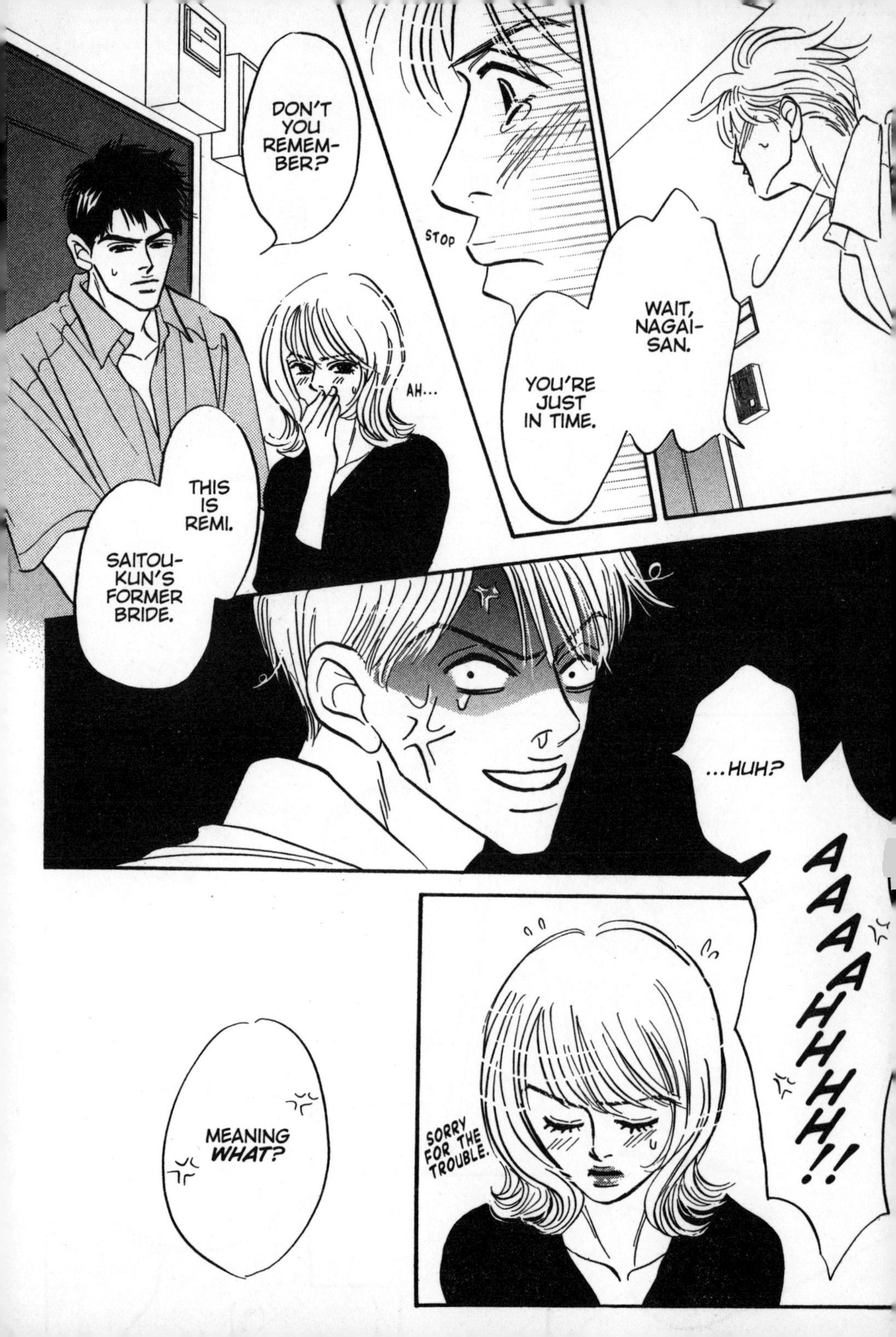
STOP
WAIT, NAGAI-SAN.
YOU'RE JUST IN TIME.
DON'T YOU REMEMBER?
AH...
THIS IS REMI.
SAITOU-KUN'S FORMER BRIDE.
...HUH?
AAAAHHHH!!
SORRY FOR THE TROUBLE.
MEANING *WHAT*?

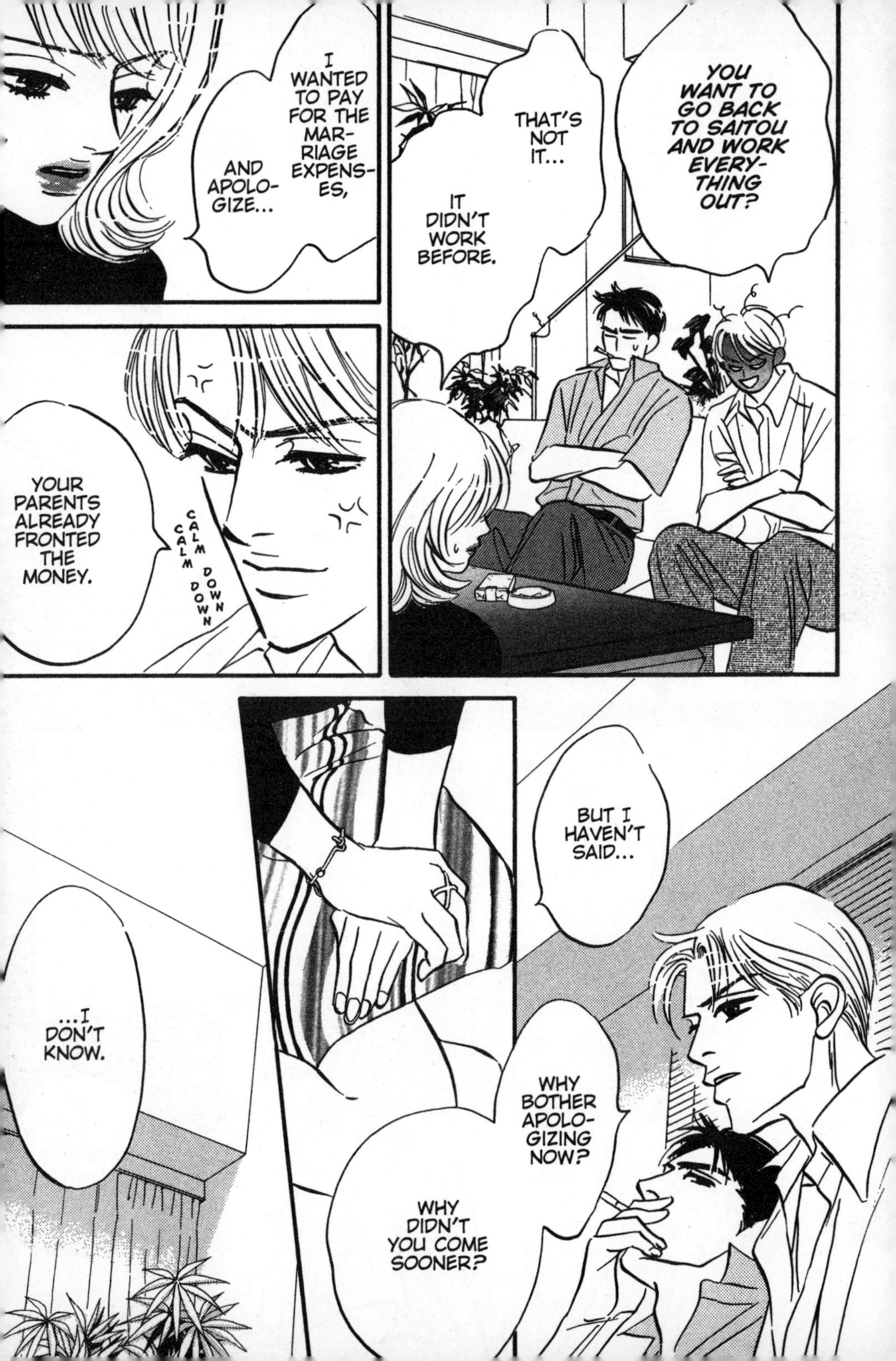
YOU WANT TO GO BACK TO SAITOU AND WORK EVERYTHING OUT?
THAT'S NOT IT...
IT DIDN'T WORK BEFORE.
I WANTED TO PAY FOR THE MARRIAGE EXPENSES,
AND APOLOGIZE...
YOUR PARENTS ALREADY FRONTED THE MONEY.
CALM DOWN CALM DOWN
BUT I HAVEN'T SAID...
WHY BOTHER APOLOGIZING NOW?
WHY DIDN'T YOU COME SOONER?
...I DON'T KNOW.

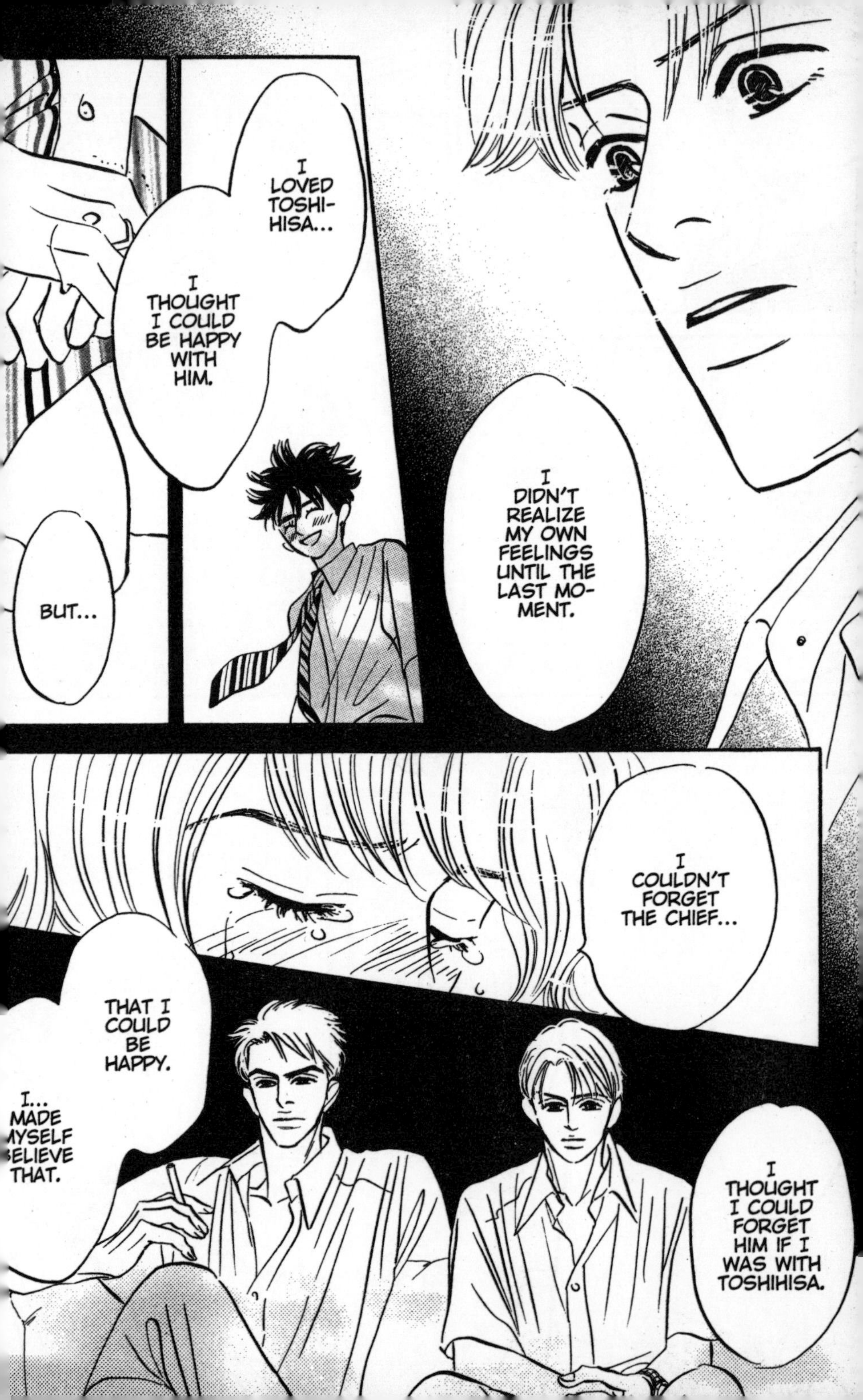
I DIDN'T REALIZE MY OWN FEELINGS UNTIL THE LAST MOMENT.
I LOVED TOSHIHISA...
I THOUGHT I COULD BE HAPPY WITH HIM.
BUT...
I COULDN'T FORGET THE CHIEF...
I THOUGHT I COULD FORGET HIM IF I WAS WITH TOSHIHISA.
THAT I COULD BE HAPPY.
I... MADE MYSELF BELIEVE THAT.

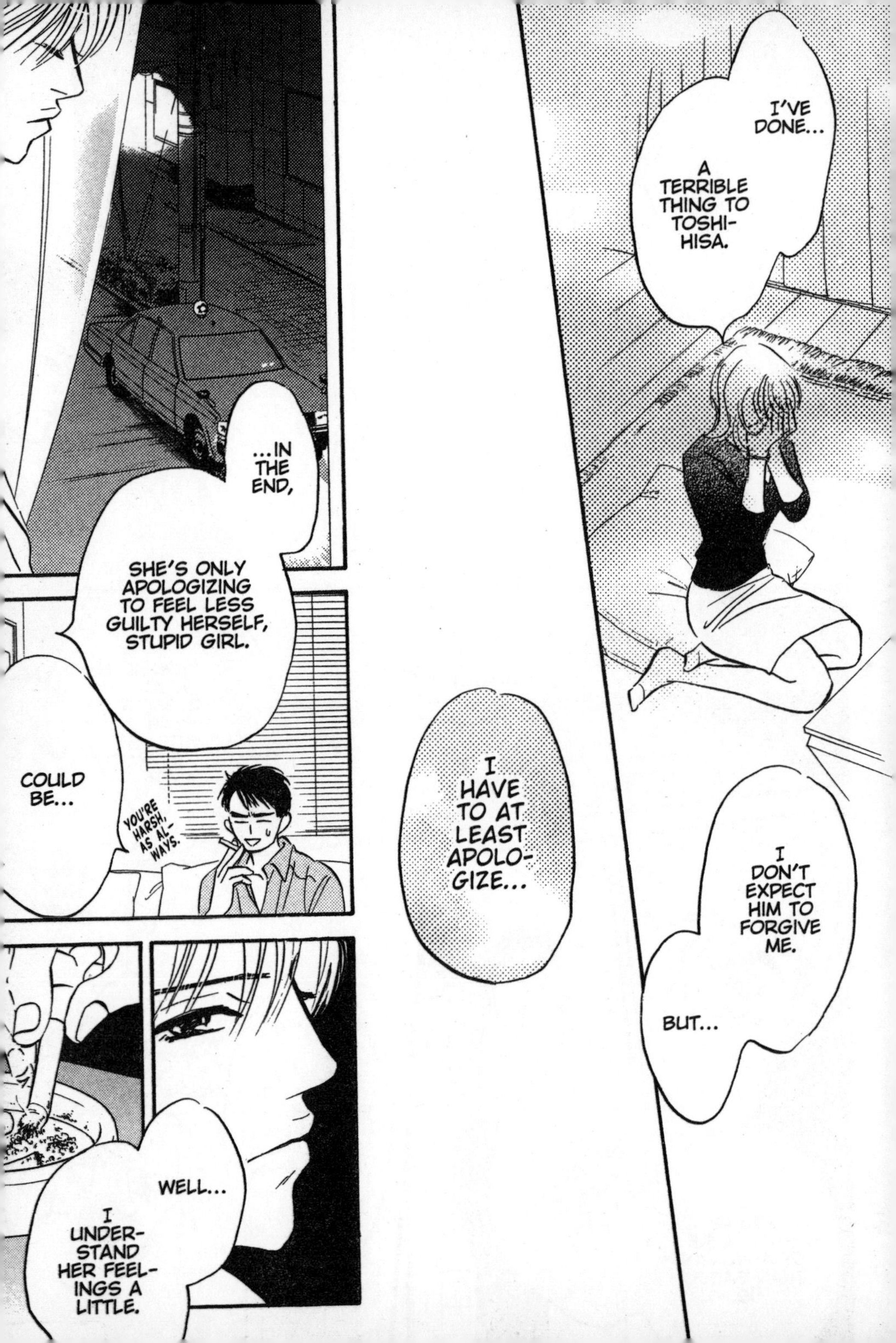
I'VE DONE...
A TERRIBLE THING TO TOSHI-HISA.
I DON'T EXPECT HIM TO FORGIVE ME.
BUT...
I HAVE TO AT LEAST APOLOGIZE...
...IN THE END,
SHE'S ONLY APOLOGIZING TO FEEL LESS GUILTY HERSELF, STUPID GIRL.
YOU'RE HARSH, AS AL-WAYS.
COULD BE...
WELL...
I UNDER-STAND HER FEEL-INGS A LITTLE.

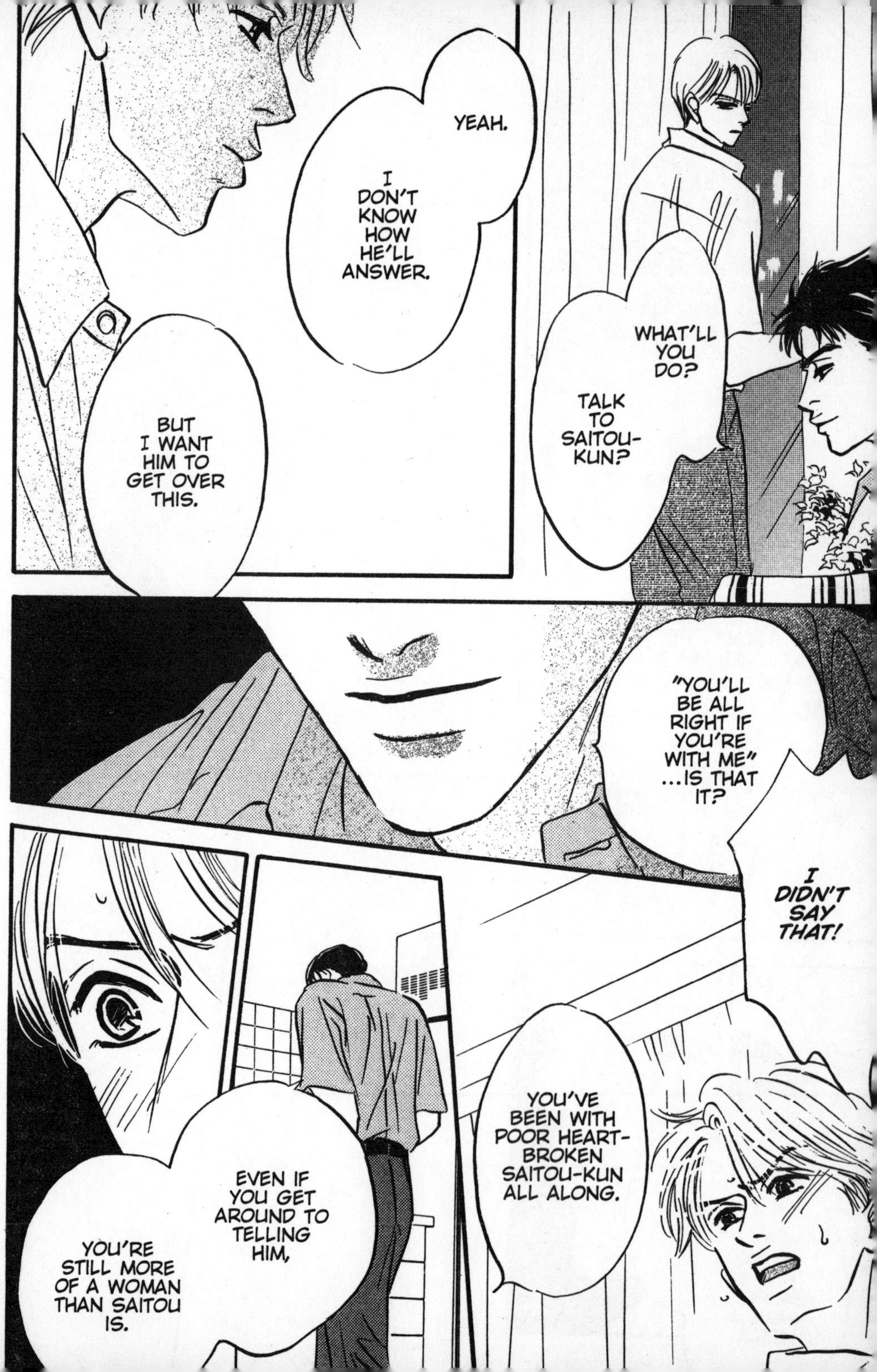
WHAT'LL YOU DO?
TALK TO SAITOU-KUN?
YEAH.
I DON'T KNOW HOW HE'LL ANSWER.
BUT I WANT HIM TO GET OVER THIS.
"YOU'LL BE ALL RIGHT IF YOU'RE WITH ME" ...IS THAT IT?
I DIDN'T SAY THAT!
YOU'VE BEEN WITH POOR HEART-BROKEN SAITOU-KUN ALL ALONG.
EVEN IF YOU GET AROUND TO TELLING HIM,
YOU'RE STILL MORE OF A WOMAN THAN SAITOU IS.

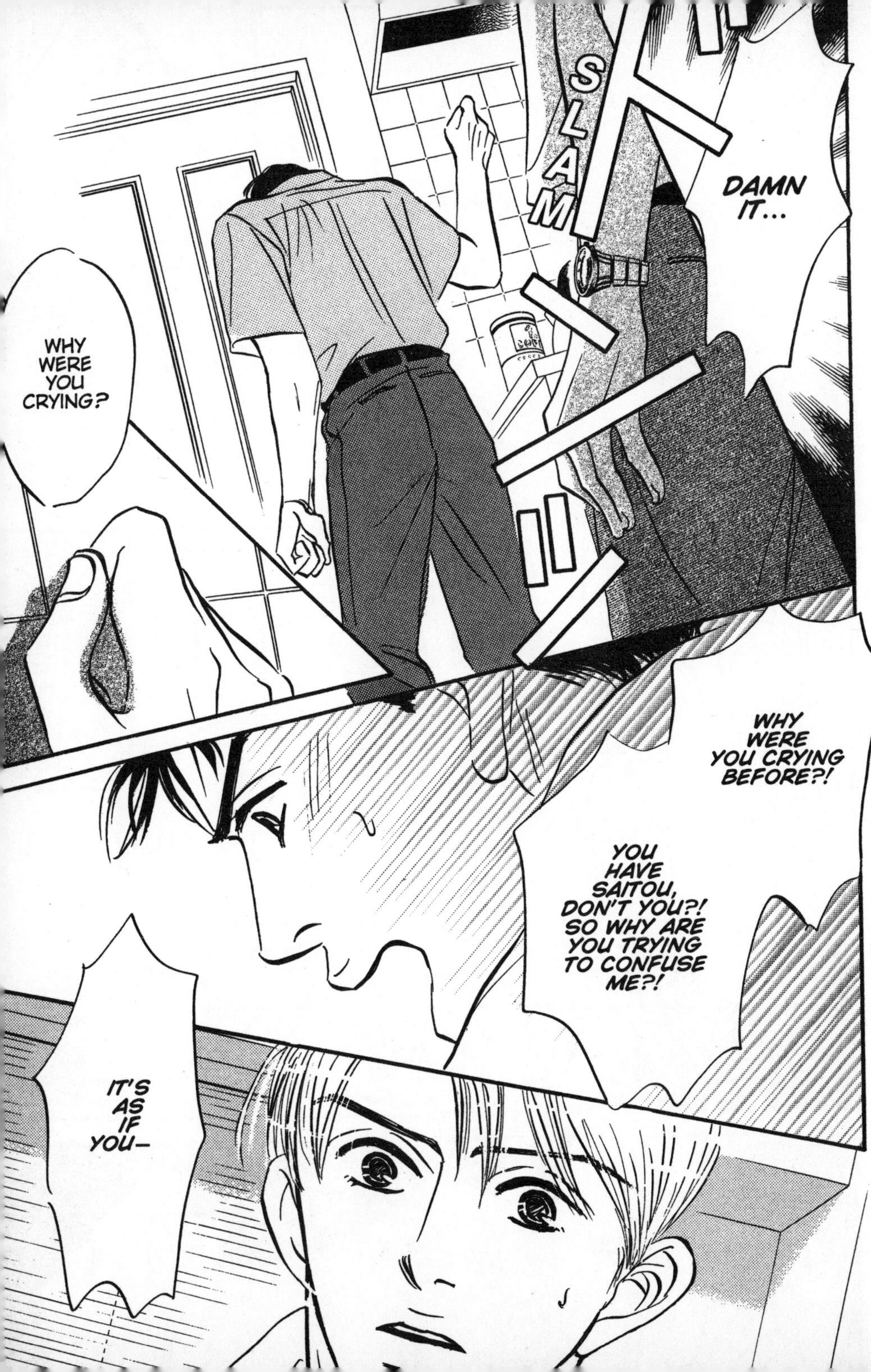
SLAM
DAMN IT...
WHY WERE YOU CRYING?
WHY WERE YOU CRYING BEFORE?!
YOU HAVE SAITOU, DON'T YOU?! SO WHY ARE YOU TRYING TO CONFUSE ME?!
IT'S AS IF YOU—

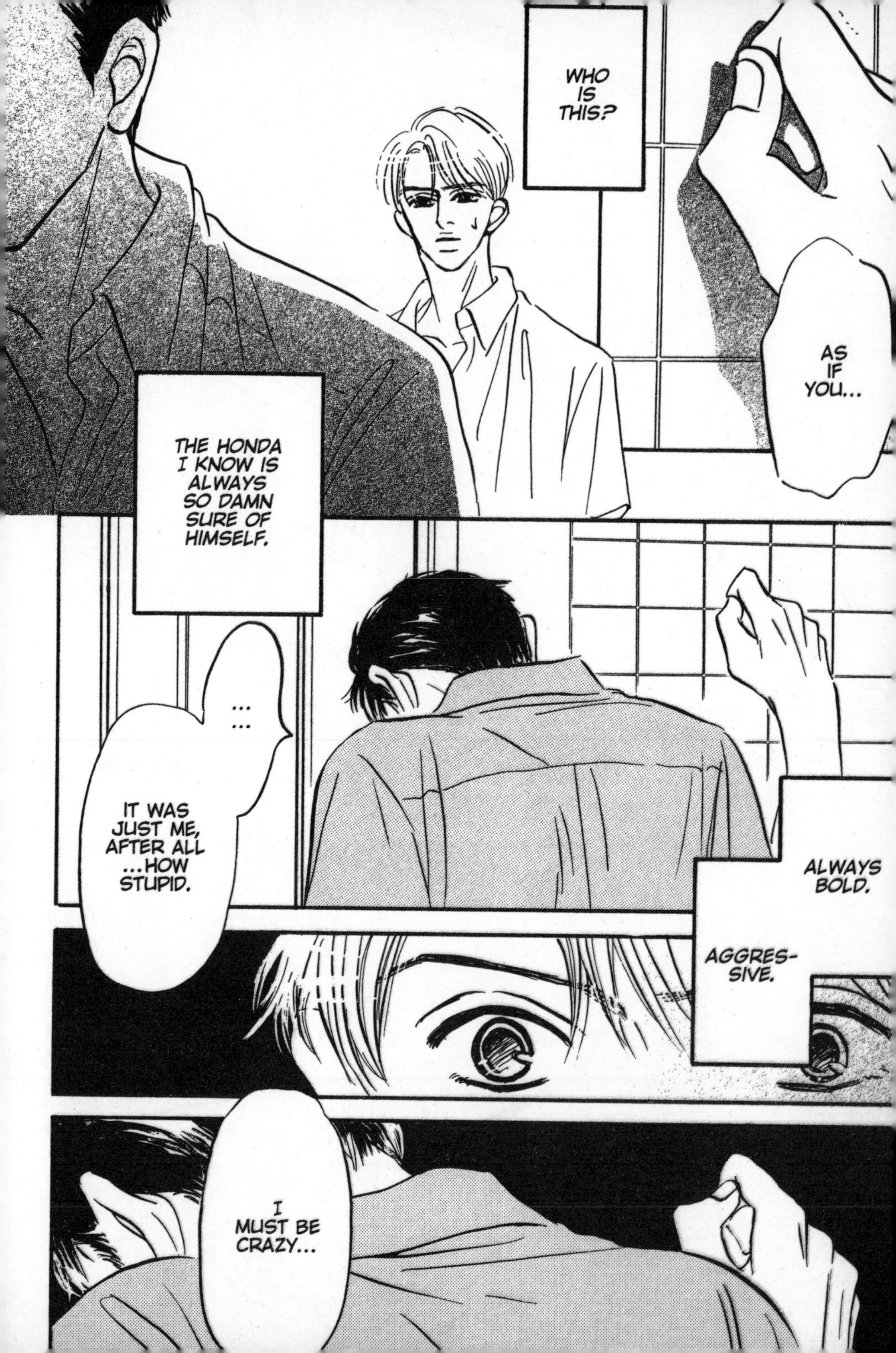
AS IF YOU...
WHO IS THIS?
THE HONDA I KNOW IS ALWAYS SO DAMN SURE OF HIMSELF.
... ...
IT WAS JUST ME, AFTER ALL ...HOW STUPID.
ALWAYS BOLD.
AGGRES-SIVE.
I MUST BE CRAZY...

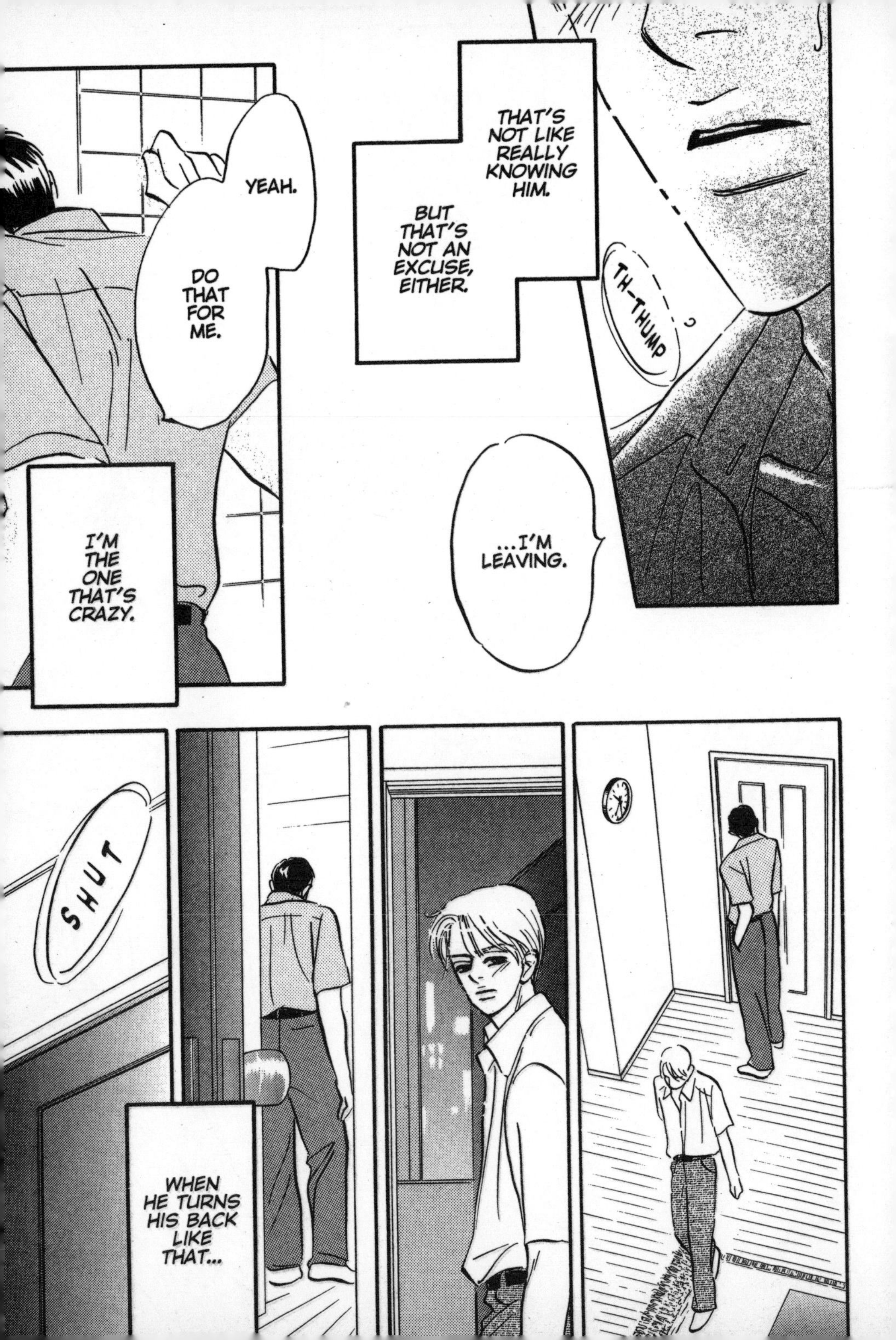
THAT'S NOT LIKE REALLY KNOWING HIM.
BUT THAT'S NOT AN EXCUSE, EITHER.
TH-THUMP
...I'M LEAVING.
YEAH.
DO THAT FOR ME.
I'M THE ONE THAT'S CRAZY.
SHUT
WHEN HE TURNS HIS BACK LIKE THAT...

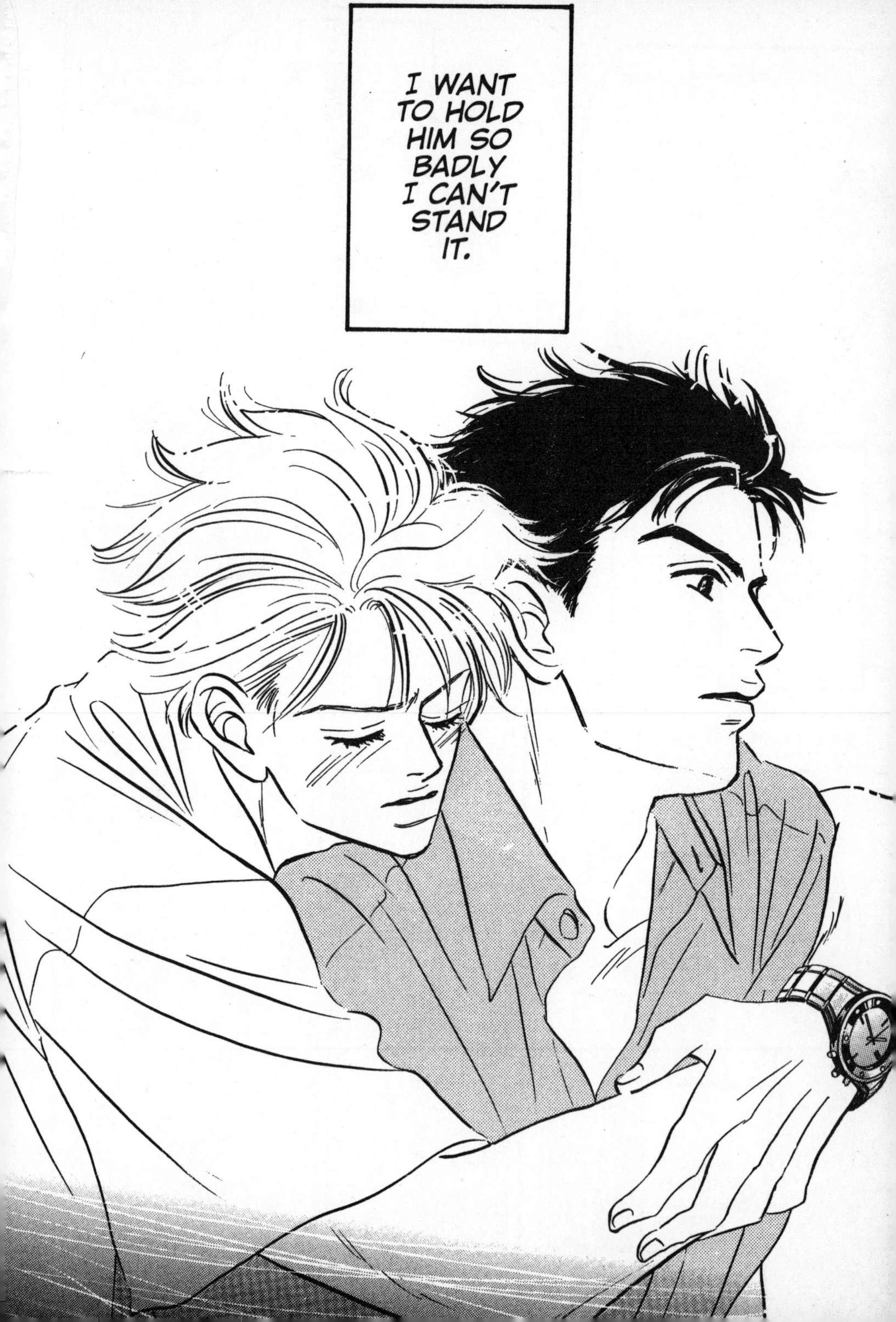
I WANT TO HOLD HIM SO BADLY I CAN'T STAND IT.

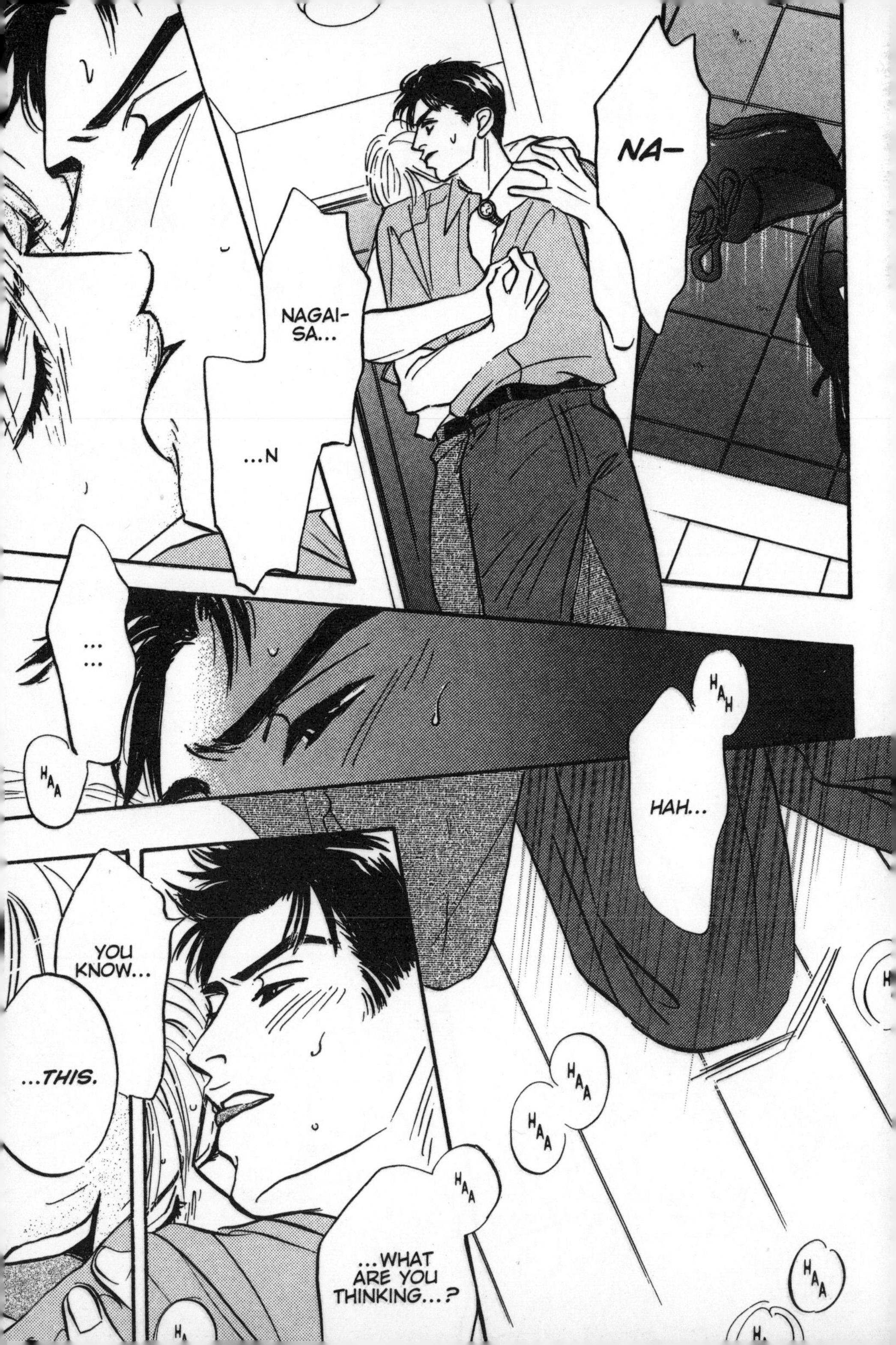
NA–
NAGAI-SA...
...N
HAH HAH
HAH...
... ...
HAA
HAA HAA
HAA
YOU KNOW...
...THIS.
HAA
...WHAT ARE YOU THINKING...?

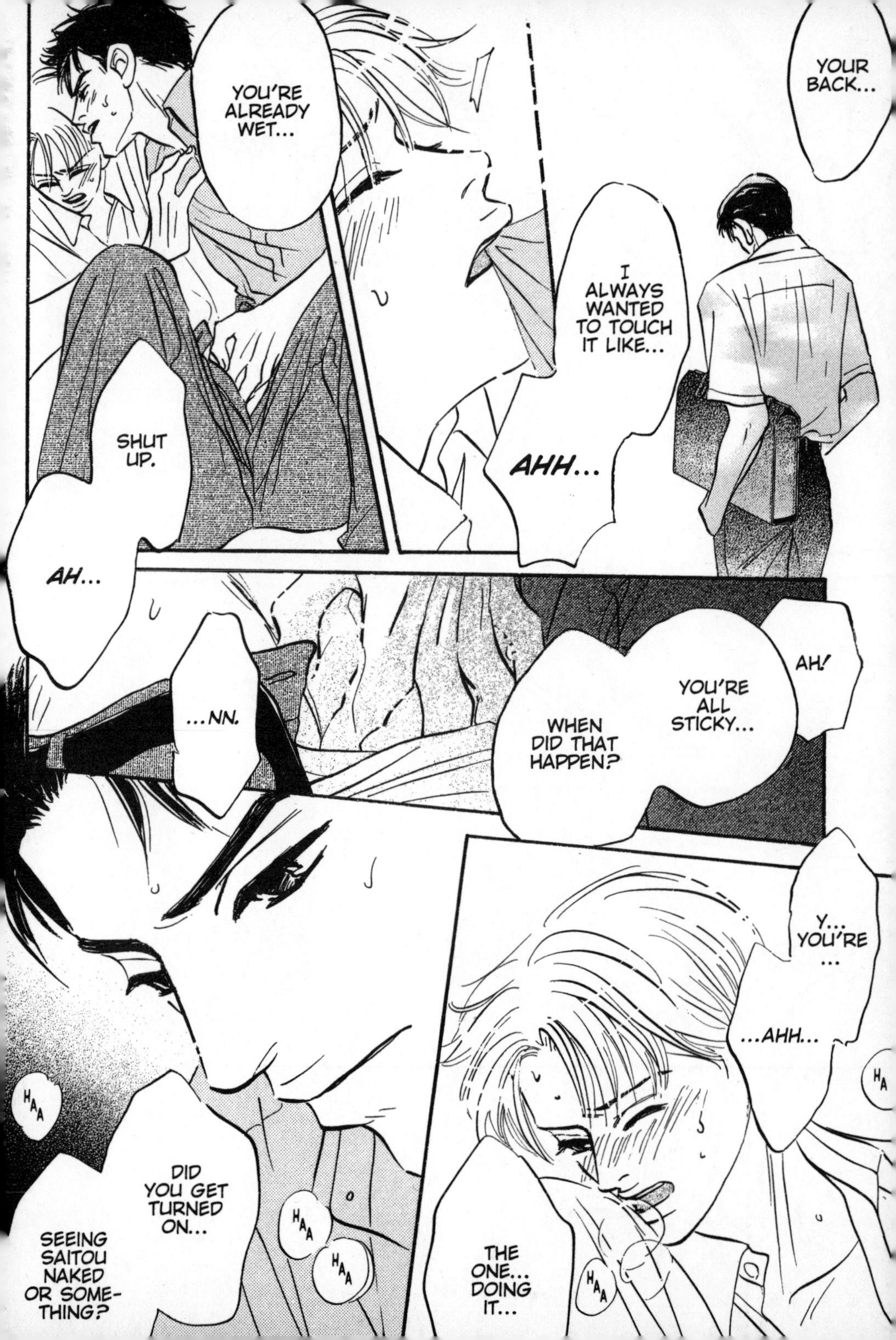
YOUR BACK...
I ALWAYS WANTED TO TOUCH IT LIKE...
AHH...
YOU'RE ALREADY WET...
SHUT UP.
AH...
AH!
YOU'RE ALL STICKY...
WHEN DID THAT HAPPEN?
...NN.
Y... YOU'RE ...
...AHH...
HA
THE ONE... DOING IT...
HAA
HAA
DID YOU GET TURNED ON...
SEEING SAITOU NAKED OR SOME-THING?
HAA
HAA

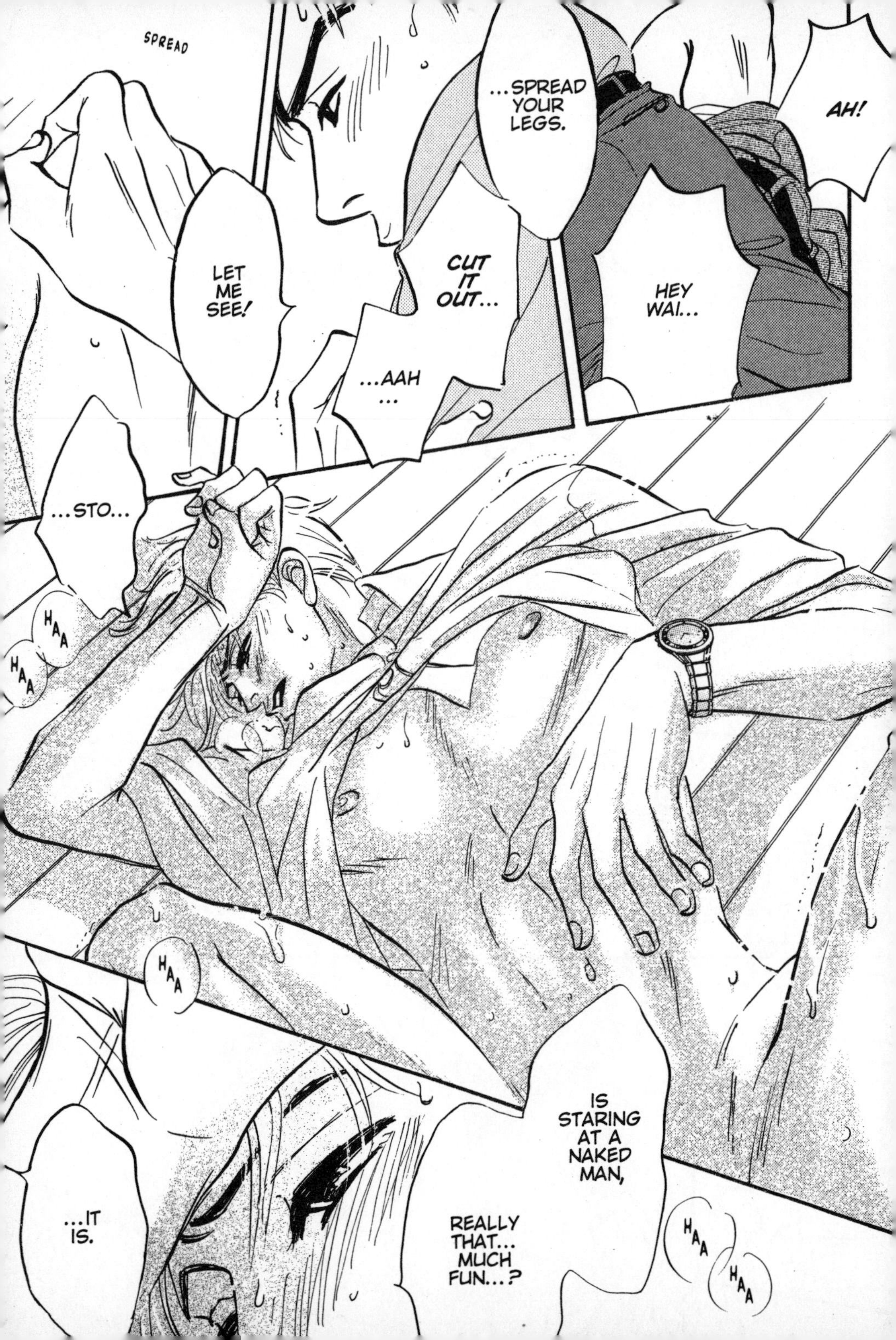
AH!
HEY WAI...
...SPREAD YOUR LEGS.
CUT IT OUT...
...AAH...
SPREAD
LET ME SEE!
...STO...
HAA
HAA
HAA
IS STARING AT A NAKED MAN,
REALLY THAT... MUCH FUN...?
HAA
HAA
...IT IS.

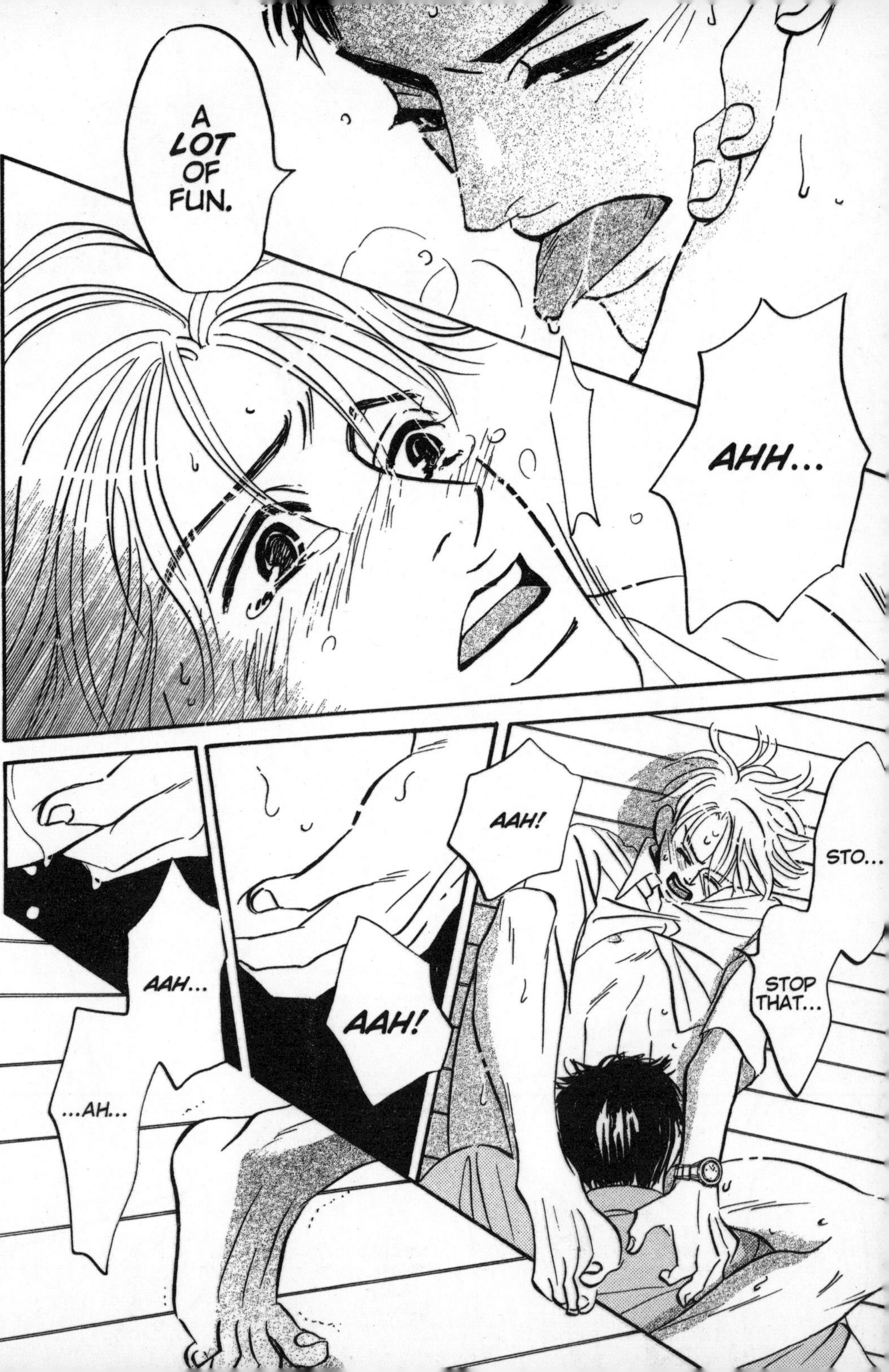
A LOT OF FUN.
AHH...
AAH!
STO...
STOP THAT...
AAH!
AAH...
...AH...

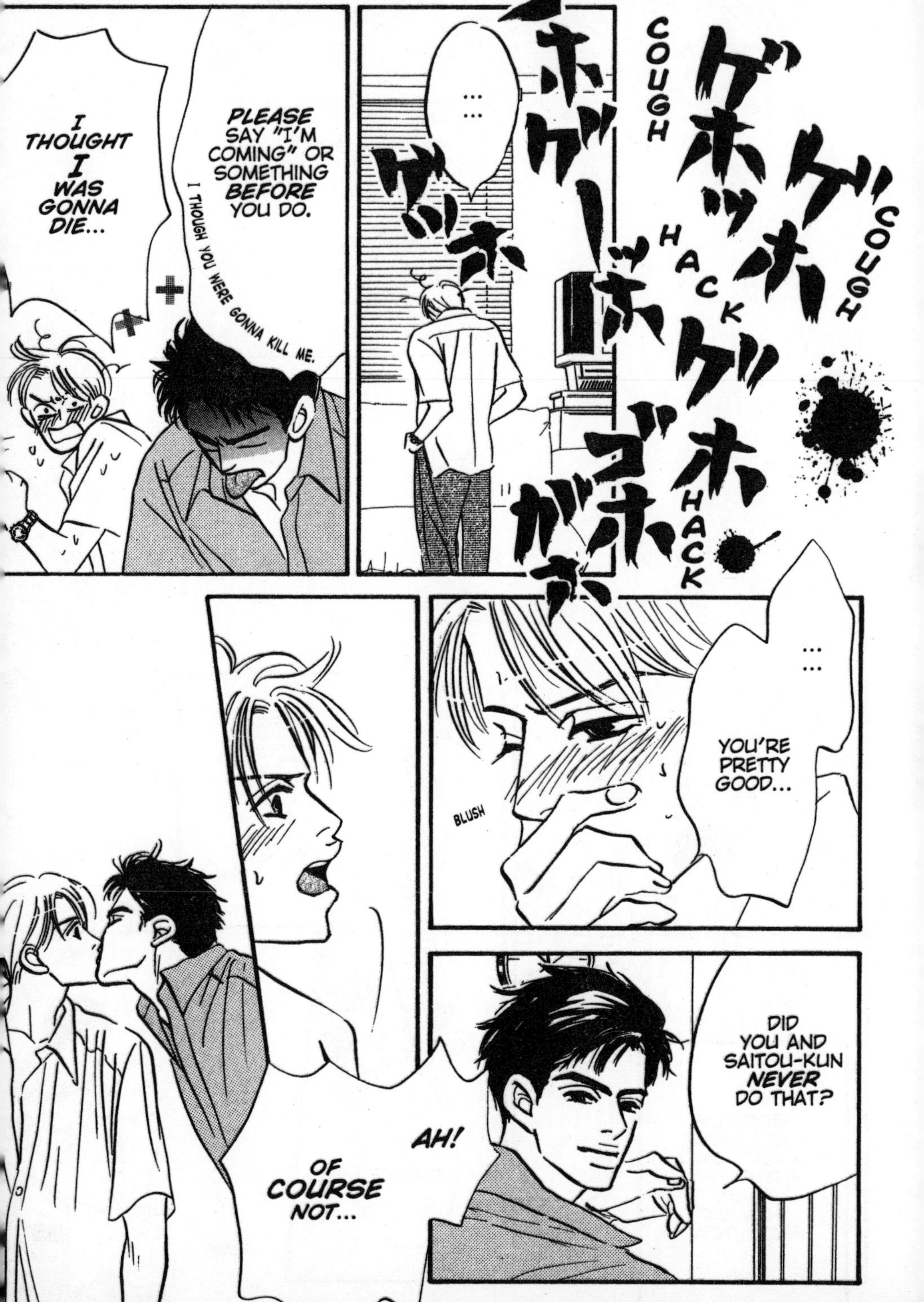

COUGH
COUGH
HACK
HACK
......
PLEASE SAY "I'M COMING" OR SOMETHING BEFORE YOU DO.
I THOUGH YOU WERE GONNA KILL ME.
I THOUGHT I WAS GONNA DIE...
......
YOU'RE PRETTY GOOD...
BLUSH
DID YOU AND SAITOU-KUN NEVER DO THAT?
AH!
OF COURSE NOT...

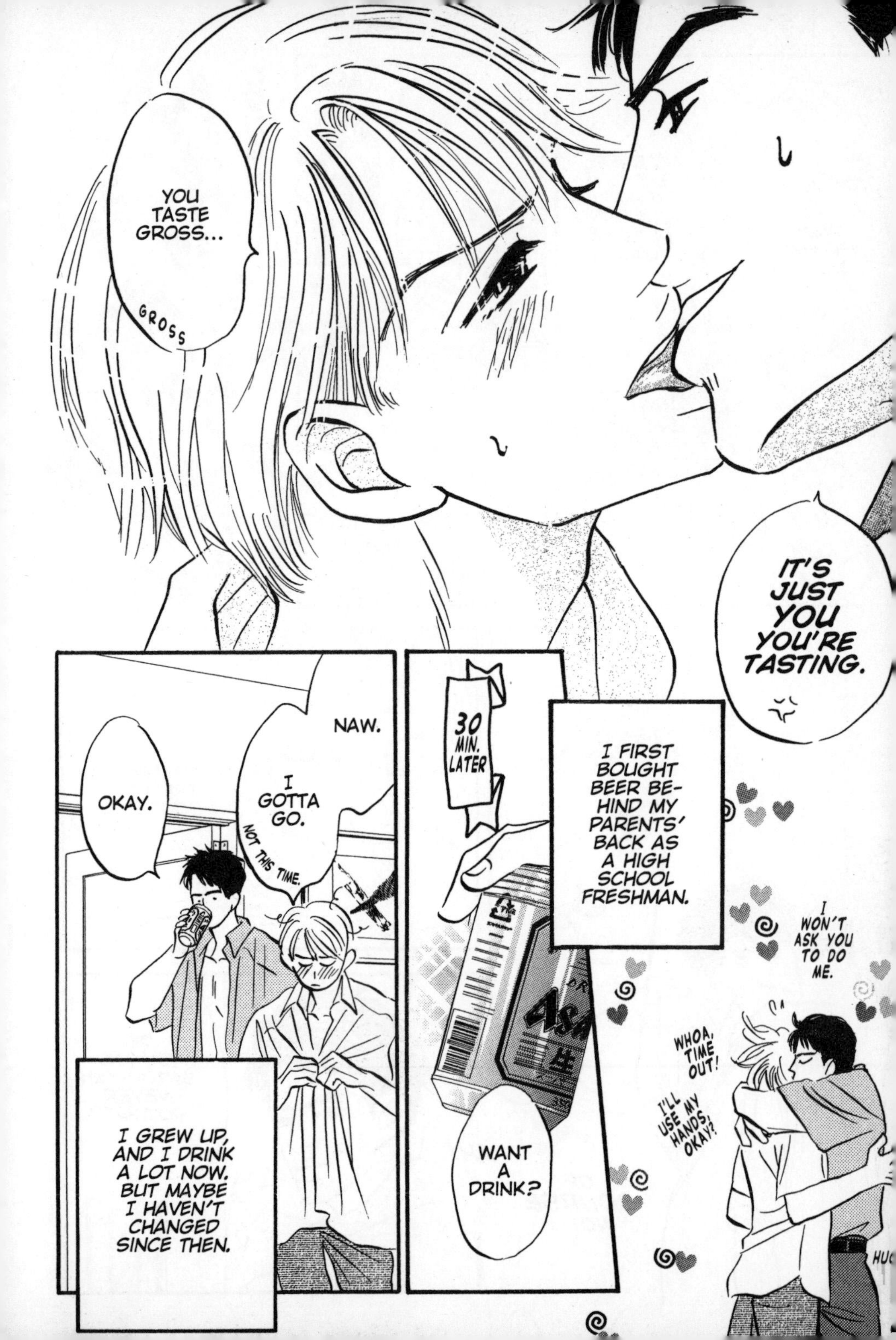
YOU TASTE GROSS...
GROSS
IT'S JUST YOU YOU'RE TASTING.
WHOA, TIME OUT!
I'LL USE MY HANDS, OKAY?
I WON'T ASK YOU TO DO ME.
30 MIN. LATER
I FIRST BOUGHT BEER BE-HIND MY PARENTS' BACK AS A HIGH SCHOOL FRESHMAN.
WANT A DRINK?
NAW.
I GOTTA GO.
NOT THIS TIME.
OKAY.
I GREW UP, AND I DRINK A LOT NOW. BUT MAYBE I HAVEN'T CHANGED SINCE THEN.

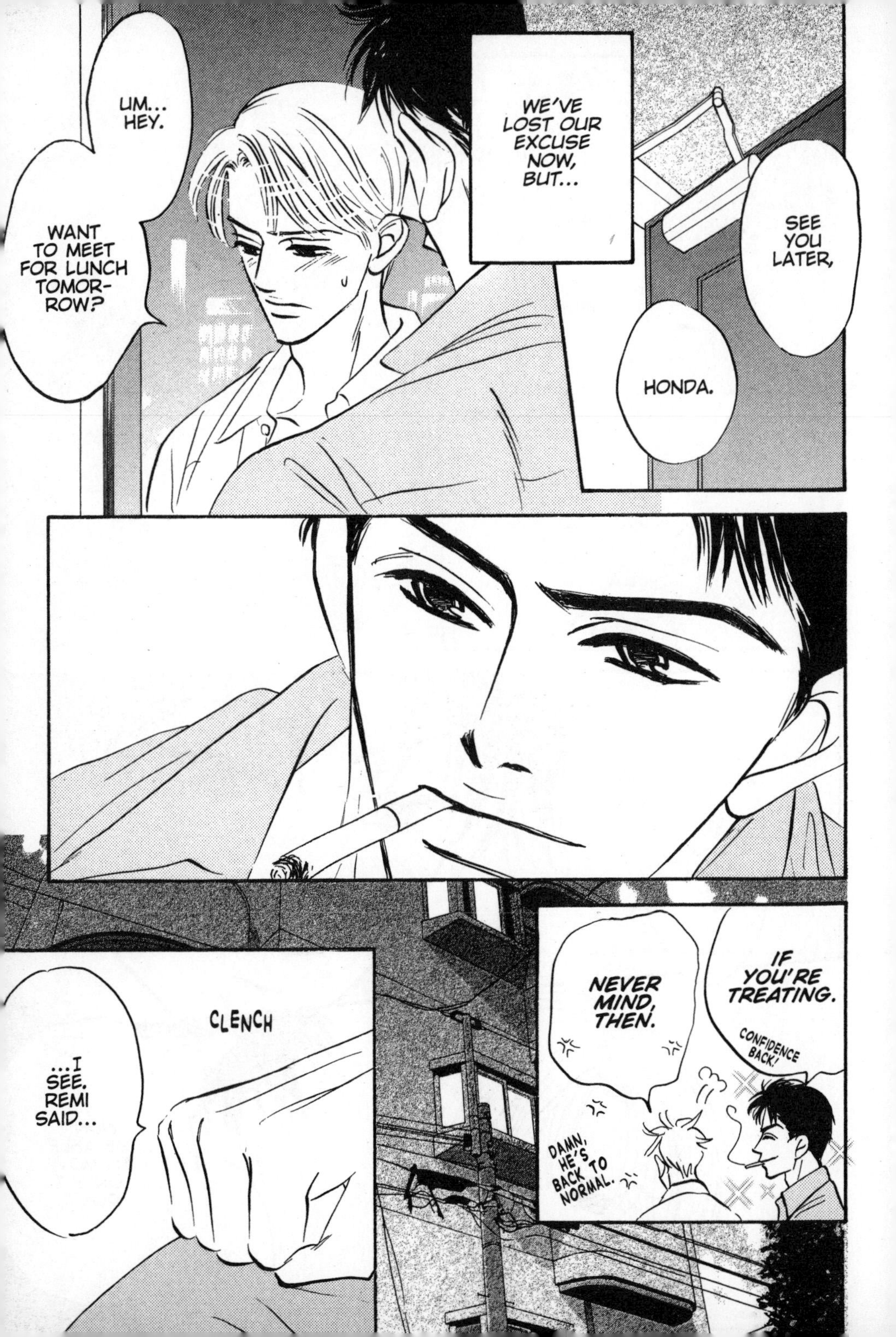
SEE YOU LATER,
HONDA.
WE'VE LOST OUR EXCUSE NOW, BUT...
UM... HEY.
WANT TO MEET FOR LUNCH TOMORROW?
IF YOU'RE TREATING.
NEVER MIND, THEN.
CONFIDENCE BACK!
DAMN, HE'S BACK TO NORMAL.
CLENCH
...I SEE. REMI SAID...

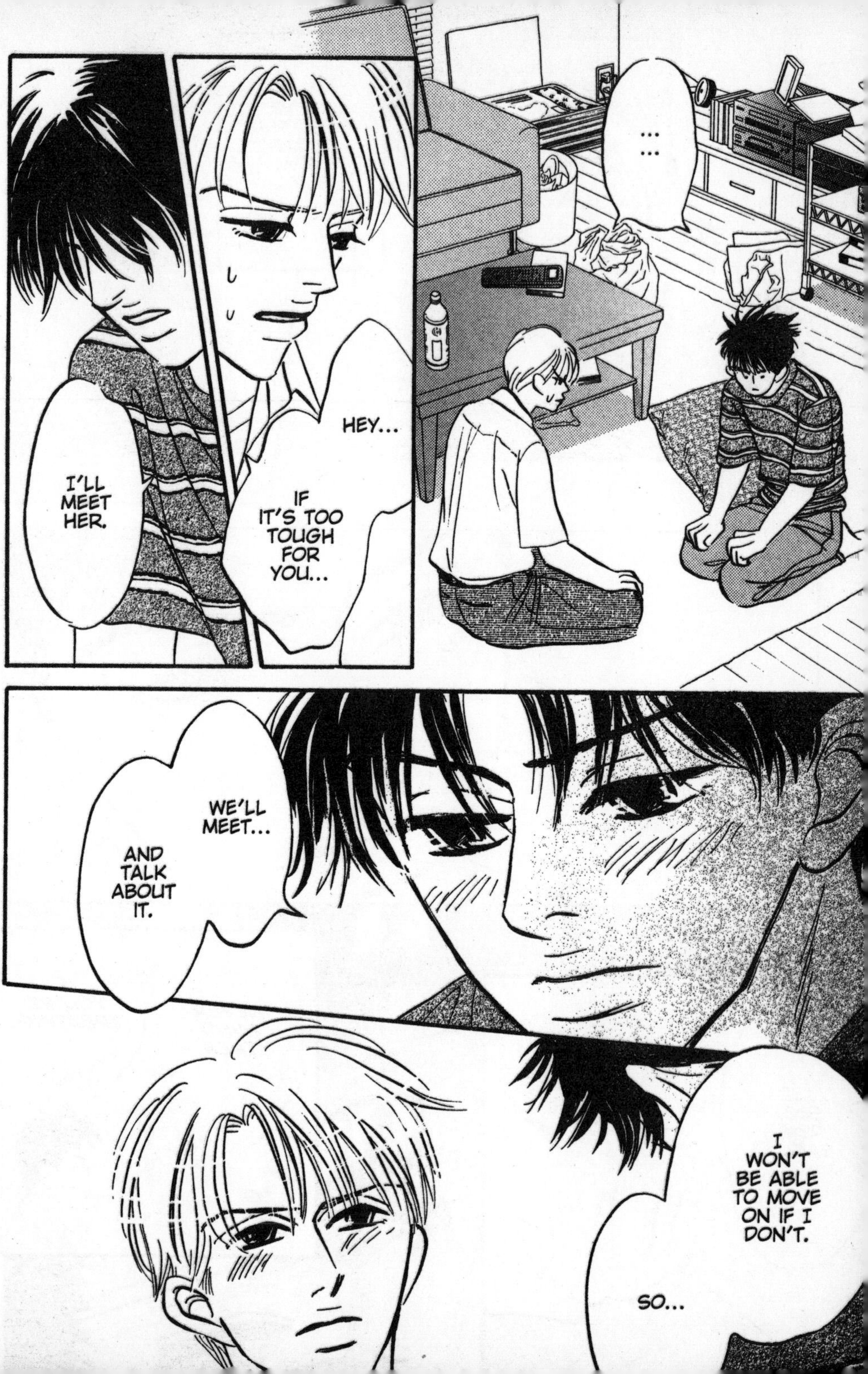

......
HEY...
IF IT'S TOO TOUGH FOR YOU...
I'LL MEET HER.
WE'LL MEET...
AND TALK ABOUT IT.
I WON'T BE ABLE TO MOVE ON IF I DON'T.
SO...

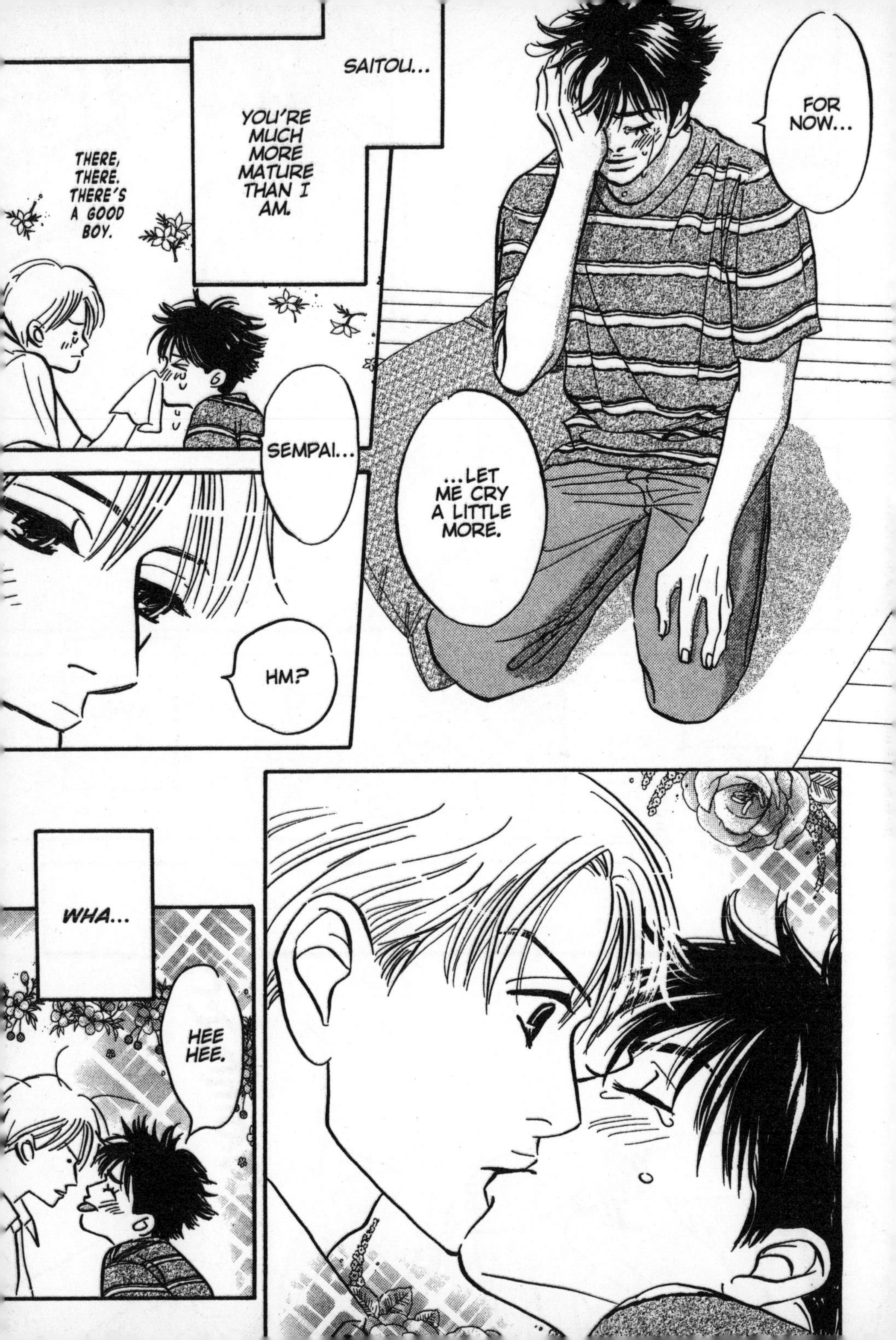
FOR NOW...
...LET ME CRY A LITTLE MORE.
SAITOU...
YOU'RE MUCH MORE MATURE THAN I AM.
THERE, THERE. THERE'S A GOOD BOY.
SEMPAI...
HM?
WHA...
HEE HEE.

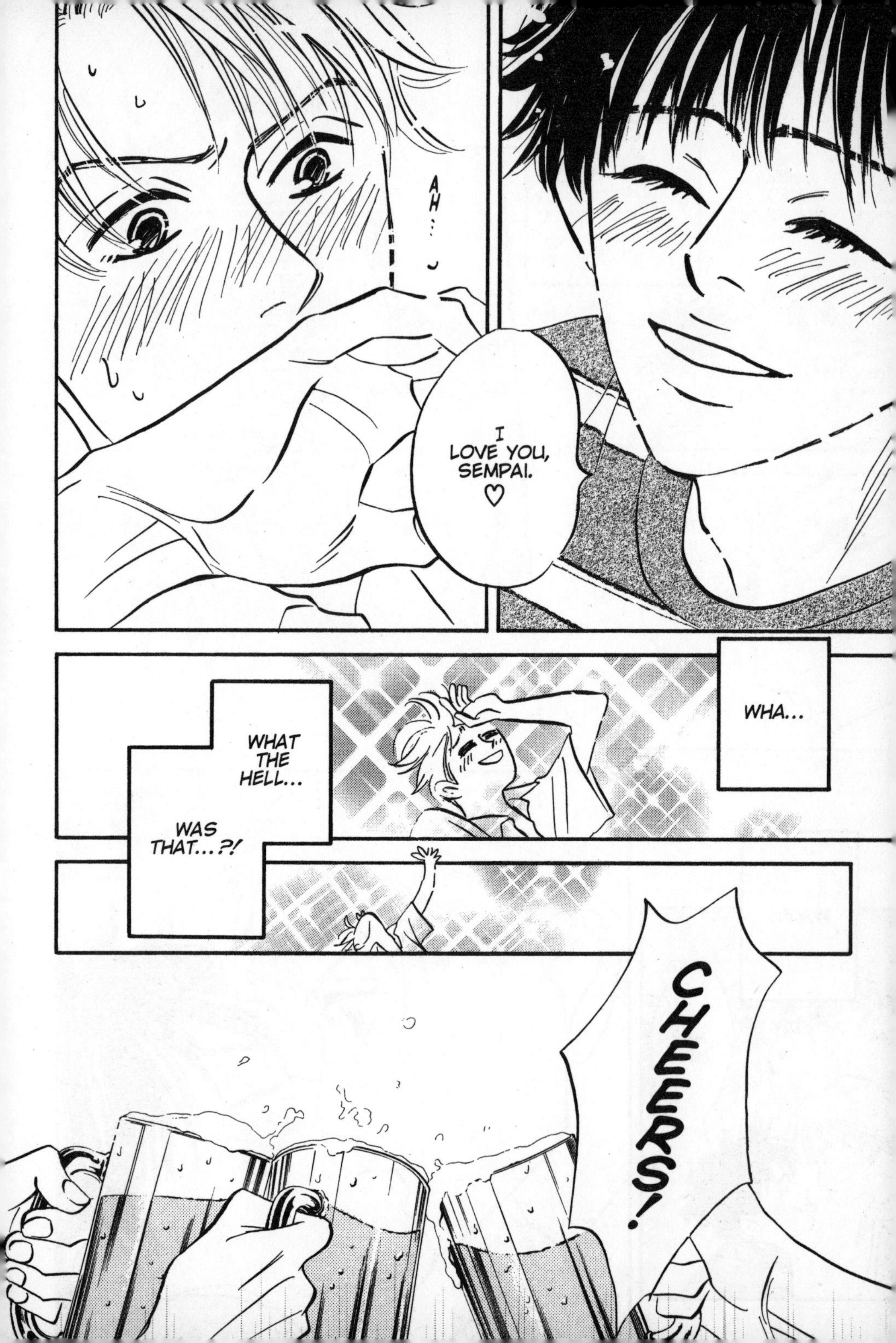
I LOVE YOU, SEMPAI. ♡
AH...
WHA...
WHAT THE HELL...
WAS THAT...?!
CHEERS!

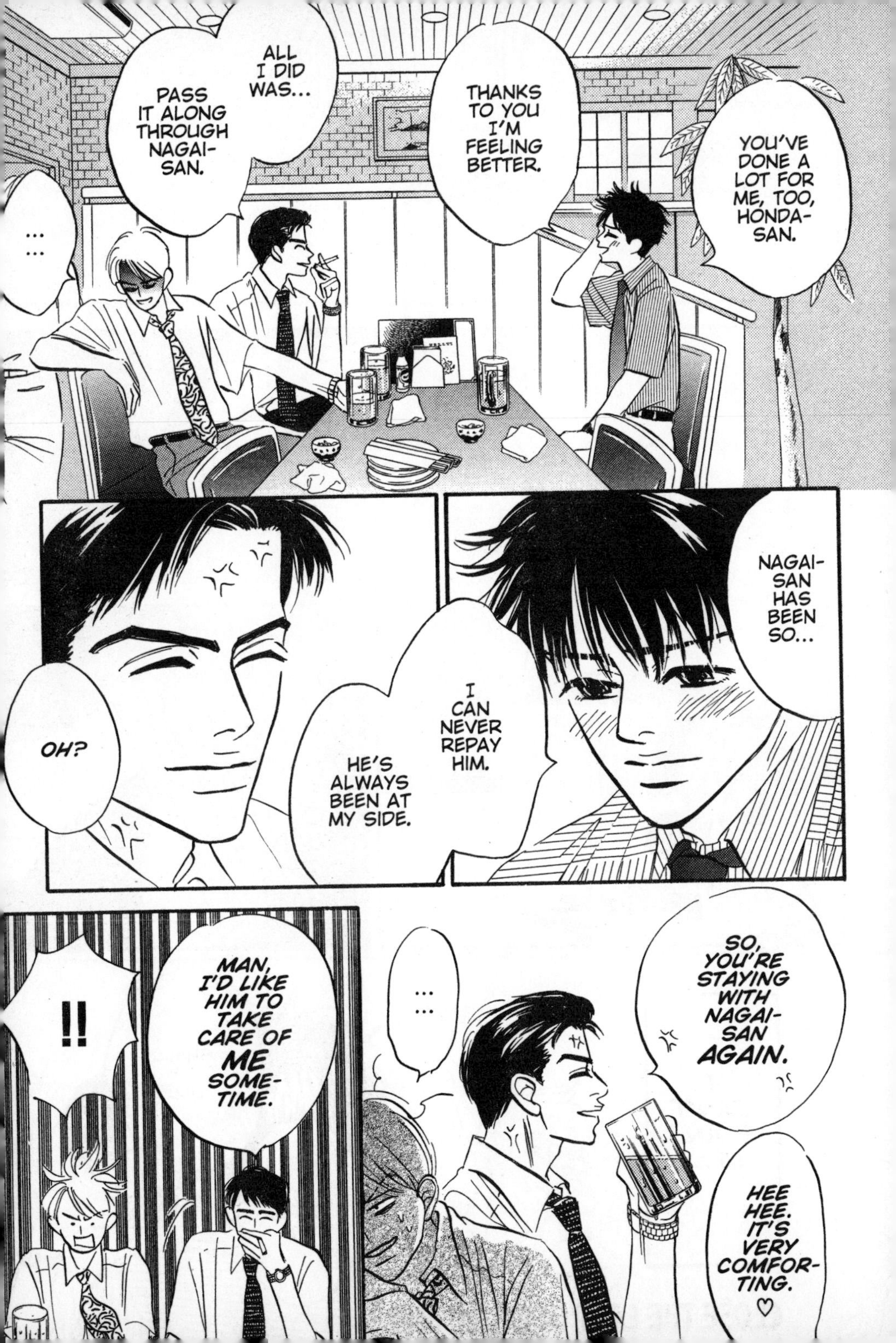
YOU'VE DONE A LOT FOR ME, TOO, HONDA-SAN.
THANKS TO YOU I'M FEELING BETTER.
ALL I DID WAS...
PASS IT ALONG THROUGH NAGAI-SAN.
......
NAGAI-SAN HAS BEEN SO...
I CAN NEVER REPAY HIM.
HE'S ALWAYS BEEN AT MY SIDE.
OH?
SO, YOU'RE STAYING WITH NAGAI-SAN AGAIN.
HEE HEE. IT'S VERY COMFORTING. ♡
......
MAN, I'D LIKE HIM TO TAKE CARE OF ME SOMETIME.
!!

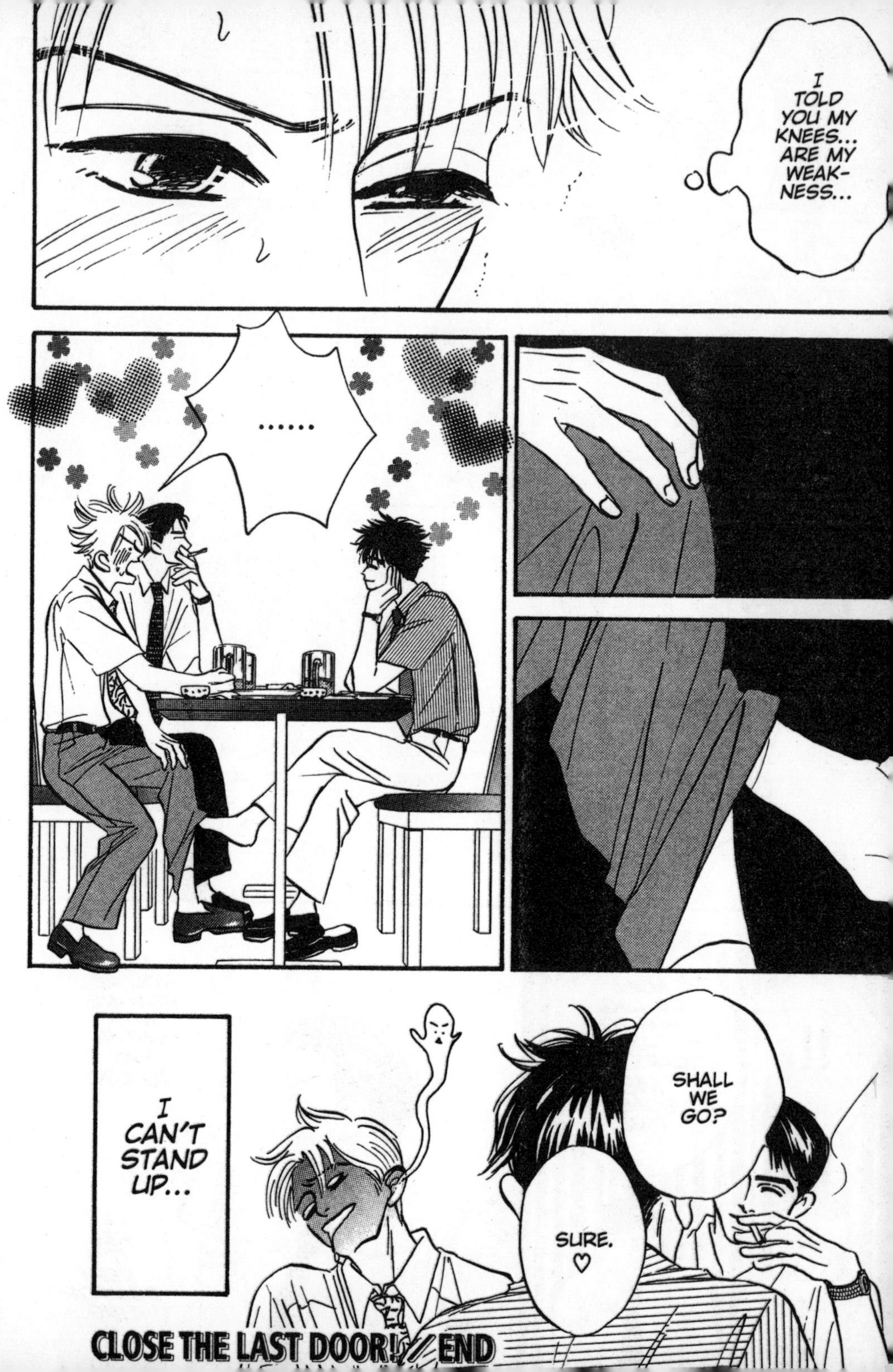
I TOLD YOU MY KNEES... ARE MY WEAK-NESS...
......
SHALL WE GO?
SURE. ♡
I CAN'T STAND UP...
CLOSE THE LAST DOOR!! END

CLOSE THE LAST DOOR!

◆EXTRAS◆

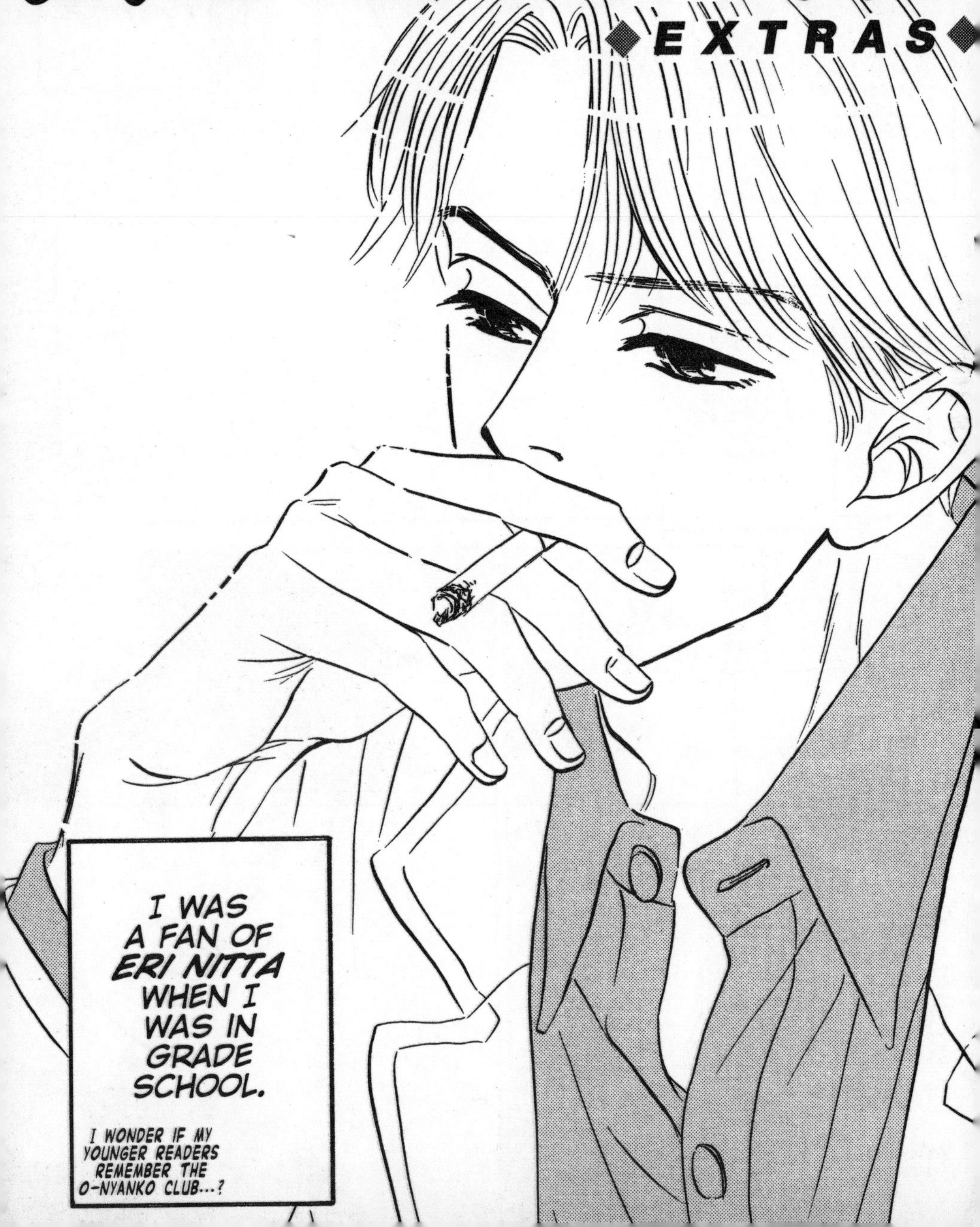
I WAS A FAN OF *ERI NITTA* WHEN I WAS IN GRADE SCHOOL.
I WONDER IF MY YOUNGER READERS REMEMBER THE O-NYANKO CLUB...?

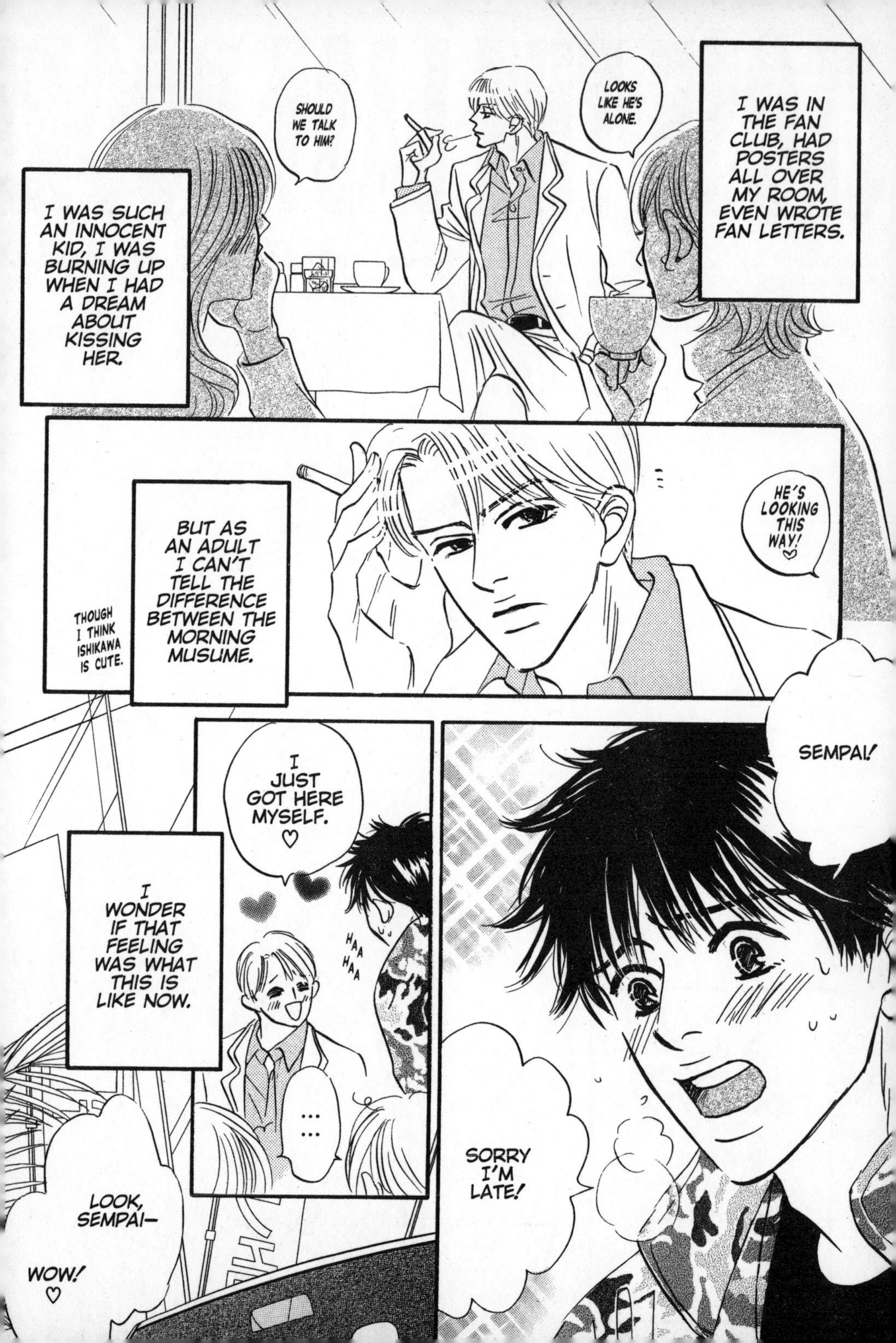
I WAS IN THE FAN CLUB, HAD POSTERS ALL OVER MY ROOM, EVEN WROTE FAN LETTERS.
LOOKS LIKE HE'S ALONE.
SHOULD WE TALK TO HIM?
I WAS SUCH AN INNOCENT KID, I WAS BURNING UP WHEN I HAD A DREAM ABOUT KISSING HER.
HE'S LOOKING THIS WAY! ♡
BUT AS AN ADULT I CAN'T TELL THE DIFFERENCE BETWEEN THE MORNING MUSUME.
THOUGH I THINK ISHIKAWA IS CUTE.
SEMPAI!
SORRY I'M LATE!
I JUST GOT HERE MYSELF. ♡
HAA HAA
I WONDER IF THAT FEELING WAS WHAT THIS IS LIKE NOW.
......
LOOK, SEMPAI—
WOW! ♡

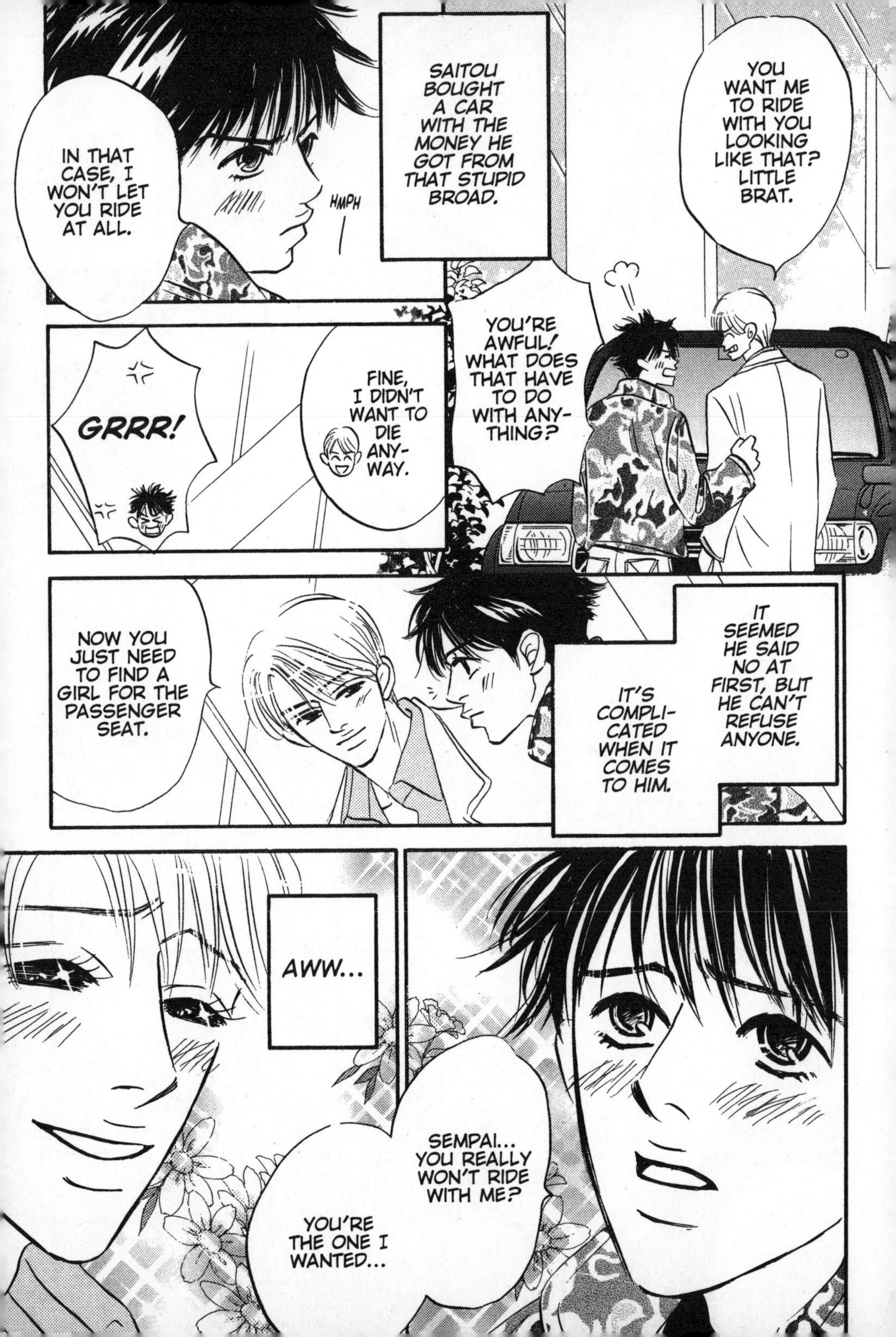
YOU WANT ME TO RIDE WITH YOU LOOKING LIKE THAT? LITTLE BRAT.
SAITOU BOUGHT A CAR WITH THE MONEY HE GOT FROM THAT STUPID BROAD.
YOU'RE AWFUL! WHAT DOES THAT HAVE TO DO WITH ANYTHING?
HMPH
IN THAT CASE, I WON'T LET YOU RIDE AT ALL.
FINE, I DIDN'T WANT TO DIE ANYWAY.
GRRR!
IT SEEMED HE SAID NO AT FIRST, BUT HE CAN'T REFUSE ANYONE.
IT'S COMPLICATED WHEN IT COMES TO HIM.
NOW YOU JUST NEED TO FIND A GIRL FOR THE PASSENGER SEAT.
SEMPAI... YOU REALLY WON'T RIDE WITH ME?
YOU'RE THE ONE I WANTED...
AWW...

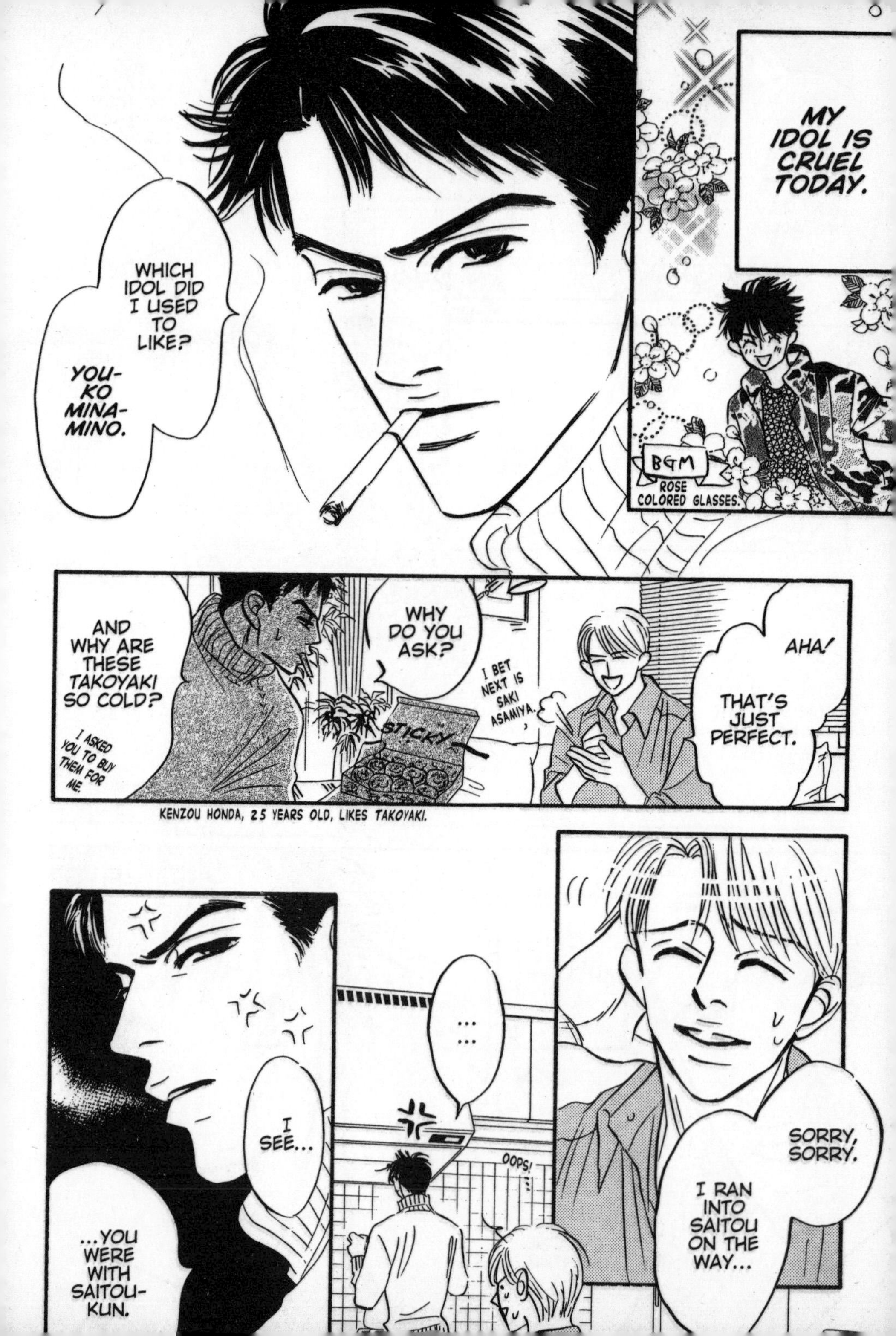
MY IDOL IS CRUEL TODAY.
BGM
ROSE COLORED GLASSES.
WHICH IDOL DID I USED TO LIKE?
YOU-KO MINA-MINO.
AHA!
THAT'S JUST PERFECT.
I BET NEXT IS SAKI ASAMIYA.
WHY DO YOU ASK?
AND WHY ARE THESE TAKOYAKI SO COLD?
STICKY
I ASKED YOU TO BUY THEM FOR ME.
KENZOU HONDA, 25 YEARS OLD, LIKES TAKOYAKI.
SORRY, SORRY.
I RAN INTO SAITOU ON THE WAY...
......
OOPS!
I SEE...
...YOU WERE WITH SAITOU-KUN.

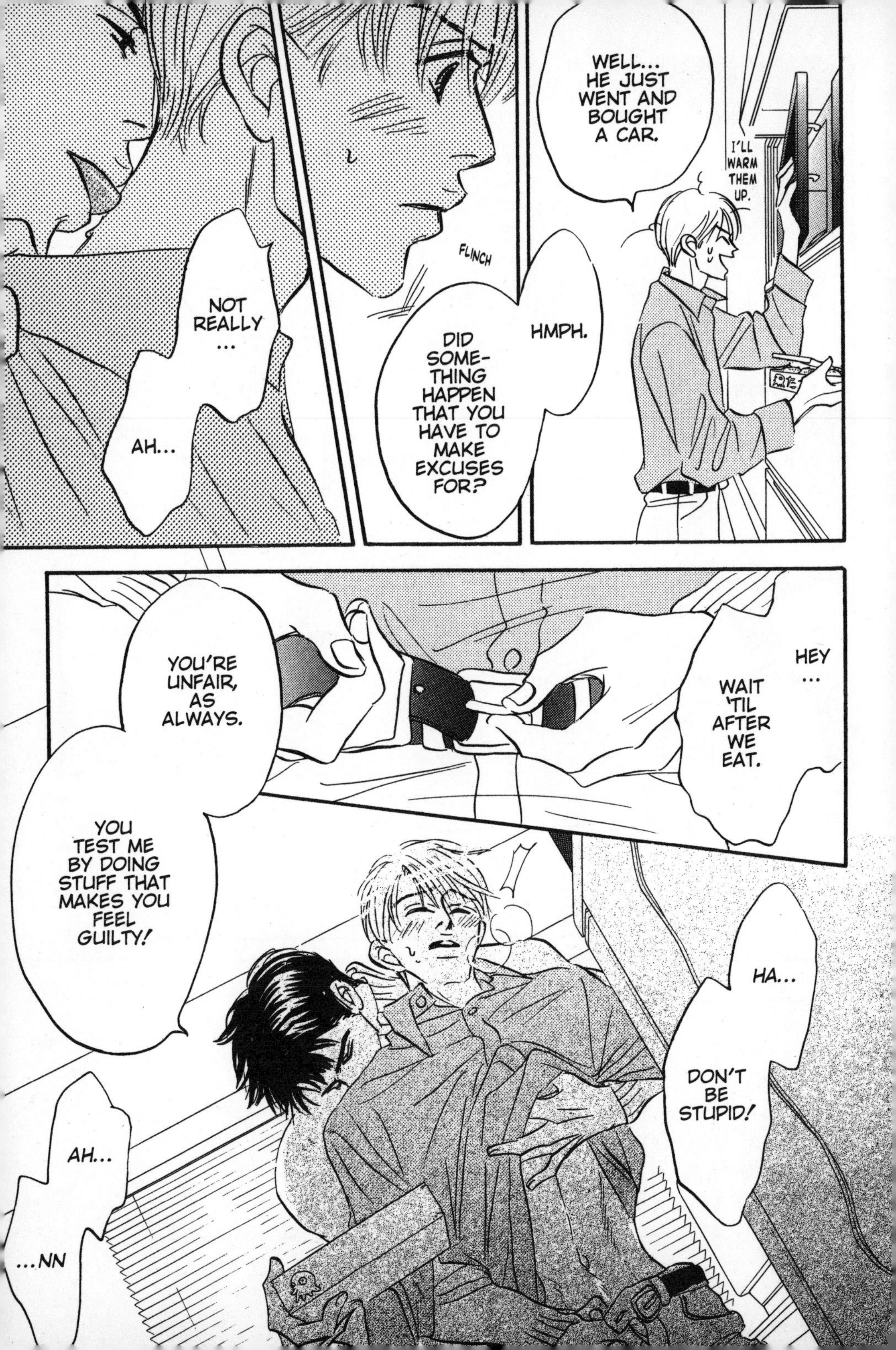
WELL... HE JUST WENT AND BOUGHT A CAR.
I'LL WARM THEM UP.
FLINCH
HMPH.
DID SOME-THING HAPPEN THAT YOU HAVE TO MAKE EXCUSES FOR?
NOT REALLY ...
AH...
HEY ...
WAIT 'TIL AFTER WE EAT.
YOU'RE UNFAIR, AS ALWAYS.
HA...
DON'T BE STUPID!
YOU TEST ME BY DOING STUFF THAT MAKES YOU FEEL GUILTY!
AH...
...NN

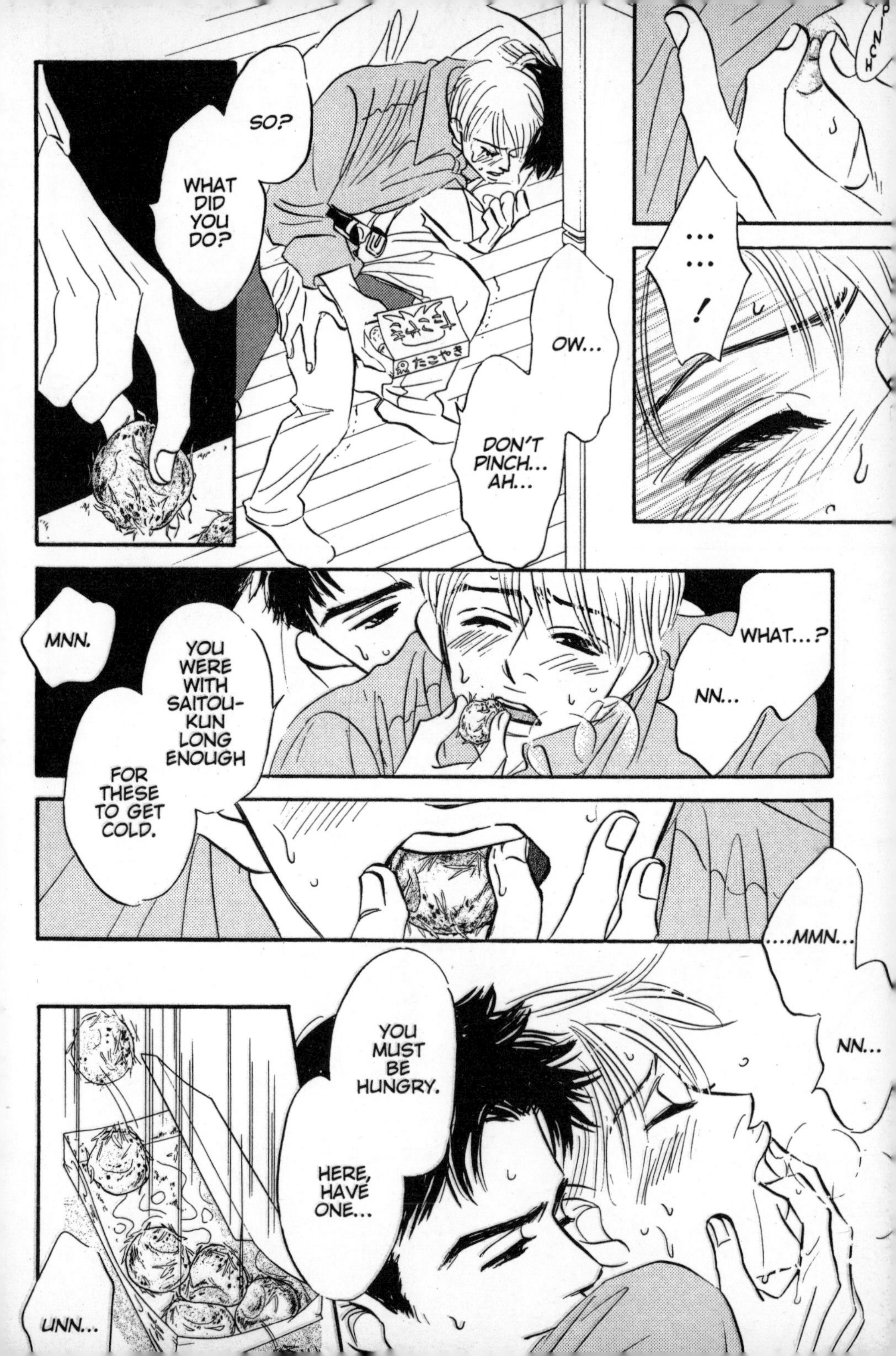
PINCH
...
...
!
SO?
WHAT DID YOU DO?
OW...
DON'T PINCH... AH...
WHAT...?
NN...
YOU WERE WITH SAITOU-KUN LONG ENOUGH
FOR THESE TO GET COLD.
MNN.
....MMN...
NN...
YOU MUST BE HUNGRY.
HERE, HAVE ONE...
UNN...

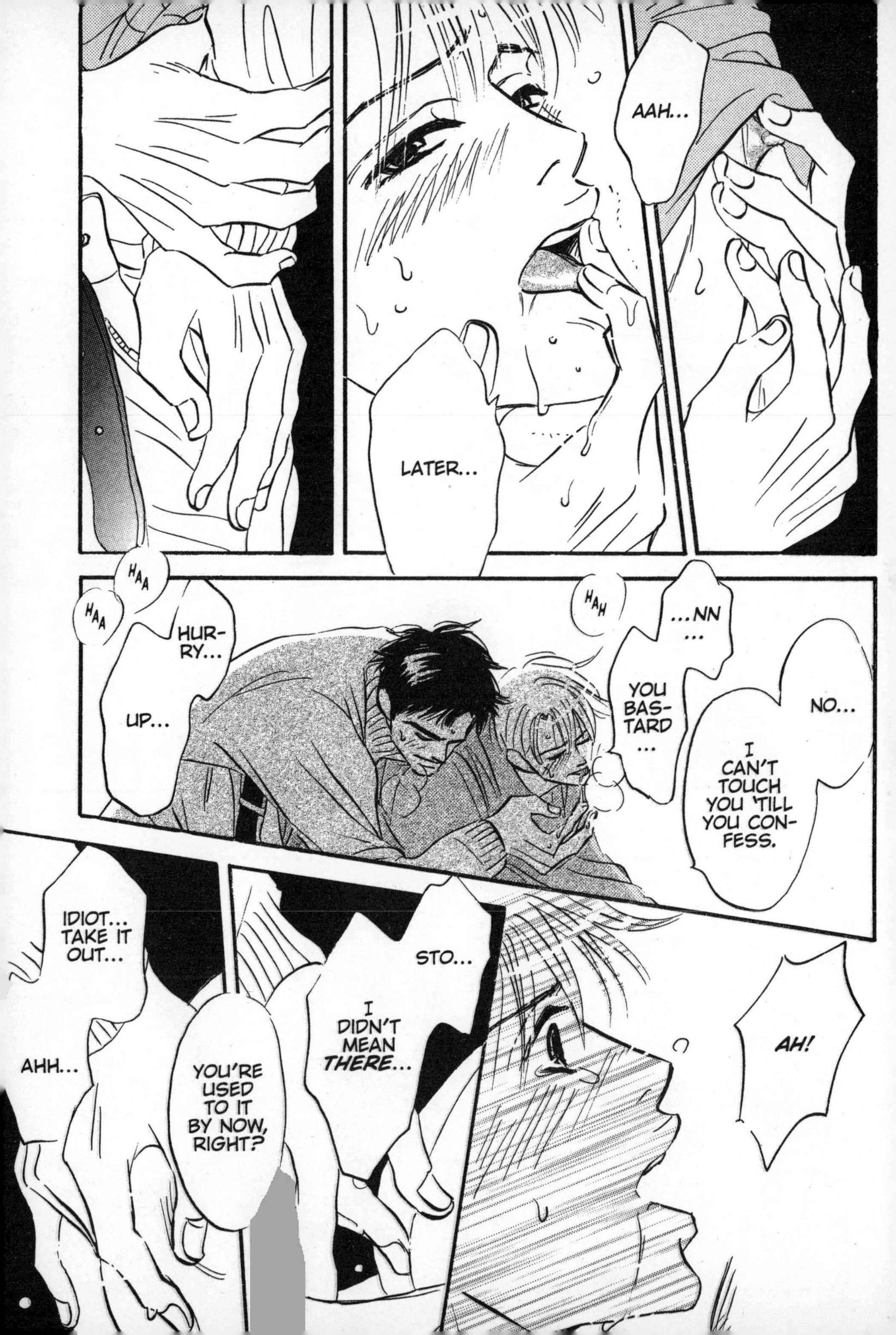
AAH...
LATER...
HAH
...NN ...
NO... I CAN'T TOUCH YOU 'TILL YOU CONFESS.
YOU BASTARD ...
HURRY... UP...
HAA HAA
AH!
STO...
I DIDN'T MEAN *THERE*...
YOU'RE USED TO IT BY NOW, RIGHT?
IDIOT... TAKE IT OUT...
AHH...

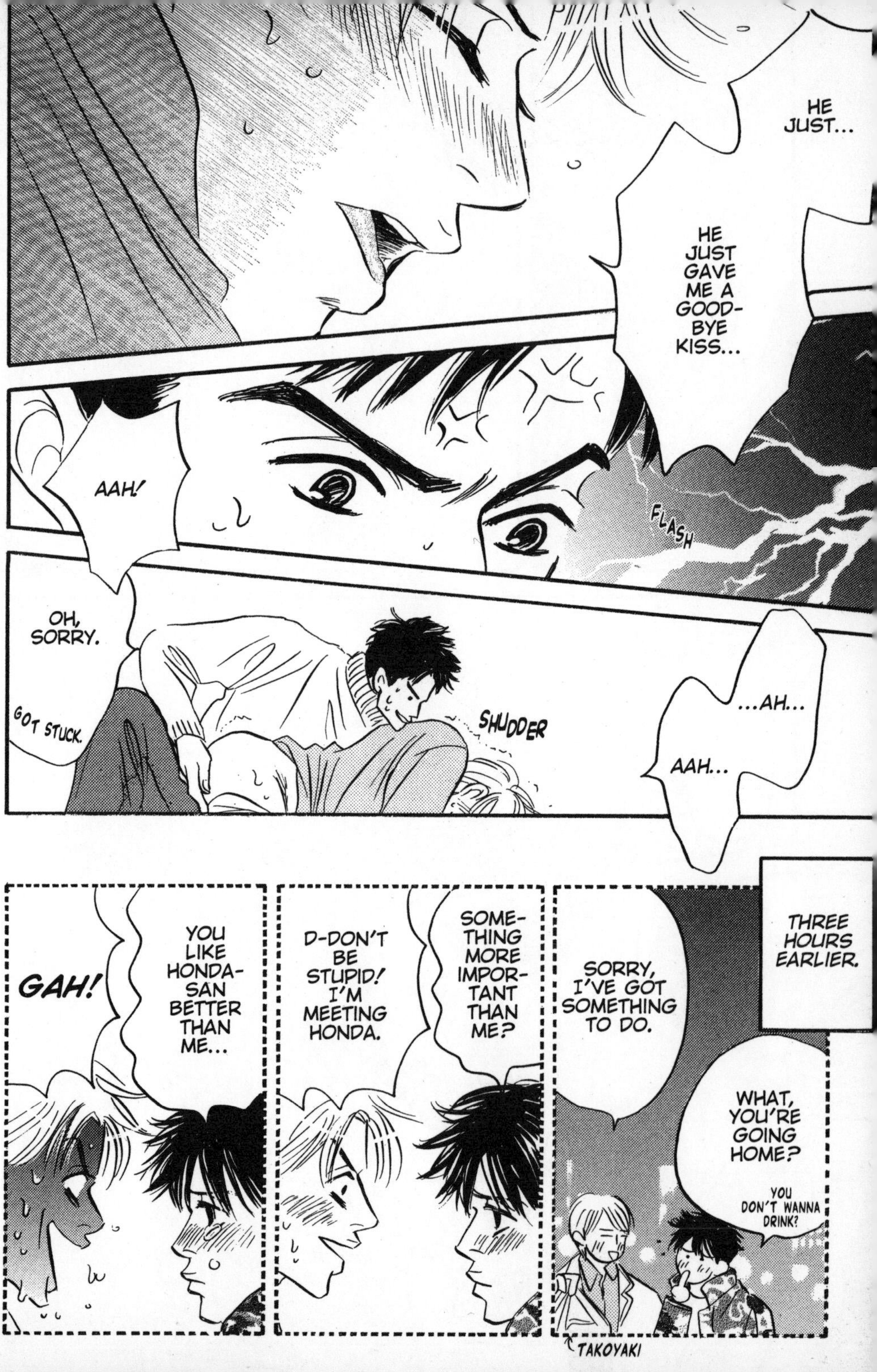
HE JUST...
HE JUST GAVE ME A GOOD-BYE KISS...
AAH!
FLASH
...AH...
AAH...
SHUDDER
OH, SORRY.
GOT STUCK.
THREE HOURS EARLIER.
WHAT, YOU'RE GOING HOME?
YOU DON'T WANNA DRINK?
SORRY, I'VE GOT SOMETHING TO DO.
TAKOYAKI
SOME-THING MORE IMPOR-TANT THAN ME?
D-DON'T BE STUPID! I'M MEETING HONDA.
YOU LIKE HONDA-SAN BETTER THAN ME...
GAH!

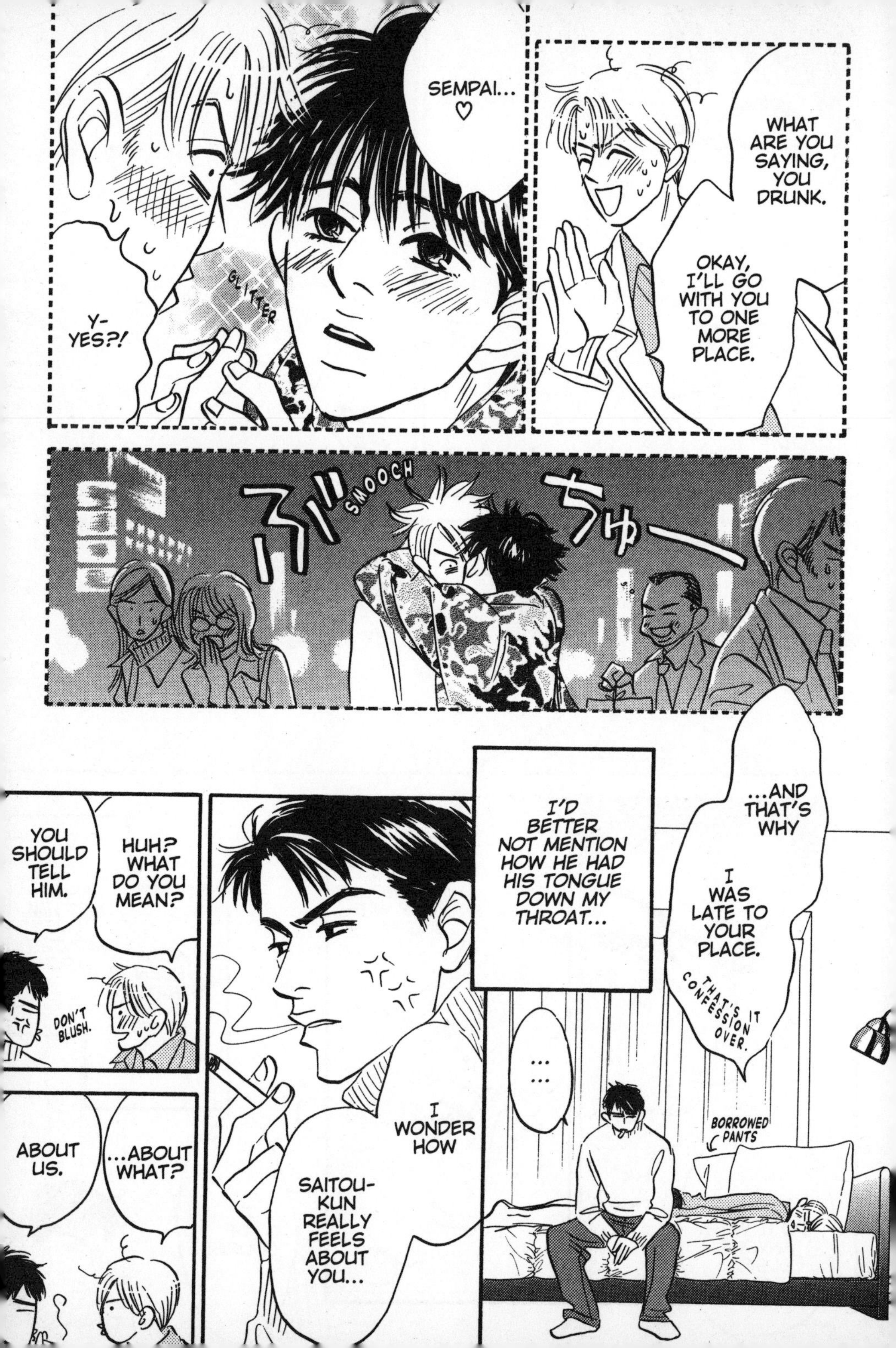
WHAT ARE YOU SAYING, YOU DRUNK.
OKAY, I'LL GO WITH YOU TO ONE MORE PLACE.
SEMPAI... ♡
GLITTER
Y-YES?!
ぶちゅー
SMOOCH
...AND THAT'S WHY
I WAS LATE TO YOUR PLACE.
THAT'S IT CONFESSION OVER.
I'D BETTER NOT MENTION HOW HE HAD HIS TONGUE DOWN MY THROAT...
......
BORROWED PANTS
I WONDER HOW
SAITOU-KUN REALLY FEELS ABOUT YOU...
HUH? WHAT DO YOU MEAN?
YOU SHOULD TELL HIM.
DON'T BLUSH.
...ABOUT WHAT?
ABOUT US.

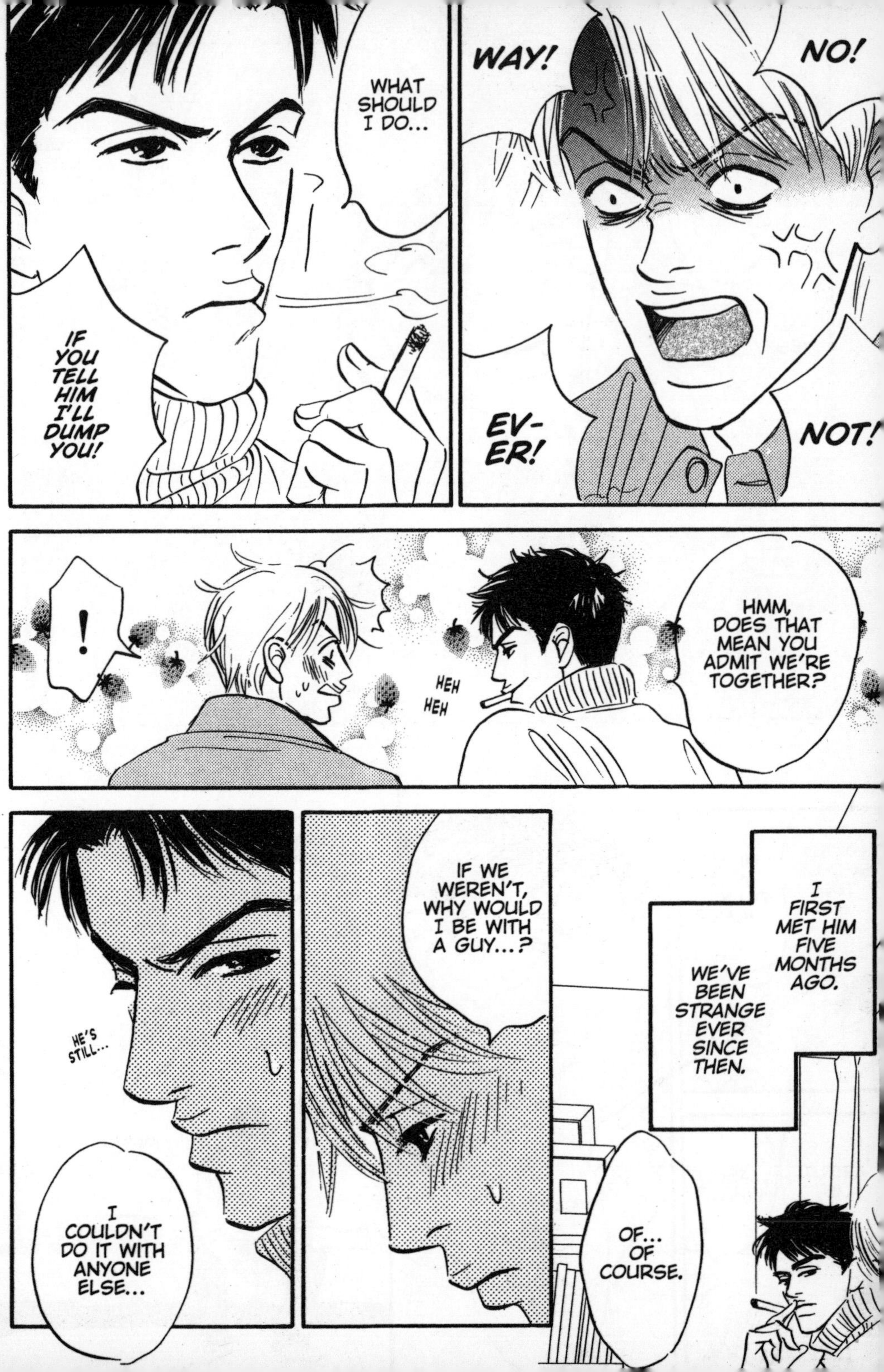
NO!
WAY!
NOT!
EV-ER!
WHAT SHOULD I DO...
IF YOU TELL HIM I'LL DUMP YOU!
HMM, DOES THAT MEAN YOU ADMIT WE'RE TOGETHER?
HEH HEH
!
I FIRST MET HIM FIVE MONTHS AGO.
WE'VE BEEN STRANGE EVER SINCE THEN.
OF... OF COURSE.
IF WE WEREN'T, WHY WOULD I BE WITH A GUY...?
HE'S STILL...
I COULDN'T DO IT WITH ANYONE ELSE...

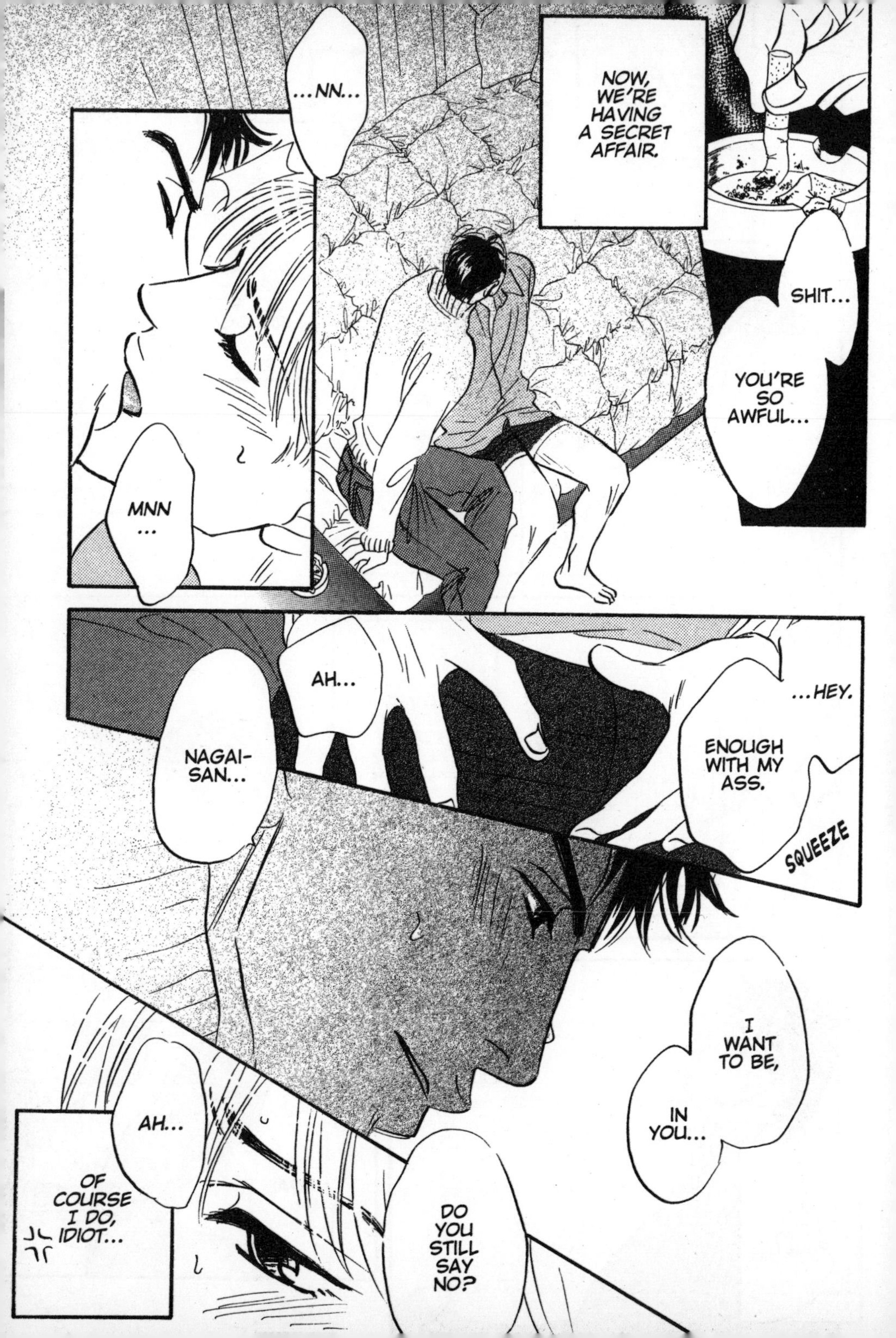
NOW, WE'RE HAVING A SECRET AFFAIR.
SHIT...
YOU'RE SO AWFUL...
...NN...
MNN ...
...HEY.
ENOUGH WITH MY ASS.
SQUEEZE
AH...
NAGAI-SAN...
I WANT TO BE,
IN YOU...
DO YOU STILL SAY NO?
AH...
OF COURSE I DO, IDIOT...

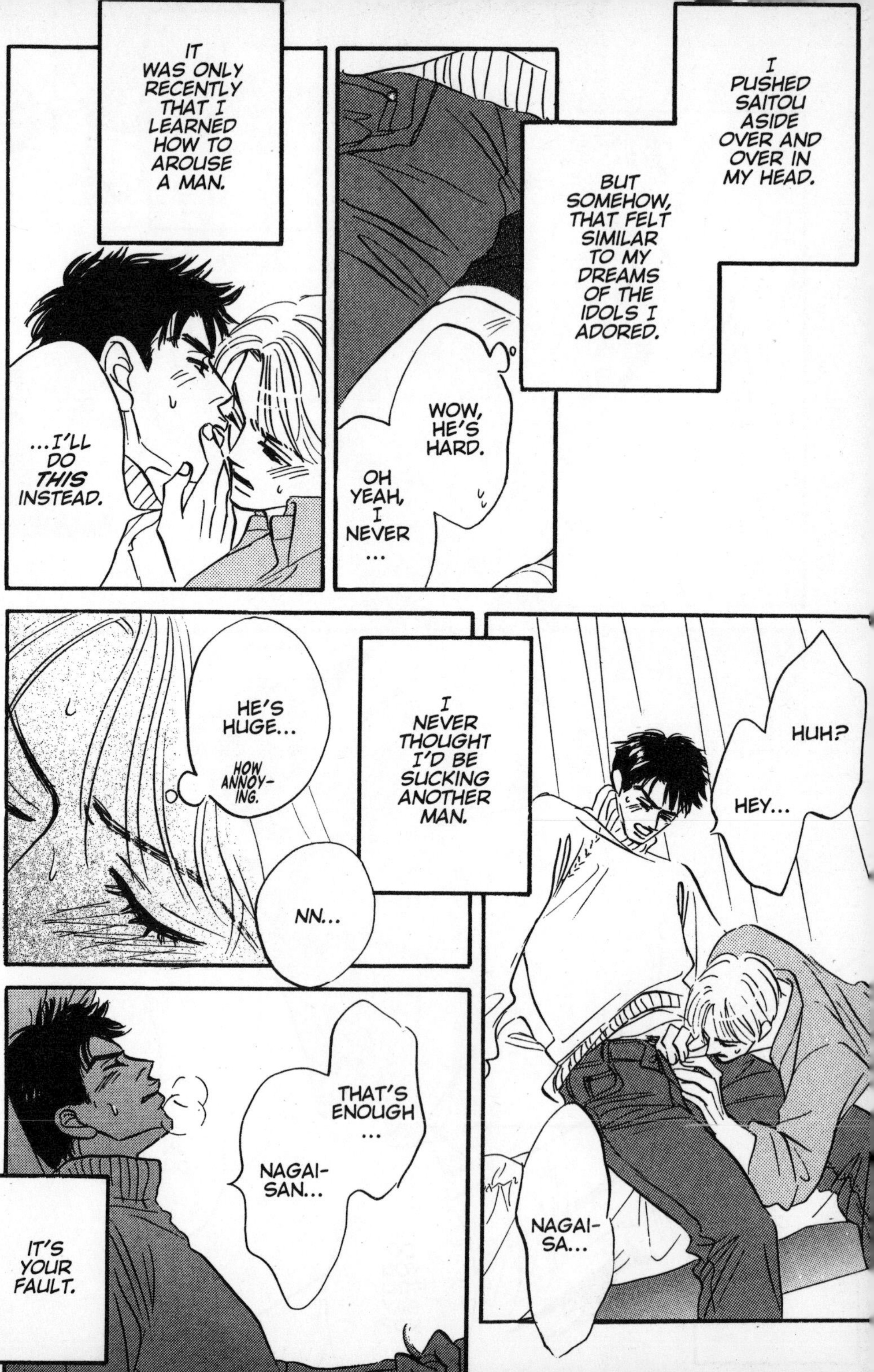
I PUSHED SAITOU ASIDE OVER AND OVER IN MY HEAD.
BUT SOMEHOW, THAT FELT SIMILAR TO MY DREAMS OF THE IDOLS I ADORED.
WOW, HE'S HARD.
OH YEAH, I NEVER...
IT WAS ONLY RECENTLY THAT I LEARNED HOW TO AROUSE A MAN.
...I'LL DO *THIS* INSTEAD.
HUH?
HEY...
NAGAI-SA...
I NEVER THOUGHT I'D BE SUCKING ANOTHER MAN.
HE'S HUGE...
HOW ANNOY-ING.
NN...
THAT'S ENOUGH...
NAGAI-SAN...
IT'S YOUR FAULT.

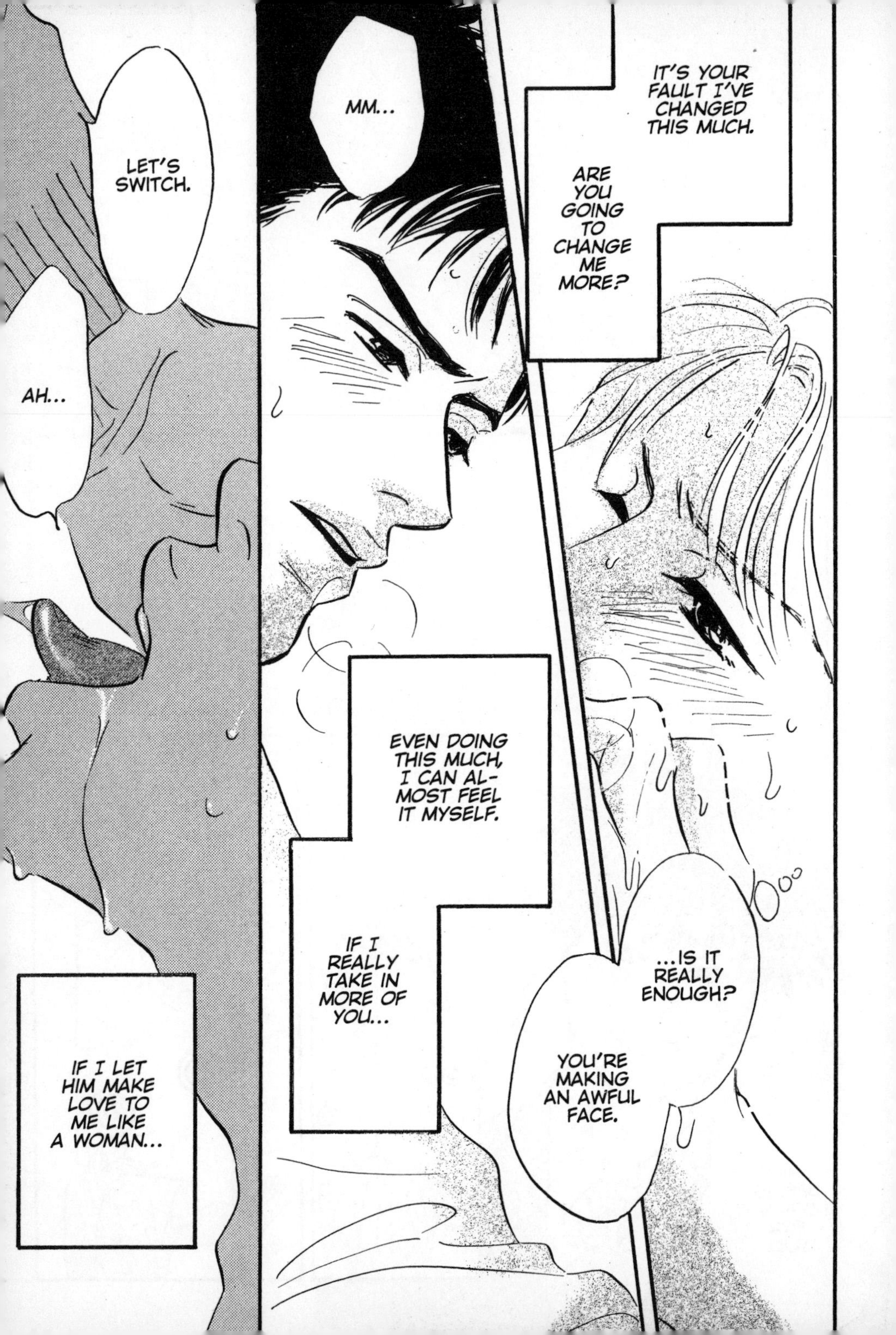
IT'S YOUR FAULT I'VE CHANGED THIS MUCH.
ARE YOU GOING TO CHANGE ME MORE?
...IS IT REALLY ENOUGH?
YOU'RE MAKING AN AWFUL FACE.
MM...
EVEN DOING THIS MUCH, I CAN AL-MOST FEEL IT MYSELF.
IF I REALLY TAKE IN MORE OF YOU...
LET'S SWITCH.
AH...
IF I LET HIM MAKE LOVE TO ME LIKE A WOMAN...

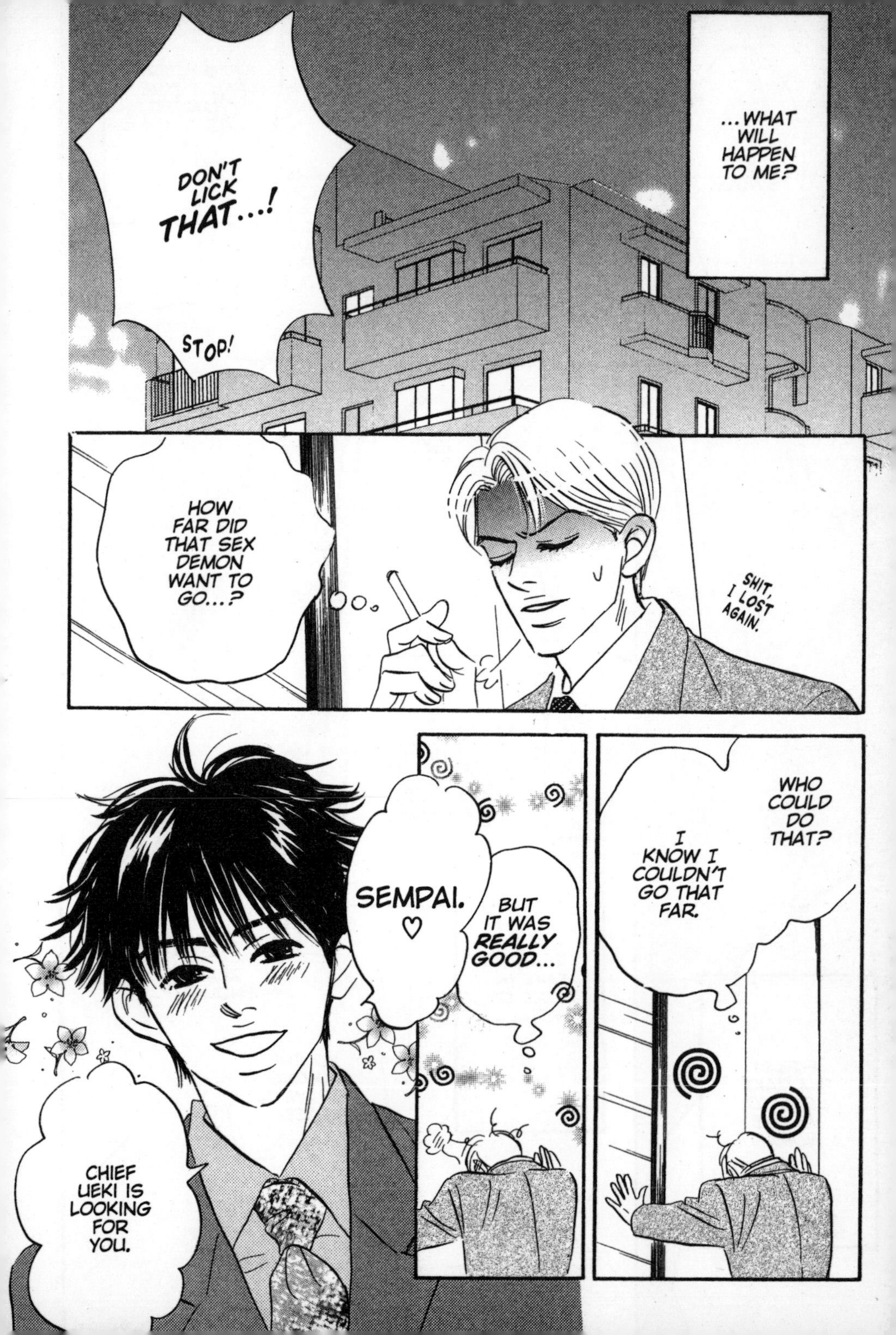
...WHAT WILL HAPPEN TO ME?
DON'T LICK THAT...!
STOP!
SHIT, I LOST AGAIN.
HOW FAR DID THAT SEX DEMON WANT TO GO...?
WHO COULD DO THAT?
I KNOW I COULDN'T GO THAT FAR.
BUT IT WAS REALLY GOOD...
SEMPAI. ♡
CHIEF UEKI IS LOOKING FOR YOU.

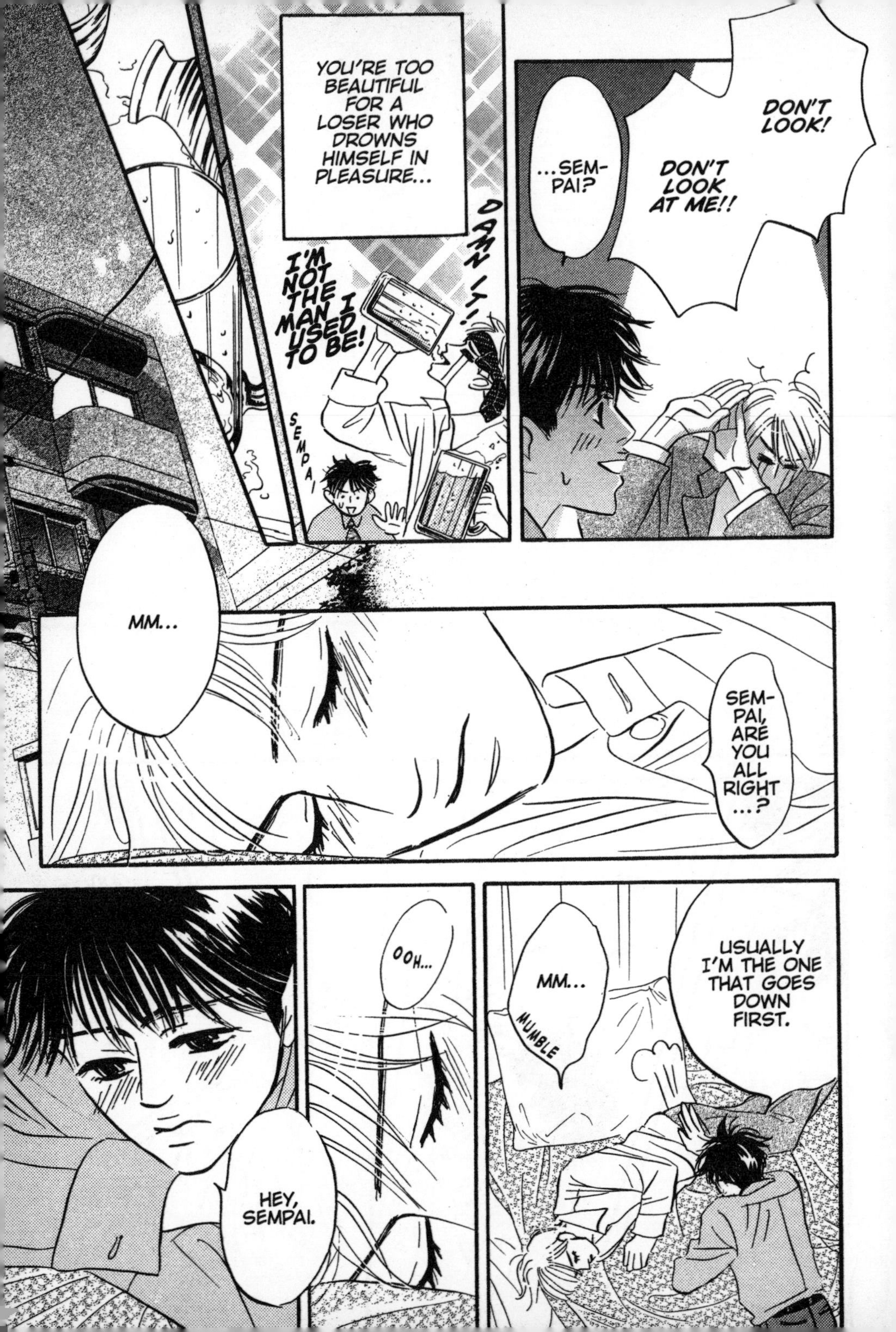
DON'T LOOK!
DON'T LOOK AT ME!!
...SEM-PAI?
YOU'RE TOO BEAUTIFUL FOR A LOSER WHO DROWNS HIMSELF IN PLEASURE...
DAMN IT!!
I'M NOT THE MAN I USED TO BE!
SEMPAI
SEM-PAI, ARE YOU ALL RIGHT ...?
MM...
USUALLY I'M THE ONE THAT GOES DOWN FIRST.
MM...
MUMBLE
OOH...
HEY, SEMPAI.

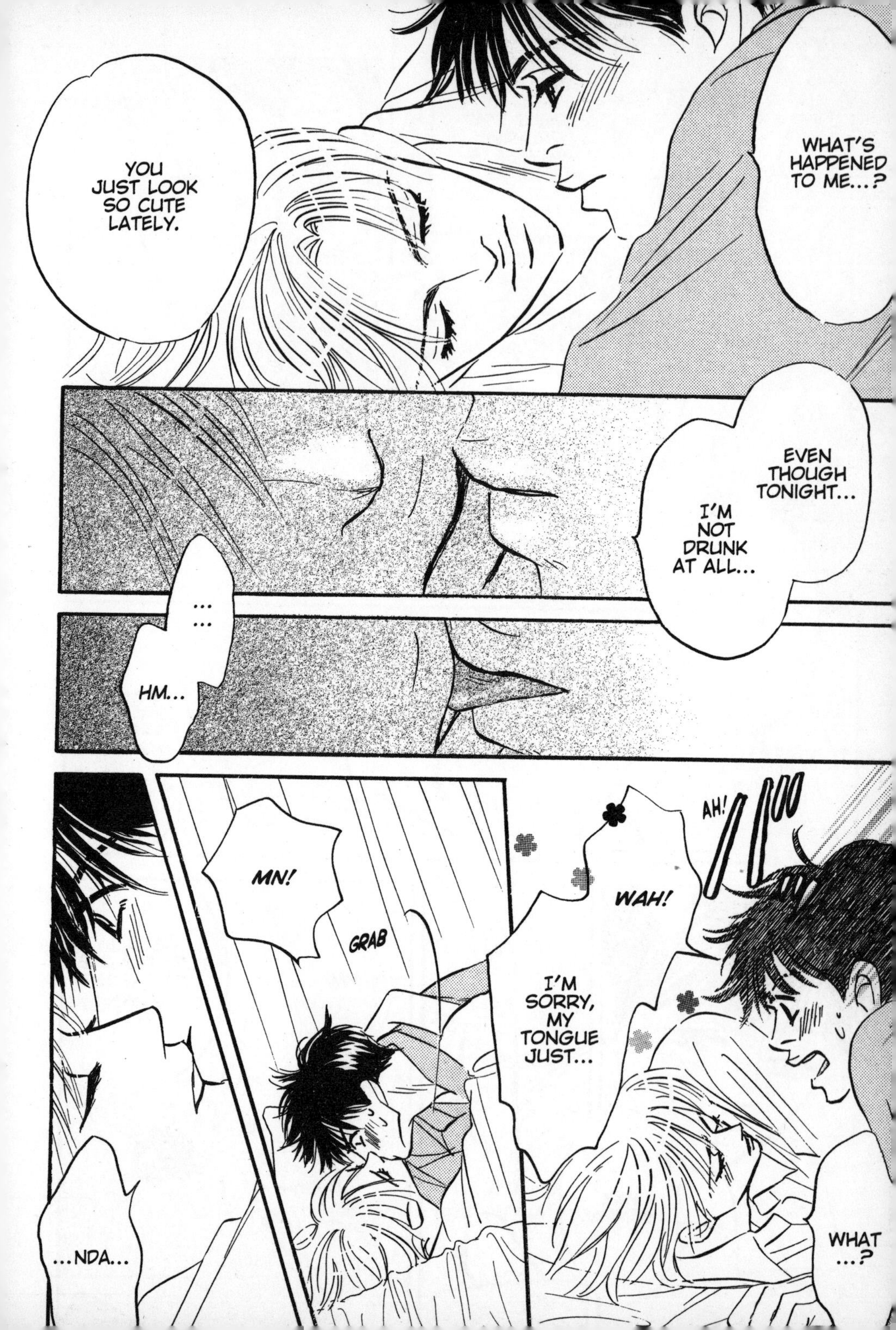
WHAT'S HAPPENED TO ME...?
YOU JUST LOOK SO CUTE LATELY.
EVEN THOUGH TONIGHT...
I'M NOT DRUNK AT ALL...
...
...
HM...
AH!
WAH!
I'M SORRY, MY TONGUE JUST...
WHAT ...?
MN!
GRAB
...NDA...

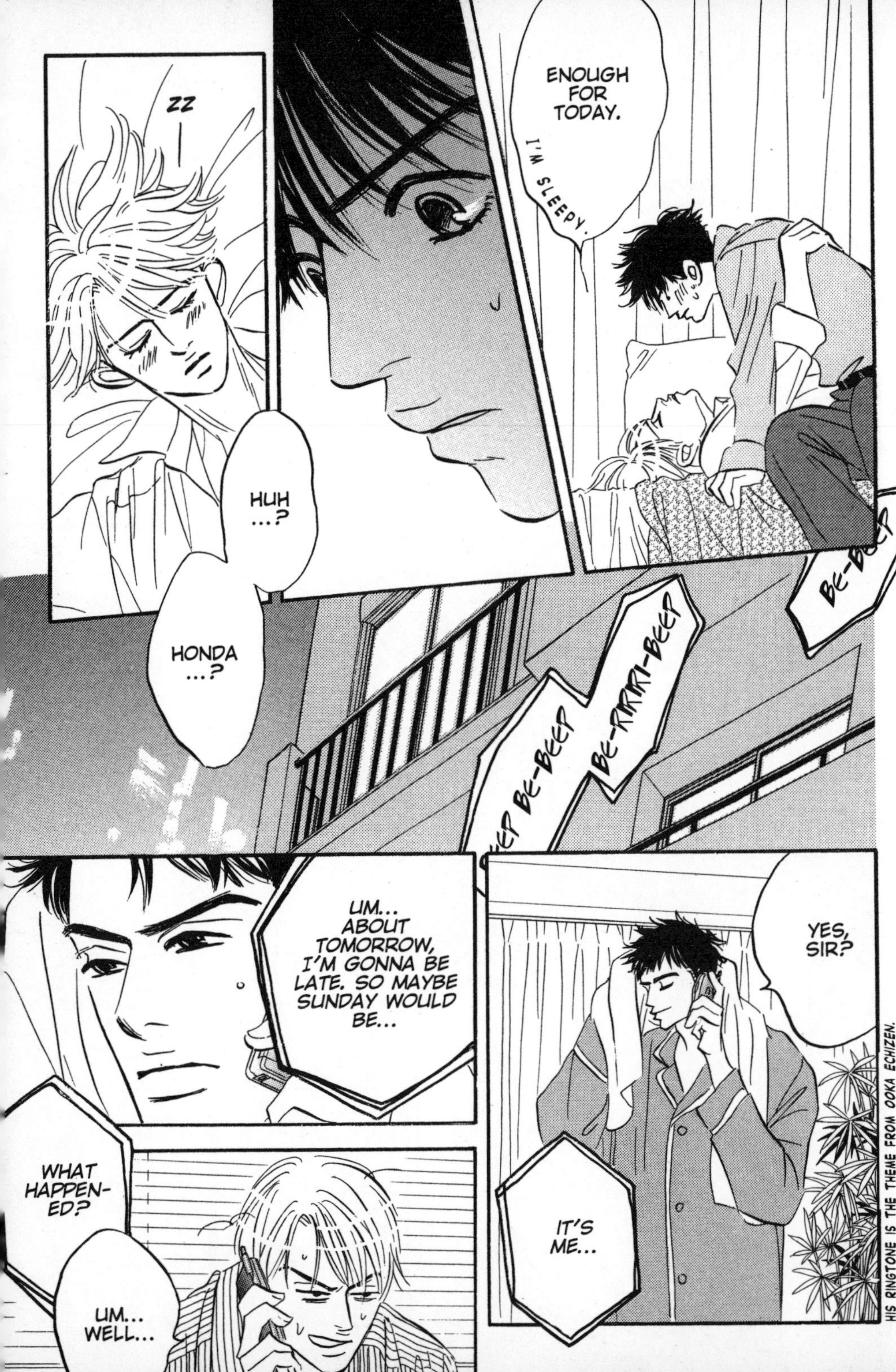
ENOUGH FOR TODAY.
I'M SLEEPY.
ZZ
HUH...?
HONDA...?
BE-BEEP
BE-RRRRI-BEEP
...EEP BE-BEEP
YES, SIR?
IT'S ME...
UM... ABOUT TOMORROW, I'M GONNA BE LATE. SO MAYBE SUNDAY WOULD BE...
WHAT HAPPEN-ED?
UM... WELL...

HIS RINGTONE IS THE THEME FROM *OOKA ECHIZEN.*

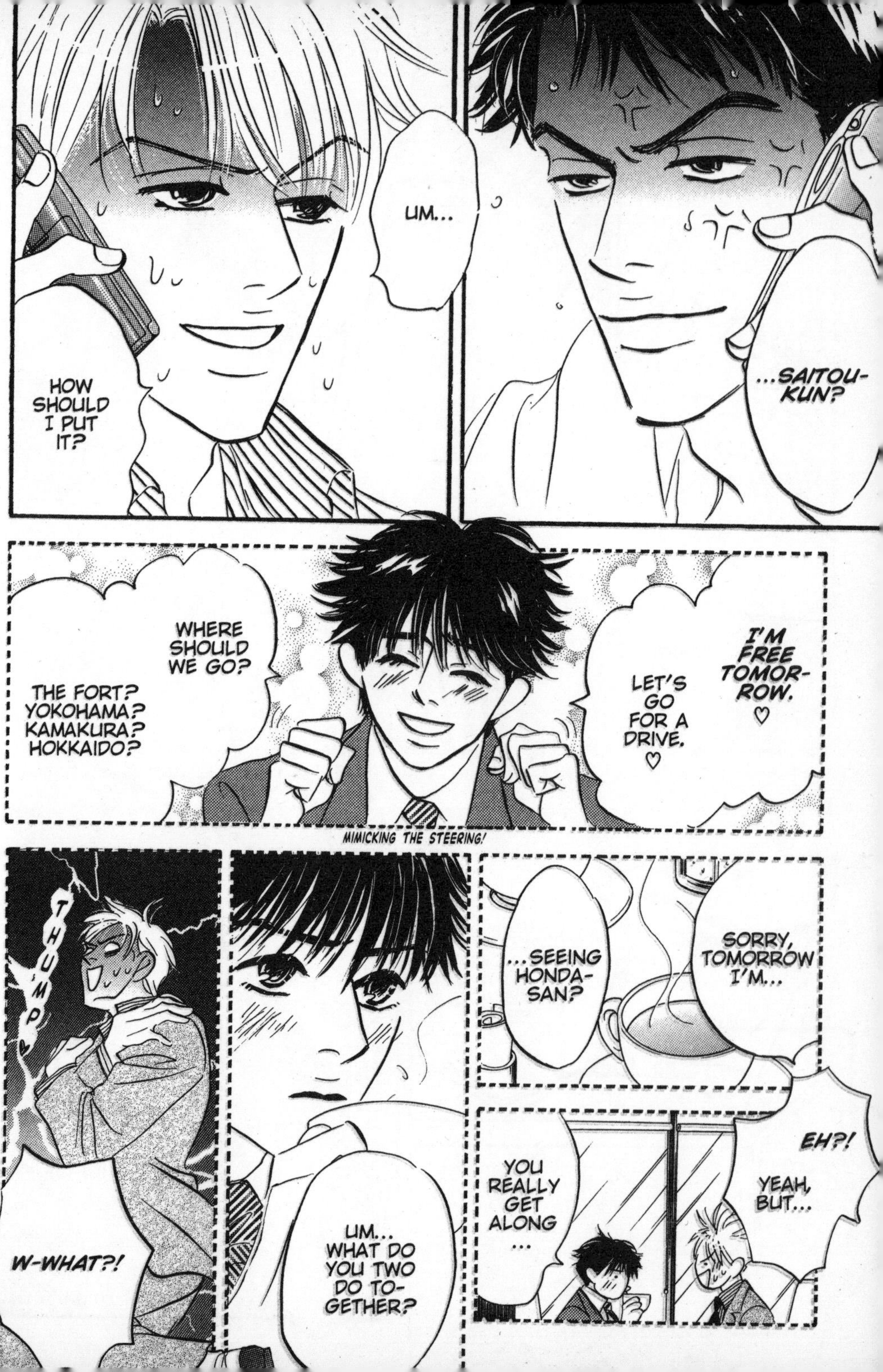
...SAITOU-KUN?
UM...
HOW SHOULD I PUT IT?
I'M FREE TOMORROW. ♡
LET'S GO FOR A DRIVE. ♡
WHERE SHOULD WE GO?
THE FORT? YOKOHAMA? KAMAKURA? HOKKAIDO?
MIMICKING THE STEERING!
SORRY, TOMORROW I'M...
...SEEING HONDA-SAN?
EH?!
YEAH, BUT...
YOU REALLY GET ALONG ...
UM... WHAT DO YOU TWO DO TOGETHER?
THUMP ♡
W-WHAT?!

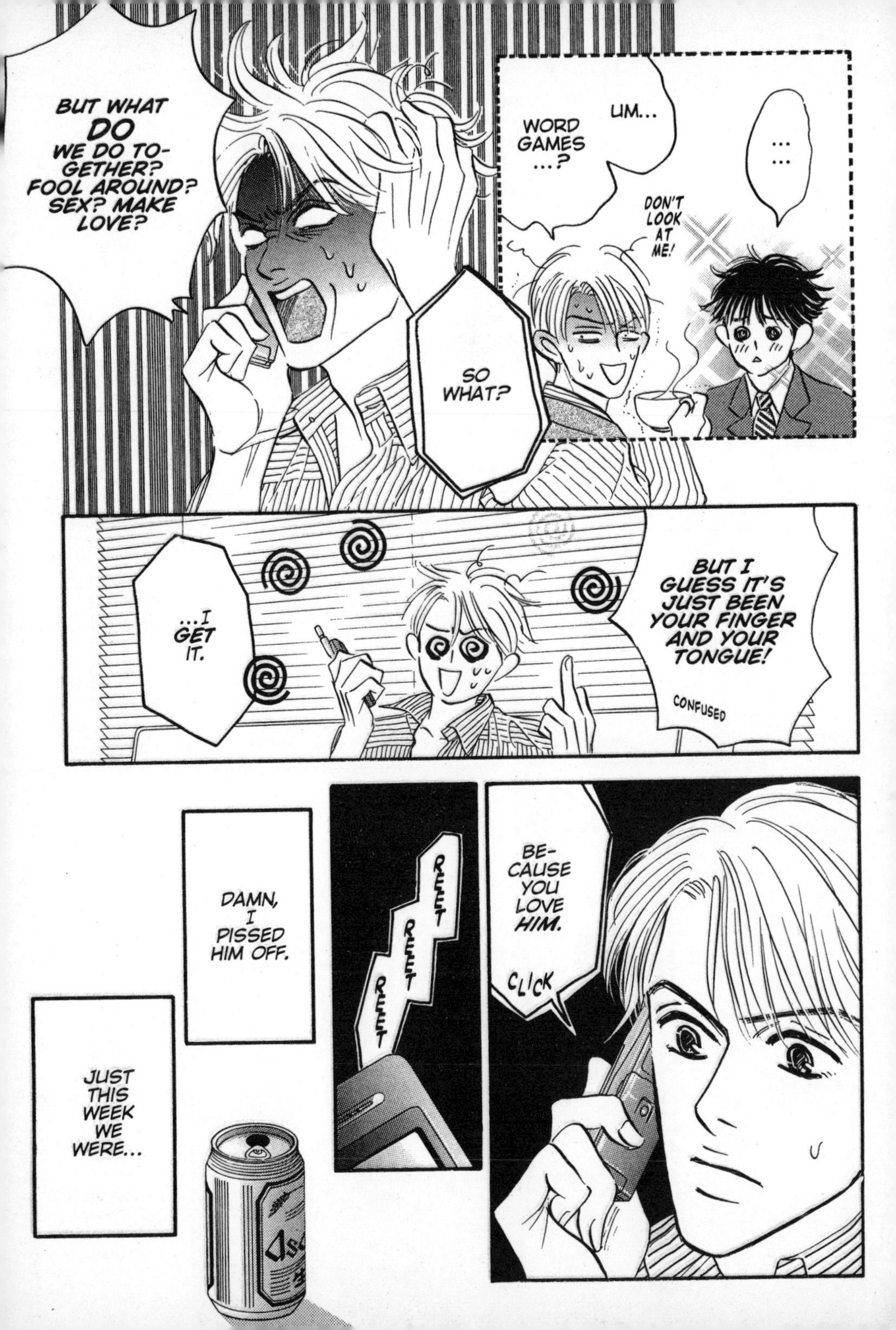
BUT WHAT DO WE DO TOGETHER? FOOL AROUND? SEX? MAKE LOVE?
UM... WORD GAMES ...?
... ...
DON'T LOOK AT ME!
SO WHAT?
BUT I GUESS IT'S JUST BEEN YOUR FINGER AND YOUR TONGUE!
CONFUSED
...I GET IT.
BECAUSE YOU LOVE HIM.
CLICK
REEET REEET REEET
DAMN, I PISSED HIM OFF.
JUST THIS WEEK WE WERE...

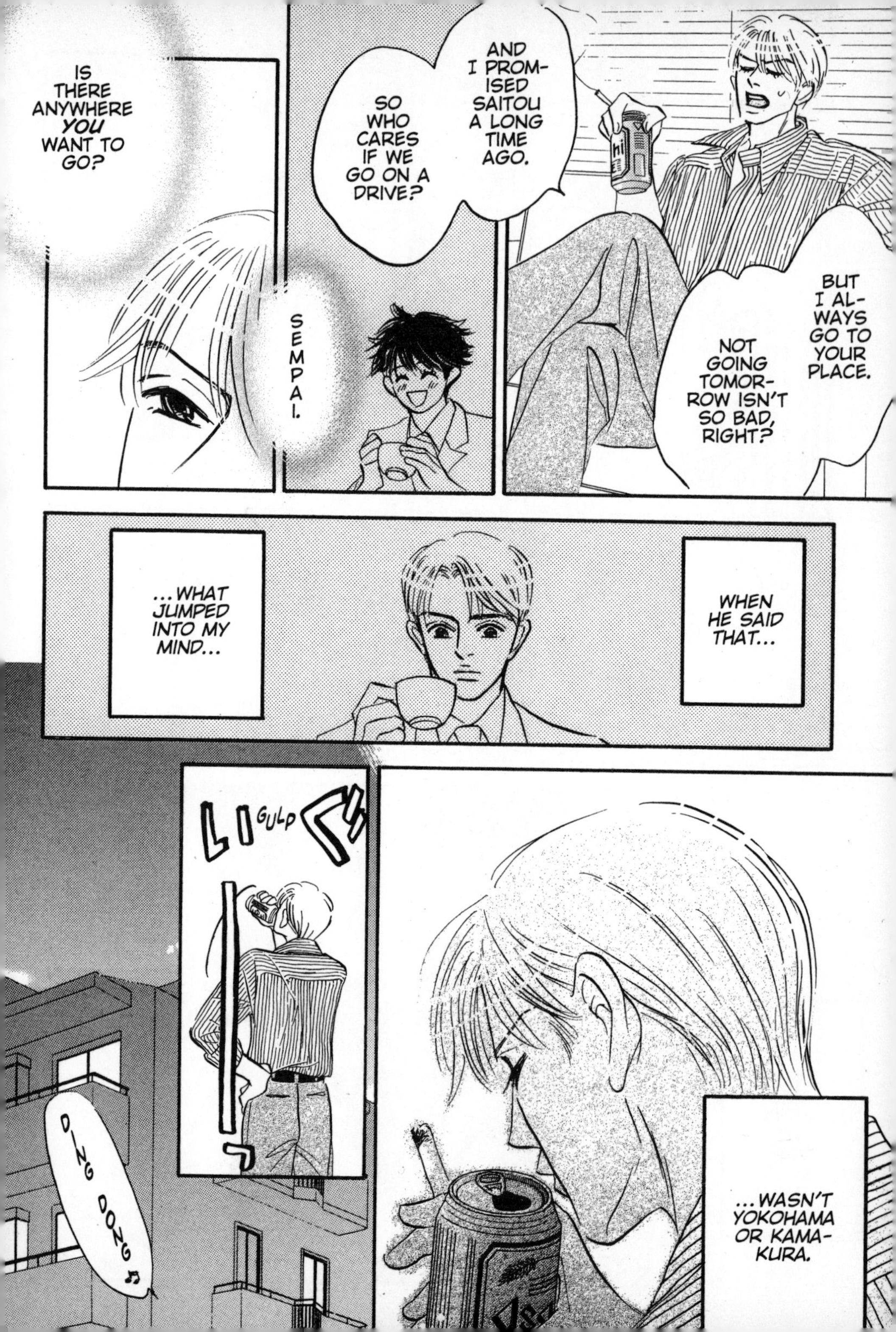
BUT I ALWAYS GO TO YOUR PLACE.
NOT GOING TOMORROW ISN'T SO BAD, RIGHT?
AND I PROMISED SAITOU A LONG TIME AGO.
SO WHO CARES IF WE GO ON A DRIVE?
SEMPAI.
IS THERE ANYWHERE *YOU* WANT TO GO?
WHEN HE SAID THAT...
...WHAT JUMPED INTO MY MIND...
...WASN'T YOKOHAMA OR KAMAKURA.
GULP
DING DONG ♫

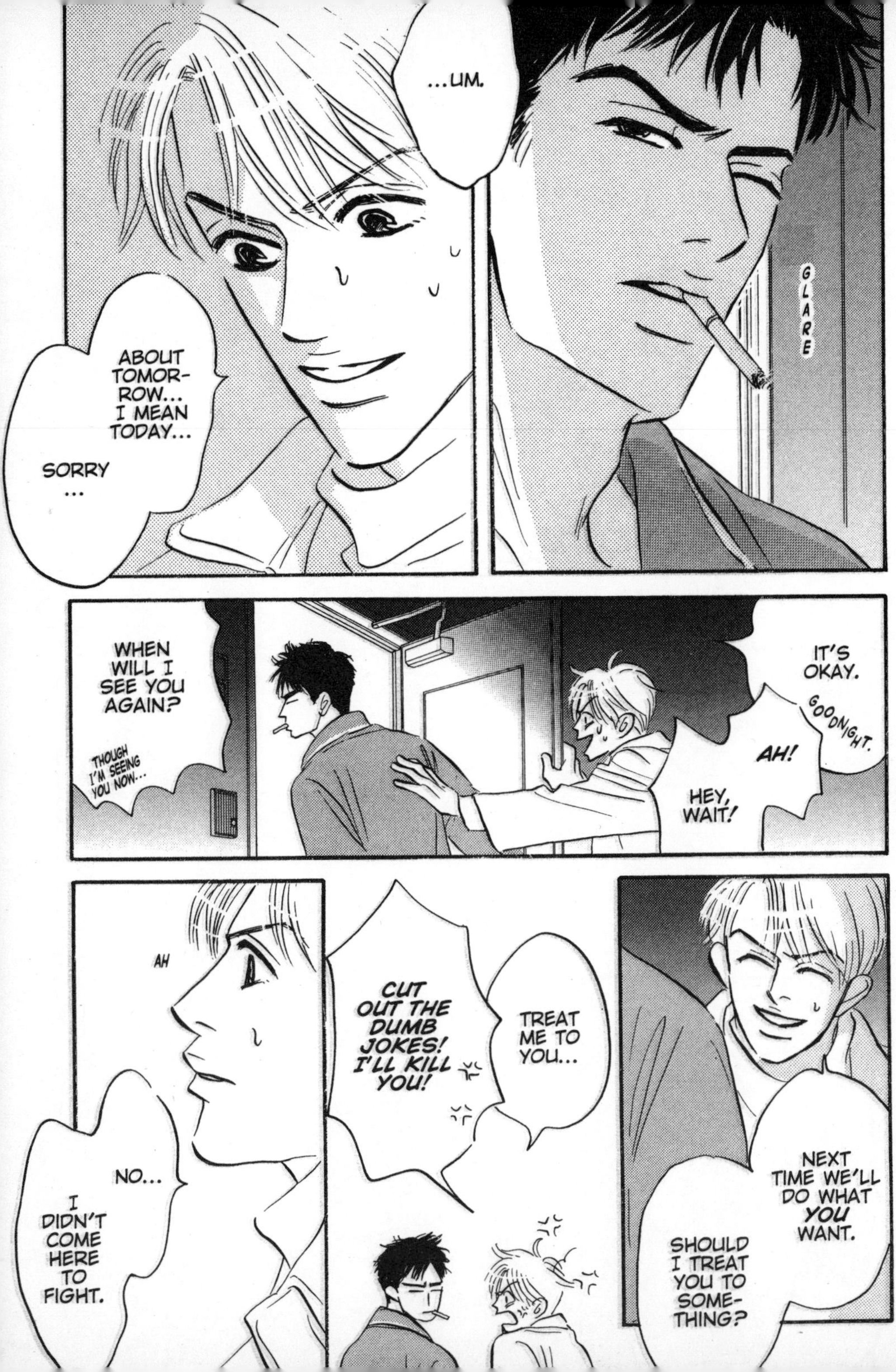
G L A R E
...UM.
ABOUT TOMORROW... I MEAN TODAY...
SORRY ...
IT'S OKAY.
GOODNIGHT.
AH!
HEY, WAIT!
WHEN WILL I SEE YOU AGAIN?
THOUGH I'M SEEING YOU NOW...
NEXT TIME WE'LL DO WHAT *YOU* WANT.
SHOULD I TREAT YOU TO SOMETHING?
TREAT ME TO YOU...
CUT OUT THE DUMB JOKES! I'LL KILL YOU!
AH
NO...
I DIDN'T COME HERE TO FIGHT.

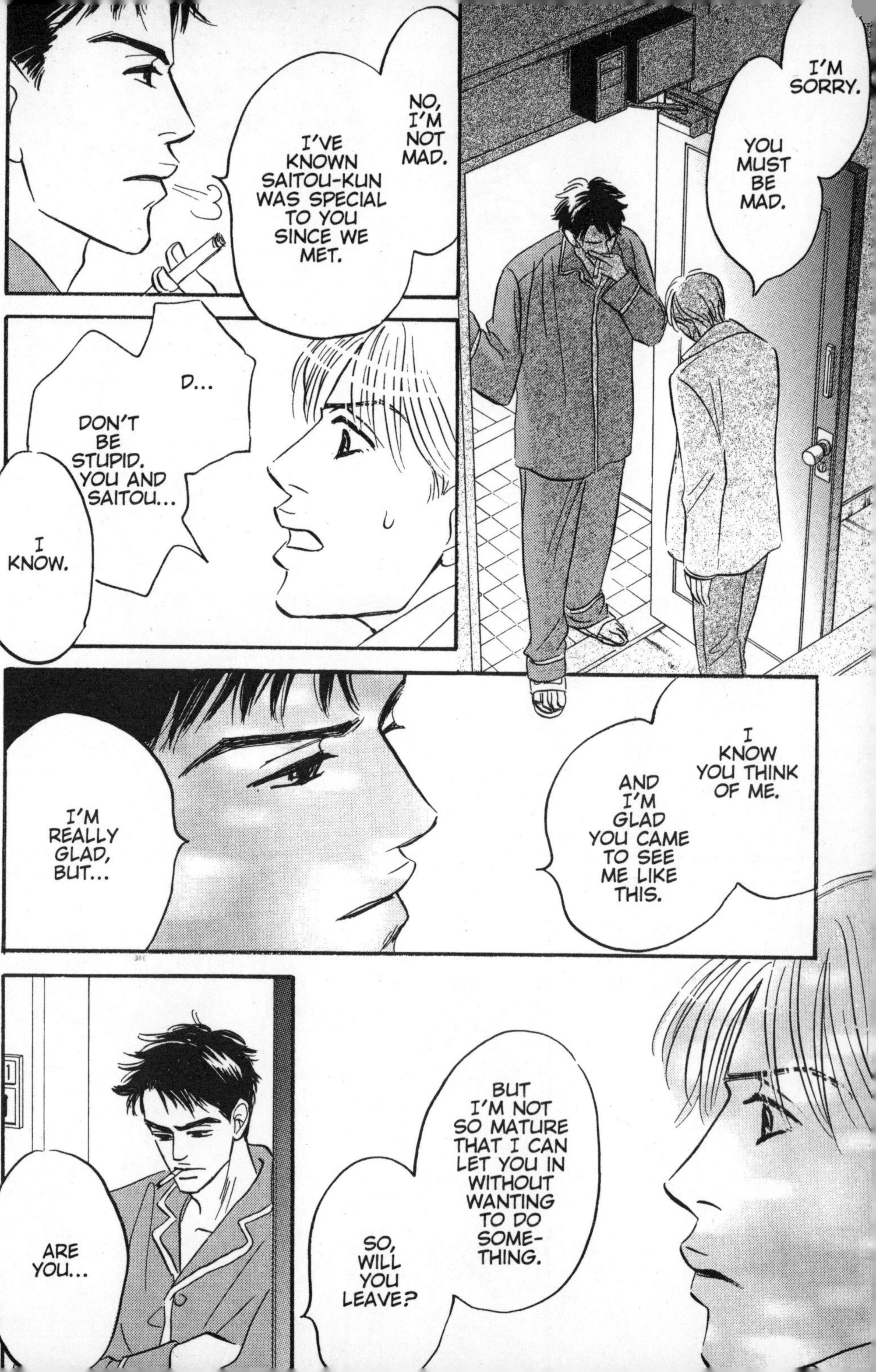
I'M SORRY.
YOU MUST BE MAD.
NO, I'M NOT MAD.
I'VE KNOWN SAITOU-KUN WAS SPECIAL TO YOU SINCE WE MET.
D...
DON'T BE STUPID. YOU AND SAITOU...
I KNOW.
I KNOW YOU THINK OF ME.
AND I'M GLAD YOU CAME TO SEE ME LIKE THIS.
I'M REALLY GLAD, BUT...
BUT I'M NOT SO MATURE THAT I CAN LET YOU IN WITHOUT WANTING TO DO SOME-THING.
SO, WILL YOU LEAVE?
ARE YOU...

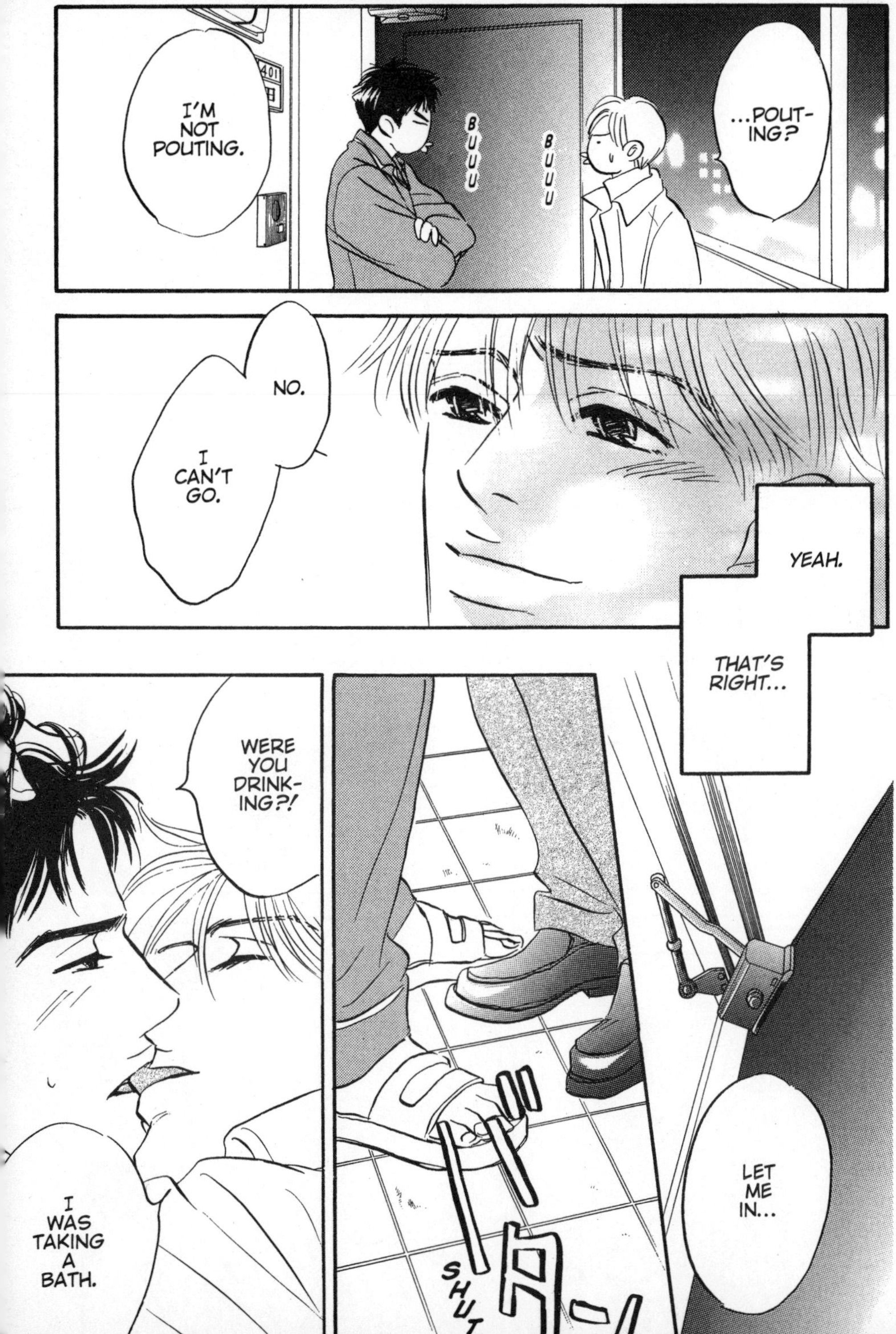
...POUT-ING?
BUUU
BUUU
I'M NOT POUTING.
YEAH.
THAT'S RIGHT...
NO.
I CAN'T GO.
LET ME IN...
SHUT
WERE YOU DRINK-ING?!
I WAS TAKING A BATH.

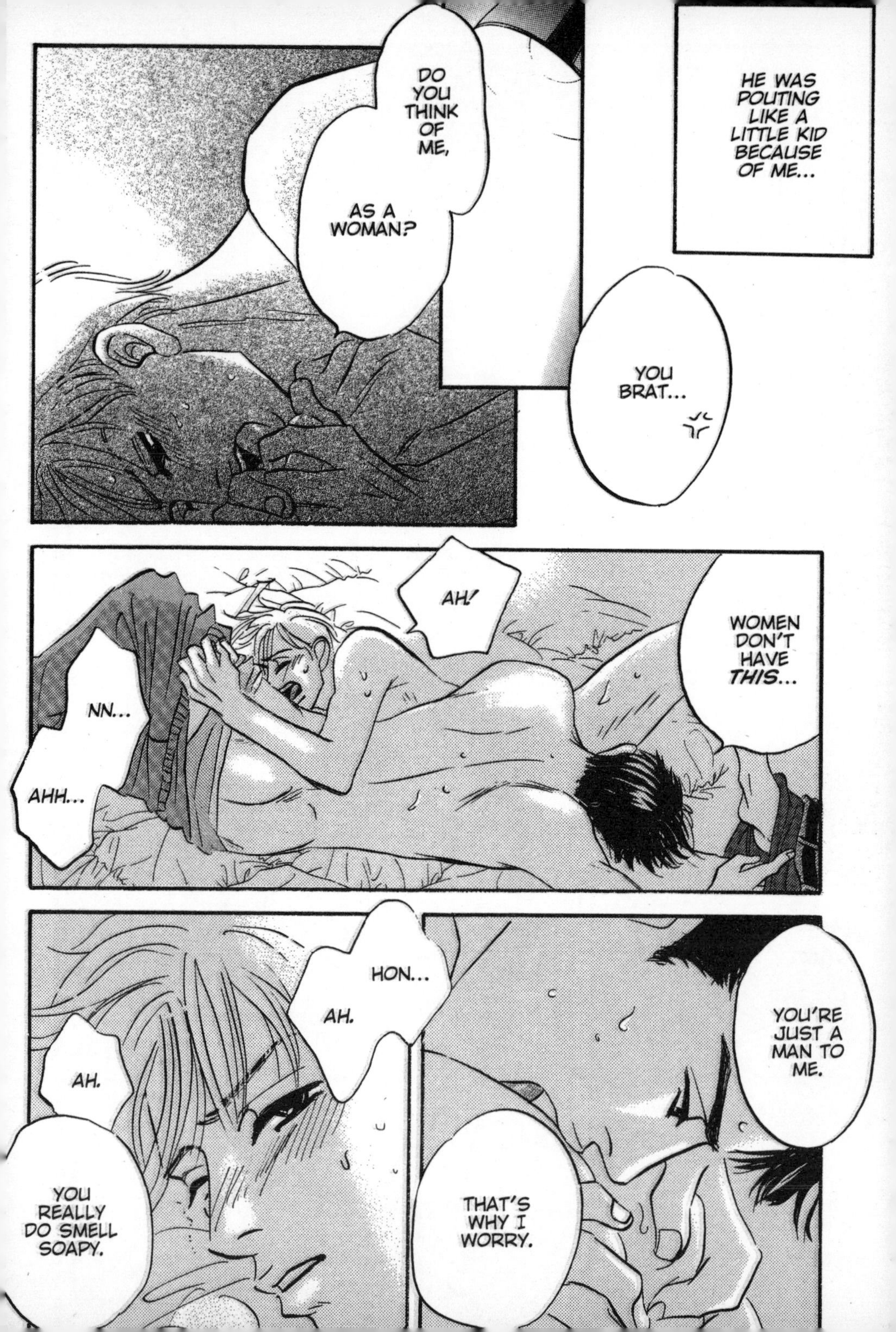
HE WAS POUTING LIKE A LITTLE KID BECAUSE OF ME...
DO YOU THINK OF ME,
AS A WOMAN?
YOU BRAT...
WOMEN DON'T HAVE ***THIS***...
AH!
NN...
AHH...
YOU'RE JUST A MAN TO ME.
THAT'S WHY I WORRY.
HON...
AH.
AH.
YOU REALLY DO SMELL SOAPY.

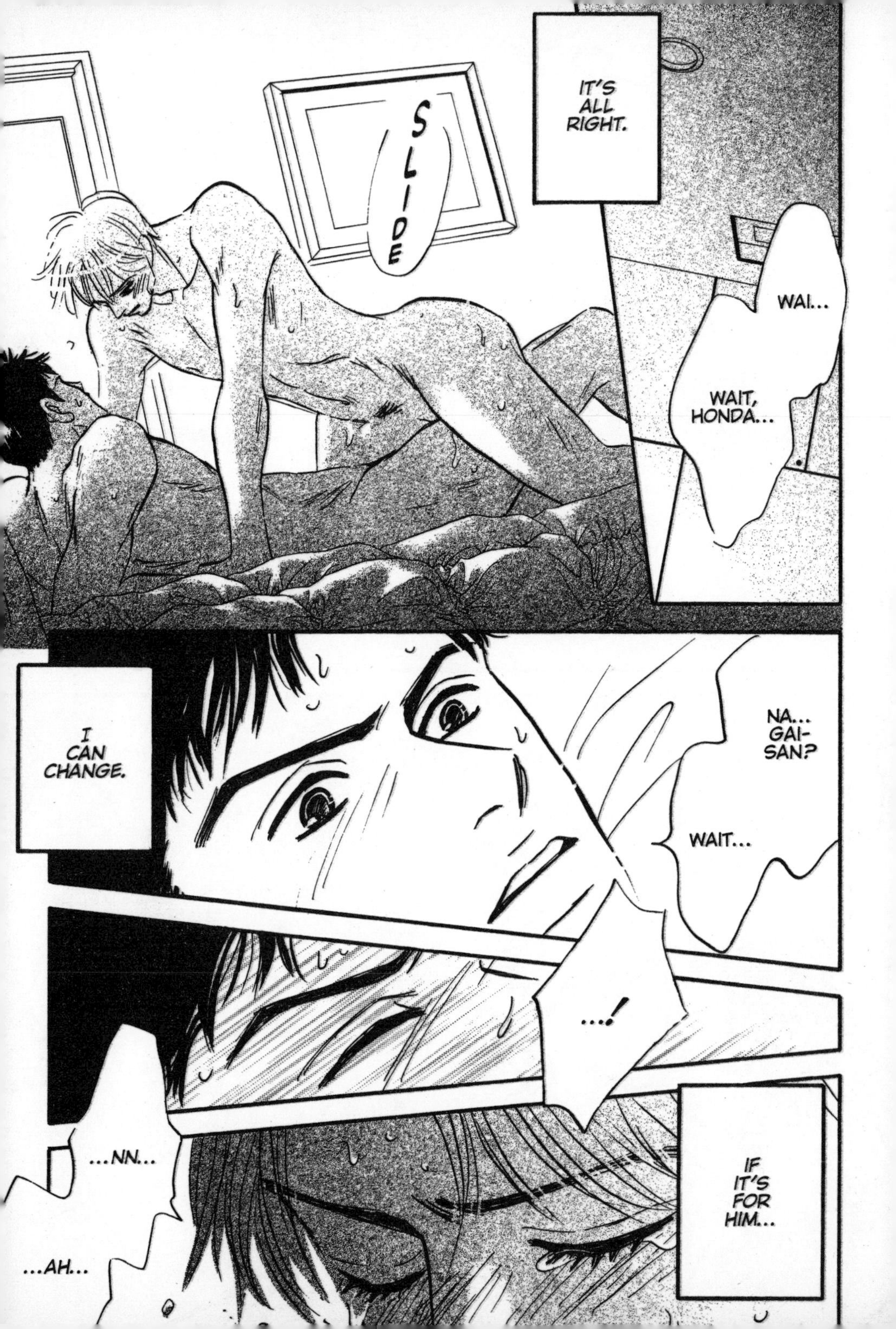

IT'S ALL RIGHT.
WAI...
WAIT, HONDA...
SLIDE
NA... GAI-SAN?
WAIT...
I CAN CHANGE.
...!
IF IT'S FOR HIM...
...NN...
...AH...

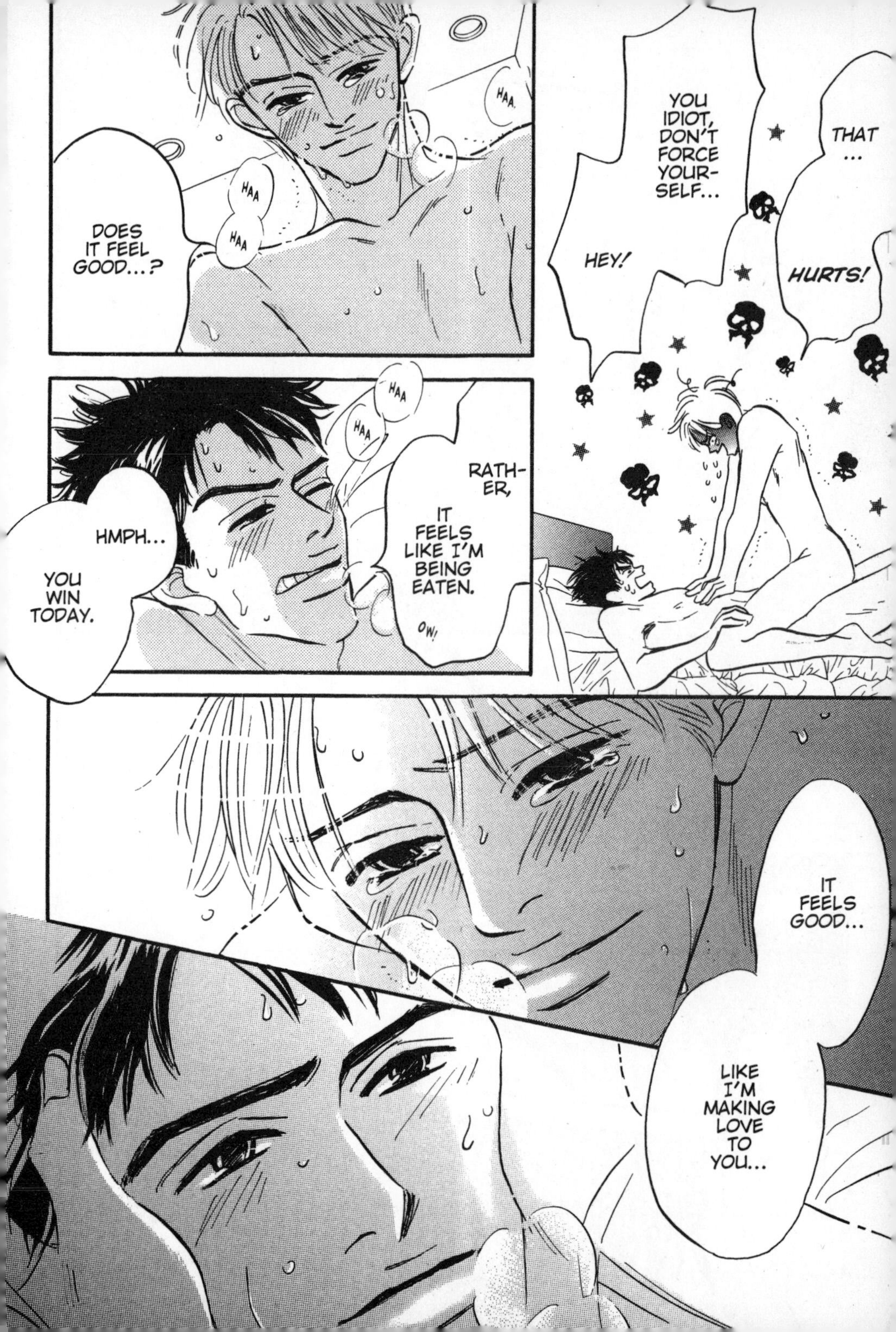
THAT ... HURTS!
YOU IDIOT, DON'T FORCE YOUR-SELF...
HEY!
HAA.
HAA
HAA
DOES IT FEEL GOOD...?
HAA
HAA
RATH-ER,
IT FEELS LIKE I'M BEING EATEN.
OW!
HMPH...
YOU WIN TODAY.
IT FEELS GOOD...
LIKE I'M MAKING LOVE TO YOU...

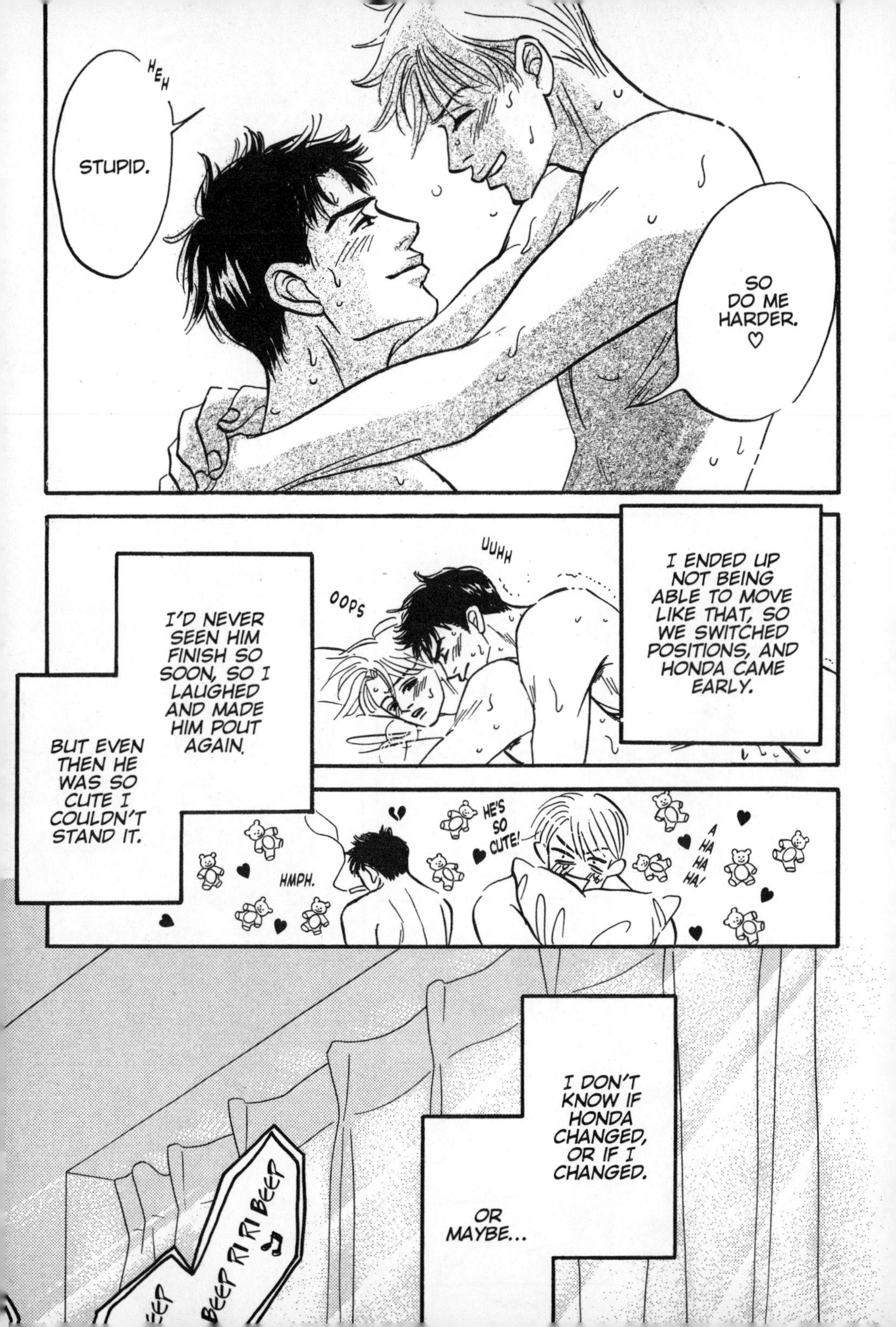
SO DO ME HARDER. ♡
HEH
STUPID.
I ENDED UP NOT BEING ABLE TO MOVE LIKE THAT, SO WE SWITCHED POSITIONS, AND HONDA CAME EARLY.
UUHH
OOPS
I'D NEVER SEEN HIM FINISH SO SOON, SO I LAUGHED AND MADE HIM POUT AGAIN.
BUT EVEN THEN HE WAS SO CUTE I COULDN'T STAND IT.
A HA HA HA!
HE'S SO CUTE!
HMPH.
I DON'T KNOW IF HONDA CHANGED, OR IF I CHANGED.
OR MAYBE...
BEEP RI RI BEEP ♪

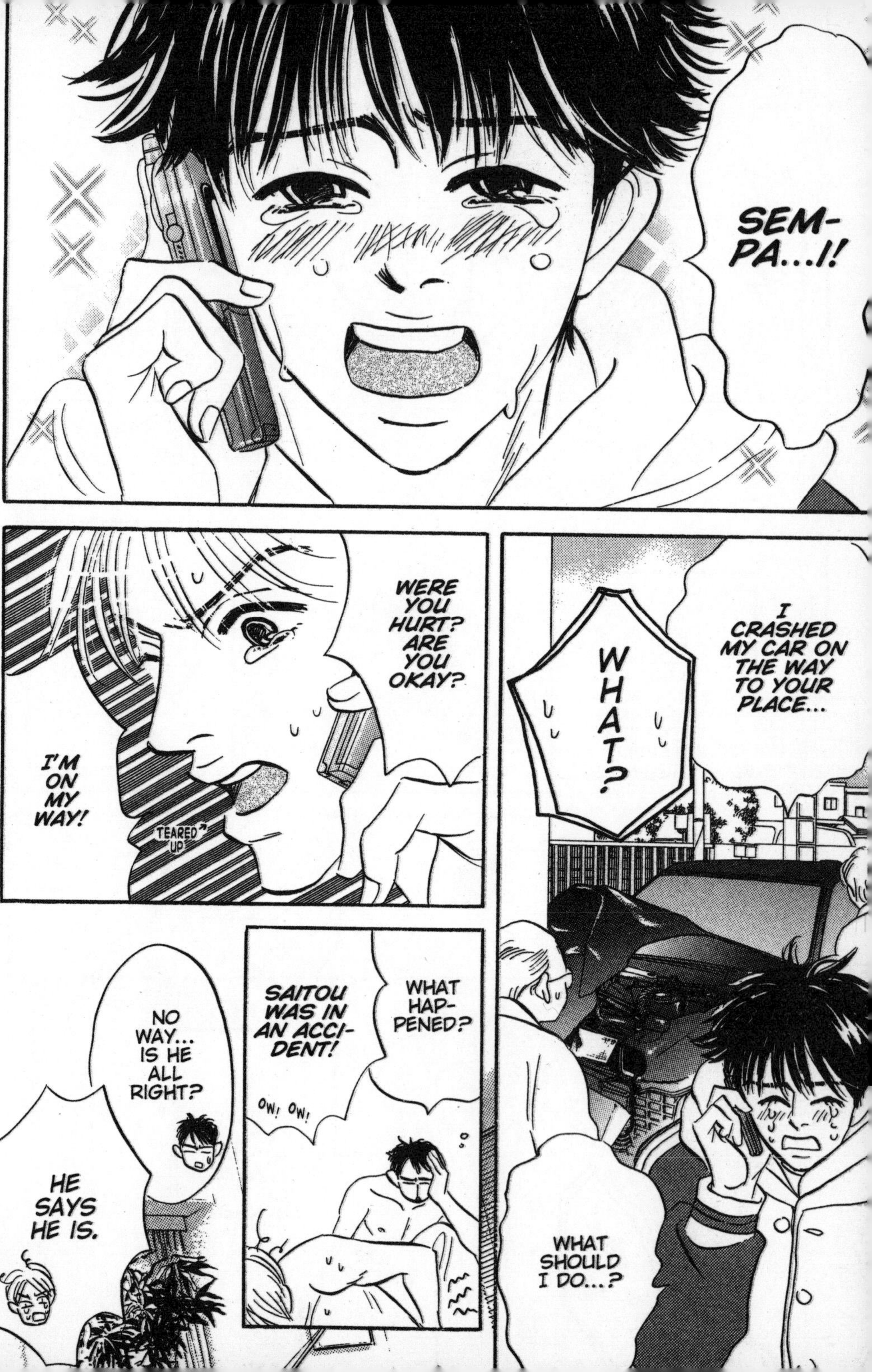
SEM-PA...I!
I CRASHED MY CAR ON THE WAY TO YOUR PLACE...
WHAT?
WHAT SHOULD I DO...?
WERE YOU HURT? ARE YOU OKAY?
I'M ON MY WAY!
TEARED UP
WHAT HAP-PENED?
SAITOU WAS IN AN ACCI-DENT!
OW! OW!
NO WAY... IS HE ALL RIGHT?
HE SAYS HE IS.

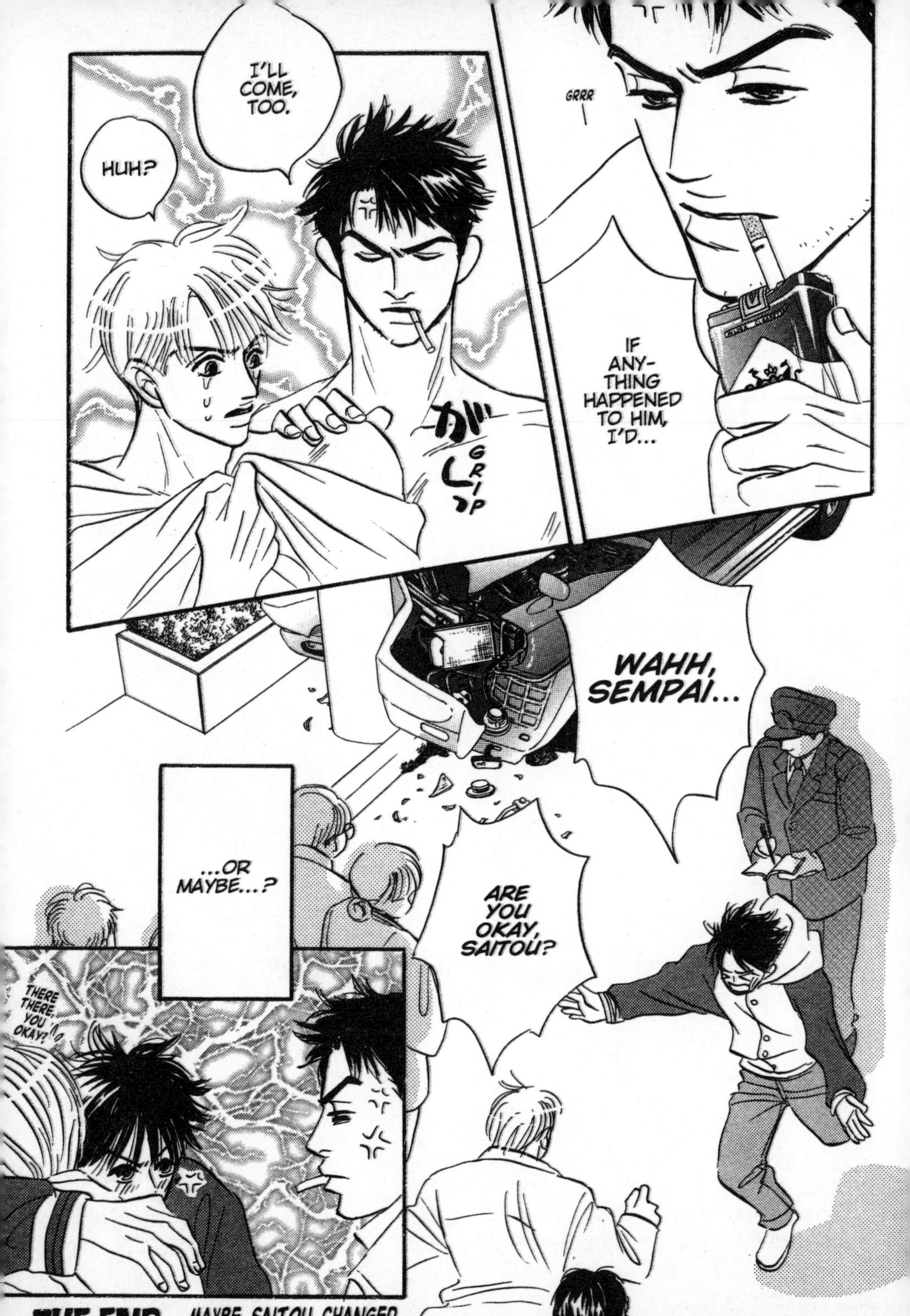
GRRR
IF ANY-THING HAPPENED TO HIM, I'D...
I'LL COME, TOO.
HUH?
がしっ
GRIP
WAHH, SEMPAI...
ARE YOU OKAY, SAITOU?
...OR MAYBE...?
THERE THERE, YOU OKAY?

THE END MAYBE SAITOU CHANGED.

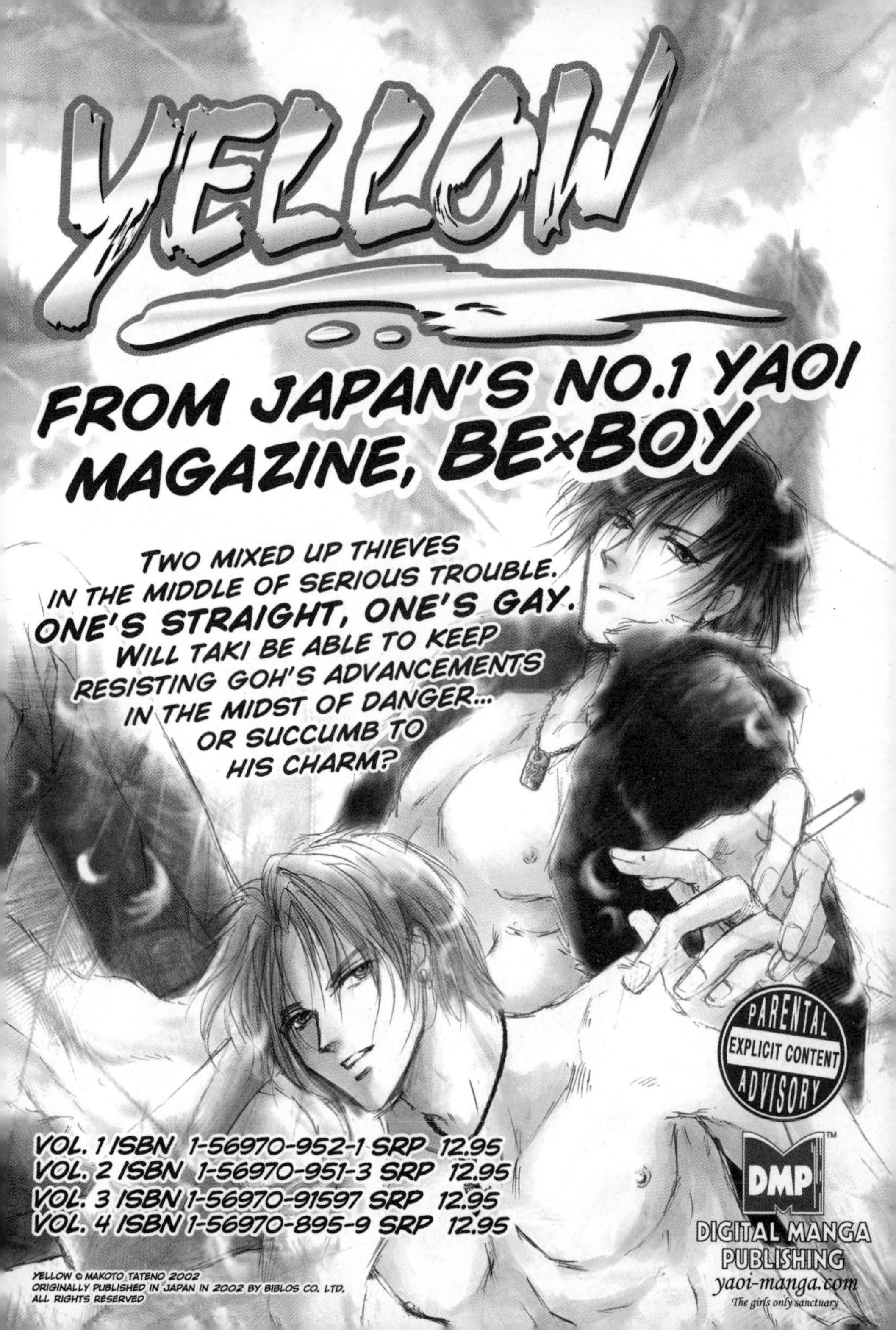
YELLOW
FROM JAPAN'S NO.1 YAOI MAGAZINE, BE×BOY
TWO MIXED UP THIEVES IN THE MIDDLE OF SERIOUS TROUBLE.
ONE'S STRAIGHT, ONE'S GAY.
WILL TAKI BE ABLE TO KEEP RESISTING GOH'S ADVANCEMENTS IN THE MIDST OF DANGER... OR SUCCUMB TO HIS CHARM?
PARENTAL EXPLICIT CONTENT ADVISORY
VOL. 1 ISBN 1-56970-952-1 SRP 12.95
VOL. 2 ISBN 1-56970-951-3 SRP 12.95
VOL. 3 ISBN 1-56970-91597 SRP 12.95
VOL. 4 ISBN 1-56970-895-9 SRP 12.95
DMP
DIGITAL MANGA PUBLISHING
yaoi-manga.com
The girls only sanctuary
YELLOW © MAKOTO TATENO 2002
ORIGINALLY PUBLISHED IN JAPAN IN 2002 BY BIBLOS CO. LTD.
ALL RIGHTS RESERVED

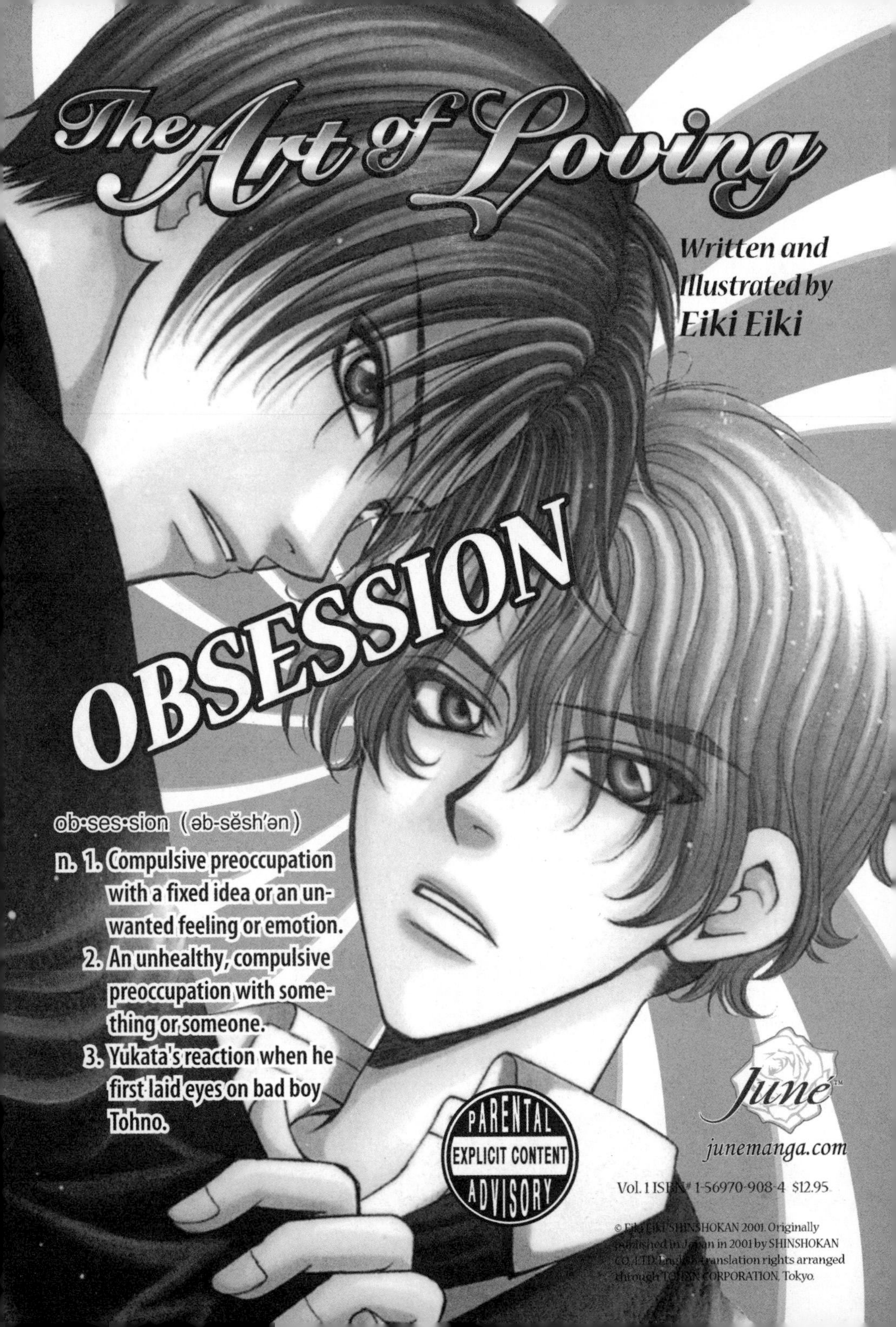

The Art of Loving

Written and
Illustrated by
Eiki Eiki

OBSESSION

ob·ses·sion (əb-sĕsh'ən)

n. 1. Compulsive preoccupation
with a fixed idea or an un-
wanted feeling or emotion.
2. An unhealthy, compulsive
preoccupation with some-
thing or someone.
3. Yukata's reaction when he
first laid eyes on bad boy
Tohno.

PARENTAL
EXPLICIT CONTENT
ADVISORY

June™

junemanga.com

Vol. 1 ISBN# 1-56970-908-4 $12.95

© Eiki EIKI SHINSHOKAN 2001. Originally
published in Japan in 2001 by SHINSHOKAN
CO., LTD. English translation rights arranged
through TOHAN CORPORATION, Tokyo.

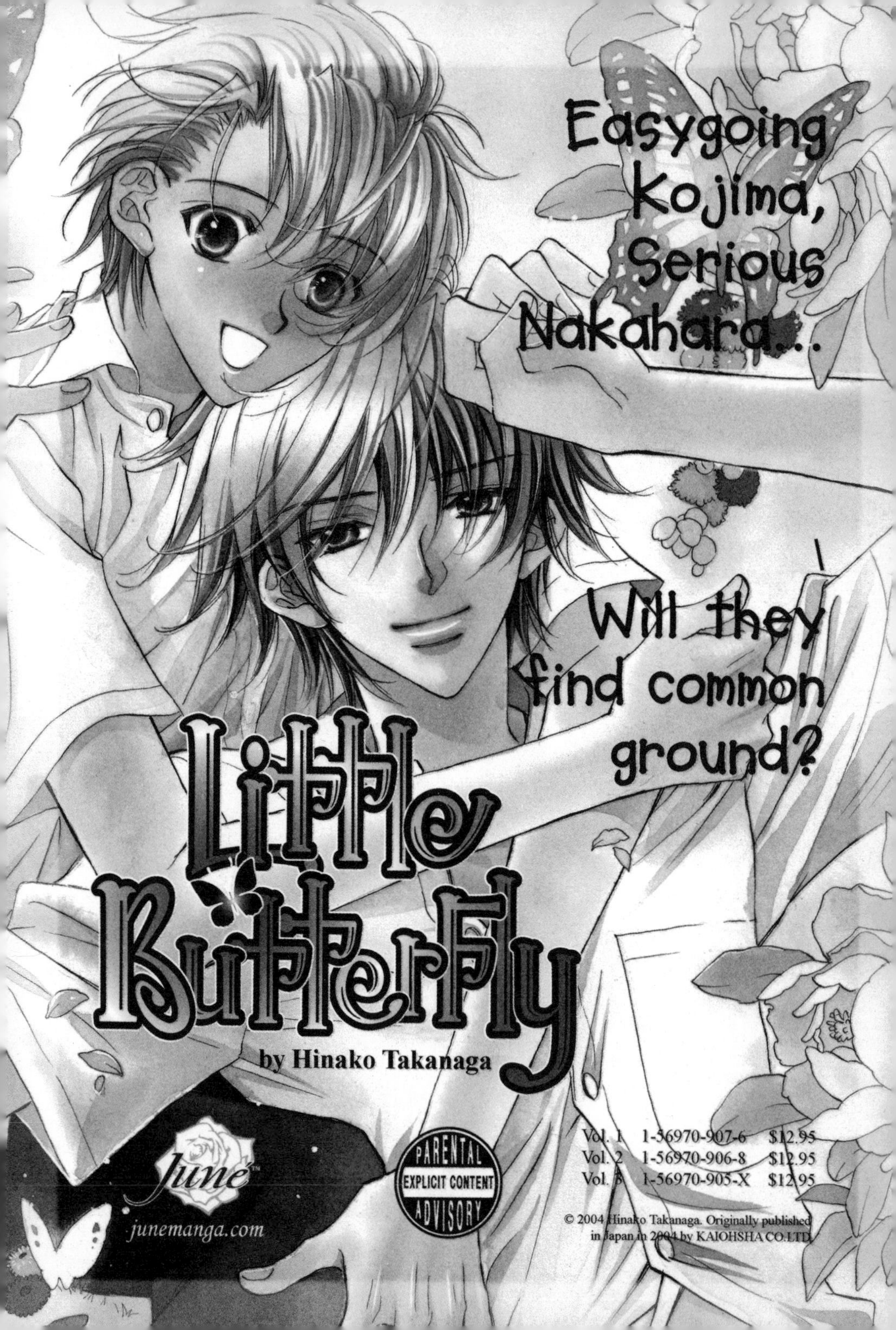
Easygoing Kojima, Serious Nakahara...
Will they find common ground?
Little Butterfly
by Hinako Takanaga
June™
junemanga.com
PARENTAL ADVISORY EXPLICIT CONTENT
Vol. 1 1-56970-907-6 $12.95
Vol. 2 1-56970-906-8 $12.95
Vol. 3 1-56970-905-X $12.95
© 2004 Hinako Takanaga. Originally published in Japan in 2004 by KAIOHSHA CO.LTD.

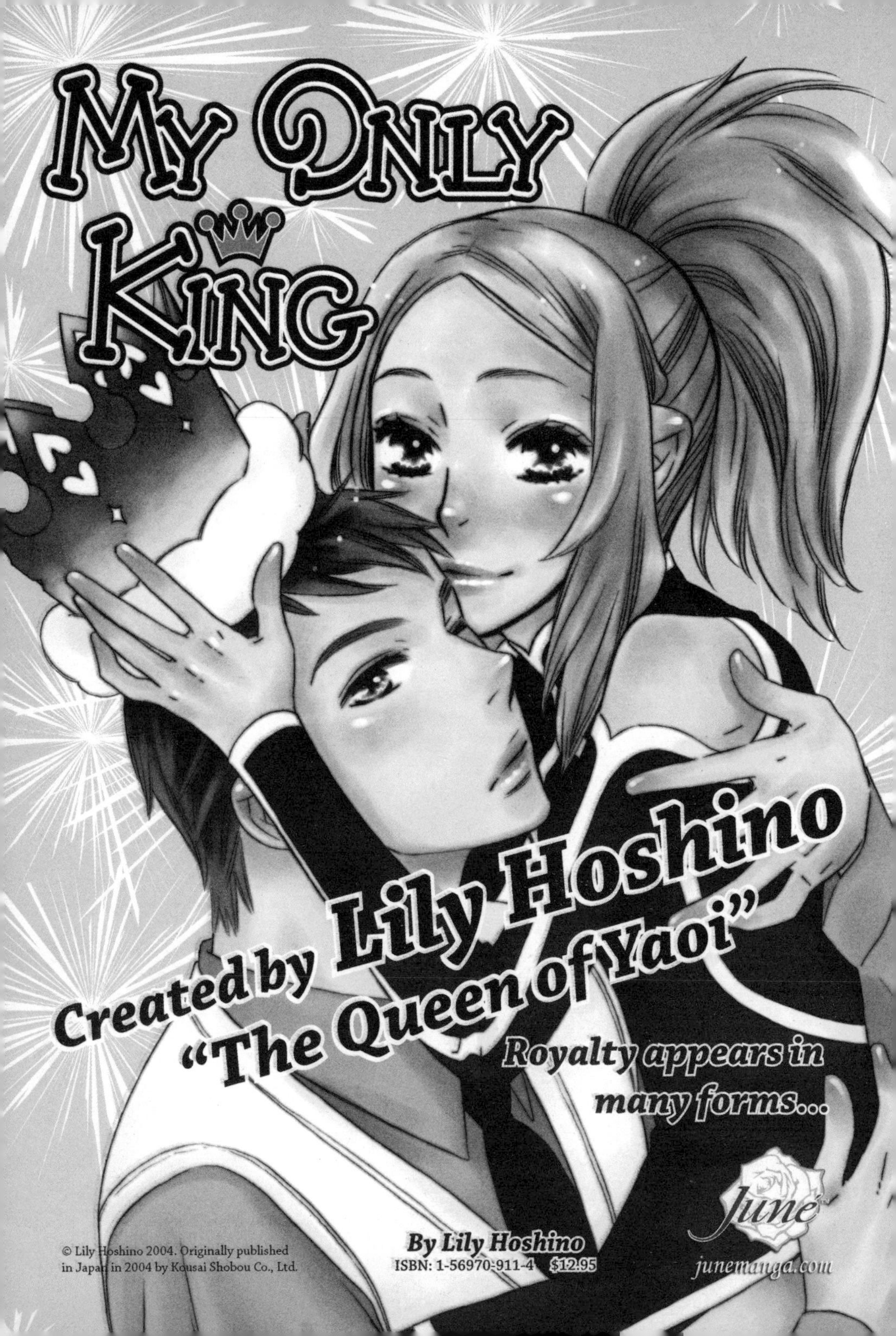
MY ONLY KING
Created by Lily Hoshino
"The Queen of Yaoi"
Royalty appears in many forms...
June
By Lily Hoshino
ISBN: 1-56970-911-4 $12.95
junemanga.com
© Lily Hoshino 2004. Originally published in Japan in 2004 by Kousai Shobou Co., Ltd.

STOP

This is the back of the book!
Start from the other side.

NATIVE MANGA
readers read manga
from *right to left*.

If you run into our *Native Manga* logo on any of our books... you'll know that this manga is published in it's true original native Japanese right to left reading format, as it was intended. Turn to the other side of the book and start reading from right to left, top to bottom.

Follow the diagram to see how its done. *Surf's Up!*

NATIVE MANGA

READ RIGHT TO LEFT